The Draft Common Frame of Reference as a "Toolbox" for Domestic Courts

Marta Santos Silva

The Draft Common Frame of Reference as a "Toolbox" for Domestic Courts

A Solution to the Pure Economic Loss Problem from a Comparative Perspective

Springer

Marta Santos Silva
Faculty of Law
University of Osnabrück
Osnabrück, Germany

ISBN 978-3-319-52922-6 ISBN 978-3-319-52923-3 (eBook)
DOI 10.1007/978-3-319-52923-3

Library of Congress Control Number: 2017939569

Printed on acid-free paper

This Springer imprint is published by Springer Nature
The registered company is Springer International Publishing AG
The registered company address is: Gewerbestrasse 11, 6330 Cham, Switzerland

Foreword

I met Dr. Marta Santos Silva when she was a promising student at the Law School of the Portuguese Catholic University in Oporto and have followed, with great interest, her subsequent steps as a bright young scholar. I was, therefore, deeply honoured by her invitation to write a small foreword to this book, which focuses on the concept of loss in tort law and, particularly, so-called pure economic loss.

James Gordley[1] pointed out that, although there may be valid reasons to deny recovery of pure economic loss, the exclusionary rule "was adopted for reasons which commended themselves to the 19th century conceptualists".

The exclusionary rule is a recent one but despite the new wording it is, to some extent, an old problem. Compensation for pure economic loss was admitted in the Middle Ages and resulted in heated debate.[2] Conversely, Christian von Bar, in his fundamental work, "The Common European Law of Torts",[3] rightly stated that the Portuguese Civil Code, "like the more modern codes of other European nations, (. . .) is marked by a certain legal eclecticism". Although strongly influenced by the German doctrine and the German Civil Code, the Portuguese legislator did not blindly follow in the footsteps of the BGB and, as a result, Article 483 of the Portuguese Civil Code, in spite of a strong German influence,[4] must not be seen as a general clause with a restrictive scope. To the contrary, it must be read in conjunction with other legal rules that may be called upon to broaden the concept of an unlawful act that can provide a basis for reparation of a loss. This explains von Bar's remark that "although the Portuguese law of delict appears rather conservative in some areas, it nevertheless reacted very 'positively' to a number of recent developments concerning the principles of liability law".[5] Recently, the Portuguese

[1]Gordley (2006), p. 263.

[2]*ibid.*, p. 266 ff.

[3]von Bar (1998a), p. 33.

[4]*ibid.*

[5]*ibid.*, p. 36.

Supreme Court has seen fit to award reparation for pure economic loss, in a case where the wrongdoer acted with the intent to cause a loss to his or her neighbour.[6]

This book provides useful insights into the possibility of legitimising the recourse to the DCFR, as well as offering a comprehensive overview of the methods used by both scholars and courts in Portugal. It is an attempt to adapt a Code with a lifespan of half a century and to cautiously modernise the possibility of recovering pure economic loss without forgetting that "one person should not have to subsidise another's vulnerability".[7] It also represents a fair assessment of the role of the judge, torn between the need to adapt the law to an ever-changing world and the lack of political legitimacy in countries of the Civil Law tradition.

Júlio Gomes, L.LM. (Columbia University), DPhil (Oxford) Judge at the Portuguese Supreme Court, Invited Law Professor at the Portuguese Catholic University, Member of the Study Group on a European Civil Code's Co-ordinating Group and Advisory Council.

[6]STJ 8 September 2016, proc. 1952/13.6TBPVZ.P1.S1.

[7]Gordley (2006), p. 284.

Preface

In this book, I undertook the daunting task of referring in English to terms taken from Civil Law legal systems ("legal irritants", as some call them).[8] This is a perilious undertaking because English, "the *lingua franca* of modern times"[9] unconsciously carries with it the baggage of concepts and principles of Common Law.[10] Therefore, for the sake of clarity, I have opted to express myself in mainly descriptive legal English.[11] Most of the terms here were used in line with the terminology proposed by the Draft Common Frame of Reference. Whenever the translation of a term was disputed, I included the concept as expressed in the native language of the system in which it originated.

As regards case law, I refer to the first page of the decision, followed by each cited page in turn. Whenever a paper-format source is not named for a decision of a Portuguese court, it can be understood that the decision is only available in electronic format through the legal database of the Portuguese Ministry of Justice.[12]

Osnabrück, Germany | Marta Santos Silva

[8]Teubner (1998), pp. 11–32.

[9]von Bar (2000c), p. 69.

[10]See von Bar (1998a), p. 383; Swann (2003), pp. 2–3; von Bar (2011b), p. 391.

[11]On the importance of a descriptive drafting style, see von Bar (2009d), p. 56.

[12]http://www.dgsi.pt (accessed 31 March 2017).

Acknowledgments

This book is an adapted version of the doctoral thesis submitted and defended on 8 February 2016 at the University of Osnabrück. It is the result of several years of research at the European Legal Studies Institute and the Centre of European Law and Politics (in Osnabrück and Bremen, Germany, respectively). The research and publication was partly financed through a doctoral fellowship of the *Fundação para a Ciência e a Tecnologia – Ministério da Ciência, Tecnologia e Ensino Superior de Portugal* (SFRH/BD/38610/2007). The final stages of research and drafting were facilitated by the generous flexible work arrangements agreed by Prof. Manuela Magalhães from the University Portucalense Infante D. Henrique (Porto, Portugal) and Prof. Christoph Schmid (Bremen).

The completion of this book would have not been possible without the patient guidance of Prof. Christian von Bar to whom I am, at many levels, greatly indebted. I am also sincerely grateful to Prof. Schulte-Nölke for the helpful comments and suggestions for improvement, as well as to Prof. Thomas Große, for chairing the doctoral committee assessing my Ph.D. and raising many relevant connections between the topics therein and Public Law.

My thanks also to several people with whom I had very fruitful discussions of the ideas and challenges in the book during the drafting process. I would particularly like to thank: Dr Rui Cascão, for his endless availability to dissect the most disputed issues and the overall structure of the book; Supreme Court Judge António Fonseca Ramos, for his patience in several lengthy discussions of the most recent case law decisions of the Portuguese Supreme Court, and lastly, Supreme Court Judge Professor Júlio Gomes, for his bright insights and input, for drafting the foreword of this book and for his tireless support for my career.

I also owe a debt of gratitude to those colleagues and friends who engaged in many long discussions about the particular issues addressed by this book.

To: Supreme Court Judge Prof. Graça Trigo, Prof. Gert Brüggemeier, Prof. Manuel Carneiro da Frada, Prof. Luisa Antoniolli, Prof. Stathis Banakas, Prof. Nieves Fenoy, Prof. Fernando Torrão, Dr Carlos Nóbrega, Dr Celia Martinez, Dr Fernando Sá, my thanks for your invaluable input.

A special word of thanks goes to Dr Sabine Mehlmann of the Ph.D. Career Center at the University of Osnabrück. She guided me through the preparation of the doctoral thesis and under her careful tutelage I managed to avoid embodying Penelope, undoing and redoing the woven (thesis') web.

The unconditional support of my family and friends gave me the strength to endure and reach the end of this, at times, seemingly endless marathon. My final and most heartfelt thanks, then, to my parents, for their support and their anxiety on my behalf through my nail-biting and head-scratching moments; to my good friend Diana, who ran with me, on her own track, in that last against-the-clock academic sprint and, lastly, to Goran, for supporting me in every possible way and making me believe in the impossible. I share with him the merits of this achievement.

Introduction

"When I use a word," Humpty Dumpty said, in rather a scornful tone, "it means just what I choose it to mean — neither more nor less."

"The question is," said Alice, "whether you can make words mean so many different things."

"The question is," said Humpty Dumpty, "which is to be master — that's all."

Lewis Carroll, "Through the Looking-Glass, and What Alice Found There" (1871)

Three decades ago, a well-known Portuguese legal sociologist wrote that "we live in a time of legal porosity".[13] This sentiment remains current insofar as the present-day Portuguese regime of non-contractual liability is concerned.

This regime, provided for in the Portuguese Civil Code, is less than fifty years old. However, it is deeply embedded within the philosophy of the secular German Civil Code (*Bürgerliches Gesetzbuch*). Both revolve around the cornerstone of the historical concept of unlawfulness (*ilicitude*, *Rechtswidrigkeit*), whose fundamental view is that the legislature intended to restrict the protection of pure economic interests.

The spectrum of economic interests worthy of legal protection in the eyes of the courts has diversified in recent years, as unprecedented industrial and technological development multiplied the risk of damage being inflicted. Within this context, the requirement of unlawfulness has revealed itself to be *porous*, with multiple facets into which liability seeps.

In fact, "forced" to deal with unlawfulness as a requirement of liability, courts have skillfully influenced the concept through the use of general clauses and open-ended concepts on the one hand, and through the extension of contract law devices to the field of non-contractual liability, on the other. The proliferation of legal developments has moved the application of the concept away from the intent of the legislature, which was to provide for strict filters on the liability of pure economic loss. A regime traditionally thought to be conservative in theory—and which

[13]Sousa Santos (1987), p. 298. See also Markesinis (2006), p. 1364 and Violante (2011), p. 343.

maintains this façade in general[14]—has come close in nature to the systems which provide for a general clause of liability. This development has the potential to lead to the progressive opening of the "floodgates" of litigation,[15] burdening both the judicial system and, often, the person inflicting the harm, with a liability that may be disproportionate to his or her actual fault. The expansion of the requirements of liability, as provided for by law, may also ultimately affect those citizens with a pervasive risk of liability, with an associated further impact as far as insurance policies are concerned. Too, the considerable judicial creativity makes it more difficult to foresee the outcomes of cases and can potentially lead to the application of different rules to cases with similar facts. A consistent, objective and self-comprising framework, which is a requirement for legal certainty and equality before the law, seems to be lacking in the non-contractual area of the civil liability system.

In spite of this, the requirement of unlawfulness and the law of non-contractual liability in general, have not been amended since their promulgation and entry into force in Portugal. Academics acknowledge the legal developments leading to the expansion of liability—a more detailed discussion of which can be found in § 5—but a systematic and critical approach to such expansion remains necessary.

This book analyses whether or not the solution to the legal problems caused by the requirement of unlawfulness may involve the Draft Common Frame of Reference (DCFR). The DCFR consists of a comprehensive set of principles, definitions and model rules, including a Book on "non-contractual liability arising out of damage caused to another", and which—as part of its "toolbox" function—aims to assist national courts in solving national disputes (see analysis under § 3 below). More specifically, the research question investigates whether Portuguese courts *could* and *should* informally consider[16] the concept of "legally relevant damage" in the adjudication of domestic disputes, particularly in light of the current stalemate created by the question of the protection of pure economic interests.

The interpretation of Portuguese rules on non-contractual liability arising out of damage caused to another in the light of the DCFR, within the process of adjudication, is yet to be considered. The hypothesis should be measured in light of the abandonment of the concept of a Common European Sales Law (CESL) by the European Commission and the reluctance to reduce a harmonised European private law instrument to a digital single market instrument. Several EU Member States have, however, publicly endorsed the idea of a non-binding toolbox (as will be seen in § 3 below), and this is also relevant to the discussion.

This book presents its arguments in three parts.

The first part deals with the first element of the research question, which consists of a *macro-analysis* of the possible role of the DCFR, in particular in the Portuguese private legal system. The second part addresses the second element of the research

[14]Bussani and Palmer (2003a), p. 532.

[15]Spier and von Bar (1998b).

[16]On the "informal Europeanisation of private law", see von Bar et al. (2009), Intr. 8, p. 9.

question, and is a *micro-analysis*[17] of this possible role, that is, it presents an assessment of the role of the DCFR in one of its main original concepts, that of "legally relevant damage". The third and final part of this book weighs and comments on the arguments presented in the first two parts.

Part I ("*The Portuguese Civil Code Through the Prism of the Draft Common Frame of Reference*") considers whether or not Portuguese courts *could* use the DCFR in the adjudication of legal disputes. It gives a brief overview of the historical evolution of Portuguese codified law and its openness towards foreign sources of law. It explores the evolutionary process which culminated in the approval of the present-day Civil Code and the extent to which the latter was influenced by the BGB, as well as the general opinion towards a European Civil Code and the convergence of European private laws in general (*§ 1—Portuguese Codified Law and Its Broad-Minded Attitude Towards Comparative Law and Jurisprudence from a Historical Perspective*). Following the historical overview, the book outlines the theoretical framework that binds Portuguese courts in the present-day adjudication process. As such, it describes and analyses the system of sources of law, as well as the accepted methods of legal interpretation and integration provided for in the Portuguese Civil Code (*§ 2—Judges as Key Players in the Development of European Private Law*).

The final section of Part I discusses the extent to which Portuguese courts can use the DCFR as a source of law in the adjudication process. An examination of courts' analysis of the Portuguese Civil Code in the light of foreign legal systems is presented, and the DCFR itself is assessed in more detail, namely, its nature and purpose, together with its current and potential impact on the case law of Portuguese courts (*§ 3—A Role for the DCFR in Domestic Adjudication*).

After discussing if Portuguese courts *could* use the DCFR in the adjudication of legal disputes in preference to Portuguese sources of law, the question arises as to whether or not Portuguese courts *should* use the DCFR, using the example of the concept of "legally relevant damage" as a potential mechanism to bring to an end the stalemate created by the category of pure economic loss.

Part II ("*A Plea for the Informal Acceptance of the Concept of 'Legally Relevant Damage' as a Way to Break the Stalemate Created by the Category 'Pure Economic Loss'*") begins with an overview of the Portuguese regime of non-contractual liability arising out of damage caused to another, the general rule of liability and its respective requirements, in particular the requirement of *ilicitude* (*§ 4—General Remarks on the Non-Contractual Liability Regime Arising out of Damage Caused to Another in the Portuguese Civil Code*). The next section analyses the extent to which the present-day framework of liability—based upon the requirement of unlawfulness—, copes with the compensation of relevant pure economic interests (*§ 5—Drawbacks of Unlawfulness and Compensation of Pure Economic Loss*). In the subsequent section, the main aspects of Book VI of the DCFR, specifically the basic rule and its particular features, are analysed (*§ 6—General Remarks on the*

[17] For similar terminology, see Zweigert and Kötz (1998), pp. 4–5.

Non-Contractual Liability Regime Arising out of Damage Caused to Another in the Draft Common Frame of Reference (PEL Liab. Dam.).

The last section of Part II analyses the real protagonist of this book, namely, the cutting-edge concept of legally relevant damage, examining how, in the absence of a category of "pure economic loss", pure economic interests are protected by Book VI of the DCFR (*§ 7—Reception of the DCFR's Concept of "Legally Relevant Damage" and its Potential for the Protection of Pure Economic Interests*).

Part III ("*Critical Remarks: Cutting the Gordian Knot with the DCFR*"), the third and last part of this book, presents a critical analysis of the legal problems raised in Parts I and II (*§ 8—The Deadlock of Pure Economic Loss and the Quest for a Solution*), including the arguments specifically discussed in Part I (*§ 9—Could Portuguese Courts use the DCFR over National Sources of Law?*) and Part II (*§ 10—Should the Portuguese Courts use the DCFR's concept of "Legally Relevant Damage"?*).

As for the scope of the book, Part I touches on topics in the areas of Legal History, Constitutional Theory, Philosophy of Law, Legal Methodology, *inter alia*. Their importance and impact are visible throughout the arguments here, although such references are not intended to be exhaustive.

The central issue is non-contractual liability arising out of damage caused to another involving fault. A closer examination of the claims surpassing this theoretical playing field is outside the scope of this particular book and is left for future analysis.

Contents

Abbreviations and Acronyms

AAFDL	Associação Académica da Faculdade de Direito de Lisboa (Portugal)
Aa. Vv.	Auctores varii (various authors)
ABGB	Allgemeines Bürgerliches Gesetzbuch (Civil Code, Austria)
AC	Appeal Cases (House of Lords, London), cited by year, book and page
AcP	Archiv für die civilistische Praxis (Tübingen), cited by number, year and page
Admin.	Administração (Macau), cited by number, year and page
AJCL	The American Journal of Comparative Law (Baltimore/Berkeley), cited by volume, year and page
ALJ	Austrian Law Journal (Graz), cited by number, year and page
ALSLS	Amsterdam Law School Legal Studies Research Paper (Amsterdam), cited by number, year and page
AmJCL	The American Journal of Comparative Law (Ann Arbor), cited by volume, year and page
AöR	Archiv des öffentlichen Rechts (Tübingen), cited by number, year and page
Apud	In the writings of
Ariz. L. Rev.	Arizona Law Review (Tucson), cited by volume, year and page
Art.(s)	Article(s)
AS	Análise Social (Lisbon), cited by volume, year and page
AT	Allgemeiner Teil (general part)
B2B	Business-to-business
B2C	Business-to-consumer
BAGE	Entscheidungen des Bundesarbeitsgerichts (Decisions of the Federal Labour Court, Germany), cited by first page of the decision and page referenced
Bd.	Band (volume)

BEUC	Bureau Européen des Unions des Consommateurs (The European Consumer Organisation)
BFD	Boletim da Faculdade de Direito da Universidade de Coimbra (Magazine of the Law Faculty of the University of Coimbra, Portugal), cited by volume, year and page
BGB	Bürgerliches Gesetzbuch (Civil Code, Germany)
BGBl	Bundesgesetzblatt (Official Journal issued by the Ministry of Justice, Germany, Bonn/Cologne), cited by part and page
BGH	Bundesgerichtshof (Federal Court of Justice, Germany)
BGHZ	Amtliche Sammlung der Entscheidungen des Bundesgerichtshofs in Zivilsachen (Decisions of the German Federal Court of Justice in civil matters), cited by volume and page
BolMinJus	Boletim do Ministério da Justiça (Bulletin of the Ministry of Justice, Lisbon), cited by volume, year and page
BT	Besonderer Teil (special part)
BverfGE	Amtliche Sammlung der Entscheidungen des Bundesverfassungsgerichts (Decisions of the Federal Constitutional Court of Germany), cited by volume, first page of the decision and page referenced
Cass.	Corte Suprema di Cassazione (Court of Cassation, Italy)
CC	Código Civil Português (Civil Code, Portugal), DL 47344 of 25 November 1966, published in DR, 1st Ser., no. 274 (1966), pp. 1883–2086, with amendments
CCP	Code of Civil Procedure; abbreviation used coherent for the following Codes: CCP 2013, Código de Processo Civil (Portugal), approved by the Act 41/2013 of 26 June 2013, published in DR, 1st Ser., no. 121 (2013), pp. 3518–3665, with amendments; CCP 1961, Código de Processo Civil (Portugal), approved by the DL 44129 of 28 December 1961, published in DR, 1st Ser., no. 299 (1961), pp. 1783–1962
CCrim	Criminal Code, Código Penal (Portugal), approved by the DL 400/82 of 23 September 1982, republished by Act 59/2007 of 4 September 2009, published in DR, 1st Ser., no 170 (2007), pp. 6181, 6258
CDP	Cadernos de Direito Privado (Braga), cited by number, year and page
CEJ	Centro de Estudos Judiciários (Portugal)
CES	Centro de Estudos Sociais; E-cadernos CES (Coimbra), cited by number, year and page
CESL	Common European Sales Law
cf.	Confer
CFR	Common Frame of Reference
Ch.	The Law Reports. Chancery Cases, cited by year, volume and page

chap(s).	Chapter(s)
CISG	United Nations Convention on Contracts for the International Sale of Goods
CJ	Colectânea de Jurisprudência (Collection of case law, Coimbra), cited by volume, year and page
CJICL	Cardozo Journal of International and Comparative Law (New York), cited by volume, year and page
CJ(ST)	Colectânea de Jurisprudência. Acórdãos do Supremo Tribunal de Justiça (Collection of case law, rullings of the Supreme Court of Justice, Coimbra, Portugal), cited by volume, year and page
CLJ	The Cambridge Law Journal (Cambridge), cited by volume, year and page
Colum. J. Eur.	The Columbia Journal of European Law (New York), cited by volume, year and page
com.	Comment
Comm.	Chambre commerciale, financière et économique de la Cour de cassation (Cour de cassation) (commercial, financial and economic division of the Court of Cassation)
CONPEDI	Conselho Nacional de Pesquisa e Pós-Graduação em Direito (Brazil)
Const.	Constitution; abbreviation used coherent for the following Constitutions: Constituição da República Portuguesa, CRP (Constitution of the Portuguese Republic) approved by the Constitutional Act 1/2005 of 12 August 2005, 1st Ser., no. 155 (2005), pp. 4642–4686, with amendments; Grundgesetz, GG, Basic Law for the Federal Republic of Germany, promulgated on 23 May 1949 (Federal Law Gazette, p. 1 ff.), with amendments
contrib.	Contributor(s)
coord.	Coordinator(s)
Corte Cost.	Corte Costituzionale (Constitutional Court of Italy)
CPRP	Constituição Política da República Portuguesa (Political Constitution of the Portuguese Republic of 1933) approved by the Decree 22241 of 22 February 1933, published in the DR, 1st Ser., no. 43 (1933), pp. 227–236
CS	Código de Seabra (Portugal), approved by the Charter of 1 July 1867
CSOH	Court of Session Outer House (Scotland), cited by year and page
CT	Código do Trabalho (Portuguese Labour Code), approved by the Act 7/2009 of 12 February 2009, published in 1st Ser., no. 30, pp. 926–1029, with amendments
DCFR	Draft Common Frame of Reference
DG	Directorate-General
Dir	O Direito (Lisbon), cited by volume, year and page
Dir(s).	Director(s)

Dir.just.	Direito e Justiça (Lisbon), cited by year and page
DL	Decreto-lei (Decree-law) (Portugal)
DR	Government gazette (Lisbon, Portugal), named Diário do Govêrno from 1 January 1869 until 9 April 1976 and Diário da República since 10 April 1976, cited by number, year and series
EC	European Community
ECJ	European Court of Justice (Luxembourg)
ECR	European Court Reports (Luxembourg)
ed.(s)	Edition, editor(s)
Edinburgh LRev	The Edinburgh Law Review (Edinburgh), cited by volume, year and page
EEC	European Economic Community
e.g.	Exempli gratia (for example)
EGTL	European Group on Tort Law
EJCL	Electronic Journal of Comparative Law (Maastricht/Tilburg/Utrecht), retrieved from http://www.ejcl.org and cited by volume, year and page
EJLE	European Journal of Law and Economics (New York), cited by volume, year and page
EJLS	European Journal of Legal Studies (Fiesole), cited by volume, year and page
ELF	The European Legal Forum (Munich), cited by volume, year and page
ELJ	European Law Journal (Oxford/Malden), cited by volume, year and page
ELSI	European Legal Studies Institute (Osnabrück, Germany)
ERA Forum	ERA Forum Journal of the Academy of European Law (Trier), cited by volume, year and page
ERCL	European Review of Contract Law (Berlin), cited by volume, year and page
ERPL	European Review of Private Law (Deventer), cited by volume, year and page
et al.	et alii (and others)
EU	European Union
EuR	Europarecht (Baden-Baden), cited by year, issue and page
Europa e dir. priv.	Europa e diritto privato (Milan), cited by number, year and page
EuZW	Europäische Zeitschrift für Wirtschaftsrecht (Munich/Frankfurt), cited by year and page
f.(f.)	Following page(s)
FDUL	Faculdade de Direito da Universidade de Lisboa (Law Faculty of the University of Lisbon)
Foro it.	Il Foro Italiano, Raccolta di giurisprudenza civile, commerciale, penale, amministrativa (Rome), cited by year, volume and column

Foro pad.	Il Foro Padano, Rivista di giurisprudenza e di dottrina (Milan), cited by volume, year and page
fn(n).	Footnote(s)
GPR	Zeitschrift für Gemeinschaftsprivatrecht (Cologne/Heidelberg/Munich/Frankfurt am Main), cited by volume, year and page
Giur.it.	Giurisprudenza Italiana (Turin), cited by year, part, section and column
Giust. Civ. Mass.	Giustizia Civile. Massimario annotato della Cassazione (Milan), cited by year and page
G.U.	Gazzetta Ufficiale (Government gazette, Italy, Rome)
Harv.ILJ	Harvard International Law Journal (Cambridge), cited by volume, year and page
ibid.	ibidem (in the same place)
ICLQ	International and Comparative Law Quarterly (London), cited by volume, year and page
i.e.	id est (that is to say)
IJVO	Internationale Juristenvereinigung Osnabrück (Osnabrück), cited by number, year and page
InDret	Review on the Analysis of Law, retrieved from http://www.indret.com/en/ and cited by number and year
Intr.	Introduction
IrLE	International Review of Law and Economics (Amsterdam), cited by volume, year and page
ISLR	The Irish Student Law Review (Dublin), cited by volume, year and page
JA	Juristische Arbeitsblätter, Zeitschrift für Studenten und Referendare (Munich/Berlin/Bielefeld/Frankfurt am Main/Berlin/Cologne), cited by year and page
JBl	Juristische Blätter (Vienna), cited by year and page
JCL	Journal of Comparative Law (London), cited by volume, year and page
JI	Juridica International (Tartu), retrieved from http://www.juridicainternational.eu/ and cited by volume, year and page
J.Law & Soc	Journal of Law and Society (Cardiff), cited by volume, year and page
JLS	The Journal of Legal Studies (Chicago), cited by volume, year and page
J.Rev	The Juridical Review (Edinburgh), cited by volume, year and page
JTLP	Journal of Transnational Law and Policy (Tallahassee/Buffalo), cited by volume, year and page
Jura	Jura. Juristische Ausbildung (Berlin), cited by year and page
JuS	Juristische Schulung. Zeitschrift für Studium und Referendariat (Munich/Frankfurt am Main), cited by volume, year and page

JZ	JuristenZeitung (Tübingen), cited by volume, year and page
KB	King's Bench
KF	Karlsruher Forum. Supplement to VersRAI (Karlsruhe), cited by year and page
Legal Affairs	Legal Affairs (n. p.), retrieved from http://www.legalaffairs.org and cited by year
LGDJ	Librairie générale de droit et de jurisprudence (French publishing company)
LQR	The Law Quarterly Review (London), cited by volume, year and page
LR	Legal Roots, cited by volume, year and page
Minn.L.Rev.	Minnesota Law Review (Minneapolis), cited by volume, year and page
MJ	Maastricht Journal of European and Comparative Law (Antwerp/Baden-Baden), cited by volume, year and page
MLR	The Modern Law Review (London), cited by volume, year and page
n.d.	No date
NJA	Nytt juridiskt arkiv (Supreme Court reports, Sweden)
NJW	Neue Juristische Wochenschrift (Munich/Frankfurt am Main), cited by volume, year and page
N.n.	No name
n(n).	Note(s) or comment(s) (to article)
no(s).	Number(s); margin number(s)
n.p.	No place
NVwZ	Neue Zeitschrift für Verwaltungsrecht (Munich/Frankfurt am Main), cited by volume, year and page
NY	New York
OJ	Official Journal
OJLS	Oxford Journal of Legal Studies (Oxford), cited by volume, year and page
org(s).	Organiser(s)
para(s).	Paragraph(s)
Passim	Passim (here and there)
PECL	Principles of European Contract Law
PEL	Principles of European Law
PEL Liab. Dam.	Principles of European Law: Non-Contractual Liability arising out of Damage caused to Another
PETL	Principles of European Tort Law
p(p).	Page(s)
proc.	Processo (court case)
Prot. I	Protokolle der Kommission für die erste Lesung des Entwurfs des Bürgerlichen Gesetzbuchs (Protocol of the Commission on the first reading of the draft of the German Civil Code)

QB	The Law Reports. Queen's Bench Division (London), cited by year, book and page
RabelsZ	Zeitschrift für ausländisches und internationales Privatrecht or Rabels Zeitschrift für ausländisches und internationales Privatrecht (Hamburg), cited by volume, year and page
RCCS	Revista Crítica de Ciências Sociais (Coimbra), cited by number, year and page
RDE	Revista de Direito e Economia (Coimbra), cited by volume, year and page
RDPC	Revista Portuguesa do Dano Corporal (Coimbra), cited by volume, year and page
RE	Relação de Évora (Court of Appeal of Évora), Portugal
Recht	Recht. Zeitschrift für juristische Weiterbildung und Praxis (Bern), cited by year and page
repr.	Reimpressão (reprint)
Rev.int.dr. comp.	Revue international de droit comparé (Paris), cited by volume, year and page
RFDUL	Revista da Faculdade de Direito da Universidade de Lisboa (Lisbon), cited by number, year and page
RG	Relação de Guimarães (Court of Appeal of Guimarães), Portugal
RGZ	Amtliche Sammlung der Entscheidungen des Reichsgerichts in Zivilsachen (Decisions of the German Imperial Court in civil matters, Berlin), cited by volume and page
RHDI	Revue Hellénique de Droit International (Athens), cited by volume, issue and page
RIL	Revista de Informação Legislativa (Brasília), cited by volume, year and page
Riv.dir.eur.	Rivista di Diritto Europeo (Rome), cited by volume, year and page
RJLB	Revista Jurídica Luso-Brasileira (Lisbon), cited by volume, year and page
RJVV	Revista Jurídica Verba Volant, Scripta Manent (Patos), cited by volume, year and page
RL	Relação de Lisboa (Court of Appeal of Lisbon), Portugal
RLJ	Revista de Legislação e Jurisprudência, Coimbra (Portugal), cited by volume, year and page
ROA	Revista da Ordem dos Advogados, Lisbon (Portugal), cited by volume, year and page
RP	Relação do Porto (Court of appeal of Porto), Portugal
RPDC	Revista Portuguesa do Dano Corporal (Coimbra), cited by volume, year and page
Rut.LR	Rutgers Law Review (Buffalo/New Brunswick), cited by volume, year and page
SAP	Sentencia dela Audiencia Provincial (Decision of a Provincial Court)

ser.	Series
Sez. Un.	Sezioni Unite (Joint Session at the Court of Cassation, Italy)
SGECC	Study Group on a European Civil Code
S.Iur	Studia Iuridica (Coimbra), cited by year and page
SME	Small or medium enterprise
sec(s).	Section(s)
STJ	Supremo Tribunal de Justiça (Supreme Court of Portugal)
STS	Sentencia del Tribunal Supremo (Decision of the Supreme Court of Spain)
subsec(s).	Subsection(s)
subtit(s).	Subtitle(s)
suppl.	Supplement
TC	Tribunal Constitucional (Constitutional Court of Portugal)
TEEC	Treaty establishing the European Economic Community
TEU	Treaty on European Union
TFEU	Treaty on the Functioning of the European Union
Themis	Themis Revista de Direito (Lisbon), cited by volume, year and page
TI	Temas de Integração (Coimbra), cited by number, year and page
tit(s).	Title(s)
TPR	Tijdschrift voor Privaatrecht (Ghent/Leuven), cited by year and page
tranl(s).	Translation(s)
TulLRev	Tulane Law Review (New Orleans), cited by volume, year and page
UKHL	Approved judgment of the House of Lords (United Kingdom)
ULR	Utah Law Review (Salt Lake City), cited by volume, number and page
UMJLR	University of Michigan Journal of Law Reform (Ann Arbor), cited by volume, year and page
UtrLR	Utrecht Law Review (Utrecht), cited by volume, year and page
V	Versus (against)
VersRAI	Versicherungsrecht, Zeitschrift für Versicherungsrecht, Haftungs- und Schadensrecht (Karlsruhe), cited by year and page
vol(s).	Volume(s)
VVW	Versicherungswirtschaft (German publisher)
WM	Wertpapier-Mitteilungen. Zeitschrift für Wirtschafts- und Bankrecht (Frankfurt am Main/Potsdam/Essen), cited by year and page
ZERP	Zentrum für Europäische Rechtspolitik (Bremen)
ZEup	Zeitschrift für Europäisches Privatrecht (Munich), cited by number, year and page
ZfRV	Zeitschrift für Europarecht, Internationales Privatrecht und Rechtsvergleichung (Vienna), cited by year and page

ZGS	Zeitschrift für die gesamte Staatswissenschaft (Tübingen), cited by year and page
ZHR	Zeitschrift für das gesamte Handels- und Wirtschaftsrecht (Heidelberg), cited by volume, year and page
ZIP	Zeitschrift für Wirtschaftsrecht (Cologne), cited by year and page
ZRP	Zeitschrift für Rechtspolitik (Frankfurt am Main), cited by volume, year and page

Part I
The Portuguese Civil Code Through the Prism of the Draft Common Frame of Reference (DCFR)

§ 1 Portuguese Codified Law and Its Broad-Minded Attitude Towards Comparative Law and Jurisprudence from a Historical Perspective

I. The Royal Edicts (*Ordenações do Reino*)

The first historical milestone of Civil Law codification in Portugal can be found in the first comprehensive compilation of laws, the Royal Edicts (*Ordenações do Reino*),[1] in particular the Edicts of Afonso V (*Ordenações Afonsinas,* enacted in 1466), the Edicts of Manuel I (*Ordenações Manuelinas*, enacted in 1521) and the Edicts of Philip I (*Ordenações Filipinas*, enacted in 1603).

The Edicts resulted in an incomplete compilation of general laws which also suffered from lack of detail and systematisation. The Edicts extended to every socially relevant sector and thus did not have the Civil Law specialisation which characterises a Civil Code.[2]

Notwithstanding these issues, the Edicts played a significant role in the development of Portuguese Private Law.[3] The *Ordenações Filipinas*, which formed the basis of Portuguese law until the promulgation of the Portuguese civil codifications, are particularly important in this respect.

Book IV of the *Ordenações Filipinas* formed a functional equivalent to the Law of Obligations. The rules of this book were a product of their time and reflected the socioeconomic framework in which they were developed. However, the Edicts did not concern themselves with civil liability, instead concentrating on "breaches to the duty of care" in the form of *delictos* (delicts) and *perdas e interesses* (damages). These terms were deeply intertwined with criminal liability and involved financial

[1]For details on the Royal Edicts, see Sinde Monteiro (1997), p. 34 ff. and the extensive bibliography indicated there (Sinde Monteiro 1997, pp. 34 ff., 44–49) and Müller (2008), pp. 19–23. See also Zweigert and Kötz (1996), p. 106; Mota Pinto (2005), p. 84 ff.; Carvalho Fernandes (2009), pp. 51–53.

[2]Oliveira Ascensão (2013), p. 364.

[3]See Müller (2008), p. 20.

M. Santos Silva, *The Draft Common Frame of Reference as a "Toolbox" for Domestic Courts*, DOI 10.1007/978-3-319-52923-3_1

penalties, the benefit of which was re-directed to the injured party.[4] The term "*responsabilidade*" (accountability) did not appear anywhere in the Edicts.[5] Gaps were filled through the *obligationes ex maleficio*,[6] which were taken from the *Institutiones*.[7]

II. The Pre-Codification Period

By the time nations all over Europe began to adopt and implement the French *Code Napoléon* (1804), propelling significant European legal harmonisation,[8] the Portuguese system of private law still consisted of a compilation of fragmented and disjointed sources of law in the Royal Edicts. Legislators saw two ways in which the law could be systematised: a) the adoption of the French Civil Code or b) the creation of a methodical codification of existing national Civil Law, extending to cover areas previously dealt with under other formats. In the end, the latter option prevailed.[9]

The Pombal Reform under the care of the University of Coimbra[10] took place in the wake of Enlightened Reformism (*Reformismo Ilustrado*) during the reign of Joseph I. This marked the beginning of a period of codification, culminating in the publication of the first Portuguese Civil Code in 1867.

The Civil Law Handbook of Pascoal de Melo (*Institutiones Juris Civilis Lusitani*, 1789)[11] marked the beginning of the pre-codification period. This handbook consisted of collections of Civil Law statutes which still made no reference either to delicts (which traditionally meant breach of the duty of care in the form of intention) or to consequential loss. Indeed, Pascoal de Melo first used the term in his *Institutiones Juris Criminalis Lusitani* (1815),[12] where "*delito*" is defined as an "(...) unlawful fact spontaneously committed against the sanction of the laws, that causes harm to society or to individuals and, by which, whenever possible, a person incurs an obligation of repairing the loss and suffering a penalty".[13]

---

[4] Menezes Cordeiro (2009), pp. 174–175.

[5] The term "*responsabilidade*" began to be used for legal purposes at the beginning of the twentieth century. See Menezes Cordeiro (2010a), p. 57.

[6] Samuel (2001), pp. 3–4, fn. 16.

[7] Santos Justo (2011), p. 119.

[8] Menezes Leitão (2009), p. 225.

[9] See Subtit. "III. The Civil Code of 1867" below.

[10] On the Pombal Reform, see generally Caetano (1941), pp. 299–303.

[11] Melo Freire (1853).

[12] Melo Freire (1829).

[13] Original version: "*... facto ilícito espontaneamente cometido contra a sanção das leis, prejudicial à sociedade ou aos indivíduos, pelo qual se incorre na obrigação de, se possível, reparar o dano e sofrer uma pena*", available in Pascoal de Melo, *BolMinJus* 155 (1966), pp. 43–202.

Pascoal de Mello is not the only Portuguese legal scholar who left his mark on Portuguese Civil Law. Corrêa Telles, for example, not only disseminated Portuguese translations of the works of Domat, the most renowned legal scholar of the French legal system during codification, but he also wrote the seminal *Digesto Portuguez* (1835),[14] the structure and conceptualisations of which clearly influenced the French Civil Code.

According to the *Digesto*, "[a]s rule, he or she who, intentionally or by serious fault, harms another's person or goods must pay damages" and "[i]f the fault is light, only the direct loss – *i.e.*, the loss which resulted from the harm – shall be repaired".[15] In this understanding, "fault" (*culpa*) is used in Domat's sense of *faute*.

Another important figure of the Portuguese codification era was Coelho da Rocha. His *Instituições de Direito Civil Portuguez* (1848)[16] were inspired by the works of the German legal scholar Ferdinand Mackeldey (*Manuel de Droit Romain*).[17] This resulted in the transfer of the Law of Obligations (and therefore civil liability) to the general part of the *Instituições*, and civil liability has been included in the general section ever since. In fact, Coelho da Rocha is recognised as the first lawyer to provide an explicit, independent analysis of civil liability, including non-contractual liability. Section VII of his *Instituições* contained the discussion of "obligations resulting from unlawful acts" ("*Das obrigações resultantes dos actos illícitos*").[18] In this section, he referred expressly to the Practical Treaty of Evaluations and Damage (*Tractado pratico das avaliações e dos damnos*) of Souza de Lobão,[19] which provided for the assessment and provision of damages, thereby complementing the Royal Edicts. In § 132 Coelho da Rocha defined unlawful facts ("*factos illicitos*") as "(. . .) not only the positive facts, which are expressly forbidden and sanctioned by the law (*delicta*), but also the omissions of the duties of each and all, to which the law does not consent whenever they may result in damage, or damage caused to third persons (*quasi delicta*)".[20]

When Coelho da Rocha wrote the *Instituições*, the Act of Good Reason (*Lei da Boa Razão*) was already in force.[21] This act can be considered a "meta-rule" designed to facilitate the system until codification, and it represents the state of

[14]Corrêa de Telles (1845).

[15]Original version: "457. *Em regra aquelle que de proposito, ou por culpa grave offende a outro em sua pessoa ou bens, deve pagar-lhe damnos e interesses. (e).* 458. *Se a culpa for leve, deve pagar-lhe sómente a perda immediata, que resultou da offensa (f)*" (Corrêa de Telles 1845, p. 75).

[16]Coelho da Rocha (1857).

[17]*ibid.*, V.

[18]Coelho da Rocha (1857), pp. 89–96.

[19]Souza de Lobão (1826), p. 107, part II *apud* Menezes Leitão (2009), p. 225.

[20]Original version: "§ *132. (. . .) Entendem-se por factos illicitos: 1.° não só os factos positivos, que são expressamente prohibidos e castigados pelas leis (delicta); 2.° mas tambem as omissões dos deveres de cada um, que as leis não consentem, quando d'ellas póde resultar damno, ou perda a outrem (quasi delicta) (. . .).*"(Coelho da Rocha 1857, p. 89).

[21]The Act of Good Reason was enacted on 18 August 1769 by Joseph I.

law in eighteenth-century Portugal. The Act provided that, where doubt existed in respect of the applicability of a law in accordance with the principle of Good Reason, the courts could apply the law only if it was part of the modern jurisprudence of a civilised nation, where "civilised nation" was read as "Christian nation".[22]

These scholarly contributions provided the only guidance on civil liability of the codification period. This scarcity of sources and guiding principles of civil liability might have been the reason why Ferreira Borges included the "loss for the non-performance of commercial contracts" (*perdas e damnos por inexecução de contracto mercantile*) in the Portuguese Commercial Code of 1833.[23]

III. The Civil Code of 1867

1. Contents and Structure

The academic work of three generations of legal scholars throughout the codification period laid the foundations for the groundwork in formal codification of Portuguese law.[24]

Queen D. Maria II entrusted the task of collating a civil code to António Luíz de Seabra, Viscount of Seabra and judge at the Court of Appeal of Porto.[25] The latter founded and chaired a commission of legal scholars with the sole purpose of revising and extending existing laws to compile a civil code.[26] On 26 June 1867, the Chamber of Deputies (*Câmara de Deputados*) approved the Portuguese Civil Code, which was immediately promulgated by King Luis I of Portugal through the *Carta de Lei* of 1 July 1867.[27] The *Código de Seabra*[28] (Seabra's Code) entered into force on 22 March 1868,[29] finally replacing the Royal Edicts.

Menezes Cordeiro argues that the first Portuguese Civil Code had both a Roman pedigree and an underpinning Jusracionalist system.[30] Indeed, it is convincingly

---

[22] Müller (2008), pp. 25–28; Reis Marques (2009), pp. 159–170; Machado Cabral (2010), p. 6117 ff.

[23] Menezes Cordeiro (1996b), p. 448, fn. 214.

[24] Menezes Cordeiro (2010a), p. 17.

[25] Zweigert and Kötz (1996), p. 107; Menezes Cordeiro (2004), p. 32, fn. 44.

[26] For details on the creation and functioning of this commission, see Menezes Cordeiro (1999), pp. 117–118; Mota Pinto (2005), p. 83.

[27] Zweigert and Kötz (1996), p. 107.

[28] Codigo Civil Portuguez (1868).

[29] On the drafting process and promulgation of the Civil Code of 1867, see Menezes Cordeiro (1987), pp. 117–119.

[30] Menezes Cordeiro (2004), p. 32. Cf. also Zweigert and Kötz (1996), p. 107. For details on the roots of the Seabra's Code, see Miranda Barbosa (2006a), pp. 156–165.

argued[31] that the Seabra's Code adopted the style of the French Civil Code (1804),[32] and could thereby have affiliated itself with the French legal family.[33] However, it is clear that the Seabra's Code was also influenced by the codes of the Enlightenment era, namely the Prussian Civil Code (1794) and the Austrian Civil Code (1811).[34]

The influence of the French Civil Code in the Seabra's Code may be explained in two ways. Firstly, by the mid-nineteenth-century Germany had not yet experienced a period of codification. Secondly, German legal scholars, moved by the rising nationalist sentiment characterising the early period of the German Historical School of Jurisprudence, began to use their own language, making their writings less accessible to Portuguese scholars, who were routinely trained in Latin.[35]

In terms of structure, the Seabra's Code diverged markedly from the French Civil Code. Inspired by the *Institutiones*, the French Code had been structured along the lines of sections concentrating on "Persons", "Things" and "Actions". By contrast, the Seabra's Code revolved around the individual as an active subject (*sujeito de direito*) engaged in a legal relationship. Accordingly, it was divided into four parts: Part I referred to civil capacity (*Da capacidade civil*), Part II to the acquisition of rights (*Da acquisição dos direitos*), Part III to property rights (*Do direito de propriedade*)[36] and, finally, Part IV referred to the infringement of rights and related compensation (*Da offensa dos direitos e da sua reparação*). Each of these four parts was divided into several books with the exception of Parts I and II, which were contained within the same volume.

Other suggested influences on the Seabra's Code were the Prussian Land Law, the ABGB and the Sardinian Civil Code.[37] Even though academic opinion has agreed on many of the international influences on the creation of the Seabra's Code, Art.16 CS apparently prevented recourse to foreign law to fill legal gaps. It read: "If the questions on rights and obligations cannot be solved, neither by the text of the law, neither by its spirit, neither by analogous cases, provided for in other Portuguese laws, they will be decided by the principles of Natural Law, according to the

[31]Sinde Monteiro (1997), p. 34; Menezes Cordeiro (2004), p. 33; Ferreira de Almeida and Morais Carvalho (2013), p. 50.

[32]According to Müller, the Viscount of Seabra used almost half of the *Code Civil* as a template for the draft of the Seabra's Code (Müller 2008, p. 47). In fact, it is argued that the Seabra's Code even included literal translations of rules of the French Civil Code (Menezes Cordeiro 2004, p. 33).

[33]As Alpa put it "*[i]l Codice Francese è padre di molti figli*" (Alpa 2007, p. 28). See also Wengler (1967), p. 64; Alpa (2005), p. 13. On the "parent-child" relationship between Portugal and Italy, see von Bar (2013), p. 5.

[34]Ferreira de Almeida and Morais Carvalho (2013), p. 50. For details on the principles guiding the Seabra's Code see Miranda Barbosa (2006a), pp. 156–165.

[35]Miranda Barbosa (2006a), pp. 162–163.

[36]To Seabra, "ownership" (*propriedade*) meant "enjoyment of rights" (*gozo dos direitos*). See art. 2167 CS.

[37]Cabral de Moncada (1995), p. 119, fn. 5.

circumstances of the case".[38] Art.16 CS stated that solutions to legal problems were to be developed strictly within the Portuguese legal order itself[39] or, as a last resort, by referring to principles of Natural Law.

2. *Regulation of Civil Liability*

Book I of Part IV of the Seabra's Civil Code dealt with civil liability (*Da responsabilidade civil*). The Seabra's Code governed non-contractual liability exhaustively. With forty-two provisions on the topic (Arts. 2361–2403) it was considered "the most elaborate codification of the law of delict of its time".[40]

Its fundamental principle, as expressed in Art. 2361 CS, read that "[e]veryone who infringes or affronts another person's rights must repair the injured person for every damage caused to him or her".[41] Based on this, only the infringement of a subjective right (i.e., the power or capacity of a person, arising from Objective Law and usually aimed at protecting a legally relevant interest) led to an entitlement to compensation. This meant that the simple infringement of an interest or even a legal provision would not be enough to lead to assumption of liability,[42] just as it is today.[43]

This rule was widely criticised. Many argued that the rule was incomplete as it made no mention of the element of fault, which was recognised by the Portuguese legal scholarship as a requirement of liability.[44] Such absence might have been justified by the inherent difficulty of translating the term "*faute*" as contained in the *Code Civil*.[45] At any rate, by excluding it from the fundamental principle on civil

---

[38]Original version: "*Se as questões sobre direitos e obrigações não podérem ser resolvidas, nem pelo texto da lei, nem pelo seu espirito, nem pelos casos analogos, prevenidos em outras leis, serão decididos pelos principios de Direito Natural, conforme as circunstancias do caso*" (Codigo Civil Portuguez 1868, p. 5).

[39]Almeida Costa (2012), p. 447.

[40]von Bar (1998a), p. 24. The extension of the non-contractual liability regime contrasted with the "reduced importance" of such regime for society in the late nineteenth century. See Preamble of the DL 33908 of 4 September 1944, DR, 1st Ser., no. 196 (1944), p. 833.

[41]Original version: "*Todo aquelle, que viola ou offende os direitos de outrem, constitue-se na obrigação de indemnisar o lesado, por todos os prejuízos que lhe cause*"(Codigo Civil Portuguez 1868, p. 392).

[42]Antunes Varela (2000), p. 530; Pestana de Vasconcelos (2007), p. 159, fn. 39.

[43]On the general principles and requirements of non-contractual liability arising out of damage caused to another, see Part II, Tit. § 4, Subtit. IV below.

[44]Correia de Jesus (1968), p. 48.

[45]Menezes Cordeiro (1996b), p. 453.

liability, the Viscount of Seabra "set aside part of the lessons of the French Code",[46] diverging both structurally and systematically from the latter.[47]

At the same time, the *lex Aquilia* was in force in several German territories, and made no distinction between unlawfulness and fault.[48]

3. Revision Process and External Influences

a) The Reception of Pandectism

The Seabra's Code was in force for almost one hundred years. It had an important influence on the Portuguese Civil Law scholarship of the late-nineteenth-century and resulted in the creation of several legal journals[49] based on scholarly analysis and discussion of its development and use. Together with the Royal Edicts, therefore, the Seabra's Code represented a milestone in the development of the present-day Civil Code.

At the beginning of the twentieth century, the Civilian system of Portugal shifted alignment from the Napoleonic tradition of Civil Law to the Germanic tradition of Civil Law.[50]

This occurred initially through the translation of the BGB into French[51] by Bufnoir and then through the original text, as the custom of reading texts in the native German spread within the universities. As a result, Portuguese legal scholars became acquainted with the German Civil Code and its innovative legal institutions.[52]

Guilherme Alves Moreira (1861–1922) made the revolutionary move of introducing the Pandectist school of legal science to Portugal[53] and this change in the philosophical landscape extended to non-contractual liability.[54]

From the citations included in his seminal work *Instituições do Direito Civil Português*, it is evident that Guilherme Alves Moreira consulted several foreign laws and a wide variety of international jurisprudence.[55] Pandectist-influenced

---

[46]Almeida Costa (2012), p. 438.

[47]See, however, Ranieri (2003), pp. 1442–1443, 1445 and fn. 70.

[48]For further details, see Münch-Komm-Wagner (2013), § 823, no. 1.

[49]See Menezes Cordeiro (2004), p. 37. That was the case of *Revista de Legislação e Jurisprudência*, which still exists today.

[50]For more details on the foreign influences on the Seabra's Code, see Zweigert and Kötz (1996), pp. 106–107; Menezes Cordeiro (1999), pp. 123–126; Miranda Barbosa (2006a), pp. 164–165.

[51]On the role of legal translation, see generally Ranieri (1977), pp. 1487–1504 (p. 1487 ff.).

[52]Menezes Cordeiro (2004), pp. 38–39. See further von Bar (1982), pp. 638–641.

[53]Menezes Cordeiro (2004), p. 37; Pinto Monteiro (2006), p. 69. But cf. Müller (2008), p. 39. With further reference on the Pandects, see Menezes Cordeiro (1987), p. 131 ff.

[54]Menezes Leitão (2009), p. 229. Due to the important contribution of Moreira, he was considered as a candidate for "(. . .) the founder of the Portuguese modern civil scholarship". See Almeida Costa (2012), p. 517.

[55]Vaz Serra (1962), p. 24.

literature from Italy, the works of the German *Pandektenrechtler* and the BGB are some influences that can be readily identified.[56]

The *Instituições* provide a clear timeline of the arrival and reception of Pandectism in Portugal. They show: a) the preference for Italian and German legal scholarship over French scholarship (namely Chiovenda, Windscheid, Dernburg and von Jhering);[57] b) increased awareness of the BGB and its classifications, particularly the general part of obligations; and, finally, c) the reception of new legal institutions (*culpa in contrahendo*, doctrine of *negotiorum gestio*, the law of unjustified enrichment and the dualist model of civil liability) and doctrinal improvement in general[58] in the Portuguese legal system.

In the first official edition of the *Instituições* (1907), three requirements for civil liability were identified—unlawfulness, fault and damage.[59] The scheme of liability proposed by von Jhering,[60] based in the distinction between unlawfulness (*objektives Unrecht, injúria objetiva*) and fault (*subjektives Unrecht, injúria subjetiva*) was adopted.[61] Several legal scholars, such as Vaz Serra, Cabral de Moncada, Pereira Coelho and Galvão Telles, subsequently adopted this distinction in their work and writings.[62] The separation of unlawfulness and fault can still be found in the current civil liability scheme.[63] Indeed, today, a two-way distinction is made where unlawfulness concerns a value judgment of the *conduct* (act or omission) of the agent or the result of such conduct, and where fault relates to a value judgment of the agent him or herself.[64]

As a result of the teachings of Guilherme de Moreira, practically all of the Portuguese Civil Law scholarship accepted the Germanic model.[65] A new doctrine had blossomed, bringing innovative solutions to modern questions[66] and the Portuguese Civil Law system forged ahead with bravely[67] replacing its old-fashioned Napoleonic "attire" with something a little more "*en vogue*".

---

[56] Müller (2008), p. 58.

[57] Nevertheless, the doctrines of Saleilles were also received. See Menezes Cordeiro (1999), p. 118.

[58] Menezes Cordeiro (2010a), pp. 71–72.

[59] Alves Moreira (1907), § 45 (p. 585 ff.) *apud* Menezes Cordeiro (1996b), p. 455, fn. 245.

[60] von Jhering (1867). See also von Caemmerer (1968), p. 126 ff.

[61] See, in detail, Menezes Cordeiro (1996b), p. 432 ff. and 451 ff. For details on the distinction between unlawfulness and fault see Part II, Tit. § 4, Subtit. IV, Secs 4 and 5 below.

[62] Menezes Leitão (2009), p. 228, fn. 629. But see Pessoa Jorge (1995), p. 70; Mota Pinto (1966), pp. 243–247. Pessoa Jorge (1995), p. 70.

[63] Menezes Cordeiro (1996b), p. 434. See also Menezes Cordeiro (2010b), p. 331.

[64] Cf. Almeida Costa (2008), p. 579.

[65] As was the case for Gomes da Silva (1944, p. 99 ff. and p. 168 ff.), Lopes Navarro (1948, p. 31) and Pereira Coelho (1950, p. 60 ff.).

[66] Menezes Cordeiro (2004), p. 52.

[67] According to von Bar, Portugal was one of the few countries that had the "courage" to distance itself, "albeit gingerly", from the French Code Civil (von Bar 1998a, pp. 23–24). But cf. Menezes Cordeiro (2010a), p. 73.

b) The Revision of 1930

The Seabra's Code sustained its most significant change in modern times through Decree 19126, passed in 16 December 1930.[68] Despite including amendments to 117 rules, the Decree is nevertheless considered a failure for a number of reasons.

Firstly, the revised Code did not reflect the economic and social reality of its day, nor the significant dogmatic transformations of the Portuguese political panorama.[69] This failure to reflect the context of its day was further exacerbated by the approval of the Political Constitution of the Portuguese Republic (CPRP) of 1933. The new constitution legitimised the rule of the *Ditadura Nacional*, a political regime directed by military authorities, which had been in power since 1926, thus putting the *Estado Novo* ("New State") formally in place.[70]

Secondly, even though the influence of the Pandect movement had been well established in research and teaching, the Decree stated that the structure and system of the Code would not be changed, as it constituted a "real monument of national reputation".[71]

Thirdly, of the many provisions amended, only two were concerned with civil liability. This already foreshadowed the growing need for further revisions in this area.

c) The Reception of *danno ingiusto* in Portuguese Civil Liability Law

The uncodified Act of 1942 on the civil liability of medical practitioners is of particular relevance to the history of Portuguese civil liability law.[72]

According to Art. 28 of the Act: "The doctor who, in such capacity, causes to someone, with intention or negligence, a *dano injusto*, must repair it". This provision, which extended to "the medical auxiliaries and to those who, even though not having a proper title, exercise medicine", was openly based upon Art. 2043 of the Italian Civil Code, approved earlier that same year.

---

[68]DR, 1st Ser., no. 292 (1930), pp. 2427–2440.

[69]Vaz Serra, *BolMinJus* 2 (1947), p. 25. Cf. Wengler (1967), p. 64.

[70]This authoritarian regime, which was qualified by some as Fascist, by others as a conservative dictatorship (Hespanha 1986a, p. 109), aimed to create a "new order", free from the "vices of Liberalism, Rationalism and Marxist contamination" (Rosas 2001, p. 1037). The foundations of *Estado Novo* were: a) God, as the guiding principle; b) Homeland (*Pátria*) and the Family as uniting elements; c) Work, as individual contribution for collective good, and d) Authority, as the element mediating between individuals and the values which went beyond them (Jesus Cunha 1994, p. 86).

[71]Müller (2008), p. 58.

[72]Decree 32171 of 29 July 1942, DR, 1st Ser., no. 175 (1942), pp. 991–994.

By bringing together the *violação* (*iniuria*, *Verletzung*) and the *dano* (*danno*, *Schaden*),[73] the Act of 1942 on the civil liability of medical practitioners departed from the French model, where factual damage consisted of a requirement for civil liability[74] without further *quid*.[75]

This was a novel formula for Portuguese law and it highlighted the shortcomings of the eighteenth-century-legal framework, according to which only the act which infringed subjective rights led to reparations.[76]

More specifically, the infringement of certain interests should have led to the need for reparation.[77] By considering every interest as worthy of legal protection irrespective whether or not it was expressly set out in the law, the Italian Civil Code encompassed a far broader protection of subjective positions than that of the BGB.[78]

The expression "*dano injusto*", as contained in Art. 28 of the Act of 1942 on the civil liability of medical practicioners, was ambiguous[79] and has led to widely differing interpretations in the Italian legal scholarship.[80] The fact that the concept of *ingiustizia* applies to *danno* (effect) and not to its cause (the *fatto*) has been particularly criticised.[81] The view that unlawfulness relates to the conduct itself is still the prevailing position in Portugal, in line with the German position since the works of the First Commission for the draft of the BGB.[82]

---

[73]Gozzi (2006), p. 24. For a critical account see Bargagna and Busnelli (2001), p. 318.

[74]Castronovo (2006), p. 9.

[75]Gozzi (2006), p. 126.

[76]Some scholars hold that if a fact does not violate a right, no damage results from that fact, in the legal sense. That is the case in Portugal (Pereira Coelho 1950, p. 67) and in Italy (Castronovo 1997, p. 128).

[77]Antunes Varela (2000), p. 531. According to traditional legal scholarship, only subjective rights led to a duty to compensate (Gozzi 2006, p. 23, fn. 17). However, this theory was called into question. As described in Gozzi (2006), p. 23, fn. 17, it was suggested that the core of the *danno ingiusto* contained: the absence of defences (Schlesinger 1960, p. 336 ff.); all typical cases where an infringed interest is protected (Sacco 1960, p. 1420 ff.); the violated interests which the court considers protected in each particular case (Rodotà 1964, p. 183 ff.); both unlawfulness and fault (Cian 1966); and the evaluation of the interests at stake (Trimarchi 2007, p. 107).

[78]Gozzi (2006), p. 22.

[79]For details on the ambiguity of the Act of 1942 on the civil liability of medical practitioners, see *ibid.*, p. 23, fn. 17.

[80]Initially, the expression was understood in similar fashion as § 823(1) BGB, in other words as referring to an absolute right (Cass. 8 May 1971, no. 1318, Giur.it. 1973 I, 1, pp. 1125, 1133) but currently it is generally defined as a loss which is caused *contra ius* (against a legally protected interest) and *non iure* (in the absence of a defence and execution of right). The courts decide, *in casu*, which interests the law should protect. See von Bar (2000a), p. 241. See Cian (1966), p. 139 and Visintini (1967), p. 1 ff.

[81]Antunes Varela (2000), p. 532. This is the prevailing view in the Italian legal scholarship (Cian 2014, p. 2238 f.) Nevertheless, Busnelli argues that the *ingiustizia* refers to both the damage and the fact (Busnelli 1993, p. 14).

[82]In Prot. I 969 (Jakobs and Schubert 1983, 876) the Commission decided: "That requirement [fault] is not to refer to the damage itself, but to the objective unlawfulness (...)". See BGH 30 May 1972, *VersR*, pp. 938–939. This theory is not applicable to the causation of a pure economic loss within § 826 BGB (Münch-Komm-Wagner 2013, § 823, no. 2).

d) The General Revision of 1944

The movement for general revision of the Seabra's Code was launched with the DL 33908[83] of 4 September 1944.[84] In its Preamble, the DL included an extensive list of reasons for reform.

The Code was deemed overly ambiguous, leaving too much room for interpretation. It was also seen as outdated in relation to the uncodified legislation which had been enacted in the previous years.[85]

The Seabra's Code was not necessarily intended to set out the best solutions, which was particularly "incomprehensible" given that the sources of the Code provided for "more perfect and reasonable" solutions.[86]

The Preamble to the DL also highlighted the fact that the new code should consider including important legal concepts, such as the contract for the benefit of third parties, precontractual liability and *abus de droit*.[87] These demands were again influenced by the BGB.

The legislative technique of the Seabra's Code was poor, with a lack of uniformity in the way concepts were employed. This was a marked contrast to the techniques of the BGB which was considered "full of safe formulae".[88]

The Preamble to the DL 33908 further stated that the Seabra's Code did not take a position on whether the code should be complete for the sake of legal certainty (*certeza e segurança jurídicas*), or whether it should leave the task of developing the guidelines provided by statutes to the courts through case law. It questioned if the courts should be "creating the law aimed at regulating the hypotheses which are not comprised in the statutory rule".[89]

The result of this debate was the decision to shift the direction of Portuguese law from the individual-centered civil code (like that of the French Civil Code) to a more social kind of civil code (such as the BGB), because the "law should serve the interests of the community at large".[90]

---

[83]DR, 1st Ser., no. 196 (1944), pp. 830–836.

[84]Vaz Serra (1947), p. 26.

[85]Preamble of the DL 33908 of 4 September 1944, p. 831 (no. 3 *lit.* a) and pp. 831–832 (no. 3 *lit.* b), respectively. Some of these statutes are listed in Mota Pinto (2008a), p. 32, fn. 16.

[86]Preamble of the DL 33908 of 4 September 1944, p. 832 (no. 3 *lit.* c).

[87]*ibid.*, p. 832 (no. 3 *lit.* d).

[88]*ibid.*, p. 833 (no. 3 *lit.* e).

[89]*ibid.*, p. 833 (no. 2).

[90]*ibid.*, pp. 833–834. Vaz Serra, *BolMinJus* 2 (1947), p. 29. On the transition from a liberal and anthropocentric paradigm of Civil Law (Seabra's Code and *Code Civil*) to the conservative and social-centric paradigm (BGB and *Codice Civile*), see generally Correia de Mendonça (1982), p. 852 ff. See also Nogueira da Silva (2007), pp. 24–27.

The regulation of civil liability had only just begun,[91] and the industrial revolution and capitalism demanded new spheres of allocation of responsibility to be added to the existing rules.[92] Many of these rules had developed on a case-to-case basis and were disjointed in nature. The rules allegedly made the code appear "more similar to the compilations of the past than to the real codes of (...) our time".[93]

The repeated references to the German Civil Code and German legal solutions in the Preamble was a consequence of the introduction of the Pandect scholarship into Portuguese general legal understanding. This, together with the substantial and structural deficiencies of the Seabra's Code, opened the way for the preparation of a new civil code along the lines of the German version.[94]

IV. The Civil Code of 1966

1. The **travaux préparatoires** *of Vaz Serra and the German Influence in the General Principle of Non-Contractual Liability Arising Out of Damage Caused to Another*

The process of creation of the present-day Civil Code followed a long gestation period, lasting more than two decades.[95]

Adriano Paes da Silva Vaz Serra, who had held the position of Minister of Justice since 1940, presided over a Commission to revise the Code. This Commission was comprised of legal scholars with practical experience as lawyers or consultants. Among these scholars were such notables as Andrade,[96] Pires de Lima[97] and Cunha.[98] The Commission took on the task of engaging in the studies necessary for the preparation of the new civil code.[99]

---

[91]Menezes Cordeiro (1999), p. 126 ff.

[92]Reis Marques (2009), pp. 216 and 217.

[93]DL 33908 of 4 September 1944, p. 832.

[94]Mota Pinto (2005), p. 82; Menezes Leitão (2009), p. 235.

[95]Mota Pinto (2008a), p. 26.

[96]For the role of Manuel de Andrade in the preparation of the Portuguese Civil Code of 1966, see generally Sinde Monteiro (1997).

[97]For the role of Pires de Lima in the revision of the Seabra's Code, see Correia de Mendonça (1982), p. 831, fn. 4.

[98]Vaz Serra, *BolMinJus* 2 (1947), p. 31.

[99]Correia de Mendonça (1982), p. 849.

Based on long, comprehensive studies,[100] Vaz Serra, who was heavily influenced by German legal scholarship,[101] extended the preliminary projects (*anteprojetos*) to the area of the Law of Obligations. Many considered the *travaux préparatoires* an exercise in "impressive" comparative studies,[102] "a truly exhaustive work and the most complete work in the Portuguese jurisprudence on the Law of Obligations (...)".

Vaz Serra was lauded as "the father of the Civil Code of 1966", which was named the Vaz Serra's Code (*Código de Vaz Serra*) in his honour.[103] Curiously, in the preamble to the first Decree-Law to revise the original version of the Portuguese Civil Code, the drafters referred to an "overestimation of the value of the study of comparative law".[104]

One particular work had a significant influence on the new draft of the fundamental principle of non-contractual liability arising from damage caused to another in the present-day Civil Code (Art. 483 CC) and its subsequent doctrinal interpretation.[105] According to the work "Requirements of civil liability",[106] civil liability results from an unlawful (*antijurídico*) human act, *i.e.* a human act which is directly or indirectly against the provisions of the legal order.[107] Vaz Serra opted for an understanding based on the German Civil Code, as opposed to a French-style general clause. He considered that the latter "only partially" satisfied its obligations of regulation.[108] In the same piece of work, Vaz Serra wrote that a person's property (*património*) is not protected as such. What he meant was that, apart from the cases of infringement of property rights (*maxime*, the right of ownership), other infringements of rights over patrimonial assets would only lead to reparation if they breached a statute aimed at protecting patrimonial interests or otherwise resulted from a breach of a contractual duty.[109]

---

[100] These studies were published in *Boletim do Ministério da Justiça*, the official newsletter of the Ministry of Justice, and are listed in chronological order in Almeida Costa (2006a), pp. 26–31. For details on the *travaux préparatoires* of Vaz Serra see von Lillienskiold (1975), pp. 22–28. See also Vaz Serra, *BolMinJus* 2 (1947), pp. 24–76.

[101] See especially: Vaz Serra (1955), pp. 98–126; Vaz Serra (1958a), pp. 259–303; Vaz Serra (1959c), pp. 5–303; Vaz Serra (1959i), pp. 345–360; Vaz Serra (1959h), pp. 381–444; Vaz Serra (1959f), pp. 21–99; Vaz Serra (1959a); Vaz Serra (1959b), pp. 5–322; Vaz Serra (1960d), pp. 37–137.

[102] von Lillienskiold (1975), p. 22; von Bar (2004a), p. 128.

[103] Menezes Cordeiro (2004), pp. 42 and 58.

[104] According to Pessoa Jorge, this was due to the refusal of the EEC to allow Portuguese accession in 1962 (Pessoa Jorge 1975–1976, p. 14).

[105] For details on Portuguese non-contractual civil liability arising out of damage caused to another, see Part II, Tit. § 4, Subtit. IV below.

[106] Vaz Serra (1960d), pp. 37–137.

[107] *ibid.*

[108] *ibid.*, pp. 44–45 and 65 ff.

[109] Vaz Serra (1960d), pp. 45–46.

It seems clear, therefore, that the influence of German Pandectism on Vaz Serra's *travaux préparatoires* led to the revelation of the existence of other realities beyond subjective rights, such as directly or indirectly protected interests.

2. The Contributions of Pires de Lima and Antunes Varela and the Enactment of the New Civil Code

a) A Social-Oriented and More Open Civil Code

Pires de Lima and Antunes Varela significantly revised the *travaux préparatoires* of Vaz Serra.[110]

Antunes Varela, appointed Minister of Justice in 1955, was the author of two global projects on Private Law in 1963 and 1965.[111] On 26 November 1966 he presented a project to the *Assembleia Nacional*[112] which was described as having a strong social orientation, expressed "in the careful limitation of the principles of freedom of contract and freedom of will, in the significant thickening of the imperative rules aimed at averting the dangers of economic and social inequality among the subjects of the legal relationship, in the greater importance given to the dictates of good faith and fair dealing and the postulates of commutative property and (...) the more frequent appeal which the law does to *aequitas*". In contrast to the earlier codifications, Varela also expressed "the reaction against the legal positivism, expressed in the open, honest confession of the insufficiency of the law before the problems under the rule of law, in the legal relevance of other legislation and the recognition that other disciplinary orders of human conduct existed within the space usually reserved for the legitimate State sovereignty".[113]

The new code was approved and published through DL 47344 on 25 November 1966.[114] The Portuguese Civil Code of 1966 entered into force on 1 June 1967 (Art. 2(1) CPRP), on the occasion of the centenary of the Seabra's Code.[115] It

---

[110]Menezes Cordeiro (1999), p. 129. Cf. also von Lillienskiold (1975), p. 23 ff.

[111]These projects were known as *Anteprojecto do Direito das Obrigações, Primeira Revisão Ministerial* and *Anteprojeto do Direito das Obrigações, Segunda Revisão Ministerial* (Preliminary Project of the Law of Obligations, First Ministerial Revision and Preliminary Project of the Law of Obligations, Second Ministerial Revision, respectively). In the first Ministerial Revision, non-contractual liability was regulated in Arts. 462 to 490 and Arts. 541 to 549 CC; in the second Ministerial Revision, non-contractual liability was regulated in Arts. 483 to 510 and Arts. 562 to 572 CC. See von Lillienskiold (1975), pp. 24–26.

[112]*ibid.*, pp. 24–25.

[113]Antunes Varela (1966), p. 11. See also Leitão (2008), pp. 129–130.

[114]DL 47344 of 25 November 1966, DR, 1st Ser., no. 274 (1966), pp. 1883–2086.

[115]See Correia de Mendonça (1982), p. 851; von Bar (1998a), p. 22, fn. 16.

thus belongs, together with the Swiss (1907), the Greek (1940) and the Italian (1942) civil codes, to a group of codification projects called the "late codifications".[116]

Through the Ministerial Order (*Portaria*) 22869 of 4 September 1967 (Art. 1)[117] the reach of the Portuguese Civil Code was extended to the overseas provinces, *i.e.* the archipelago of Cape Verde; Guinea-Bissau; São Tomé and Príncipe and respective dependencies; St. John the Baptist of Ouidah (today, Ouidah); Cabinda; Angola;[118] Mozambique;[119] Portuguese India; Macau and Timor.[120] Indeed, colonisation served as a vehicle for the spread of Portuguese legal culture throughout the world,[121] creating its long-term potential as part of the core of Civil Law in Europe.[122]

b) German Structure and Drafting Style

The Portuguese Civil Code is divided into five books,[123] each corresponding to the Germanic classifications of legal relationships as contained in Private Law,[124] namely: a general part,[125] obligations, property rights, family rights and rights of inheritance.

Book I (General Part) contains an introductory set of rules dealing with the general principles of Civil Law in Portugal.[126] The law of natural persons (Tit. II, Subtit. I, Chap. I) includes rules on legal personality. A general personality right (*direito geral de personalidade*) is provided for in Art. 70 CC. Book I regulates the social-oriented *abus de droit* and general *clause d' ordre public*, which are also

---

[116] Menezes Cordeiro (1999), pp. 123 ff.

[117] Ministerial Order 22869 of 4 September 1967, DR, 1st Ser., no. 206 (1967), pp. 1582–1583.

[118] Art. 1(2) CPRP.

[119] Art. 1(3) CPRP.

[120] Art. 1(4) CPRP, where it entered into force on 1 January 1968 (Art. 2 CPRP), revoking all civil legislation concerning the matters regulated by the Civil Code (Art. 3 CPRP).

[121] Ferreira de Almeida and Morais Carvalho (2013), p. 46.

[122] Baldus (2012), p. 105. This potential has not yet been fully realised (cf. von Bar 2014a, p. 474).

[123] On the structure of the BGB, see Zweigert and Kötz (1996), pp. 144–147, in particular p. 144; Dias Pereira (2005), pp. 623–627; Rüthers and Stasler (2014), pp. 5–8; Bork (2016), p. 33 ff.; Brox and Walker (2016), pp. 24–26.

[124] On the Germanic classification of Civil Law, see Pessoa Jorge (1995), p. 13; Menezes Cordeiro (2004), p. 43.

[125] On the controversy of the BGB adopting a general part, see Zweigert and Kötz (1996), pp. 144 ff.; Pinto Monteiro (2006), p. 59; Menezes Cordeiro (2010a), pp. 17–119.

[126] This general part contains, broadly, the same subjects as the BGB, with the exception of Private International Law, which the latter does not include.

included in the BGB. The exercise and protection of rights, however, are said to have been influenced by the Italian Civil Code.[127]

Book II corresponds to the "Law of Obligations" (*Direito das Obrigações*) and contains the features, effects and performance of legal obligations. It is divided into two parts: the first regulates obligations in general, while the second regulates each contract type individually. The first part is deemed to have been heavily influenced by the Italian Civil Code[128] which, in turn, was based on the French Civil Code.[129] Book II regulates civil liability (*responsabilidade civil*, Arts. 483 ff. CC), *negotiorum gestio* (*gestão de negócios*, Arts. 464 ff. CC) and the law of unjustified enrichment (*enriquecimento sem causa*, Arts. 473 ff.), which is also regulated by the BGB.

The second part of Book II regulates each contract type individually, and also provides for all of the securities for the performance of obligations (Arts. 601 ff. CC). This is in contrast to Germany, where such regulation can be found in Book III.

The Law of Things (*Direito das Coisas*) is laid out in Book III. Here the Civil Code regulates the right of ownership and possession, in particular.[130] Of the five books, it is here that the Italian influence is most apparent.[131]

Book IV focuses on Family Law (*Direito da Família*) and provides for those legal rules which are connected to the structure, organisation and protection of the family, as well as the obligations and rights arising from these relationships.

Finally, the Law of Succession (*Direito das Sucessões*), found in Book V, deals with the transfer of property, rights and obligations following a person's death.

Although this structure was not without its critics,[132] it is still used today when designing and outlining the study of Civil Law in Portugal.[133] The criticism has not, therefore, been considered decisive.[134] However, the German structure of both codes leaves it very open to external elements, and thereby attracts almost permanent efforts towards reform.[135]

---

[127] Magri and Medeiros Nóbrega (2014), p. 5.

[128] Murillo (2001–2002), p. 176. One of the examples of inspiration taken from Italian Law is Art. 493(2) CC (Losses caused by things, animals or activities), according to which the person who causes losses to a third party while exercising a dangerous activity shall compensate him or her unless he or she shows that every measure required by the circumstances to prevent the loss was taken. The presumption of fault is thus very difficult to rebut (Vaz Serra 1959g, pp. 361–380).

[129] See further Castronovo (1997), p. 3; von Bar (1998a), p. 23; Rübesamen (2000), pp. 17–18; Alpa (2007), pp. 28–29.

[130] For an overview, see Caramelo Gomes and Medeiros (2011).

[131] See Magri and Medeiros Nóbrega (2014), p. 6 ff.

[132] Menezes Cordeiro (2004), p. 57.

[133] See Menezes Cordeiro (1999), p. 129; Antunes Varela (2000), pp. 35–39; Almeida Costa (2006a), p. 161.

[134] Vaz Serra, *BolMinJus* 2 (1947), p. 34. For further remarks on the influence of the French and the German models in Portuguese law, see Menezes Leitão (2009), p. 225 ff. On the French and German legal models, see generally von Bar (1998a), p. 21 ff.

[135] See Menezes Cordeiro (2004), p. 54; Mota Pinto (2005), p. 85 ff.

As explained above,[136] the rules of the present-day Civil Code reflect, in particular, the influence of the BGB[137] and German legal scholarship.[138] Nevertheless, the similarities between both civil codes extend to other fields as well. That is the case for the legislative techniques used in the Portuguese Civil Code, which can also be found in the BGB.

In fact, the Portuguese legislature opted for general-abstract terms (*cláusulas gerais*) and open-ended concepts (*conceitos indeterminados*)[139] as legal formulation blueprints, as is the case with the BGB. Such terms and concepts have been considered a sort of "cysts [sic] of uncertainty (...)" that would ensure the "formulation, adequacy and durability of the law".[140] They were considered necessary to provide the Code with "greater guarantees of survival (...) against the inevitable fluctuations of uncodified legislation or against the uncontrolled free will of the legislature without legal endorsement".[141] The use of general-abstract terms in the Portuguese Civil Code was aimed at allowing solutions to vary according to the changing circumstances of each case and context.[142]

Finally, the Portuguese Civil Code is considered to contain the same technical, specialised language as that used in the BGB.[143]

3. The Carnation Revolution in 1974 and the Revision of the Civil Code in 1977

By the time of its 50th anniversary in 2016, the Portuguese Civil Code had already been revised more than 60 times.

---

[136]See Tit. § 1, Subtit. IV, Sec. 2, Subsec. b) above.

[137]More on the influence of the BGB on the present-day Portuguese Civil Code may be found in von Bar (1999c), pp. 3 and 7; Miranda Barbosa (2006a), pp. 109–113.

[138]The influence of German scholarship has extended past the promulgation of the Portuguese Civil Code (Ferreira de Almeida and Morais Carvalho 2013, p. 52) and is still visible in the acceptance, *de iure condendo*, of several legal institutions, as Part II, Tit. § 5, Subtit. III, Sec. 3 below will show.

[139]For more on Portuguese legislative techniques, see Menezes Cordeiro (1999), p. 126 ff. On the characteristics of the BGB, see Brox and Walker (2016), p. 17.

[140]Correia de Mendonça (1982), p. 846. See also Vaz Serra, *BolMinJus* 2 (1947), p. 39.

[141]Antunes Varela (1966), p. 31.

[142]Vaz Serra, *BolMinJus* 2 (1947), pp. 24–76. On the abstract-general style of the BGB, see Zweigert and Kötz (1996), p. 143 ff.; Schwab and Löhnig (2012), p. 16 ff.; Bork (2016), p. 36 ff.; Brox and Walker (2016), p. 24; Schmidt (2016), pp. 6–13. Due to the presence of such terms and concepts, the Portuguese Civil Code is considered one of the most abstract codes in Europe. See Hesselink (2001), p. 10 and fn. 3.

[143]For further remarks on the language style of the Portuguese Civil Code, see Correia de Mendonça (1982), p. 846 ff.

One of these revisions was particularly important. It was introduced by the DL 496/77 of 25 November 1977[144] and it took place in the context of political, economic and social change in Portugal following the 1974 Carnation revolution.

The revolution of 25 April 1974 brought democracy to Portugal and one of the first goals of its key players was to draft a new constitution. This Constitution came into force on 25 April 1976 and it reflected the political and ideological choices of the time, namely, the socialist ideal.[145] Thanks to the peaceful character of the revolution, the underlying political, economic and social tensions were channelled into legal discourse. While the pre-revolution law had suffered a perceived crisis of legitimacy, it remained largely in force.

Two opposing discursive strategies existed in the field of law at the time, one corresponding to the revolutionary project and the other to the conservative project.

The revolutionary project advocated the fundamental transformation of legal speech. It highlighted the importance of the teleological interpretation of the law and introduced the concept of "revolutionary legality" (*legalidade revolucionária*). This concept corresponded to an unwritten source of law, the hierarchical value of which was higher than the value of pre-revolutionary law.[146]

The conservative project was strongly legalist. It argued for an approach which, in line with the Judicial Magistrates Charter, subjugated the judge's sense of justice to the demands of the written text of the law.

In the end, the conservative project prevailed. After the Constitution entered in force (at a time where several signs of the revolutionary project still persisted), the judge could not update *in concreto* the constitutional principles. It had to be done by legislative order through the legislature.[147]

Art. 293(1) and (3) Const.[148] launched the reform of the Portuguese Civil Code. To do this, the government charged a Commission with the revision of the *travaux*

---

[144]DL 496/77 of 25 November 1977, DR, 1st Ser., no. 273-suppl. 1 (1977), pp. 1–50.

[145]Hespanha (1986b), p. 319; Kern (2010), pp. 547–548.

[146]Hespanha (1986b), p. 331.

[147]*ibid.*, p. 336. In the aftermath of the approval of the Constitution, the Natural Law supporters developed the "theory of the normative implications of concepts and words" (*teoria das implicações normativas dos conceitos e das palavras*), according to which doctrinal concepts in the Constitution had autonomous normative efficacy. The dominant role was played by the concepts of "material constitution" (*constituição material*) and "rule of law" (*Estado de Direito*). This allowed for the enlargement and correction of the will of the constitutional legislature, submitting it to doctrinal criteria or criteria of comparative law, similar to the development which took place in the democracies of Western Europe, such as that of the Federal Republic of Germany. After successive governments stated their intention to accede to the EEC, European Law became the (more positivist) substitute for the references to the material constitution, aimed at devaluing the legislative criteria and submitting them to a legal order which went beyond Positive Law (Hespanha 1986b, pp. 339–340).

[148]This article read: "1. The law which precedes the entry into force of the Constitution stays in force, provided that it is not contrary to the Constitution or the principles which it enshrines. (...) 3. The adaptation of the preceding rules concerning the exercise of the rights, freedoms and guarantees provided for the Constitution will be concluded until the end of the first legislative

préparatoires. This Commission drafted a bill, which was approved by Parliament in July 1977 and published in November that same year (DL 496/77 of 25 November 1977) before entering into force in April 1978. The decree-law largely exceeded the initial intentions of merely adapting the Code to the constitutional legislation with respect to the exercise of rights, liberties and guarantees. It also deeply transformed Family Law.[149]

4. The Evolution of the Civil Code Since the 1980s and Perspectives on Reform

The Portuguese Civil Code of 1966 was criticised for being a "rather backward-looking, conservative work", despite significant reforms to the original text.[150]

This condemnation may have had its root in several possible causes. Firstly, the fact that the legislature had opted to regulate classical Civil Law alone, leaving Labour Law and Commercial Law[151] (as was the case with the Italian *Codice Civile*)[152] untouched. Secondly, the fact that the legislature included Family Law and the Law of Successions in the Code, similar to the legal systems of the remaining Southern European countries.

Another objection was the fact that the Code adopted the Pandectist structure of the BGB, as well as its sets of concepts.[153] Indeed, ever since the promulgation of the Portuguese Civil Code, legislature, courts and legal scholars had been leaning towards German legal solutions.[154] The prevailing legal scholarship envisaged German Law as the "legal calculating machine *par excellence*"[155] and as the ultimate source of novel developments, gradually to be assimilated into the Portuguese Law of Obligations.[156]

---

session [15 June 1977]". Original version available through http://www.parlamento.pt/parlamento/documents/crp1976.pdf (accessed 31 March 2017).

[149] Hörster (2004b), p. 61; Magalhães Collaço (2004), p. 28; Oliveira Ascensão (2013), p. 374. See also Guimarães (1986), pp. 575–577 and Moura Ramos (2004), p. 736.

[150] Zweigert and Kötz (1996), p. 107.

[151] For details on the codification of Commercial Law in Portugal, see Reis Marques (2009), pp. 201–208.

[152] Wengler (1967), p. 65.

[153] Zweigert and Kötz (1996), p. 107. It could be argued that such criticism was a mere "fashion symptom, diffused among many German comparatists, of disagreeing with German law and only praising foreign laws" (Canaris 2006, p. 25). But cf. von Bar (2011a), p. 429.

[154] Menezes Cordeiro (2004), p. 53.

[155] See Schwarz (1950), p. 8.

[156] For details on the German novel developments that Portuguese law adopted, see Part II, Tit. § 5, Subtit. III, Sec. 3 below.

In recent decades, the Portuguese Civil Code has undergone several revisions, in particular in the field of Family Law.[157] As far as the Law of Obligations is concerned, the amendments to the binding promise to contract (*contrato-promessa*),[158] lease contract (*contrato de arrendamento*)[159] and strict liability for road traffic accidents[160] are good examples of matters which have recently been revised.

Certain civil matters have "escaped" the Civil Code, sometimes regrettably.[161] Product liability[162] was one—among many others—that "gained strength and lived on"[163] after being separated from the Civil Code.[164] Most of these bodies of law resulted from the transposition of European Union Directives.[165] According to some critics, the long-lasting effect of these Directives and the extension of their scope sometimes disturbs the domestic structure of civil codes.[166]

Despite such criticisms, prevailing opinion holds there to be no need for comprehensive reform of the Civil Code.[167]

---

[157]Particularly worthy of mention are: a) the Divorce law, Act 61/2008 of 31 October 2008, DR, 1st Ser., no. 212 (2008), pp. 7633–7638; b) the Act 9/2010 of 31 May 2010, DR, 1st Ser., no. 105 (2010), p. 1853, which recognised same-sex marriages, and c) the Act 23/2010 of 30 August 2010, DR, 1st Ser., no. 168 (2010), pp. 3764–3768, as amended by the Act 31/2012 of 14 August 2012, DR, 1st Ser., no. 157 (2012), pp. 4411–4452, which approved measures for the protection of non-marital partnerships.

[158]DL 236/80 of 18 July 1980, DR, 1st Ser., no. 164 (1980), pp. 1723–1724, as amended by DL 379/86 of 11 November 1986, DR, 1st Ser., no. 260 (1986), pp. 3381–3383.

[159]Act 6/2006 of 27 February 2006, DR, 1st Ser., no. 41 (2006), pp. 1558–1587 as amended by the Act 31/2012 of 14 August 2012, DR, 1st Ser., no. 157 (2012), pp. 4411–4452, which also reinstated the residential tenancy law into the Civil Code (Book II, Tit. I, Chap. 4).

[160]DL 190/85 of 24 June 1985, DR, 1st Ser., no. 142 (1985), pp. 1666–1667; DL 14/96 of 6 March 1996, DR, 1st Ser., no. 56 (1996), p. 444, which transposed Third Council Directive 90/232/CEE of 14 May 1990 on the approximation of the laws of the Member States relating to insurance against civil liability in respect of the use of motor vehicles [1990] OJ L 129, pp. 33–35.

[161]Menezes Cordeiro (2004), p. 59; Mota Pinto (2008a), p. 25.

[162]DL 383/89 of 6 November 1989, DR, 1st Ser., no. 255 (1989), pp. 4880–4882, as amended by DL 131/2001 of 24 April 2001, DR, 1st Ser., no. 96 (2001), p. 2337, which transposed Council Directive 85/374/EEC of 25 July 1985 on the approximation of the laws, regulations and administrative provisions of the Member States concerning liability for defective products, OJ L 210, pp. 29–33, as amended by Directive 1999/34/EC of the European Parliament and of the Council of 10 May 1999, OJ L 141, pp. 20–21.

[163]Pires da Rosa (2008), p. 17.

[164]Here, the Portuguese legislature diverged from the German legislature, which included the subject in the BGB. See the critical approach of Lebre de Freitas (2008), p. 11.

[165]Mota Pinto (2008a), pp. 33–35.

[166]See Hesselink (2001), p. 45. This is due to the fact that Directives are usually tailored for specific business activities, while national regulations follow legal classification criteria. See von Bar (2002f), p. 267. Cf. also von Bar (1999d), p. 149.

[167]Lebre de Freitas (2008), p. 11; Pires da Rosa (2008), p. 17.

Firstly, the Civil Code is not considered to be particularly dated.[168] Secondly, it can be argued that comprehensive reform already took place in the aftermath of the drafting of the constitution.[169] Thirdly, since the direct aftermath of the promulgation of the Vaz Serra's Code,[170] claims have been made that a general reform would entail more doctrinal and case law development than that which has been achieved so far.[171] Finally, it has been admitted that it would not be possible, either in the short or medium-term, to organise a set of *travaux préparatoires* such as those available when the present-day code was designed. A general reform would require[172] the compilation of such *travaux préparatoires* by means of comparative law.[173]

a) The Role of Portuguese Scholars in the Modernisation of the Civil Code

In 2002, three possible means of implementing a reform of the Portuguese Civil Code were put forward.[174] These three alternatives were: a) reform through piecemeal adjustments; b) a global revision of the Civil Code; or c) the recodification of the whole of private law, leading to the emergence of a new civil code.[175]

Only a small group of scholars publicly endorse a wholesale revision of the Civil Code, in particular with respect to Family Law, the Law of Persons and the Law of Obligations. According to this group, insofar as civil liability is concerned, a reform would need to tackle the preconditions of civil liability and the topic of remedies.[176] Some of the scholars who defended a complete revision of the Civil Code argued that it contains an "outdated" set of specific rules which were inspired by even older formulations of the Code. These rules were passed in a social context adapted to a predominantly rural life in economic isolation,[177] in stark contrast with the current social reality. Other scholars urge wholesale reform as a "condition of survival" against the risk of the disintegrative effect of "European updates".[178]

---

[168] Mota Pinto (2008a), p. 29. But see Menezes Cordeiro (2004), p. 59.

[169] Mota Pinto (2008a), p. 29.

[170] Cunha (1966), p. 315.

[171] Mota Pinto (2008a), pp. 37 and 46. See also Menezes Cordeiro (1999), p. 124. A sign of the "immaturity" of the doctrinal development would be the fact that there is as yet only one full comprehensive commentary on the Civil Code, Pires de Lima and Antunes Varela (2010) (Mota Pinto 2008a, p. 46, fn. 40).

[172] Mota Pinto (2008a), pp. 37–38.

[173] Menezes Cordeiro (2004), p. 200.

[174] Menezes Cordeiro (2002–2003), pp. 31–44.

[175] These alternatives were "*solução fraca*" ("weak solution"), "*solução média*" ("balanced solution") and "*solução forte*" ("strong solution"), respectively (Menezes Cordeiro 2004, pp. 60–65).

[176] *ibid*., pp. 63–64.

[177] Ferreira de Almeida (2008), pp. 346–347.

[178] Menezes Cordeiro (2004), pp. 200–201. On this "disintegrative effect", see generally Joerges (1999).

In light of the experience of the Portuguese Code of Civil Procedure (CCP) of 2013, small sections of legal academia advocate a "civil recodification".[179] This would lead, among other things, to the unification of private law, the reorganisation of Civil Law, and the update of legal matrices.[180]

In May 2003, the Bureau of Legislative Policy and Planning of the Ministry of Justice (*Gabinete de Política Legislativa e do Planeamento do Ministério da Justiça*)[181] concluded an agreement with the main Portuguese law faculties. This research group was tasked with undertaking research on the Portuguese Civil Code in order to assess the necessity and desirability of a reform of the civil code and "downstream legislation".[182]

Even though the then Minister of Justice endorsed a wholesale revision of the Code, no goals or deadlines were established for the project. Despite this, the group's conclusions led to a discussion of a possible reform of Portuguese Civil Law.[183]

Among the reasons presented by the Bureau for launching this research were: a) the "discomfort of seeing the Civil Code successively emptied through the adoption of baffling legislation, very often due to the urgency of transposing European Directives which would hardly be compatible with a revision of the Civil Code"; b) the fact that other national legal systems which have inspired the Portuguese Civil Code, namely German and Italian Law, have modernised their own civil codes; c) the initiatives of the European Parliament and the European Commission towards a more coherent and harmonised European contract law; and d) the significant economic and social changes that the country has undergone in recent years.[184]

Another motivation for the launch of the inquiry was the intention to ensure that any new civil code would have the structural capability of influencing a possible future European Civil Code.[185] Within a European context, this incentive is curious and unusual, with other Member States paying greater attention to adapting their existing domestic civil codes to a harmonised set of European rules—the reverse process.[186]

---

[179]Menezes Cordeiro (2004), p. 59.

[180]*ibid.*, p. 65.

[181]Since 2011, it is called *Direção Geral da Política de Justiça* (General Direction of the Policy of Justice).

[182]Ferreira de Almeida and Morais Carvalho (2013), p. 71. The formal involvement of universities in this inquiry highlights the continuing high regard for scholarship within the modern Portuguese legal system in the context of legislative reforms (for details on the high regard for scholarship within the modern Portuguese legal system see Tit. § 2, Subtit. II, Sec. 3, Subsec. b) below. This same regard can be found in almost all Romano-Germanic Civil Law systems.

[183]Mota Pinto (2008a), p. 37.

[184]See Caramelo Gomes and Medeiros Nóbrega (2011), p. 618.

[185]Gabinete do Ministério da Justiça (2005), p. 5.

[186]That was the case for Germany, which included some of the European solutions through the reform of the Law of Obligations of 2001–2002. Outside Europe, the Civil Code of Macau is

Portugal seems to have been acutely aware of its potential to become a "laboratory for legal Europe".[187] This is explained by the argument that Portuguese legal thinking, despite showing a remarkable interest in foreign solutions,[188] remains embedded in a nationalist conception of the private legal system, where national law is ultimately regarded as the only "valid" law[189] and should, at best, function as a role model for other European nations.

At any rate, very little attention was given to the subject of non-contractual liability arising out of damage caused to another[190] in the tender dossier.[191] The inquiry asked a single question on the compensation of non-economic loss, that being whether Art. 496(1) CC should expressly refer to non-economic loss and, if so, in which terms and with which justification.[192]

In spite of this, three of the four universities consulted suggested changes to the rules of non-contractual liability in their preliminary reports. Both the Law Faculty of the University of Coimbra and the Law Faculty of the Portuguese Catholic University considered that "some clarifications would be possible as far as the topic of civil liability is concerned".[193] Additionally, the Law Faculty of the Nova University of Lisbon appealed to a "unifying and clarifying" opinion on the aim of compensation.[194] Finally, the scholars of the Law Faculty of the Nova University of Lisbon argued that Art. 494 CC (limitation of compensation in the case of fault) should be repealed and Art. 496 CC (non-economic loss) adapted accordingly.[195]

Despite the results of the protocol, there have been no legislative amendments to the Portuguese Civil Code with respect to non-contractual liability arising out of damage caused to another. The legislature continues to opt for "piecemeal and

particularly worthy of mention. It originally consisted of an adapted version of the Portuguese Civil Code. On the reform of the Civil Code of Macau, see generally Jian (1995), pp. 319–341.

[187]Baldus (2012), p. 105.

[188]See Magri and Medeiros Nóbrega (2014), pp. 2–4.

[189]Jansen (2010), p. 151. There are legal scholars who consider Portuguese legal scholarship to be closed in a "self-referential introspection" (Hesselink 2012, p. 11; von Bar 2013, p. 9). For the difficulties in dealing with nationalism in this context, see von Bar (2008b), p. 5.

[190]Hereinafter, non-contractual liability arising out of damage caused to another, a formulation which closely follows the title of Book VI of the DCFR, which will be analysed under Part II, Tit. § 6, Subtit. II and Tit. § 7.

[191]Menezes Leitão (2009), p. 278.

[192]For further details on Art. 496 CC, see Part II, Tit. § 4, Subtit. IV, Sec. 2 below.

[193]See Gabinete do Ministério da Justiça (2005), pp. 25–29 and 69–73, respectively.

[194]According to scholars from the Law Faculty of the Nova University of Lisbon, there must be an express option for a *repairing* aim of compensation or for a *punitive* aim of compensation. Such an option is necessary to put an end to the difficulties of interpretation and the different solutions applied by the courts, particularly insofar as the compensation of pure economic loss is concerned.

[195]Gabinete do Ministério da Justiça (2005), pp. 85–86 and 94.

surgical"[196] transpositions of European directives,[197] which are more often than not integrated into the national legal system by way of uncodified legislation.

Many critics argue that specific bodies of laws, particularly the law of non-contractual obligations and non-contractual liability arising out of damage caused to another, are in need of reform. The social and economic framework on which the original version of the Civil Code was based has changed significantly, as has the Portuguese legal order.[198] Fifty years on, the Portuguese Civil Code remains a point of pride for Portuguese academics. However, the lack of legislative action in moving towards a revision of the Civil Code stands in stark contrast to the considerable judicial innovation which has taken place.[199]

In 2016 and 2017, the publication and entry in force of the Portuguese Civil Code were commemorated. Some of the members of the National Commission who organised such commemorations[200] (*Comissão Nacional do Código Civil*)[201] declared that "due to the high technical and scientific quality that it still shows today, the Civil Code is a matter of pride for all the Portuguese legal community" (Pinto Monteiro) and "one of the masterpieces of the Portuguese legislation" (Alarcão).[202]

b) Position Towards a European Civil Code and the Process of Harmonisation of European Private Law

The considerable contribution of Portuguese legal scholars to the Europeanisation movement started in the 1980s, when Magalhães Colaço (preceeding Ferreira de Almeida) joined the "Lando Commission".[203] They were followed by Gomes and Sinde Monteiro (who joined the Co-ordinating Group of SGECC), Pinto Monteiro

[196] Pires da Rosa (2008), p. 18.

[197] As was the case of DL 59/2004 of 19 March 2004, DR, 1st Ser., no. 67 (2004), pp. 1550–1551, which transposed the Second Council Directive 84/5/CEE of 30 December 1983 on the approximation of the laws of the Member States relating to insurance against civil liability in respect of the use of motor vehicles, OJ L 8, pp. 17–20.

[198] Pires da Rosa (2008), p. 18.

[199] On judicial innovation within the Law of Obligations, and particularly the compensation of pure economic loss, see Part II, Tit. § 5, Subtit. III, Sec. 3 below.

[200] For a complete list of these commemorations, see http://www.stj.pt/noticias/687-comemoracoes-do-50o-aniversario-do-codigo-civil?format=pdf (accessed 31 March 2017).

[201] The members of the Commission who organised the commemorations of the Civil Code are: Alarcão (Professor at the Law Faculty of the University of Coimbra and President of this Commission); Supreme Court Judge and President Henriques Gaspar; Fraga (President of the Portuguese Bar Association), Pinto Monteiro (Professor at the Law Faculty of the University of Coimbra) and Menezes Cordeiro (Professor at the Law Faculty of the University of Lisbon).

[202] UDireito, *Comissão organiza Comemorações dos 50 anos do Código Civil*, July, 29th 2015, available through http://www.udireito.com/2015/comemoracoes-dos-50-anos-do-codigo-civil/ (accessed 31 March 2017).

[203] For details on the Lando Commission, see Tit. § 3, Subtit. II, Sec. 1, Subsec. b) below.

and Mota Pinto (members of the Acquis Group), as well as Cristas and several junior researchers who provided national notes for the working teams of the SGECC.[204]

In Portugal in recent years, several national and international conferences have discussed new developments in the Europeanisation process.

Portuguese legal scholarship has, from an early stage, shown itself to be a significant player in the process of Europeanisation.

In the immediate aftermath of the Presidency Conclusions of the Tampere European Council (October 1999), which requested "an overall study (...) on the need to approximate Member States' legislation in civil matters",[205] the University of Coimbra[206] held the conference "A Civil Code for Europe".[207] This was the first conference in Portugal that acknowledged the ongoing process of Europeanisation. This was the first of several conferences organised in Portugal in the years that followed.[208]

Publications in highly ranked journals on DCFR issues and on a possible future European Civil Code, are frequent and regular. Some of these arguments reflect a clear opposition to a European Civil Code,[209] which is sometimes characterised as potentially representing "significant cultural loss".[210] Others hold that the uniformisation of Civil Law would step outside of EU competencies, which justifies the piecemeal approach of EU regulations in this field and the imposition of a merely scientific (not political) approach to this issue.[211]

---

[204]Namely, Cascão, Pereira, Couto Guedes, Braga and Santos Silva. See von Bar et al. (eds) (2008), p. 41 ff.

[205]Available through http://www.europarl.europa.eu/summits/tam_en.htm (accessed 31 March 2017). For details on the approximation of Member States' legislation in civil matters see Tit. § 3, Subtit. II, Sec. 1, Subsec. a) below.

[206]Appropriately, the location of the conference was the oldest university in Portugal, which remains one of the world's oldest operating universities.

[207]This conference was organised by Sinde Monteiro.

[208]The Law of Trust, as envisaged by the DCFR, was presented to the academic community in February 2009 at the 11th International Congress and 14th Ibero-American Congress of Roman Law at the Law Faculty of Lisbon. The topic was again included in the programme two years later, at the conference "New tendencies in Financial Law. The impact of trust", organised at the University Portucalense in Oporto (by Martinez de Campos and Santos Silva). The conference "A European Law of Obligations? The Influence of the DCFR" (organised by Afonso and Guichard), which took place in Porto in September 2014, included papers on the DCFR presented by Portuguese and foreign legal scholars, judges and practitioners.

[209]Mota Pinto (2008a), p. 30. Some legal scholars consider it more feasible to provide solely for a European Code of Contract Law (Pinto Monteiro 2006, p. 73). Other scholars even talked of a "decline" in the codifying movement. See Reis Marques (2006), p. 89 *passim*. But see Hondius (1997), p. 455 ff.

[210]Menezes Cordeiro (1996a), pp. 887–912; Miranda Barbosa (2015), p. 251. For criticism of a European Civil Code, see also Calvão da Silva (2001–2002), pp. 272–273.

[211]Sinde Monteiro (2002), p. 51.

Other, more "pro-Europeanists" scholars,[212] defend the view that a European Civil Code is desirable, even necessary. They suggest that legal scholars are best qualified to lead the creation of a full European Civil Code, although they recognise that this is unlikely to occur in the near future.[213]

There are also those who take intermediate positions on the issue, defending a two-stage approach to a European Civil Code. The first stage should be voluntary, with a second stage being mandatory provided that it is deemed "fair and efficient".[214]

One school of thought holds that unification of non-contractual liability is necessary because of its influence on the free movement of people, goods, services and capital, as well as the need to assure balanced competition in equal conditions.[215] Others admit that the harmonisation of non-contractual liability arising out of damage caused to another is preferred to the process of transposition of Directives into national law, which has lead to "scattered orders which destroy the coherence of the system".[216]

5. *A Synthesis of Several Legal Traditions in the Present-Day Civil Code*

The question of how to classify the Portuguese Civil Law system within the legal systems (*Rechtskreise*) is highly controversial.

Some legal scholars point to its Roman origins, suggesting that modern Portuguese law fits well into the Romano legal model,[217] as was the case for its historical precedent, the Seabra's Code.[218]

Other authors claim the Portuguese Civil Code of 1966 as "the second fundamental transformation of the French Civil Code".[219]

There are also some authors who acknowledge the clear transition the Code underwent at the beginning of the twentieth century to fit with the German style, tying it irrevocably, in their eyes, to the German legal model.[220]

---

[212]For the description of the different perspectives towards European Private Law, see Hesselink (2009), p. 932 ff. and Hesselink (2012), pp. 1–41.

[213]See, for example, Menezes Leitão (2009), p. 351, fnn. 921 and 352.

[214]Silva Pereira (2004), pp. 497–608. For critics, see Menezes Leitão (2009), p. 355, fn. 929. For an overview of several positions towards a European Civil Code, see Menezes Leitão (2009), pp. 352–353, fn. 924.

[215]Carneiro da Frada (2007b), p. 354. This was recognised in the conference of Coimbra in 2000. See Viney (2002), pp. 211–225. For details on the unification of non-contractual liability law see Tit. § 6, Subtit. I below.

[216]Moura Ramos (2002), p. 311. See also von Bar (2003b), p. 385.

[217]Oliveira Ascensão (2013), pp. 153–155.

[218]Müller (2008), p. 264.

[219]Fikentscher (1975), p. 580. Similarly, van Dam (2013), p. 53.

[220]Zweigert and Kötz (1996), p. 107. For a critical account, see Menezes Cordeiro (1987), p. 305, fn. 1. See also Ebert (1978), p. 50.

Finally, other scholars speak of a *spanisch-portugiesische Sprachfamilie*[221] or a combination of Portugal, Spain, France and Italy under the sub-system of "Latin states of the West" and Germany and Austria as "states of Germanic culture".[222]

Prevailing opinion holds that the Portuguese Civil Code builds a bridge (*Kompromissmodell*) between the French and the German legal systems.[223] This reveals the importance of the Portuguese legal system within the broader comparative Private Law panorama of Europe and even the world.[224] From this perspective, Portuguese law is influenced by German doctrine "at a primary level" and by continental law at "a secondary level".[225] This school of thought, which acknowledges both the Germanic and Romano law influences, classifies Portuguese Civil Law as belonging to the "Romano-Germanic" legal family[226] or, as suggested by some legal scholars, as an autonomous sub-system of the Romano-Germanic legal model.[227]

Despite these manifold influences and attempts at classifications, it is widely held that the Portuguese Code is rather original[228] in and of itself within its own legal tradition. This view was fully reflected in the Civil Code.[229] In the Preamble to the DL 496/77 of 25 November 1977, the legislature stated that "[i]n the present revision of the Civil Code (...) there was no concern of aligning by solutions already provided for in foreign legal systems".[230] This originality does not mean that the revisions were "nevertheless tempered by the fire of foreign ideas".[231]

---

[221]Bucher (2004), p. 538. This might be due to the fact that the Portuguese Supreme Court itself indicates that Spain is a country with which Portugal "has particular affinities" (STJ 16 January 2014, proc. 6430/07.0TBBRG.S1).

[222]Ferreira de Almeida and Morais Carvalho (2013), p. 72. But see Menezes Cordeiro (2004), p. 52. On the "Lusitan legal family" or the common law of the Portuguese-speaking countries see Medeiros Nóbrega (2015), pp. 39–42.

[223]von Bar (1994c), p. 221; von Bar (2014a), p. 475. According to some, the Portuguese Civil Code adopted the contents of the French Civil Code and the structure of the BGB (Baldus 2012, p. 105), but the influence of the German Civil Code on the contents of the Portuguese Civil Code is highlighted by other scholars (Baptista Machado 1999, p. 184; Ferreira de Almeida and Morais Carvalho 2013, p. 52).

[224]von Bar (2004a), p. 128.

[225]von Bar (2011a), p. 432. But cf. Moura Vicente (2001), p. 193 and Sinde Monteiro (2007), p. 455.

[226]Castro Mendes (1982–1983), p. 260; Menezes Cordeiro (1996b), pp. 424 and 445; Menezes Cordeiro (2009), pp. 231–233.

[227]For further details on the "Lusophone system", see Menezes Cordeiro (2009), pp. 226–234.

[228]Wengler (1967), p. 64.

[229]Sinde Monteiro (1997), p. 39; Lebre de Freitas (2008). See also Menezes Cordeiro (2004), p. 53; Mota Pinto (2008a), p. 27.

[230]DL 496/77 of 25 November 1977, p. 2.

[231]Jayme (1993), p. 258.

§ 2 Judges as Key Players in the Development of European Private Law

I. The Official Speech of Judges as Adjudicators of the Law

Under Art. 202(1) Const. "The courts are the entities that exercise sovereignty with the competence to administer justice in the name of the people".[1] Several national legal regulations provide for the way in which courts are to administer justice.

The Judicial Magistrates Charter (*Estatuto dos Magistrados Judiciais*)[2] states that justice should be administered "in accordance with the sources which, under the law, it [the judicial magistrature] shall resort to" (Art. 3(1)) and that courts "decide only according to the Constitution and the law" (Art. 4(1)). The Portuguese Civil Code also refers to a "[d]uty of deciding and the duty of obeying the law" when making legal judgments (Art. 8 CC).[3]

According to these provisions, judges are expected to apply the law which is in force in Portugal in the exercise of their judicial activity.[4] This remains true when the legal texts contradict the courts' ethical and legal convictions[5] (Art. 8(2) CC) and even where these legal rules jeopardise justice.[6]

---

[1]Original version available through http://www.parlamento.pt/parlamento/documents/crp1976.pdf (retrieved 31 Mar 2017).

[2]Judicial Magistrates Charter, Act 21/85 of 30 July 1985, DR, 1st Ser., no. 173-suppl. 1 (1985), pp. 1–23, with amendments.

[3]The duty of deciding corresponds to the prohibition of *non liquet* (Art. 8(1) Const.; Art. 3 of the Judicial Magistrates Charter).

[4]See Hespanha (1986a), pp. 326, 335–336. See also Bobbio (1995), pp. 171–172; Gaspar Martinho (2011), p 58.

[5]Art. 8 of the original version of the Swiss Civil Code expressly allows courts to reject the application of legal rules due to the injustice or immorality of their contents. See Wengler (1967), p. 65.

[6]Larenz and Canaris (1995), p. 17; Vogenauer (2001), p. 151. There are several principles which give judges significant power in the development of the law. That is the case of the principle of proportionality. For details on the principle of proportionality see Alexy (2006).

M. Santos Silva, *The Draft Common Frame of Reference as a "Toolbox" for Domestic Courts*, DOI 10.1007/978-3-319-52923-3_2

In Portugal, it remains clear that courts are still expected to be "*la bouche qui prononce les paroles de la loi*".[7] In the Portuguese legal system, as in the remaining Civil Law systems, statutory law (i.e., codes and special legislation) aspire to completeness: judges must be able, within the rules of statutory law, to regulate any situation in dispute.[8] Courts are expected to select from the available set of rules the one that applies to the private legal dispute *sub judice*.[9] Within the adjudication of Civil Law disputes, courts are expected to find the solution to a case within special legislation or the flexible open-ended concepts and abstract rules of the Portuguese Civil Code.

The legal-statutory paradigm is seen as enhancing the uniform application of the law and is intended to promote legal certainty.[10] It was born from the eighteenth century understanding of the liberal democratic doctrine of the separation of powers, which calls for the *separation* between the institution in which the law is created (legislative power) and the institution where it is applied (judicial power) for governance to be legitimate.[11]

However, while in theory courts present themselves as those who merely *apply* the law, in practice they *create* law through the expansion and interpretation of its boundaries, as will be discussed in more detail below.[12]

---

[7]Montesquieu (1973), p. 176, Book XI, Chap. VI. See also BGHZ 3, 308, p. 315; BGHZ 17, pp. 266, 276; Schulze (1997), pp. 186–187; Vogenauer (2001), p. 145; Aguiar e Silva (2011), p. 150; Oliveira Ascensão (2013), p. 320. The affirmation of the absolute duty to obey the law can be explained by the fact that, with the advent of the modern State, statutes (*leis*) became the only source of law (Bobbio 1995, p. 226).

[8]Bailey et al. (2007), p. 475; Pereira Neves and Ferreira de Almeida (2007), pp. 31 and 41. The importance of statutory law is clear in Civil Law countries. It is also the case, however, in Common Law countries, where the doctrine of parliamentary sovereignty implies that no person or body—meaning judicial body—has the right "to override or set aside the legislation of Parliament" (Dicey 1915, p. 18). In England, it is held that the liberty of Englishmen lies in "the little power of the courts in explaining, altering, extending or correcting the meaning of the laws, and the great exactness with which they must be observed according to the literal meaning of the words (. . .)" (Smith et al. 1978, p. 275). See also Gordon (2015).

[9]See also Kirchhof (1976), pp. 59–61.

[10]Aguiar e Silva (2011), p. 359; Gaspar Martinho (2011), p. 66.

[11]Cf. Aguiar e Silva (2011), p. 150. See STJ 8 March 2001, proc. 98P1205. See Abrantes Geraldes (2014), p. 26. Cf. also Gaspar Martinho (2011), p. 67.

[12]See Tit. § 2, Subtit. III, Sec. 2 and Tit. § 3 below.

II. The Portuguese System of Sources of Law

1. The Monopoly of the lei *in the Sources of Law of the Portuguese System*

The concept of the separation of powers as described above signifies that, in practice, Portuguese courts are constrained by the existing set of sources of law in their decision-making power.

In the strict legal sense, there are two kinds of sources of law: the *direct* ones, defined as the methods for the creation and disclosure of legal rules and regulations,[13] and *the indirect* ones, i.e. the methods for mere disclosure of legal rules.[14] A similar distinction can be found in the German difference between *Rechtsgeltungsquellen* (sources which produce law) and *Rechtserkenntnisquellen* (sources which only state what the law is).[15]

The Act of Good Reason contains the first rules governing the hierarchy of sources of law, thereby reinforcing the supremacy of statutory law.[16] Currently, the system of sources is contained in the Civil Code.

According to Art. 1(1) CC, which had no corresponding element in the Seabra's Code,[17] statutory law and corporate law rules are the direct sources of law of the Portuguese system of Civil Law. Statutory law (*lei*) consists of "any generic rule enacted by a competent state organ"[18] (Art. 1(2) CC) and it superior among the overall system of sources of law institutionalised by the Portuguese Civil Code.[19] As well as statutes and corporate rules, prevailing legal opinion[20] considers customs (*i.e.* the modes of developing law that result from a generalised social practice) to be direct sources of law.

The Portuguese Civil Code also refers to common usages and *aequitas* in the chapter on sources of law. Within the text of the Civil Code these are distinguished from statutory law, corporate rules (and customs, when applicable), in that they are only legally relevant when expressly set out by law.[21]

Art. 3 CC refers to usages, which are mainly relevant in the field of Commercial Law, and which are distinguished from customs by the fact that they are not

---

[13]Senden (2004), p. 5.

[14]Pereira Neves and Ferreira de Almeida (2007), p. 30. See also Castro Mendes (1982–1983), p. 260; Oliveira Ascensão (2013), p. 51.

[15]Larenz (1995), p. 429.

[16]Menezes Cordeiro (2004), pp. 51–52.

[17]Carvalho Fernandes and Brandão Proença-Fontaine de Campos (2014), p. 27.

[18]It can be a national organ (such as the Parliament) or a local one. See Pires de Lima and Antunes Varela (1987), n. 1 to Art. 1 CC, p. 51.

[19]Cf. Pereira Neves and Ferreira de Almeida (2007), p. 30. For further references, see Ferreira da Cunha (1991), p. 252, fn. 31.

[20]Pereira Neves and Ferreira de Almeida (2007), p. 30.

[21]Pires de Lima and Antunes Varela (1987), n. 1 to Art.3 CC, p. 53.

recognised as mandatory.[22] Finally, Art. 4 provides for *aequitas* (*equidade, Billigkeit*). It reads that "courts can only decide according to *aequitas*: a) whenever there is a legal rule which allows it; b) whenever there is agreement between the parties and the legal relationship is not inalienable; c) when the parties had previously agreed upon reliance on *aequitas* (...)".[23]

2. The Nature and Status of aequitas

There is little agreement among scholars as far as the precise nature of *aequitas* is concerned.[24] However, this form of law is either associated with a process of "smoothing" of legal commands,[25] or to the possibility of departing from such legal commands[26] towards an individualised (but not arbitrary) decision in a case *sub judice* (the so-called "*justiça do caso concreto*").[27]

With the advent of modern codifications of law, many saw *aequitas* as threatening legal certainty, the principle of equality before the law and the principle of separation of powers.[28] This might explain the absence of an express reference to *aequitas* in the Seabra's Code. Art. 16 of the Seabra's Code contains a provision for filling lacunae, referring to aequitas only indirectly, providing that the judge should decide according to the "circumstances of the case".[29]

The Jurisprudence of Interests (*Interessenjurisprudenz*) and the doctrine of free law (*Freirechtslehre*) introduced the idea of value to legal hermeneutics, as well as the argument that the court should go beyond the spirit of the law. These doctrines boosted the re-emergence and acceptance of *aequitas* into legal awareness. *Aequitas* was openly included in the Seabra Code chapter on sources of law.[30] Currently, there are several legal concepts which accord importance to *aequitas* (such as *culpa in contrahendo* and *abus de droit*)[31] in the field of non-contractual law (Arts. 489,[32] 494, 496(3) CC).[33] This statutory recognition stands in contrast to

[22] *ibid.*, p. 54, n. 2 to Art. 3 CC.

[23] *Aequitas* is also a decision criterion whenever the parties require it within Art. 39(1) of the Act on Voluntary Arbitration (*Lei da arbitragem voluntária*).

[24] Gernhuber (1977), pp. 193 ff.; Carneiro da Frada (2012), p. 111.

[25] Carneiro da Frada (2012), p. 122.

[26] Pires de Lima and Antunes Varela (1987), n. 1 to Art. 4 CC, p. 55.

[27] Carneiro da Frada (2012), p. 143.

[28] Dias Pereira (2015), p. 100.

[29] See Tit. § 1, Subtit. III below.

[30] In Germany, the *Prinzip von Treu und Glauben* (principle of good faith) is provided for in § 242 BGB.

[31] Dias Pereira (2015), pp. 101–102 and 104 n. 33.

[32] von Bar (1994a), p. 83.

[33] See, generally, Carneiro da Frada (2012).

the lack of active discussion of the concept among Portuguese legal scholarship[34] and its omission in textbooks as a source of law.[35] The few scholars who discuss the concept do so with the suggestion that courts are only able to use the concept in limited terms.[36] The principle *dura lex, sed lex* ("the law is harsh, but it is the law") would impose such limitations, in light of the Portuguese written law.[37]

These discussions show that those theories defining law exclusively as that approved by legitimate law-makers (Positivistic Formalism and Normativism), remain popular in contemporary practice.

3. The Weight of Case Law and Legal Scholarship in the Development of the Law

Case law (*jurisprudência*) and the opinion of legal scholars (*doutrina*) are usually defined as *indirect* sources of law.[38]

In the case of legal academic scholarship, it was held that it could constitute a source of law only when it analyses the law *de iure constituto* (based upon the law in force).[39] Whenever such analysis takes place *de iure constituendo* (based upon that which might become the law in the future) the legal scholarship would no longer be simply disclosing legal rules, but would be making a legislative proposal. In such cases, it was seen as "a source of sources".[40]

a) The Conforming Influence of Case Law

In the Portuguese legal system, the decisions of Portuguese courts are not binding on other courts. The *assentos*,[41] i.e. judicial decisions aimed at the uniformisation of the law, originally had statutory general force (*força obrigatória geral*) but their

[34]Carneiro da Frada (2012), p. 114. But see Oliveira Ascensão (2013), pp. 245 ff.

[35]See Castro Mendes (1982–1983); Ferreira de Almeida and Morais Carvalho (2013). Some legal scholars consider that *aequitas* is not a source of law. See Carneiro da Frada (2012), p. 121.

[36]Cabral de Moncada (1995), p. 40.

[37]Dias Pereira (2015), p. 127, n. 92.

[38]Ferreira de Almeida and Morais Carvalho (2013), p. 47 *passim*; Oliveira Ascensão (2013), pp. 263 and 321. But see Larenz and Canaris (1995), p. 256, who consider case law a *Rechtsgeltungsquelle* (source of rights).

[39]Betti considers the process of legal interpretation a source of law in itself. See Betti (1971) *apud* Aguiar e Silva (2011), p. 287, fn. 744.

[40]Aguiar e Silva (2011), p. 287, fn. 744. For a discussion on whether or not general legal principles constitute a source of law within Civil Law see generally Hesselink (2013).

[41]Art. 769(2) CCP 1961 provided that, whenever two judgments or appellate decisions in analogous cases diverged, judges of the STJ would come together to decide on a single way of interpreting a law and outline a judgment or appellate decision adequate to apply in analogous

standing was changed in 1995[42] for violating the rule of law and interdependence of powers (Arts. 2 and 111 Const.).[43] Their use as binding precedent is currently prohibited by Art. 112(5) Const.[44]

The rule of law imposes on each of the holders of public powers that they play a specific role in the realisation of legal rules. It is the task of the legislature to define the rule in its abstract form (not in relation to a specific case) and it is task of the legal scholarship to identify and deconstruct the law's content and to influence the court in deciding on its meaning.[45] It can therefore be concluded that, implicitly and explicitly, courts themselves were precluded from defining rules.[46]

Precedent, in contrast to Common Law jurisdictions,[47] does not form a source of law in the Portuguese legal system. However, court decisions, including appellate decisions (*acórdãos*) of Portuguese courts, may generate an indication with *persuasive* effect.[48] Portuguese courts tend to adhere to a so-called "system of informal precedent",[49] which occurs particularly in cases of well-established case law (*jurisprudência constante*).[50] The existence of (freely accessible) digital databases giving access to full-length decisions[51] facilitates such convergence efforts.[52]

---

cases with statutory general force (*força obrigatória geral*). This means that this *assento* would bind every court. See Wengler (1967), p. 65; Castanheira Neves (1972), p. 134.

[42]Art. 17(1) DL 329-A/95 of 12 December 1995, DR, 1st Ser., no. 285-suppl. 1 (1995), pp. 2–269.

[43]Gaspar Martinho (2011), p. 66. See also Gomes Canotilho and Vital Moreira (1997), n. 3 to Art. 2 Const, pp. 208–209.

[44]Gomes Canotilho and Vital Moreira (Gomes Canotilho and Moreira 2010), n. 23 to Art. 112 Const, p. 68. Art. 112(4) Const. ("Normative acts") reads: "(. . .) 5. No law may create other categories of legislative act, or grant other types of act the power to interpret, complete, modify, suspend or repeal any of its precepts in a way that produces external effects." Original version available through http://www.parlamento.pt/parlamento/documents/crp1976.pdf (retrieved 31 March 2017). Some scholars consider that the *julgamento ampliado de revista* (expanded revised appellate decision), introduced by Arts. 732.°-A e 732.°-B, added to the Code of Civil Procedure by DL 329-A/95 of 12 December 1995 presents a way of ensuring uniform judicial decisions and is thus a functional equivalent to *assentos*. For details on *assentos* see Prata (2010), p. 843 f.

[45]See Sacco and Joussen (2011), p. 13 ff.

[46]Castro Mendes (1982–1983), p. 268; Oliveira Ascensão (2013), p. 319. But see Hesselink (2001), p. 12, according to which the Parliament is "the other lawmaker".

[47]Bailey et al. (2007), p. 477 ff. On the doctrine of precedent or *stare decisis,* see Goodhart (1934), pp. 40–65; Cappelletti (1981), Whittaker (2006), pp. 705–746.

[48]Ferreira de Almeida and Morais Carvalho (2013), pp. 55 and 57. See also Oliveira Ascensão (2013), p. 325.

[49]Fon and Parisi (2006), p. 520. See also Hesselink (2008b), p. 28.

[50]Fon and Parisi (2006), p. 519.

[51]The collection of decisions is available through http://www.dgsi.pt, as mentioned before (see Preface) and under the official website of the Supreme Court of Justice (http://www.stj.pt, retrieved 31 Mar 2017).

[52]See STJ 7 May 2014, proc. 436/11.1TBRGR.L1.S1.

b) The Authority of Legal Scholarship

Similar to past judicial decisions, legal scholarship is not binding on courts. Despite this, courts often make use of textbooks and specialised academic literature in their decisions.[53]

The practise of citing seminal academic works has intensified with what may be termed the gradual *academisation* of the judiciary. This phenomenon, which initially occurred in the field of Constitutional Law in Portugal and across Europe, expanded to Civil Law through the nominations of experienced and internationally active scholars to the Supreme Court of Justice,[54] such as Supreme Court Judges Sottomayor, Pizarro Beleza, Moniz and Gomes.[55]

The legal scholars' theoretical background gives them a privileged position from which to complement and enrich the letter of the law.[56] For this reason, legal scholarship has been termed "the great inspirer and freethinker".[57]

Legal scholars have always assisted the judiciary in developing workable solutions to the new problems in Private Law.[58] If the law in force does not provide for a solution to legal problems, the contribution of scholars can be considered when developing solutions *praeter legem*.[59] At other times, the law in force provides unsatisfactory solutions to new problems, in which case the courts may let the opinion of legal scholars prevail over positivist legal rules, allowing a development *contra legem* to take place. This shows that the question of whether legal scholarship can be considered an indirect source of law remains open.[60]

4. International and Supranational Sources of Law

Scholars have based the integration of primary and secondary European and International Law into the Portuguese legal order in Art. 8 Const.[61] It has been

---

[53]Ferreira de Almeida and Morais Carvalho (2013), p. 57. By contrast, there is a certain aloofness to legal scholarship as far as case law is concerned. See Oliveira Ascensão (2013), pp. 321–322. In the Common Law system, treatises are also not binding, but have been cited as authoritative guides. See Bailey et al. (2007), p. 514.

[54]On the implications of these phenomena in the use of foreign law by courts see Markesinis (2006), p. 136 ff.

[55]Supreme Court Judge Gomes was member of the Study Group on a European Civil Code's Advisory Council on Unjustified Enrichment Law and Benevolent Intervention in Another's Affairs.

[56]Betti (1971), pp. 4–5. But see Abrantes Geraldes (2014), p. 26.

[57]Ferreira da Cunha (1991), p. 352, fn. 29.

[58]Józon (2008), p. 157; Mak (2014), p. 377.

[59]Ferreira de Almeida and Morais Carvalho (2013), p. 57.

[60]López Medina (2009), pp. 285–286.

[61]In the German Constitution, Art. 25 Const. regulates the relationship between German Law and International Public Law while Art. 23 Const. is a special rule that specifically regulates the

argued that this provision is mainly aimed at preventing conflicts between the Portuguese Constitution and EU Law.[62]

Art. 8(1) Const. reads that "the rules and principles of General International Law shall form part of Portuguese Law", thus reproducing the expression originating in the Weimar Constitution,[63] which is identical to that of the present-day German Constitution (Art. 25 Const.). Leaving aside the problems that this formula creates for the relationship between national and international law (e.g. the question of the hierarchical relationship between the two, and the problem of monism v dualism),[64] the Constitution seems to have enshrined the automatic incorporation of general international law into the Portuguese legal system in Art. 8(2) Const.[65]

EU Law[66] became directly applicable to national cases when Portugal acceded to the European Community in 1986,[67] creating a situation where national, international and European rules are in force simultaneously in the Portuguese legal system, forming a set of "different and sometimes overlapping layers".[68]

The coexistence, in the same social space, of rules with differing legal weight and content,[69] that legal scholars call "plural legalism"[70] (*pluralismo jurídico*)[71]

relationship between German Law and EU Law. For details on this relationship see Basic Law for the Federal Republic of Germany (*Grundgesetz für die Bundesrepublik Deutschland*), of 23 May 1949 and published in BGBl. I, 2438, pp. 1 ff., most recently amended through Art. 1 of the Act of 23 December 2014 (BGBl.I 2438), Constitution of the German Reich (*Verfassung des Deutschen Reiches*) of 11 August 1919, published in *Reichsgesetzblatt* 1919, pp. 1383 ff.

[62]Poiares Maduro and Pereira Coutinho (2007), p. 52.

[63]Cf. Gomes Canotilho and Vital Moreira (1997), n. 3 to Art. 8. Const., pp. 254–255. The Weimar Constitution (*Weimarer Reichsverfassung*) reads: "4. The generally recognised rules of International Public Law are a binding constitutive part of the German Reich's law" (Constitution of the German Reich of 11 August 1919, *Reichsgesetzblatt* 1919, 1383, available through http://www.jura.uni-wuerzburg.de/fileadmin/02160100/Elektronische_Texte/Verfassungstexte/Die_Weimarer_Reichsverfassung.pdf (retrieved 31 Mar 2017)).

[64]For further discussion on the topic, see Hesselink (2012).

[65]Gomes Canotilho and Vital Moreira (1997), nn. 3 and 4 to Art. 8 Const., 254–256, and n. 13 to Art. 8 Const., pp. 263–264; Gomes Canotilho (2001), pp. 813–814; Kern (2010), p. 555. Art. 8 (2) Const. reads: "The norms contained in duly ratified or approved international conventions come into force *in Portuguese internal law* [emphasis added] once they have been officially published, and remain so for as long as they are internationally binding on the Portuguese state". Translation available through http://www.en.parlamento.pt/Legislation/CRP/Constitution7th.pdf (retrieved 31 Mar 2017).

[66]The sources of EU Law are multitudinous. EU Law includes both primary law (in other words, the Accession Treaties) and secondary law (Directives, Decisions, Regulations and remaining Acts listed in Art. 189 TEEC). On the unwritten European sources of law, see Bleckmann (1993), p. 825.

[67]For details on direct applicability (*aplicabilidade directa*) of EU Law see Mota de Campos and Mota de Campos (2010), pp. 361–386.

[68]Hesselink (2012), p. 26. See also Schmid (2002), p. 417.

[69]Hespanha (2012), p. 148. Plural legalism is particularly endorsed by Teubner (1997). See also Calliess and Zumbansen (2010), p. 2031.

[70]Hesselink(2012), p. 1. See also Mak (2014), p. 376.

[71]Sousa Santos (1987), p. 298; Violante (2011), p. 353.

has, at least, two consequences. Firstly, not only EU hard law, but also soft law could claim to be a separate legal system,[72] as, according to one position, "Law is whatever people identify" to be as such.[73]

Secondly, each of the coexistent legal systems could compete for normative supremacy or, at least, for the preferential application of their rules and principles.[74] Under the principle of hierarchy (which provides that in the event of conflict, the rules that occupy a higher ranking prevail over those of lower rank),[75] the relative weight of international and European rules within the national system of law must be investigated.

The Portuguese Constitution does not provide express guidance on the ranking of International Law within the hierarchy of sources of law. As a result, there has been a lively doctrinal debate as to whether International Law holds supremacy over national law.[76] Based on Art. 8(2) Const., the prevailing legal scholarship considers International Law to be hierarchically superior to ordinary national law[77] but below Constitutional Law.[78]

A further discussion centres on hierarchy and value of EU Law in relation to national law.[79] In the wake of repeated rulings of the ECJ,[80] the prevailing theory is that EU Law occupies a higher ranking than national law.[81] In practice, this is not considered a strict rule of normative supremacy leading to the invalidation of national law.[82] Instead, judges develop a preference or priority use (*princípio da*

---

[72]Hesselink (2012), p. 26.

[73]Tamanaha (2001), p. 194.

[74]See Oliveira Ascensão, who states that several legal systems can interact without excluding each other (Oliveira Ascensão 2013, p. 14).

[75]See Schilling (1994) and Gomes Canotilho (2001), pp. 694–695.

[76]Mota de Campos and Mota de Campos (2010), p. 400.

[77]Kern (2010), p. 555; Mota de Campos and Mota de Campos (2010), pp. 400–402. But see Gomes Canotilho (2001), p. 815. If the Portuguese constitutional legislature had provided for a rule similar to Art. 25 of the German *Grundgesetz*, which, as has been outlined, clearly states that Common International Law prevails over national ordinary law, this discussion would have been avoided. See Gomes Canotilho (2001), pp. 813–816 and references therein at pp. 813–814, fn. 2.

[78]Mota de Campos and Mota de Campos (2010), pp. 403–407; Oliveira Ascensão (2013), pp. 581–586. The arguments given are that the wording of Art. 8(2) Const. refers to "Portuguese internal law" and not to Constitutional Law and that constitutional amendments must be adopted within a specific democratic-based process. See Kern (2010), p. 556.

[79]Mota de Campos and Mota de Campos (2010), pp. 397–408. See also Hesselink (2008b), p. 32.

[80]See Case 6/64 *Flaminio Costa v E.N.E.L.* (*Costa v Enel*) [1964] ECR p 585; Case 249/85 *Albako Margarinefabrik Maria von der Linde GmbH & Co.* (*Albako*) [1987] ECR p 2345; Case T-231/02 *Piero Gonnelli and Associazione Italiana Frantoiani Oleari (AIFO) v Commission of the European Comunities* (*Gonnelli and AIFO v Commission*)[2004] II- II-01051. In Portuguese case law, see TC 1 February 1989, no. 89-184-P, *BolMinJus*384 (1989), p 173; STJ 31 March 1993, *CJ (ST)* 1 (1993-2), p. 49.

[81]See Gomes Canotilho and Vital Moreira (1997), n. 16 to Art. 8 Const., p. 266; Mota de Campos and Mota de Campos (2010), pp. 390–391.

[82]Gomes Canotilho and Vital Moreira (1997), n. 16 to Art. 8 Const., p. 266.

aplicação preferente, Anwendungsvorrang)[83] of EU Law in relation to national legislation.[84]

Both the automatic integration of EU Law into national law and the exclusion of the application of national rules in contravention of EU Law rules are necessary corollaries of the uniform application of EU Law, as required by the Treaties.[85] Moreover, the conflict rule in Art. 8(4) Const.[86] suggests that each EU act, irrespective of its legal nature, prevails over Portuguese internal law.[87] However, the Portuguese Constitution in its Art. 8(4) *in fine* limits such superiority of EU Law when it says: "respect for the fundamental principles of a democratic state based on the rule of law". The decisions of the Federal Constitutional Court of Germany have also been in the same vein.[88] It can be argued that this interpretation is supported by Art. 4(2) of the EU Treaty.[89]

The wording of Art. 8 Const. therefore suggests that the primacy of EU Law is not absolute. The prevailing legal scholarship endorses a "limited constitutional supremacy on the part of EU Law"[90] and it is up to the domestic judge to decide which law shall prevail.[91]

It is generally considered that in cases of conflict, domestic judges shall attempt to reconcile apparently contradictory rules by way of interpretation, whilst following the principle of conforming interpretation (*princípio da interpretação conforme*).[92] If this is not possible, they shall apply the rules of EU Law over the

---

[83]See Gomes Canotilho (2001), p. 822. For details on the relationship between Constitutional Law and EU Law see Kirchhof (1976), pp. 68–76; Cruz Villaça et al. (1991); Schilling (1996).

[84]Gomes Canotilho (2001), p. 819; Senden (2004), p. 398. See Case 106/77 *Amministrazione delle Finanze dello Stato v Simmenthal SpA* (*Simmenthal*) [1978] ECR p 629 and TC 23 February 1989, proc. 88–0290.

[85]The remaining corollary consists of the uniform interpretation and uniform validation (Mota de Campos and Mota de Campos 2010, p. 360).

[86]Art. 8(4) Const. was included in the Portuguese Constitution with the constitutional revision of 2004. It reads: "4. The provisions of the treaties that govern the European Union and the norms issued by its institutions in the exercise of their respective competences are applicable in Portuguese internal law in accordance with Union law and with respect for the fundamental principles of a democratic state based on the rule of law". Translation available through http://www.en.parlamento.pt/Legislation/CRP/Constitution7th.pdf (retrieved 31 Mar 2017).

[87]On the sources of law of the EU, see generally in the Portuguese legal scholarship Mota de Campos and Mota de Campos (2010), p. 291 ff.

[88]See, particularly BVerfGE 87, p. 155 and BVerfGE 123, p. 267 (German approval law of the Treaty of Lisbon). The *Struktursicherungsklausel* in Art. 23 I, 1, 2nd part of the Const. reads that the European Union shall be "committed to democratic, social and federal principles (. . .)". Translation available through https://www.bundestag.de/blob/284870/ce0d03414872b427e57fccb703634dcd/basic_law-data.pdf (retrieved 31 Mar 2017).

[89]Mota de Campos and Mota de Campos (2010), p. 408.

[90]Poiares Maduro and Pereira Coutinho (2007), p. 53.

[91]Cf. Gomes Canotilho and Vital Moreira (1997), nn. 26. to Art. 8 Const., pp. 272–273. For a critical account see Hespanha (2012), p. 148.

[92]The scope of this principle is determined by the cases: Case 14/83 *Sabine von Colson and Elisabeth Kamann v Land Nordrhein* (*von Colson*) [1984] ECR 01891; Case 157/86 *Mary Murphy*

conflicting domestic rules, even if the latter are of a more recent nature than the former.[93] It would therefore be the case that through the application of the cooperation principle under Art. 4(3) TEU, they would ensure the internal effectiveness of EU Law.[94]

Enforcement of EU Law is thus primarily a matter for the national courts, which are part of the judiciary of the European Union as *juges de droit commun*.[95]

III. Domestic Adjudication of Legal Disputes

1. The Role of the Judges at the Crossroads

The variety of sources of law and the plurality of interpretations which exist in the different legal systems, together with their status, sit uneasily with the nineteenth century model of the judge-official (*juiz-funcionário*) who mechanically, through "deductive juggles",[96] applied the law.[97]

In the course of the last century in Europe, it became hard to say that the separation between legislative and judicial power could be seen in practice, as

---

and others v An Bord Telecom Eireann (*Murphy*) [1988] ECR 00673; Case C-106/89 *Marleasing SA v La Comercial Internacional de Alimentación SA* (*Marleasing*) [1989] ECR I-04135. For critics, see Leible (2009), p. 229.

[93]See Case 34/67 *Firma Gebrüder Lück v Hauptzollamt Köln* (*Luck*) [1968] p. 359; *Simmenthal*. See Case 26–62 *NV Algemeene Transport en Expeditie Onderneming van Gend en Loos v Netherlands Inland Revenue Administration* (*van Gend en Loos v Netherlands Inland Revenue Administration*) [1963] ECR p. 1.

[94]See Case 33/76 *Rewe – Zentralfinanz eG and Rewe-Zentral AG v Landwirtschafts Kammer für das Saarland* (*Rewe*) [1976] ECR p 1989. In the event that courts decide that an EU rule is unconstitutional and thus not applicable, the application of national law would give rise to an infringement of the fundamental principle of the primacy of the superior legal order (Mota de Campos and Mota de Campos 2010, p. 408).

[95]Kapteyn (1997), pp. 181 and 187; Mota de Campos and Mota de Campos (2010), p. 387.

[96]Hespanha (1986b), p. 336. See also Heusinger (1975), p. 17; Laborinho Lúcio (1986); Bobbio (1995), p. 212. But see Henriques da Graça (2008), p. 12. Also, critically, Heusinger (1975), pp. 16–28, especially p. 19 ff. and Ferreira da Cunha (1991). Indeed, the compulsory indication, in the decision, of the proofs which underpinned the reasoning of the court and the respective critical examination (Art. 607 CCP 2013) is aimed at ensuring that the judge followed a logical and rational reasoning procedure in the evaluation of the proofs, and that the decision on the findings of fact is not arbitrary, detached from the sense of the rules in the light of the experience or dominated by the personal impressions, political or ideological beliefs of the judge (Henriques da Graça 2008, p. 22; Gaspar Martinho 2011, p. 59). For criticism on the excessive justification of judicial decisions, see Sousa Santos (2005), p. 274. See also Ferreira de Almeida and Morais Carvalho (2013), p. 57.

[97]Bobbio (1995), p. 212. See also Tate and Vallinder (1995), p. 13 ff.; Hesselink (2001), p. 74; Martins (2006), p. 203; Poiares Maduro (2006), p. 67; Frasheri (2010), p. 134.

courts (especially the higher courts)[98] sometimes did not limit themselves to applying the national law in force in the adjudication of cases.[99]

The German Historical School introduced, in the nineteenth century, a movement from the predominance of legislation (*Gesetzgebung*) towards the predominance of legal science (*Herrschaft der Rechtswissenschaft*).[100] Legal Exegesis has departed from the nineteenth century conceptions of law as the product of the nation state and has moved closer to law creation (*Rechtsetzung*).[101]

In line with this new philosophy of justice, courts[102] are expected to cement the legal order,[103] to "govern" social relationships through policy-making[104]and pursue the real concept of justice,[105] letting it prevail, if necessary, over and above the values of legal clarity and legal certainty.[106] Some scholars even hold that judges are obliged to do so.[107]

Despite having always been one of the most conservative institutions—particularly as far as Civil Law is concerned[108]—it can be argued that judicial (self-) restraint[109] has progressively given way to a sort of judicial "activism". In this, the limits of statutory law are becoming blurred. In addition, the risk in such empowerment[110] of courts is that the criteria on which they base their decisions may be considered biased or arbitrary.[111]

[98]Hesselink (2001), p. 12. A good example is the case of the Spanish Supreme Court of Justice, which will be described below in Tit. § 3, Subtit. II, Sec. 2, Subsec. c), bb).

[99]Hespanha (2012), p. 171. See also Larenz and Canaris (1995), p. 519 ff. and Oliveira Ascensão (2013), p. 589 ff.

[100]von Savigny (1814), Sandström (1989).

[101]Odersky (1999), p. 3.

[102]Gaspar Martinho (2011), p. 66 *passim*.

[103]Oliveira Ascensão (2013), p. 321. See also Zenha Martins (2011), pp. 196–197.

[104]See Colombi Ciacchi (2014), pp. 120–134, particularly p. 125.

[105]See also Ferreira da Cunha (1991), pp. 348 and 353.

[106]Laborinho Lúcio (1986), p. 294. On the other hand, in Germany, they tend to be applicators rather than improvers of the law (Kropholler 1975, p. 68).

[107]For a detailed account see von Bar and Markesinis (1981), in particular pp. 7 ff., 51. See also Mak (2014), pp. 379–380.

[108]Dias and Almeida (2007), pp. 4 and 6.

[109]Garapon (1998), p. 54.

[110]It is argued that the failure of democratic regimes as welfare states may explain the increased involvement of the courts in public administrative affairs in recent decades. While on the one hand, public opinion is said to have perceived a certain lack of transparency, on the other hand, there are claims of a loss of efficiency of social protection and the protection of rights by the State. See Dias and Almeida (2007), pp. 4 and 6.

[111]Hespanha (2012), pp. 172–173.

2. "*Judge-Made*" *Law*

Although courts avoid speaking of the creation of legal rules,[112] modern non-contractual liability is in large part based on the decisions of judges.[113] Scholars talk of "judge-made law" (*Richterrecht,*[114] *richterliche Rechtsfortbildung*)[115] when referring to law resulting from judicial decisions.[116] Judge-made law is identified with "judicial legislation or interpretation justified by the current needs of the community".[117]

Scholars have separated "judicial law-making" into two groups, based on its departure from statutory law. The first group comprises those cases in which court decisions are apparent from the *ratio legis* of the statute (*gesetzesimmanente Rechtsfortbildung*).[118] The second group contains those decisions which go beyond the *ratio legis* by referring to evidence taken from the global legal order and its underlying legal principles (*gesetzesübersteigende Rechtsfortbildung*).[119]

The legislature does not provide a comprehensive answer on the limits of "judicial law-making"[120] but, in general, the *contra legem* development of the law in the broad sense, i.e. including both statutes and the constitution, is not admitted.[121] Similarly, decisions founded on individual reasons of public policy or affecting the normative independence of the legislature are not openly discussed nor acknowledged.[122]

Despite the provisions of the Constitution and the Judicial Magistrates Charter, judicial decisions in Portugal are considered "widely creative and truly constitutive".[123] It is said that judges have been participating in the determination of the

---

[112]Cf. Martins (2006), p. 204.

[113]See von Bar (1996a), p. 4.

[114]BVerfGE 38, 386, p. 397; BVerfGE 59, 231, p. 257; BGH *NJW* 1999, p. 2290.

[115]BVerfGE 82, 6, p. 12; BAGE 24, 177. Heusinger (1975), pp. 53 ff.; Grosche (2011), p. 85 ff. See also BVerfGE 82, 6, p. 12; BAGE 24, 177.

[116]Heusinger (1975), p. 53.

[117]von Bar and Markesinis (1981), p. 41. For alternative terms see Vogenauer (2001), p. 144 and references therein.

[118]Larenz and Canaris (1995), pp. 187–261.

[119]Vogenauer (2001), p. 142.

[120]von Savigny (1814), p. 239; Vogenauer (2001), p. 149.

[121]BVerfGE 35, 263, p. 280; BVerfGE 79, 283, p. 290; BVerfGE 84, 212, p. 228 f. See also Vogenauer (2001), pp. 148–149.

[122]See BVerfGE 3, 225, p. 239; BVerfGE 20, 162, p. 219; BVerfGE 25, 167, p. 183 f.; BVerfGE 34, 269, p. 292; BVerfGE 49, 304, pp. 318–320 and 323; BVerfGE 57, 220, p. 248; BVerfGE 66, 116, p. 138; BVerfGE 69, 315, p. 372; BVerfGE 71, 354, p. 362 f.; BVerfGE 82, 6, p. 12 f.; BGH *NJW* 1967, 343, p. 351. See also Vogenauer (2001), p. 142, pp. 149 and 151.

[123]See also, for Germany, Drobnig (1999b), p. 146. See also Rangel (2001), pp. 15–16; Ribeiro de Albuquerque (2011), p. 218. See also Ferreira da Cunha (1991), p. 348; Bobbio (1995), p. 173; Gaspar Martinho (2011), pp. 58–59.

meaning of the law (which the legislature thereby only *pre*-determines)[124] and have remained open to policy considerations (*rechtspolitische Überlegungen*).[125]

In spite of the above-mentioned developments, the role of courts in Europe is still not clear today. On the one hand, it is recognised that they have a major role to play in the development of private law—some argue than an even bigger role than the legislature.[126] It is claimed that "the judiciary is in a better position to fine-tune contract law rules than the legislative power as the courts' responsibility of handling actual cases forces them to come up with practicable solutions", and that there is a "'quantitative dominance' of judge-made law in the field of contract law".[127] On the other hand, however, the separation of powers and the superiority of the democratically elected legislature are steady, general principles of the legal order.[128] For this reason, a certain trend remains of concealing innovative judicial input under the veil of legal interpretation.[129]

3. Legal Interpretation as the Cornerstone of Adjudication

The abstract language and open-ended concepts in the Portuguese Civil Code foster the development of law by the courts.[130] Abstract language gives the judge the opportunity to explore several possible legal paths[131] while open-ended concepts are said to allow him or her to "complete" the legal rule passed by the legislature.[132] It is thus often difficult to draw the line between true "judicial law-making" and simple interpretation (*reine Auslegung*).[133]

---

[124]Laborinho Lúcio (1986), p. 2. It is referred to a "dynamic interpretation" of the law (Bobbio 1995, p. 213).

[125]See, generally, von Bar and Markesinis (1981).

[126]Mak (2014), p. 391.

[127]Grigoleit (2015), p. 252.

[128]A good example of these practices is the fact that lower courts deal with the questions of fact and questions of law, while higher courts deal only with the latter (Hesselink 2001, p. 12). For the question of whether judicial activism is legitimised by the principle of separation of powers itself see Schmid (2008), p. 85 ff.

[129]Scholars have referred to "constrained activist judges" to characterise those judges who do not wish to disrespect the law but whose works on an interpretation are different than those traditionally used (Kennedy 1996, p. 792 ff.). Such judges opt for a pragmatic approach, in other words they base their decisions on the effects that they are likely to have, rather than on the wording of a pre-existing rule. Cf. Frasheri (2010), pp. 134–135, fn. 17.

[130]Józon (2008), p. 156; Lambert-Faivre and Porchy-Simon (2011), p. 41.

[131]Cf. Menezes Cordeiro (2004), p. 54. See also Gomes Canotilho (2001), p. 98.

[132]Menezes Cordeiro (2004), p. 54; Hesselink (2008b), p. 28.

[133]von Savigny (1814), pp. 238 and 329 f.;Vogenauer (2001), p. 142. However, the supporters of the objective interpretation theory consider that the latter occurs every time the result of an interpretation remains to be found within the meaning of the rule at issue. For further references see Vogenauer (2001), p. 141, fn. 891.

"Interpretation" can be defined as the extraction of the law, i.e. the applicable rule within the legal system,[134] or as the results that arise from such extraction (*Rechtsfindung*).[135] The common understanding of legal interpretation is closely related to the legal-statutory paradigm.

Portuguese scholars usually categorise interpretation based upon its authorship. They differentiate between *legislative* interpretation (as well as customary interpretation or interpretation based upon *usus*), *doctrinal* interpretation and *judicial* interpretation. Whereas legislative interpretation is legally binding, the importance of the remaining two groups relies on their hermeneutical-methodological merits. Doctrinal and judicial interpretations approach the law in two separate ways. Within doctrinal interpretation, the concrete legal problem is treated in a dogmatic-systematic manner. Judicial interpretation treats the law from the perspective of the specific case *sub juditio*. The different kinds of interpretation are said to complement each other.[136]

Legal interpretation uses several elements[137] which, in the Romano-Germanic legal systems, result from doctrinal construction.

Varying sources have influenced these elements or canons of interpretation.[138] Nevertheless, they remain the same as those put forward by Savigny's "*System des heutigen Römischen Rechts*"(1840)[139] and have only been expanded by the *Interessenjurisprudenz*.[140]

The methods of legal interpretation are: the *logical* element (genetic representation of the sequence of thoughts of the legislature); the *grammatical* element (representation of the legal language used); the *historical* element (representation of the historical context of the legal rule); the *systematic* element (representation of the position of the legal rule in the legal system and the benefit that the legal rule brings

---

[134]Bobbio (1995), p. 214.

[135]According to a more restricted definition, interpretation consists of the meaning of the law, in other words the effects of the foregoing extraction of the contents of law (Łętowska 2010, p. 32).

[136]Castanheira Neves (2010), p. 34 ff.

[137]Following the Portuguese tradition, "elements of interpretation" (*elementos de interpretação*) is used instead of "interpretation methods" (*métodos de interpretação*). See Poiares Maduro (2007), pp. 1–21. But see Hesselink (2010), pp. 451–459.

[138]See also Zweigert (1949), pp. 5–6.

[139]See von Savigny (1814), pp. 213–215. See also Hespanha (2012), p. 451; Ferreira de Almeida and Morais Carvalho (2013), pp. 59–60. For a thorough analysis of the development of the criteria of legal interpretation see Vogenauer (2001), p. 438 ff.

[140]It is argued that these criteria gathered momentum in the middle of the twentieth century, with Larenz and Forsthoff. See Vogenauer (2001), p. 441.

to the overall system) and the *teleological* element (*ratio legis* or scope of the rule).[141] These elements remain active in Portugal today.[142]

a) The Elements of Interpretation in the Portuguese Civil Code

Portuguese scholarship categorised the different arguments judges may use to illuminate the vision of the legislature or the law.[143] Art. 9 CC ("Interpretation of the law") refers to such interpretative criteria and thus lays down the rules of legal interpretation:

1. Interpretation shall not be limited to the letter of the law, but must reconstruct, from the texts, the legislative thought, having particular account of the unity of the legal system, the circumstances in which the law was enacted and the specific conditions of the time when it was applied.
2. However, the interpreter cannot consider the legislative thought that does not have a minimum of verbal correspondence to the letter of the legal text, albeit imperfectly expressed.
3. In the determination of the meaning and scope of the law, the interpreter shall presume that the legislature enacted the most appropriate solutions and knew how to express the respective thought adequately.

The origin of these categories can be found jointly with Thomasius and Savigny. Based upon Art. 9(1) CC, the judge shall be sensitive to two elements: the letter of the law (*letra da lei*) on the one hand, and its spirit (*espírito da lei*) on the other. The spirit of the law can be further broken down into: the historical element ("circumstances in which the law was enacted"); the systematic element ("unity of the legal system") and rational or teleological element ("scope of the law").[144]

Art. 9 CC, which goes back to the first edition of the Civil Code, was not immediately applied to cases after the Civil Code entered into force. As this was an innovation in relation to the corresponding rule in the Seabra's Code, it began to be applied only when the new generation of lawyers could understand its normative message.[145]

---

[141]von Savigny (1951), p. 25 ff.; Larenz and Canaris (1995), p. 153.

[142]The twofold classification of Thomasius (seventeenth-eighteenth century) between the grammatical and logical element only prevails in France. See also Vogenauer (2001), p. 438 ff., in particular pp. 441–442.

[143]*ibid.*, p. 438.

[144]For details on the elements of interpretation see Kirchhof (1976), pp. 65–66; Bobbio (1995), pp. 214–215; Baptista Machado (1999), pp. 181 – 185; Ferreira de Almeida and Morais Carvalho (2013), p. 71.

[145]Menezes Cordeiro (2004), p. 50.

aa) Grammatical Element

The grammatical element, or letter of the law (*letra da lei, Gesetzeswortlauts,*[146] *Wortsinn*),[147] i.e. the meaning of an expression or a combination of words in common or legal usage,[148] has been an interpretation criterion since Roman times (*verba legis*).[149]

The letter of the law holds an important position in the Portuguese Civil Code, as shown by Art. 9(2) CC. Indeed, it is both the point of departure for each interpretation[150] and the boundaries drawn around the interpretative task.[151] It can be said that, as for the latter, the letter of the law has a negative role, that of eliminating the interpretations which do not have any support, correspondence or resonance in the text of the law.[152]

However, different terms often imply various possible meanings, creating doubt in the reader.[153] The judge must then attend to the context of the rule, to its nature or to the circumstances in which it was enacted,[154] i.e. to the historical element.

bb) Historical Element

The historical element (*Geschichte*[155]) refers to the short-term political, social and economic circumstances which influenced the creation of the legal rule.[156]

It includes the legislative background to the legal rule (*Entstehungsgeschichte der Norm*), which may be discovered through the minutes of the legislative debates that led to promulgation, and through the preceding laws (*Vorgeschichte der Norm*).[157] The historical element also encompasses the intention of the legislature, i.e. the authors of the legislative text and the members of the advisory committees (*vontade do legislador, Wille des Gesetzgebers*).[158]

---

[146]Vogenauer (2001), p. 442.

[147]Larenz and Canaris (1995), p. 320 f.

[148]ibid., p. 141.

[149]Vogenauer (2001), p. 442.

[150]Larenz and Canaris (1995), p. 141 *passim*.

[151]Meier-Hayoz (1951), p. 42. See also Larenz and Canaris (1995), p. 145.

[152]Baptista Machado (1999), p. 189.

[153]Larenz and Canaris (1995), pp. 142–143.

[154]ibid., pp. 141–142, 145.

[155]Vogenauer (2001), p. 443. An alternative, longer formulation to "*Geschichte*" is "*Regelungsabsicht, Zwecke und Normwertstellung des historischen Gesetzgebers*" (Larenz and Canaris 1995, p. 328 f.).

[156]Baptista Machado (1999), p. 190. The circumstances which influenced the creation of the legal rule include, in particular, the regulatory intent, aim and standardised conceptions of the historical legislature (Larenz and Canaris 1995, p. 149).

[157]Vogenauer (2001), pp. 443–447. Access to the legislative background of a legal rule is possible through the bills and their explanatory notes and consultation minutes.

[158]Larenz and Canaris (1995), p. 150.

As for the legislative framework of the law, the present-day Portuguese Civil Code is backed by a great number of *travaux préparatoires*, which Portuguese scholars and courts consider carefully in their works and decisions. This is despite the criticism that claims resorting to the historical element in statutory interpretation resembles a form of cherry-picking, a kind of "looking out over a crowd and picking out your friends".[159]

An interpretation cannot be based solely upon the historical element. Such an interpretation would most certainly be unfeasible due to the length of the period of time passed since the enactment of the legal provisions being interpreted.[160] The judge is therefore advised to employ additional elements of interpretation, such as the systematic element.

cc) Systematic Element

The systematic element (*Bedeutungszusammenhang des Gesetzes*[161] or *Zusammenhang*)[162] comprises the context of the law, in other words, the external systematics and conceptual framework surrounding the law.

The importance of this element is evident,[163] with some authors considering the court to be bound by it even when engaging in legal interpretation,[164] stating that the result reached through legal interpretation should be fixed, to ensure uniformity of solutions.[165] In this opinion, the meaning of a legal rule mostly reveals itself when it is interpreted within the external system to which it belongs.[166] Among the several possible interpretations, the one chosen should be the one which preserves its substantive integrity, in line with the remaining provisions.[167]

---

159 The comparison is authored by Judge Harold Leventhal (Tushnet 2006, p. 1276, fn. 3). But see Schulze (1997), p. 193.

160 Larenz and Canaris (1995), p. 166.

161 ibid., pp. 324–328.

162 Vogenauer (2001), p. 447.

163 Larenz and Canaris (1995), p. 145 ff.

164 Baptista Machado (1999), p. 191. But cf. Vogenauer (2001), p. 447 ff.

165 Baptista Machado (1999), p. 176.

166 Nevertheless, the legal rule, as part of a specific legal system, sometimes deviates from its underlying conceptual scheme. That is the case when rules are located outside their "natural habitat", which happens, for instance, when property law rules are to be found within the law of non-contractual obligations in the Civil Code (Arts. 623 ff. CC) or the rules on qualification in International Private Law are found in Book I of the Civil Code.

167 Larenz and Canaris (1995), p. 146. In Germany, the systematic element has been classified into several sub-elements, namely: the narrow regulatory context (*engerer Regelungszusammenhang*); the broader regulatory context (*weiterer gesetzlicher Regelungszusammenhang*); interpretation in line with general legal principles; interpretation in line with higher ranking positive law; interpretation in line with International Public Law; comparative interpretation and interpretation in line with the *ius commune*. See Vogenauer (2001), pp. 447–453. These elements have been defended since the first German monographies on legal interpretation (Forster 1613, Book II, Chap. V, II, 1042 *apud* Vogenauer 2001, p. 450, fn. 152).

Here, the "external system" (*äußere Systematik*) does not consist only of domestic laws (starting with constitutional rules),[168] but also those foreign laws which served as inspiration for domestic laws (as would often be the case with the BGB within non-contractual liability law). It is argued that the rules of legal systems providing innovative and effective legal solutions for modern problems should also be considered as part of such external systems.[169]

The importance of the context and the respective conceptual framework may only be apparent in relation to the scope of a particular law. The systematic element is thus said to anticipate the teleological element.[170]

dd) Teleological Element

An interpretation based on the teleological element (purposive interpretation)[171] concerns the *ratio legis*, defined variously as the aim (*Zweck*) envisaged by the legislator[172] or the "reasonable grounds" of a regulation ("*vernünftiger Grund*").[173] This type of legal interpretation is found in German jurisprudence since the nineteenth century and has been recognised as an important aspect of legal interpretation since the turn of the twentieth century.[174] In Portugal, use of this interpretation element became widespread in legal scholarship from the early twentieth century onwards, following its use by Baptista Machado[175] and Castanheira Neves.[176]

The teleological element aligns with a normative construction formed of both an *objective* and a *subjective* component. The objective component consists of the purpose of the legislation within the democratic structure at the time of interpretation. The subjective component corresponds to the policy orientations, i.e. the intention of the legislature at the time the legislation was promulgated.

The analysis of the subjective element, based on the language of the text (letter of the law) and the circumstances at the time of promulgation (historical element)—is imposed by the importance of the legislation in a democracy.[177] In

[168] Ferreira de Almeida and Morais Carvalho (2013), p. 60. For details on legal interpretation in accordance to the Constitution see Larenz and Canaris (1995), pp. 159–163.

[169] Cf. Ferreira de Almeida and Morais Carvalho (2013), pp. 36–37.

[170] Larenz and Canaris (1995), pp. 148–149. On systematic interpretation see, generally, Höpfner (2008).

[171] "Teleological interpretation" and "purposive interpretation" are used interchangeably, although "teleological interpretation" is more commonly used with respect to EU Law (Conway 2012, p. 20).

[172] Baptista Machado (1999), p. 182.

[173] Larenz and Canaris (1995), p. 336.

[174] Vogenauer (2001), pp. 453, 456–457.

[175] Baptista Machado (1999), p. 1999.

[176] Castanheira Neves (2010).

[177] Cf. Vogenauer (2001), pp. 188–189, 238.

non-contractual law, where the outcome of an interpretation arising from the objective and the subjective elements differ, the subjective element shall prevail.

This does not seem to be the prevailing opinion, however. When referring to this method of legal interpretation, Larenz called it "objective-teleological" (*objektiv-teleologische*), implying that the legislature itself is not aware of the meaning of the norm, and that such meaning is only revealed through a construction of the legal scholarship.[178] The aim of the legislature often corresponds to the purposes of the law itself and involves balanced legal rules, i.e. rules which take note of the interests involved. The objective-teleological criterion of interpretation involves two sub-criteria: the factual context of the rule, over which the legislature has no influence, and the ethical-legal principles which are behind the rule and which reveal its aim.[179]

Art. 9(1) CC refers expressly to the objective-teleological element, when it states that interpretation shall take into account the "specific conditions of the time where it [the statute] is applied". This form of interpretation allows for the meaning of a law to evolve in light of changes occurring after its initial promulgation[180] (*interpretação atualista* or contemporary-based interpretation).[181] The law must adjust the legal order to social change ("acceleration of history")[182] all the while avoiding the charge of acting as an unauthorised extension to the exclusive domain of the legislature.[183]

Legal theorists allow for the supremacy of law and through it the analysis of the subjective element. However, within the teleological interpretation, the subjective purpose is not to be given a prominent role, as the objective-teleological interpretation reflects the development of the legal system through history.[184] Indeed, it is argued that democracies impose an obligation on the judge to safeguard the fundamental values of the legal system. In cases where the legislative text is of a certain type (i.e. where it has a specific content, age or type of regulation), the judge may be entitled, or expected, to disregard the intention of the legislature in deciding upon the law, to safeguard these fundamental values.[185]

---

[178] Larenz and Canaris (1995), p. 336. See also Baptista Machado (1999), p. 183.

[179] Larenz and Canaris (1995), p. 333.

[180] Baptista Machado (1999), pp. 190–191. It is argued that the German legislature achieved the same effect by not regulating the interpretation criteria in the BGB and leaving the determination of the interpretation criteria exclusively to the legal scholarship and case law (Schulze 1997, p. 187).

[181] See Zweigert (1949), p. 6.

[182] Baptista Machado (1999), p. 223.

[183] See dissenting opinion to settling case law decision 6/2014 of 22 May 2014, DR, 1st Ser., no. 98 (2014), 2926, p. 2938.

[184] Barak (2005), p. 388.

[185] Schulze (1997), p. 189.

ee) The Relationship Between the Different Elements of Interpretation

The judge is not obliged to select a single interpretation criterion: he or she can also combine them, in particular as they often support one another in the task of interpretation.[186]

There is no rigid hierarchy between the different criteria,[187] they are "guiding points of view with different weights".[188] Nevertheless, legal scholars have suggested guidelines to follow in the task of interpretation.

According to one of the prevailing methods, the letter of the law indicates the *possible* interpretation(s). As there is usually more than one interpretation, the judge must resort to the systematic element. If the judge considers there is still room for different interpretations, he or she must opt for the interpretation best suited to the intention of the legislature and the aim of the legislation (teleological element).[189]

Art. 9 CC sets out a similar reasoning, stating that the judge is expected to "reconstruct" the legislative thought in accordance with the limits provided by the law. Although, as described above, the letter of the law serves as the departure point and limit for interpretation, the spirit of the law takes precedence. Accordingly, extensive, restrictive and even corrective interpretation of legal rules are allowed.[190]

The legislature opted for a solution of "cautious ambiguity" in this debate. Although it has never adopted a clear position along the schism between objectivists and subjectivists,[191] a certain preference for the objective component of the teleological element, i.e. the *mens legis* (the meaning of the law) as opposed to the *mens legislatoris* (the meaning of the legislator), is evident in Art. 9(3) CC.[192]

Art. 9(3) CC imposes on the judge the need to presume that the legislature enshrined the right decisions and expressed them adequately within the text.[193] This view seems to be confirmed by Andrade, who was personally responsible for the draft law leading to the current wording of Art. 9 CC and who wrote:[194] "[i]n Art. 9 CC it was not intended to mark an entirely defined attitude as far as the interpretation method is concerned (. . .)". The intention of the scholar responsible

---

[186] See von Savigny (1814), p. 215.

[187] Larenz and Canaris (1995), p. 166. This is the prevailing view in the legal scholarship. See references in Larenz and Canaris (1995), p. 166 and fn. 70.

[188] Larenz and Canaris (1995), p. 163.

[189] *ibid.*, p. 333.

[190] Ferreira da Cunha (1991), p. 350.

[191] Andrade (1961), p. 150; Menezes Cordeiro (2010a), p. 28. For further details on objectivism and subjectivism see Baptista Machado (1999), pp. 177–181.

[192] Baptista Machado (1999), p. 189.

[193] Aguiar e Silva (2011), pp. 369–370.

[194] Menezes Cordeiro (1999), pp. 149–150.

for the *travaux préparatoires* of Book I was, instead, to "still leave vague a considerable space for the free investigation of the learned jurists".[195]

b) Results of Interpretation

Through the use of the above-mentioned elements, the judge will reach a particular decision.

When the meaning derives directly and definitively from the letter of the law, the judge undertakes a declarative interpretation (*interpretação declarativa*). However, when he or she makes the decision that the letter of the text falls short of the spirit of the law, he or she may, through *a pari* or *a fortiori* arguments, engage in an extensive interpretation (*interpretação extensiva*). On the other hand, when the judge feels that the letter of the law goes beyond the spirit of the law, he or she may choose to undertake a *restrictive* interpretation (*interpretação restritiva*), because "when the reason for the law ceases, the law itself ceases".[196] Such "corrections" of the letter of the law to adjust it to the spirit of the law through, respectively, a teleological extension and a teleological reduction, correspond to a "development of the law based upon the law" (*gesetzesimmanenten Rechtsfortbildung*).[197]

The judge engages in a deductive interpretation (*interpretação enunciativa*) when he or she deduces from the rule a normative message which it contains only tenuously, for example through an *a maiore ad minus* argument ("the law which allows the most also permits the least"), an *a minore ad maius* argument ("the law which forbids the least also forbids the most") or an *a contrario* argument (which deduces a principle from an exception).[198]

In rare cases, where the legal rule blatantly fails to convey the spirit of the law, the judge is entitled to engage in what is called a corrective interpretation (*interpretação corretiva*). When there is an unresolved conflict between two legal rules, the judge is entitled to repeal one rule (*interpretação revogatória*).[199]

It follows, therefore, that interpreting legislation involves a certain degree of creative mental activity.[200] More particularly, by taking into account the past and the present context of the rule, the Portuguese legislature supports the concept that interpretation consists in the "process of looking forward and looking back, a so-called mutual clarification".[201]

---

[195] Andrade (1961), p. 150. For details on this quarrel see Baptista Machado (1999), pp. 177–181. For a thorough list of references on legal interpretation, see Ferreira da Cunha (1991) pp. 348–350, fn. 27.

[196] *Cessante ratione legis cessat ipsa lex* (Gratian).

[197] Larenz and Canaris (1995), p. 153.

[198] Baptista Machado (1999), pp. 185–188.

[199] *ibid.*, p 186.

[200] *ibid.*, p 199.

[201] Larenz and Canaris (1995), pp. 142, 148.

4. Integration Through Reasoning by Analogy and Creation of a Judicial Rule

Legal interpretation is the task carried out by the judge whenever laws are applied to a specific case. It consists of what can be read within one rule (or sets of rules) that regulate a particular situation. Where this is not the case, the judge shall either proceed to reasoning by analogy (which involves appealing to rules not initially aimed to regulate that particular situation) or to legal rule creation.[202] Reasoning by analogy, as well as rule creation, demonstrates the need to appeal to rules not initially intended to regulate a situation, or even to new rules created by the judge.

Both reasoning by analogy (and legal rule creation) and legal interpretation are at the heart of the process of adjudication (Art. 205(1) Const.)[203]and they are sometimes considered to be the same act.[204]

Whenever the judge cannot fit an individual case within the available legal rules, he or she is faced with lacunae. These may be caused by lack of sufficient knowledge of the relevant facts of the case. They can also be due to the lack of a legal solution for a case or to the lack of a *reasonable* legal solution,[205] as previously described.

In the canons of traditional legal positivism, the law must provide judges with a legal solution for every question with which they are confronted. If the question cannot be addressed by a general rule, the solution must be drawn from past precedents (*analogia legis*) or from the general legal principles of the legal system (*analogia juris*).[206] The solution in the Portuguese Civil Code for the problem of lacunae follows this principle in general, but as will be seen below, it sometimes goes beyond.

a) Reasoning by Analogy

Art. 10 CC provides for the closing of lacunae:

1. Cases not foreseen in the law shall be regulated in accordance with the norm applicable to analogous cases.

---

[202]Ferreira de Almeida and Morais Carvalho (2013), p. 59.

[203]This article reads that "1. Court rulings that are not merely administrative in nature shall set out their grounds in the form laid down by law". Original version available through http://www.parlamento.pt/parlamento/documents/crp1976.pdf (retrieved 31 Mar 2017).

[204]Zweigert (1949), pp. 9–10. Indeed, the traditional legal scholarship considers integration to be qualitatively similar to interpretation, but a specific kind of interpretation (ibid.). The concept of interpretation adopted by the ECJ includes interpretation in a strict sense and the development of the law (Hesselink 2008b, p. 25, fn. 69). Therefore, it is sometimes called "extra-textual interpretation" or "integrative interpretation" (Bobbio 1995, pp. 214–215).

[205]Varela (2011), p. 171 f.

[206]Bydlinski and Bylinski (2012), p. 477 ff.

2. There is reasoning by analogy whenever the reasons justifying the regulation of the case mentioned in the law apply to the unregulated case.
3. In the absence of an analogous case, the situation shall be solved in accordance with the norm that the interpreter would have created if he or she had to legislate within the spirit of the system.

The first two paragraphs show that filling the lacunae should be done with the use of precedent.[207] The first recourse to reasoning by analogy as a primary way of filling lacunae[208] is justified by the principle of equality before the law (which states that similar cases must be decided similarly) and by the principle of legal certainty. Certainty under the law is greater under legal harmonisation, where precedent is used across cases (*uniformidade de julgados*), than would be the case under *aequitas* or the general principles of law.[209]

While filling lacunae through reasoning by analogy, judges usually resort to national statutes, even if such statutes are yet to be enacted when the case is presented.[210]

Many argue that the similarity between the already regulated case and the as-yet unregulated case depends on justifications for the legal solution rather than the formal similarity of the cases.[211] This seems to suggest that a non-domestic or non-statutory solution could equally be applied through reasoning by analogy.

b) Creation of a "Judicial Rule"

As mentioned above, traditional legal positivism relies on reasoning by analogy to resolve situations where there is no legal solution to a particular case.

The Portuguese Civil Code is often deemed to explicitly break with this interpretation by allowing lacunae to persist after no solution can be found through reasoning by analogy.[212]

Perhaps influenced by the Swiss Civil Code[213] (as well as the prohibition of *non liquet*),[214] Art. 10(3) CC provides that, in the absence of an analogous case, courts are expected to create a hypothetical legislative rule within the spirit of the legal

[207]For further indications on filling the lacunae with the use of precedent see Kirchhof (1976), pp. 59–67.

[208]As mentioned before, not deciding is not an option, due to the prohibition of the *non-liquet* decision in both the CC (Art. 8(1) Const.) and the Judicial Magistrates Charter (Art. 3(2) Const.).

[209]Baptista Machado (1999), p. 202.

[210]Vaz Serra (1969), pp. 158–165.

[211]Pires de Lima and Antunes Varela (1987), n. 2 to Art. 10 CC, p. 59.

[212]Varela (2011), p. 179.

[213]ibid., p. 180.

[214]See dissenting opinions to settling case law decision 6/2014 of 22 May 2014, p. 2939.

system.[215] This "secondary rule of adjudication"[216] provides the judge with the creative power to decide the case *sub iuditio* whenever reasoning by analogy is ineffective. The decision must be found within the domestic legal system, as is the case for reasoning by analogy.[217]

Supporters of traditional legal positivism argue that the reference to the "spirit of the system" (*espírito do sistema*) consists of a legal value judgment.[218] Others, however, argue that this reference was made solely to demarcate the framework for the integration of gaps in the Portuguese legal system.[219]

Where an analogous solution cannot be found, the judge is not referred to *aequitas* by the legislature.[220] Instead, the legislature made the interpreter responsible for creating a "(legal) rule",[221] although only an *ad hoc* rule for the case *sub judice*, which is neither binding on that same court nor any other court, lower or higher in the hierarchy.[222] These rules created by the court are a way of incorporating general principles of law into the Portuguese legal system. It also justifies their exclusion from the Article of legal integration as it stands in the present-day Civil Code,[223] in contrast to the Seabra's Code.

Some argue that Art. 10(3) CC shows that the law is no longer an exclusive product of the Parliament, but, rather, that it is a time of "legislative paroxysm".[224] The sentiment challenges the official discourse on the role of courts, which denies them any function of normative creation.[225]

---

[215] Andrade (1963), p. 138 ff.; Ferreira de Almeida and Morais Carvalho (2013), p. 60. According to Art. 1 of the Swiss Civil Code: "§ 2 - In the absence of a provision, the court shall decide in accordance with customary law and, in the absence of customary law, in accordance with the rule that it would make as legislature. § 3 - In doing so, the court shall follow established legal scholarship and case law". Translation available through http://www.admin.ch/ch/e/rs/2/210.en.pdf (retrieved 31 Mar 2017).

[216] Varela (2011), pp. 170–171.

[217] Grochowski (2013), p. 98.

[218] Cabral de Moncada (1995), p. 166 ff.

[219] Varela (2011), p. 180. Cf. also Andrade (1946), p. 291.

[220] Art. 4 CC governs the circumstances in which courts can decide in accordance with *aequitas*: "(. . .) a) whenever there is a legal provision which allows it; b) whenever there is agreement of the parties and provided that the legal relationship is not personal [*indisponível*]; or c) whenever the parties had previously convened to resort to *aequitas*, in the terms applicable to arbitration clauses".

[221] Vaz Serra, *BolMinJus* 2 (Serra 1947), p. 39. See also Ferreira de Almeida and Morais Carvalho (2013), p. 56.

[222] Baptista Machado (1999), p. 203. However, it is argued that the court shall act *as if* the *rationes decidendi* of the court decision would ground an indeterminate number of future decisions (Kriele 1979, p. 35; Baptista Machado 1999, p. 204, fn. 2).

[223] Baptista Machado (1999), pp. 204–205.

[224] Ribeiro de Albuquerque (2011), p. 231. It is argued that the principle of legality of judicial activity should be revised accordingly (Rangel 2001, pp. 14–16).

[225] Ferreira de Almeida and Morais Carvalho (2013), p. 57.

§ 3 A Role for the DCFR in Domestic Adjudication

I. The Interpretation of the Portuguese Civil Code in Conformity with Comparative Law

1. Culture of Routine and Permeability

Until the beginning of the nineteenth century, the use of comparative law[1] arguments (*komparative Auslegung*) was, as a rule, forbidden.

In the 1950s, following the strong plea for "comparative law as a universal method of interpretation",[2] comparative law became an independent element in legal interpretation. Since then, it has been endorsed by a significant proportion of the European scholarship,[3] including Portuguese legal scholars.[4]

Nevertheless, courts still do not use comparative law based arguments in general in their decisions.[5] There are several reasons for this reluctance.

Firstly, foreign legal systems are often considered to be unrelated to the national legal order.[6]

Secondly, a certain European trend towards "intellectual unilateralism" can be observed.[7] Courts seem to have a certain reticence in relation to the use of solutions

---

[1]For a definition of "Comparative Law", see Zweigert and Kötz (1996), p. 1 ff.

[2]Zweigert (1949), pp. 5–21.

[3]Zweigert and Kötz (1996); Schulze (1997), p. 183; Drobnig (1999a); Odersky (1999), p. 1 ff., 2; Vogenauer (2001), p. 453; von Bar (2004a), p. 129.

[4]Baldus (2012), p. 105. See also Menezes Cordeiro (2009), pp. 145 and 146.

[5]Schulze (1997), p. 184; von Bar (2004a), pp. 124–125. On the impact of foreign precedents in judicial reasoning see Reed, *LQR* 124 (2008), pp. 253–273; Groppi (2013).

[6]See von Bar (2010b), p. 8. See also von Bar (2014a), p. 476.

[7]The expression has been used in the context of Common Law. See Markesinis (2006), p. 1347. "Legal narcissism" is also mentioned. See von Bar (2004a), pp. 124–125; von Bar (2013), p. 6.

M. Santos Silva, *The Draft Common Frame of Reference as a "Toolbox" for Domestic Courts*, DOI 10.1007/978-3-319-52923-3_3

based in other legal systems,[8] showing an apprehension of "being swamped by foreign influences and losing a knowledge power base".[9] This stance might be a consequence of a lack of in-depth knowledge of other legal systems, making it harder for legal actors to incorporate foreign elements in their day-to-day work.[10]

Thirdly, the use of foreign law is potentially cumbersome, onerous and time-consuming,[11] particularly when it involves a language barrier.[12] One argument is that the endorsement of individual rights stemming from the democratisation of civil society,[13] together with limited technical and human resources,[14] has led to a significant number of cases burdening judges.[15] The result has been a culture of routine, in which courts are compelled to re-use the legal arguments of previous cases[16] and which limits their interest in seeking solutions in foreign systems.

In fact, there is still insufficient support for the use of comparative law to generate a need for further research and information in public institutions. At the European level—and despite the extensive efforts of some European academic institutions—,[17]there is still no Pan-European database providing free and easy access to the decisions of every European Supreme Court, as there is for decisions connected to the CISG.[18] The creation of a database where decisions could be displayed in every European language or, at least, in English and in French,[19] to be used as an auxiliary argument by other national courts in the adjudication process, has been endorsed.[20]

Although these reasons also apply to Portuguese courts, particularly courts of first instance and courts of appeal, it is worth noting that the Portuguese Supreme

---

[8]See von Bar (2011a), p. 437.

[9]von Bar (2013), p. 6.

[10]Violante (2011), p. 341.

[11]von Bar (2009b), p. 33; von Bar (2009d), p. 60.

[12]von Bar and Lando (2001), pp. 218, 220.

[13]Freitas do Amaral (2000), p. 248.

[14]Laborinho Lúcio (1986), p. 297; Gaspar Martinho (2011), pp. 65–66.

[15]See von Bar (2004a), pp. 124–125.

[16]Sousa Santos (2005), p. 275.

[17]The Institute of Global Law of University College London and the Institute of Transnational Law of the University of Texas jointly run a website where French, German, Austrian and Israeli legal materials (including leading judicial decisions) in the fields of constitutional, administrative, and private law can be found. See http://www.utexas.edu/law/academics/centers/transnational/work_new/ (retrieved 31 March 2017). See also Markesinis and Fedtke, *TulLRev* 80 (2005–2006), pp. 113–114.

[18]See the database CLOUT, provided for UNCITRAL (http://www.uncitral.org/uncitral/en/case_law.html, retrieved 31 March 2017).

[19]Although English may be the *lingua franca* of the current young adult generation, that is not the case for the judges of the Portuguese Supreme Court, most of whom belong to a generation more fluent in French. See also Gridel (2003, p. 3), according to whom French is the truly European Union language).

[20]von Bar (2004a), p. 418.

Court of Justice often refers to comparative law materials in its decisions and extrajudicial writings,[21] thus showing a willingness to look abroad for inspiration. This happens despite the fact that the Documentation and Comparative Law Office (*Gabinete de Documentação e Direito Comparado*) of the Prosecutor's Office of the Republic (*Procuradoria Geral da República*)—the authority serving as the "receiving agency" for international legal information on procedure and judicial systems since 1986[22]—has already been considered unable to cope with demands for information.[23]

2. Use of Comparative Arguments

Traditionally, courts do not usually make use of comparative law within their jurisdictions. However, there are two groups of cases which can be seen as notable exceptions.[24]

In the first group ("classic situations"),[25] the court is under a *duty* to apply comparative law techniques. This occurs when the case contains a foreign element.[26] Where a transnational dispute is in question, courts often analyse and apply foreign law as a matter of course, because they are bound to do so by domestic conflict rules or general principles common to the EU Member States.[27]

In the second group of cases ("cases of inspiration"),[28] courts reference foreign decisions even when not bound to do so under the rules of their own system, i.e. on a voluntary basis.[29]

---

[21]On the reference, by judges, to extrajudicial writings, see Moitinho de Almeida n.d.; Abrantes Geraldes (2007b); Sousa Dinis (2009), pp. 51–68.

[22]The European Convention on Information on Foreign Law, open for signature by the Member States of the Council of Europe in London in June 1968, provided that the Parties shall supply information on their law, procedure and judicial systems when problems of foreign law arise in the course of legal proceedings. This Convention was ratified by Portugal and entered into force in November 1978.

[23]Freitas do Amaral (2000), p. 254.

[24]For a thorough analysis of the use, by courts, of foreign law in selected European countries (plus Canada and South Africa), see Markesinis and Fedtke, *TulLRev* 80 (2005–2006), pp. 11–167.

[25]von Bar (2004a), p. 125. The first group of cases where courts make use of comparative law within their jurisdictions is also called "situations of impact" (Violante 2011, p. 343).

[26]See Case 9/69 Claude Sayag and S.A. Zurich v Jean-Pierre Leduc, Denise Thonnon and S.A. La Concorde. (*Sayag/Leduc*) [1969] ECR 329. See also Schulze (1997), p. 186 ff.; von Bar (2004a), p. 125; Markesinis and Fedtke, *TulLRev* 80 (2005–2006), pp. 17–18; Bartman (2009), pp. 111–112.

[27]Art. 340(2) TFEU reads: "(...) In the case of non-contractual liability, the Union shall, in accordance with the general principles common to the laws of the Member States, make good any damage caused by its institutions or by its servants in the performance of their duties". See Consolidated Version of the Treaty on European Union and the Treaty on the Functioning of the European Union of 26 October 2012[2012] OJ C 326, pp. 1–390.

[28]Violante (2011), p. 343.

[29]Schulze (1997), p. 186.

As mentioned above, references to foreign legal systems are increasing in Portuguese courts,[30] even though this occurs mostly in cases of particular complexity or importance.[31]

Such references to comparative law extend beyond the so-called "cosmopolitan"[32] legal disciplines and have entered more traditional fields of law, such as Family Law and the Law of Persons.[33] There has been progressively greater recognition of the importance that the "transnational realities have had and have been having in the decisions on civil liability in several Member States of the Union",[34] thus, particularly in this legal field, a European approach is now favoured.[35]

a) Countries Called Upon for Comparison

When selecting the foreign jurisdiction for comparison, the judge can employ various criteria, such as linguistic, geographical or political proximity.

One possible criterion for comparison is based on similar culture.[36] The Portuguese Supreme Court of Justice usually opts for a choice of jurisdictions with similar legal systems (*sistemas jurídicos afins*), particularly those which most influenced the construction or development of the legal institution under analysis.[37] This appeals to the systematic element of interpretation, which was discussed in detail above.[38] Generally, the Court calls upon Italian,[39] French[40] and German[41]

[30]For the use of comparative arguments in German courts, see generally Drobnig (1999b). See also, with examples, Schulze (1997), p. 185.

[31]von Bar (1998a), pp. 415–416; von Bar (2004a), p. 127; Violante (2011), p. 351. Similarly to the STJ, the Portuguese Constitutional Court reveals a significant openness to external elements of international and foreign jurisdictions. The Constitutional Court uses these elements "repeatedly and in a methodologically sophisticated fashion" (Violante 2011, p. 345).

[32]According to Zweigert, "cosmopolitan" (*weltläufig*) legal fields are Contract Law and Commercial Law (Zweigert 1949, p. 12 ff.).

[33]STJ 27 June 1995, proc. 087207; STJ 17 April 2008, proc. 08A474. See also Markesinis and Fedtke, *TulLRev* 80 (2005–2006), p. 110.

[34]STJ 9 September 2010, proc. 2572/07.OTBTVD.L1.

[35]von Bar (2004a), p. 125.

[36]Zweigert (1949); Schulze (1997), pp. 13–14 and pp. 185–186; Oliveira Ascensão (2013), p. 142.

[37]See von Bar (1998a), pp. 414–418; von Bar (2004a), p. 125.

[38]See Tit. §2, Subtit. III, Sec. 3 above.

[39]STJ 27 June 1995, proc. 087207; STJ 3 March 2010, proc. 886/8PSL.SBL1.S1; STJ 21 October 2010, proc. 1285/07.F.TJV; STJ 2 December 2013, proc. 306/10.0TCGMR.G1.S1.

[40]STJ 21 October 2010, proc. 1285/07.F.TJV; STJ 2 December 2013, proc. 306/10.0TCGMR.G1.S1;STJ 16 January 2014, proc. 6430/07.0TBBRG.S1.

[41]See STJ 9 September 2010, proc. 2572/07.OTBTVD.L1.; STJ 21 October 2010, proc. 1285/07.F.TJV; STJ 16 January 2014, proc. 6430/07.0TBBRG.

Law. However, the convenience of referring to other systems for the sake of showing the wide spectrum of applicability of a law has also been recognised.[42]

b) Object of Comparison and Weight of Comparative Arguments

The comparative element can consist, simultaneously, of the rules, the legal scholarship and case law of the country in question, or a combination of some or all of those elements.[43]

Just as in other European courts, Portuguese courts have given a limited weight to foreign cases when adjudicating at the domestic level.[44] For the most part, they merely briefly state the foreign solution, without critical assessment.[45] Reference to foreign law is generally found in the *obiter dicta*,[46] not generating any substantial weight for the final decision,[47] as would be the case if it were integrated into the precedent forming part of the decision (*ratio decidendi*). This has therefore raised the question of whether, in the cases where courts merely state the foreign solutions, the comparative method can be said to be used at all.[48]

c) Critical and Supportive Arguments

The use of comparative methods in adjudication has given rise to an intense discussion within legal scholarship.

The most frequent argument brought forward is the lack of democratic legitimacy of comparative reasoning in the adjudication of national disputes. According to this view, courts are not allowed to search for normative guidance in foreign

---

[42] Ferreira de Almeida and Morais Carvalho (2013), pp. 36–37. See also Zweigert (1949), p. 19.

[43] Schulze (1997), p. 185.

[44] See STJ 22 October 2009, proc. 409/09.4YFLSB; STJ 21 October 2010, proc. 1285/07.F.TJV; STJ 16 January 2014, proc. 6430/07.0TBBRG.S1.

[45] Józon (2008), p. 157.

[46] Foreign law has been considered "mere decoration". See Tushnet (2006), p. 1277. See also Posner (2004) and cf. von Bar (2013), p. 56.

[47] See, *e.g.*, STJ 21 October 2010, proc. 1285/07.F.TJV. Sometimes the court openly acknowledges the foreign solution, but decides in a different way. See STJ 7 May 2014, proc. 1070/11.TBVCT.G1.S1.

[48] Markesinis and Fedtke (2005–2006), p. 128. This may change over time, given the gradual rise of scholars to the Supreme Court of Justice (See Art. 55(3) b) of Judicial Magistrates Charter), as decisions with significant numbers of foreign sources begin to increase. STJ 5 June 2013, proc. 192/10.0TTVNF.P1S1; STJ 30 September 2014, proc. 844/09.8TVLSB.L1.S1. Also, quite impressively, Supreme Court Judge João Bernardo declared, in a STJ's decision: "It is certainly not common that domestic courts decide according to what is decided in neighbour countries but it must be acknowledged that transnational realities have had a huge importance in the court decisions on civil liability in several EU Member States" (STJ 9 September 2010, proc. 2572/07.OTBTVD.L1).

sources of law because these have not been democratically approved at national level.[49]

Critics also point out that when one allows domestic courts to appeal to foreign laws for solutions to legal problems, the judge is given the power to choose his/her preferred solution rather than following the letter of the law. This opens the door to "solution shopping"[50] or to the "cherry picking" of legal solutions and thus to judicial discretion.[51]

On a more practical note, it has also been argued that the widening of the normative horizon to include foreign laws would undermine the predictability[52] and legal certainty principles within the national system, hamper lawyers in the execution of their duties[53] and even delay judicial procedures. Another recurring argument is the educational costs that are incurred by an appeal to foreign law, as well as the risk that references to foreign law will be made inaccurately.[54]

Those who defend the use of the comparative method by national courts present the following counter-arguments.

Firstly, "cherry-picking" already exists within the domestic system,[55] and is not, therefore, a newly introduced problem within the national framework. The simple introduction of the need to state the precise reasons underlying the decision could even go towards alleviating the overall problem.[56] With respect to the principle of predictability, and the supposed lack thereof, interpretation might become progressively more precise and open for discussion and review as courts move closer to the solutions most accepted in other European jurisdictions.[57] Within EU Law, this process of convergence should be reinforced by the possibility of a preliminary ruling.[58]

As information on foreign laws becomes more readily accessible online, education costs will decrease and become less of a problem.[59] Moreover, even though the

---

[49]Violante (2011), p. 356. See also Markesinis and Fedtke (2005–2006), p. 133 ff.

[50]For criticisms of the "cherry picking argument", see Tushnet (2006), pp. 1280–1284.

[51]Tushnet (2006), p. 1275; Violante (2011), pp. 349 and 356.

[52]The importance of predictability of the law applicable to a case is in the base of the frequent choice, by the parties, of the rules applicable to their contract. Within non-contractual liability, it is particularly important as liability insurance is concerned, both on the part of the insurance companies (in the scope and price of insurance policies) and on the part of the person wishing to buy liability insurance.

[53]von Bar (2004a), p. 127. This could turn into the violation of the principle of equality of procedural arms.

[54]Tushnet (2006), p. 1294 (but see p. 1297). With further reference to the dangers involved in the use of comparative law, see Markesinis and Fedtke (2005–2006), pp. 109–136.

[55]Markesinis and Fedtke (2005–2006), p. 127.

[56]Violante (2011), p. 352.

[57]Schulze (1997), p. 193.

[58]Case 166/73 *Rheinmühlen-Düsseldorf v Einfuhr- und Vorratsstelle für Getreide und Futtermittel (Rheinmühlen)* [1974] ECR 00033.

[59]Schulze (1997), p. 196.

present legal training of judges[60] is based mainly on domestic law,[61] comparative law courses are becoming more widespread and will hold significant influence for future generations of judges.[62]

Arguments from the field of legal hermeneutics address the problem of the lack of legitimacy of foreign sources of law. It could even be argued that the comparative sources available to the judge to support his/her interpretation of the law are part of the systematic element of interpretation,[63] as described earlier. This argument is particularly strong among those who consider individual national bodies of private law as "local manifestations of an all-encompassing whole",[64] the supporters of European Private Law as a single body of law. This leads to a further argument, namely that, in the context of systematic interpretation, the obligation to preserve the internal coherence of the national level law is no longer absolute.[65]

However, the comparative method can also be seen as part of the teleological argument.[66] This argument states that there should be an ambition to make the overall system coherent—the national within the international. They go one step further, seeing the purpose of laws to be coherent as a deep, *a priori* obligation, and thus the question of coherence between domestic and international jurisprudence becomes a non-issue.[67]

Seen within the historical element, comparative interpretation becomes an outcome of the past legislature relying on sources outside the national system. Sometimes the *travaux préparatoires* are read as taking the intention of a past legislature to rely on the legal order of other systems, such as for example, by reference to "good rules" of other countries.[68]

d) State of the Art of Comparative Argumentation

Traditionally, the comparative legal method is particularly helpful where the national law leaves a lacuna, or where the regulations are ambiguous[69] and in

---

[60]On the influence of the educational background of the judge in the reasoning and outcome of a court decision, see the groundbreaking study Watson (1991) , in particular p. 230.

[61]That is the case for the Portuguese training of prospective judges. The curriculum is available through http://www.cej.mj.pt/cej/formacao/fich-pdf/plano_de_estudos_2016_17.pdf (retrieved 31 March 2017).

[62]Cf. von Bar (2003a), p. 100. In Portugal, these are the cases of the Law Faculty of the University of Lisbon and the Law Faculty of the Nova University. In the Law Faculty of the Nova University, Comparative Law is a mandatory course and it was governed for several years by Professor Ferreira de Almeida, who integrated the Third Commission on European Contract Law.

[63]See Brugger (1994), p. 24; Alexy (1995), p. 71 ff.

[64]von Bar (2013), p. 8. See also Schulze (1997), pp. 188 and 191.

[65]See Schulze (1997), p. 195.

[66]See Kropholler (2004), p. 265; Bydlinski and Bylinski (2012), pp. 461–463.

[67]Cf. Schulze (1997), p. 194.

[68]Schulze (1997), p. 194.

[69]Drobnig (1999b), p. 146.

need of revision.[70] The majority of countries adopt a more "nationalist" (or less "Europeanist")[71] stance,[72] making little use of the comparative methods in private law.

The use of foreign legal rules in a comparative manner can also be helpful where the applicable national legal provision is perfectly clear.[73] In these cases, it is beneficial for courts to rely on comparative arguments if the rule itself was imported from a foreign or international jurisdiction[74] or when the issue under analysis is of a highly technical nature.[75] Courts should also rely on foreign solutions for reasons which extend past the immediate outcome of the case *sub judice*.[76] This would be the case when: unveiling "common principles of law"; taking account of a change in the constitution and system of values;[77] rebutting concerns about outcomes of legal solutions; confirming the workability of a legal solution; and, last but not least, providing a uniform answer to a problem faced by several countries.[78]

The use of the comparative method in any of these circumstances gives the judge a deeper understanding of national law as far as legislative policy is concerned.[79] The judge's horizons, as well as those of the authors of the *travaux préparatoires*,[80] would be expanded, and the legal discourse in general would benefit from the engagement with the comparative element.[81] Ultimately, comparative analysis would improve the law[82] and would also contribute to a shift towards a less formal, positivist approach.[83] It is perhaps for these reasons that some argue that the courts are allowed to search for inspiration in foreign legal systems[84] and even to amend or disregard national law in favour of solutions found elsewhere in Europe, based on the principle *lex specialis derogat legi generali*.[85]

---

[70] Schulze (1997), p. 186.

[71] On the distinction between the nationalist and Europeanist perspectives see, with detail, Hesselink (2012), p. 11 ff.

[72] Markesinis and Fedtke (2005–2006), pp. 90–94.

[73] See Zweigert (1949), p. 10. But see Zweigert and Kötz (1998), pp. 17–18.

[74] Schulze (1997), p. 186.

[75] See Markesinis and Fedtke (2005–2006), pp. 76–109.

[76] *ibid.*, p. 127.

[77] Schulze (1997), p. 186.

[78] Markesinis and Fedtke (2005–2006), pp. 76–109. See also Zweigert (1949), p. 11; Schulze (1997), p. 186 *passim*; von Bar (1998a), p. 414; Odersky (1999), pp. 1–4; von Bar (2013), pp. 9, 11.

[79] Castro Mendes (1982–1983), p. 79; David (2002), p. 8; Oliveira Ascensão (2013), p. 14.

[80] David (2002), p. 8; Oliveira Ascensão (2013), p. 142.

[81] Markesinis and Fedtke (2005–2006), p. 127.

[82] Drobnig (1999b), p. 146.

[83] Hesselink (2001), pp. 51–52. See also Józon (2008), p. 157. Some argue that the current period will come to be known as the "real end of legal positivism" (Safjan 2010, p. 107).

[84] Violante (2011), p. 355.

[85] Snijderns and Vogenauer (2009), p. V. On the situations which justify a comparative "dialogue" see Markesinis and Fedtke (2005–2006), pp. 76–109.

Comparative law also has the power to be an interpretative catalyst within national law.[86] Scholars speak of "judicial dialogue"[87] or a form of "cross-judicial influence"[88] to refer to the process when the persuasive strength[89] of extra-systematic legal elements[90] is recognised, "importing"[91] them for the purposes of following a specific interpretation of national law, in a structured reasoning resembling the analogical argument.[92]

More human and technical support should be provided to the highest courts of the EU Member States so that they might examine how issues have been dealt with by other legal systems, and be inspired by them.[93] The judgments of high-level courts should be widely disseminated and the European Law Institute (ELI) could have an important role in such dissemination.[94] The ELI[95] has several core tasks, among which is the duty "to provide a forum of discussion and cooperation for jurists irrespective of their vocation or occupation. Among these are scholars, judges, lawyers and other legal professionals who take an active interest in European legal development and together represent a broad range of legal traditions".[96]

Koen Lenaerts, President of the ECJ, in his keynote speech to more than 350 legal experts from all over Europe and beyond at the ELI 2016 Annual Conference, stressed the comparative law method as "*a valuable interpretative*

[86]Lollini (2007), p. 60; Violante (2011), p. 342 *passim*.

[87]Markesinis and Fedtke (2005–2006).

[88]Lollini (2007), pp. 60–61.

[89]Violante (2011), p. 343. See also Zweigert (1949), p. 14.

[90]The constitution of post-apartheid South Africa states that courts can use extra-systematic parameters for interpretation: "When interpreting the Bill of Rights, a court, tribunal or forum [...] (b) must consider International Law, and c) may consider foreign law" (Art. 39 of the Constitution of the Republic of South Africa no. 108 of 1996 with amendments, available through http://www.gov.za/sites/www.gov.za/files/images/a108-96.pdf (retrieved 31 March 2017).

[91]von Bar (2004a), p. 125.

[92]Even the representatives of the "Exclusive Legal Positivism" admit that legal systems are open systems, in other words that they contain rules with binding force, or "adopt" frameworks from one legal system to another. See Lamy Pimenta (2011), p. 273.

[93]See von Bar (2004a), p. 127.

[94]Hesselink (2009), p. 928.

[95]Schulte-Nölke (2010b), p. 55. For a characterisation of the European Law Institute, see Zimmermann (2012), pp. 309–311. The ELI thus plays the role of a "European Law Academy". See von Bar (2003b), p. 387; von Bar (2004b), p. 1231.

[96]Art. 3 II of the ELI Statute, as amended by Council Decision 2013/5 of 2 April 2013 on Election Procedure and Amendments to the Articles of Association, retrieved on 31 March 2017 from http://www.europeanlawinstitute.eu/fileadmin/user_upload/p_eli/Council/CD_2013-5__Election_Procedure_and_Amendments_to_the_Statute_pdf and ELI's Manifesto, available through https://www.europeanlawinstitute.eu/fileadmin/user_upload/p_eli/ELI_Manifesto_final_11-04-16.pdf (retrieved 31 March 2017).

tool that serves to strike the dynamic balance" between unity and diversity.[97] This seems to be a first steady step in the right direction.

II. The Interpretation of the Portuguese Civil Code in Conformity with the DCFR

The proponents of the use of comparative analysis of the law argue that it allows actors to focus on the similarities between legal systems instead of their differences, and that it demonstrates that such similarities are more (and more substantive) than the differences.[98]

Nevertheless, comparative law no longer satisfies[99] those who support the idea of a common European private legal system.[100] A new approach has arisen with the DCFR, which openly displays its comparative basis[101] while distinguishing itself markedly from comparative law in general.[102] The DCFR, which has generated an overwhelming number of academic papers and works,[103] opened another era in post-national law, the era of European Private Law.

1. Brief Consideration of the Future of the DCFR

a) Origin and Inspiration

aa) A Plan of Action Towards Harmonisation of European Patrimonial Law

The pan-European jurisdictional interaction and convergence in some legal areas that came to attention in the 1990s allowed scholars to take the lead in drawing conceptual guidelines for the development of law in Europe.[104]

---

[97]ELI, "Building the future of law in Europe on unity and diversity – 3rd day of the ELI Annual Conference 2016", available at http://www.europeanlawinstitute.eu/news/news-contd/article/building-the-future-of-law-in-europe-on-unity-and-diversity/?tx_ttnews%5BbackPid%5D=179468&cHash=3c11e9e5574c4329695052197664024c, retrieved on 31 March 2017.

[98]Zweigert (1949), p. 11; Watson (2000), p. V.; Hesselink (2001), p. 53. Cf. also, for Contract Law, Jansen (2010), p. 160.

[99]von Bar (2014b), pp. 3–9.

[100]See also Schulze (1997), p. 196.

[101]von Bar et al. (2009), Intr. 63, pp. 38–39.

[102]See von Bar (2004a), pp. 131 and 135; Jansen (2010), p. 162.

[103]For a classification of these comments on the DCFR, see Schulte-Nölke (2011), p. 12.

[104]Scognamiglio (2000), p. 338. See also Schulte-Nölke (2011), p. 17 f.

The institutional debate on the existence, scope and development of European Private Law entered legal scholarship in 1999, with the summit of Tampere, where the European Council addressed the question of the future of European Private Law. In its conclusions, the Council declared that "better compatibility and more convergence between the legal systems of Member States"[105] must be achieved, and requested "an overall study on the need to approximate Member State legislation in civil matters for eliminating obstacles to the good functioning of civil proceedings".[106]

As an answer to the European Council initiative, and in the face of the unresolved question of the extent of the legislative competences in the EU in the area of Private Law,[107] the European Commission published a Communication on the future of European Contract Law in July 2001.[108] It requested statements from Member States on the four alternatives proposed in the Communication: (a) taking no measure, leaving further development to market forces; (b) developing a kind of re-statement; (c) improving the *acquis communautaire*, or (d) creating a legislative instrument.[109] The Commission's interest lay in determining whether the diversity of contract law created an obstacle to the workings of the single market.[110]

The European Parliament responded by passing a resolution in November 2001 criticising the increased narrowing of focus on contract law alone, and requesting that the Commission construct an "action plan"[111] for the development of a European patrimonial law.[112]

---

[105] Presidency Conclusions from the Tampere European Council 15 and 16 October 1999, retrieved 31 March 2017 from http://www.europarl.europa.eu/summits/tam_en.htm#c.

[106] von Bar (2003b), p. 44. See the Presidency Conclusions from the Tampere European Council, B VII, no. 39. Just before the Tampere Summit, the Directorate-General for Research of the European Parliament commissioned an expert report on the growing difficulties caused by the implementation of EU Directives in the national legal systems (von Bar et al. 1999; von Bar 2003b, p. 43).

[107] Case C-376/98 *Federal Republic of Germany v European Parliament and the Council of the European Union* [2000] ECR I p. 8419 discussed the so-called "Tobacco Directive" (Directive 2014/40/EU of the European Parliament and of the Council of 3 April 2014 on the approximation of the laws, regulations and administrative provisions of the Member States concerning the manufacture, presentation and sale of tobacco and related products ("Tobacco Directive") and repealing Directive 2001/37/EC of 24 April 2014, OJ L 127/1, pp. 26–34).

[108] Communication of the Commission to the Council and the European Parliament on European contract law, 13 September 2001, COM(2001) 398 final, OJ C 255, p. 1 ff. "Contract law", however, was understood in a broad sense. See von Bar (2003b), p. 45.

[109] See von Bar (2003b), p. 383; von Bar (2004b), p. 1218.

[110] von Bar (2003b), p. 382.

[111] European Parliament Resolution of 15 November 2001 on the approximation of the civil and commercial law of the Member States (COM(2001) 398—C5-0471/2001 –2001/2187(COS) A5-0384/2001), retrieved 31 March 2017 from http://www.europarl.europa.eu/sides/getDoc.do?pubRef=-//EP//TEXT+REPORT+A5-2001-0384+0+DOC+XML+V0//EN, no. 9.

[112] *ibid.*, no. 14.

In this resolution, the European Parliament adopted, for the first time, a "bottom-up approach" (as opposed to a "top-down approach"), focused on the growing acceptance of regulation developing over time in the field of European Private Law and gradually becoming a binding force.[113] This resolution listed the legal areas where model rules should be formulated, and highlighted the sets of rules which should be promoted in academic training from 2005 onwards. It also highlighted the terminology that should be applied all over Europe and adopted after 2010.[114]

The European Commission answered this request in February 2003 with the launch of an "Action Plan on a More Coherent European Contract Law".[115] This demonstrated that, like the European Parliament, it, too, was concerned by the possible effects of diverse contract law systems on cross-border trade in the single market and the fragmentation arising from the piecemeal development of European law.[116] In the Communication "Action Plan", the Commission proposed three alternative measures[117] to the coherence of European Contract Law: (a) to improve the quality of the *acquis communautaire* in the area of Contract Law; (b) to promote the elaboration of EU-wide standard contract terms; or (c) to promote an optional instrument in the area of European Contract Law. Within the *acquis communautaire*, the Commission endorsed the development of a "Common Frame of Reference" (CFR), coining the term.[118] With the Communication "Action Plan", the Commission invited "feedback on the suggested mix of non-regulatory and regulatory measures" and "further reflections on an optional instrument in the area of European Contract Law".[119] This public consultation on the Commission's Action Plan received 319 response statements,[120] including more than 50 from academics, providing feedback and input to the Commission's proposal.

The Portuguese Foreign Office presented the Government's position in one concise document.[121] Here, the Portuguese Government expressed support for the

---

[113] von Bar (2003b), p. 385.

[114] See von Bar (2003b), pp. 47–48.

[115] Communication from the Commission to the European Parliament and the Council "A More Coherent European Contract Law: An Action Plan", 12 February 2003, COM(2003) 68 final, OJ C 63, 1 (hereinafter, *Action Plan*).

[116] Cf. von Bar (2004b), p. 1220.

[117] See no. 4, p. 14 ff. of the *Action Plan*.

[118] von Bar (2007), pp. 350–361; Schulte-Nölke (2009a), p. 49. See s. 4.1.1., nos. 59–68 of the *Action Plan*.

[119] See no. 98 (25) of the *Action Plan*.

[120] Annex to the *Action Plan*, Intr., para. 1. The complete list of contributions is available through http://ec.europa.eu/justice/news/consulting_public/news_consulting_0052_en.htm (retrieved 31 March 2017).

[121] Ministry of Foreign Affairs of Portugal, DG for Community Matters, Response to "A More Coherent European Contract Law – An Action Plan", retrieved 31 March 2017 from http://ec.europa.eu/consumers/archive/cons_int/safe_shop/fair_bus_pract/cont_law/stakeholders/1-8.pdf.

measures proposed by the Commission and declared it was "prepared to participate in the initiatives that will be adopted to put these measures in place". Further, it stated that "the establishment of a 'common frame of reference' is one of the most interesting measures in the proposed approach and must be one of the first to be implemented".[122] The optional instrument was considered an "innovative solution for avoiding legal disputes given that its use (. . .) would not rule out the application of the binding rules of national law".[123]

The "Joint Response of the Commission on European Contract Law and the Study Group on a European Civil Code" was one of the responses submitted.[124] This statement proposed a process separated into several distinct steps, leading to the achievement of a "comprehensive binding text", not excluding other measures of convergence. Stage 0 would consist of the creation of an effective re-statement of European patrimonial law. Stage 1 would introduce measures to promote awareness and dissemination of a non-binding formulation in the form of a "Restatement of European patrimonial Law", including recommendations to universities and national high-level courts. At this stage, the principles could be seen as general contract clauses of a public call for tenders and the European legislature would commit to adopting the system and terminology of these principles. At stage 2, measures would then be adopted that would allow the parties to choose the principles to form a legal order (dispositive European law). In stages 3 and 4 the text would become applicable by default (binding unless specifically excluded and, at the same time, mandatory European Law for cross-border transactions), and finally, at stage 5, the text would become mandatory European law for all transactions, similar to national civil codes.[125] The text did not indicate the timeframe for any of these stages or any overall timeline. This was left to the political level of decision-making.[126]

This proposal advocated a CFR in the form of "best rules", extending beyond contract law to reach "areas of private law, such as tort law (. . .) which (. . .) complete the legal framework for economic transactions and determines the totality of rights and responsibilities of the affected parties".[127]

In the responding document (Section 5.9) the role of the CFR was deemed superior to the optional instrument for a number of reasons, one of which was the "potential influence on judgments of the national courts".[128]

---

[122]*ibid.*, p. 2.

[123]*ibid.*, p. 4.

[124]See, generally, von Bar (2002f).

[125]von Bar and Lando (2001), pp. 236–237. See also von Bar (2002f), pp. 267–269, in particular p. 269.

[126]von Bar (2002f), p. 268.

[127]von Bar et al. (2002), no. 50, p. 30. See also von Bar (2003a), p. 100.

[128]von Bar (2003a), p. 100.

bb) The Conception of the Draft Common Frame of Reference

In October 2004, the European Commission published a further recommendation,[129] this time aimed at the creation and adoption of a Common Frame of Reference. It defined a set of legal terms, fundamental principles and coherent model rules, which would be instrumental in revising the *acquis* and which could provide the basis for an optional European Code of Contracts.[130]

To develop this text, the Commission funded the creation of a network of scholars (Network of Excellence "Common Principles of European Contract Law", Co-PECL), which it charged with accomplishing the submission of a DCFR, from which the EU institutions would finally select the CFR.[131] This project was intended to prepare the way for codification of general civil law principles, particularly relevant for the functioning of the single market.[132] This would later be incorporated in an EU regulation and allow the Member States to reach an agreement without affecting their national legal cultures.[133]

The DCFR was presented for the first time to the European Commission in December 2007. A preliminary draft ("interim outline edition") was published at the same time,[134] to allow for discussion of the content and open the way for amendment proposals. Most of the criticisms and suggestions were addressed by the revision of the DCFR. A more complete version ("outline edition") was then submitted to the European Commission in December 2008, and it was subsequently published in March 2009. The full edition[135] was presented in October 2009.[136]

In April 2010, the European Commission appointed an Expert Group on Contract Law,[137] tasked with distilling the relevant rules on contract from the DCFR.

---

[129]See also Communication from the Commission to the European Parliament and the Council "European Contract Law and the revision of the *acquis*: the way forward", 11 October 2004, COM (2004) 651 final, retrieved 31 March 2017 from http://eur-lex.europa.eu/LexUriServ/LexUriServ.do?uri=COM:2004:0651:FIN:EN:PDF (hereinafter, *The Way Forward*).

[130]See, in particular, the no. 62 of the *Action Plan*.

[131]von Bar et al. (2002), p. 192; Rajski (2006), p. 23. See also Moura Vicente (2008), p. 533.

[132]von Bar (2005), p. 18.

[133]von Bar (2002e), p. 68.

[134]von Bar et al. (2008). See von Bar (2008b), p. 4.

[135]von Bar and Clive (2009).

[136]See Santos Silva (2010), pp. 822–823. Some critics argued that by publishing draft rules before final rules and background material, the drafters behaved as legislatures. See Jansen and Zimmermann (2010), pp. 106–107.

[137]Commission Decision 2010/233/EU of 26 April 2010 setting up the Expert Group on a Common Frame of Reference in the area of European contract law, OJ L 105/109, pp. 101–111. This Expert Group included Schulte-Nölke from Osnabrück and Mota Pinto from Coimbra (available through http://ec.europa.eu/justice/contract/files/expert-group_en.pdf, retrieved 31 March 2017).

One month later, in the context of the Stockholm Programme, the European Council stated that "the common frame of reference for European Contract Law should be a non-binding set of fundamental principles, definitions and model rules to be used by the lawmakers at Union level to ensure greater coherence and quality in the law-making process" and invited the Commission to submit a proposal on a Common Frame of Reference.[138]

The Commission replied in July 2010, with the publication of a Green Paper on policy options for progress towards a European Contract Law for consumers and businesses.[139] Here, the Commission listed all possible options raised in the debate. These were:

a) The online publication of (non-binding) model contract rules which could be used in Europe's Single Market (option one);
b) An official (binding or non-binding) "toolbox" for EU lawmakers (option two), either as a Commission act for preparation of new legislation or amendment of existing legislation or as an inter-institutional agreement for more coherent drafting of new legislation;
c) A Commission recommendation on European Contract Law, which would call on EU Member States to include a European contract law in their national legal systems (option three);
d) A regulation setting an optional instrument of European Contract Law (or a "28th system"), which could be chosen by consumers and businesses as an alternative to the existing national contract laws, applicable in cross-border contracts or in both cross-border and domestic contracts (option four);
e) A Directive harmonising national contract laws (option five);
f) A Regulation harmonising national contract laws (option six); and
g) The creation of a European Civil Code which "would further reduce the need to fall back onto national provisions" (option seven).[140]

The Commission expressly highlighted the disadvantage of option two, namely, that legal divergences would continue to exist and that an official toolbox for lawmakers would not "ensure a convergent application and interpretation of Union contract law by the courts".[141]

In May 2011, the Expert Group on Contract Law published a feasibility study on the development of a European contract law instrument.[142] The study highlighted

---

[138]Council of the European Union, "The Stockholm Programme – An Open and Secure Europe Serving and Protecting the Citizens", 2 December 2009, retrieved 31 March 2017 from http://register.consilium.europa.eu/doc/srv?l=EN&f=ST%2017024%202009%20INIT, p. 33.

[139]Green Paper on European Union Consumer Protection COM(2010) 348 final, 1 July 2010, retrieved 31 March 2017 from http://ec.europa.eu/justice/contract/files/consultation_questionaire_en.pdf (hereinafter, *Green Paper*). See von Bar (2012b), p. 5 with criticism at p. 6 ff.

[140]*Green Paper*, pp. 7–11.

[141]*Green Paper*, p. 8.

[142]"A European contract law for consumers and businesses: publication of the results of the feasibility study carried out by the Expert Group on European contract law for stakeholders' and

that, based on the policy options provided for in the Commission's Green Paper, many respondents supported options one and two in particular. As for the scope of a potential European contract law instrument, most expressed a preference for a toolbox (option two) and an optional instrument (option 4). Of the first, most respondents chose a toolbox, which would go beyond contract law.[143]

In the aftermath of its Green Paper, the Commission carried out an impact assessment on the effects that legal diversity in contract law had for businesses and consumers.[144] The impact assessment covered areas beyond Contract Law, such as non-contractual liability.[145]

The resulting document stated that both the substitution of national laws with an optional instrument and a regulation establishing a European Civil Code were to be rejected because, firstly, they did not have sufficient support and, secondly, they affected the principles of proportionality and subsidiarity. When analysing the policy options proposed in its Green Paper, the European Commission concluded that any impact of option 2, first alternative (a "toolbox", in the sense of a Commission document for the amendment of existing legislation or preparation of future sectoral legislation) "would not be felt immediately because negotiations for new legislation or amendments to existing legislation would take time to achieve".[146]

The impact assessment concluded that the optional CESL was the preferred policy option to address the problems identified by the impact assessment, because it would reduce transaction costs and provide consumer protection.[147]

The Commission thus launched the "Proposal for a Regulation of the European Parliament and of the Council on a Common European Sales Law".[148] This law would introduce into the contract law of the Member States a second voluntary, "opt-in" regime for cross-border sales and related services in B2C and B2B

---

legal practitioners feedback", retrieved 31 March 2017 from http://ec.europa.eu/justice/contract/files/feasibility_study_final.pdf (hereinafter, *Feasibility Study*). In the Memorandum for the Italian Presidency: Consumer priorities 2014, BEUC, retrieved 31 March 2017 from http://www.beuc.eu/publications/beuc-x-2014-019_jkl_memorandum_for_the_italian_presidency.pdf, it was declared that "The European Parliament's 'health check' of the Commission's Impact Assessment found the Commission's methodology unreliable, with the quality and credibility of the data being questionable" (p. 12).

[143] *Feasibility Study*, p. 2.

[144] Executive summary of the Impact Assessment Proposal for a Regulation of the European Parliament and of the Council on a Common European Sales Law, 11 October 2011, SEC(2011) 1166 final, retrieved 31 March 2017 from http://ec.europa.eu/justice/contract/files/1_resume_impact_assesment_en.pdf (hereinafter, *Impact Assessment*).

[145] *Impact Assessment*, p. 4.

[146] *ibid.*, p. 5.

[147] *ibid.*, p. 7.

[148] Proposal for a Regulation of the European Parliament and of the Council on a Common European Sales Law, 11 October 2011, COM(2011) 0635 final—2011/0284 (COD) (hereinafter, CESL). The impact assessment was published together with the proposal on a CESL.

contracts where one of the parties is an SME. From the options presented by the Green Paper, option 4 (optional instrument) was thus preferred,[149] albeit with a narrower scope than that proposed by the drafters of the DCFR.[150] In fact, the Commission opted to focus solely on consumer contract law.

Several Member States objected to the proposal, namely UK, Austria, Belgium and Germany. Hungary, the Netherlands, Slovenia and Finland joined the protest later. They believed, among other reasons, that an optional instrument would be against the principles of subsidiarity and solidarity. Still, the European Parliament adopted a legislative resolution on an optional CESL[151] on February 2014,[152] with an even narrower scope than that of the Commission's proposal, containing only rules on the marketing of digital products and related services.[153]

In November 2014, a number of national Ministries (France, Germany, the UK, Austria, the Netherlands and Finland), delivered a joint letter expressing their disapproval of the CESL.[154] They stated that the CESL's legal basis, as well as its insertion into the existing legal order, raised "difficulties" and conflicted with the principles of subsidiarity and proportionality, that the need for such an instrument was not proven by the impact study carried by the Commission, and that the CESL itself was not comprehensive. According to these national Ministries, the CESL would "be a source of confusion and legal uncertainty". The CESL would provide for lower protection of consumers and small businesses compared to the legislation of several Member States, and would overlap with the Consumer's Rights Directive.[155] Given all those reasons, the signatory Ministries concluded that the proposed Regulation on a CESL could "not be a suitable solution to the current issues

---

[149]See Annex II, "Parameters concerning the optional instrument – For further discussion on the opportuness of this instrument" of *The Way Forward*.

[150]von Bar (2012a), p. 5. For details on the envisaged optional instrument, see von Bar (2007), 352; von Bar (2008a), p. 2; von Bar (2008b), p. 5, fn. 5; von Bar (2011c), p. 266; Zoll (2009); Zoll (2011a).

[151]European Parliament Resolution of 26 February 2014 on the Proposal for a Regulation of the European Parliament and of the Council on a Common European Sales Law (COM(2011)0635—C7-0329/2011—2011/0284(COD)) (Ordinary legislative procedure: first reading), retrieved 31 March 2017 from http://www.europarl.europa.eu/sides/getDoc.do?pubRef=-//EP//TEXT+TA+P7-TA-2014-0159+0+DOC+XML+V0//EN.

[152]Hériter (2015), pp. 363–364.

[153]Joint Brussels Office (2015), p. 2.

[154]Joint letter of the French, German, British, Austrian, Dutch and Finnish Ministries concerning the proposed legislation on a Common European Sales Law to Věra Jourová, European Commissioner for Justice, Consumers and Gender Equality (hereinafter, *Joint letter*).

[155]Directive 2011/83/EU of the European Parliament and of the Council of 25 October 2011 on consumer rights, amending Council Directive 93/13/EEC and Directive 1999/44/EC of the European Parliament and of the Council and repealing Council Directive 85/577/EEC and Directive 97/7/EC of the European Parliament and of the Council. Text with EEA relevance, OJ L 304, 22 November 2011, pp. 64–88. In the Memorandum for the Italian Presidency: Consumer priorities 2014 (see Tit. § 3, Subtit. II, Sec. 1, Subsec. b) above, in footnote), BEUC also manifested preference for the Consumer's Rights Directive as opposed to the CESL (pp. 11 and 12).

faced by stakeholders" and that in addition it "may reduce confidence in the single market".[156]

The signatory Ministries considered instead that "approaches and discussions that have been considered now for several years could well lead to the negotiation of a "toolbox" that would inspire European legislation, and which would allow national legislation to gradually achieve a common minimum standard".[157] The scope of such a toolbox would be in harmony with the scope of the DCFR.[158]

In December 2014, the Commission listed the Proposal for a Regulation of the European Parliament and of the Council on a CESL as one of the areas in need of modification, "in order to fully unleash the potential of e-commerce in the digital single market".[159]

In May 2015, the European Commission adopted a digital single market strategy,[160] demonstrating that an instrument for the regulation of the online, digital market seems to be the current priority for the European Parliament and the Commission.[161] There are still question marks over the legal format and standing of such a document and some argue that, as a result of the proposal, an optional instrument has been abandoned.[162] The ELI issued the Statement "Proposal for a Common European Sales Law (CESL)", as well as two supplements,[163] within a long-term project aimed at setting out a general approach for a detailed legislative proposal.[164]

---

[156]*Joint letter*, pp. 4–5.

[157]*ibid.*, p. 5.

[158]Joint Brussels Office (2015), pp. 1–12.

[159]Annex to the Communication from the Commission to the European Parliament, the Council, the European Economic and Social Committee and the Committee of the Regions, Commission Work Programme 2015, A New Start, 16 December 2014, COM(2014) 910 final, retrieved 31 March 2017 from http://ec.europa.eu/atwork/pdf/cwp_2015_withdrawals_en.pdf, no. 60, p. 12.

[160]See http://ec.europa.eu/priorities/digital-single-market/ (retrieved 30 August 2015).

[161]See the recent creation of the Stakeholder Consultation Group for consumer rules for online and digital purchases, available through http://ec.europa.eu/transparency/regexpert/index.cfm?do=groupDetail.groupDetail&groupID=3295 (retrieved 31 March 2017).

[162]Clive (2015).

[163]S-2-2012 Statement on the Proposal for a Regulation on a Common European Sales Law, available through http://www.europeanlawinstitute.eu/fileadmin/user_upload/p_eli/Publications/S-2-2012_Statement_on_the_Proposal_for_a_Regulation_on__a_Common_European_Sales_Law.pdf (retrieved 31 March 2017); S-4-2014 1st Supplement to the Statement on the Proposal for a Regulation on a Common European Sales Law, available through http://www.europeanlawinstitute.eu/fileadmin/user_upload/p_eli/Publications/CESL_1st_Supplement.pdf (retrieved 31 March 2017); and S-6-2015 2nd Supplement to the Statement on the Proposal for a Regulation on a Common European Sales Law, available through http://www.europeanlawinstitute.eu/fileadmin/user_upload/p_eli/Projects/Unlocking_the_Digital_Single_Market.pdf (retrieved 31 March 2017).

[164]See http://www.europeanlawinstitute.eu/home/news-contd/article/the-eli-publishes-the-2nd-supplement-to-its-cesl-statement-unlocking-the-digital-single-market/?tx_ttnews[backPid]=180991&cHash=aa76109a1cd713d1e51d9ce439909e6a (retrieved 31 March 2017).

In September 2015, delivering on its digital single market strategy, the Commission introduced two proposals for Directives on sales laws: one on the supply of digital content[165] and one on the online sale of goods.[166]

These recent developments were a topical legal issue at the European Law Institute (ELI)'s Annual Conference and General Assembly in September 2016. The discussion following the panel, "Digital Single Market: European Developments after the withdrawal of the CESL Proposal", chaired by Lord Chief Justice John Tomas, seems to have led to the generally endorsed conclusion that maximum harmonisation in such a narrow field as digital sales is not desirable, and that a more comprehensive instrument would be preferable.[167]

More than 30 years after the demand for the harmonisation of European Private Laws begun to be discussed under the leadership of Ole Lando, therefore, the current state of affairs seems to favour a broad, non-political, European patrimonial law instrument, instead of a CESL.

b) Authorship

The DCFR was prepared by the Study Group on a European Civil Code (SGECC) and the Research Group on EC Private Law (Acquis Group).

The SGECC was established in 1998[168] and built on the results achieved by the PECL. The text of these Principles, drafted by the Commission on European Contract Law ("Lando Commission"), was included in the DCFR in an expanded, revised form.[169] The SGECC was based on research into legislation, case law and legal writings from the EU national legal systems, taking into account international

[165] Proposal for a Directive of the European Parliament and of the Council on certain aspects concerning contracts for the supply of digital content, COM/2015/0634 final—2015/0287 (COD) retrieved 31 March 2017 from http://eur-lex.europa.eu/legal-content/EN/TXT/?qid=1450431933547&uri=CELEX:52015PC0634.

[166] Proposal for a Directive of the European Parliament and of the Council on certain aspects concerning contracts for the online and other distance sales of goods, COM/2015/0635 final—2015/0288 (COD), retrieved 31 March 2017 from http://eur-lex.europa.eu/legal-content/EN/TXT/?qid=1450431933547&uri=CELEX:52015PC0635.

[167] ELI, "Building the future of law in Europe on unity and diversity – 3rd day of the ELI Annual Conference 2016", available at http://www.europeanlawinstitute.eu/news/news-contd/article/building-the-future-of-law-in-europe-on-unity-and-diversity/?tx_ttnews%5BbackPid%5D=179468&cHash=3c11e9e5574c4329695052197664024c, retrieved on 31 March 2017.

[168] von Bar (2008a), p. 4.

[169] Clive (2008), p. 19; Moura Vicente (2008), p. 534; von Bar (2008a), p. 5; von Bar et al. (2008), Intr. n. 40, p. 30; Jansen (2010), p. 3 *passim*. For a summary of the differences from the PECL, see Clive (2008), p. 20 ff. On the PECL and its authorship, see Lando (1999), p. 125 ff.

conventions and the desire for uniform rules and practices. It formulated common principles of Private Law and suggested ways of surmounting the differences between the different national laws of the EU Member States.[170]

The SGECC's working groups comprised lawyers from every EU Member State, all working under the close supervision of a team leader. The groups were responsible for preparing comparative law reports, which were subsequently discussed with the SGECC's Advisory Council.

The Advisory Council was composed of leading experts in the legal fields of each working team, representing each EU Member State.[171] The Co-ordinating Group, consisting of almost 50 law professors from all over Europe,[172] analysed and discussed the comparative materials on a bi-annual basis.

From the outset, the SGECC recognised the importance of the collaboration between legal scholarship and judicial practice.[173] This acceptance might have been particularly strong because its members comprised legal practitioners and sitting judges from the respective national jurisdictions.[174]

The Acquis Group was founded in 2002 and was attended by about 30 legal scholars from the EU countries and candidate countries for accession. Its activities started in 2005 and were completed in 2010. Its role consisted of extracting the "Principles of the Existing EC Contract Law" from the *acquis communautaire*.[175] This was done not through the analysis of each EU legal system (as was the case of the SGECC), but through an analysis of the *acquis communautaire* itself. The Acquis Group also ensured the correct representation of the content of the European Directives in the DCFR.[176]

The authors of the DCFR have themselves come in for some criticism. Some legal scholars have claimed that the network of scholars working on these definitions, principles and model rules lack tradition and institutional legitimacy, which could pose a problem should the DCFR be politically approved and become binding law.[177]

[170]von Bar et al. (2002), p. 192.

[171]Cf. von Bar (2009c), pp. vii and viii.

[172]von Bar (2003b), p. 386.

[173]Zweigert (1949), p. 18.

[174]Santos Silva (2010), p. 804, fn. 8. For details on the SGECC see von Bar (2000d).

[175]Rajski (2006), p. 22; von Bar (2012b), p. 3.

[176]von Bar (2008a), p. 2. For details on the different fields of work and comparative foundations see Schulte-Nölke (2009b), pp. 11–12. On the Acquis Principles see generally Schulte-Nölke (2008). See also Zoll (2011b), pp. 559–560.

[177]Grigoleit (2015), pp. 255 and 256.

c) Scope and Contents

aa) European Patrimonial Law

The DCFR deals with the sources of legal obligations,[178] as well as aspects of Property Law.[179] It includes: (a) the general Law of Contracts; (b) the law of the most relevant particular types of contract; (c) the Law of Non-Contractual Obligations (Law of Non-Contractual Liability, the Law of Unjustified Enrichment and Law of Benevolent Intervention in Another's Affairs); (d) the Law of Credit Securities in Movables; (e) the Transfer of Ownership in Movables; and, (f) the Law of Trusts and corresponding instruments in continental legal systems.[180] It is thus commonly said that the DCFR deals with "European Patrimonial Law".[181]

The reach of the DCFR, therefore, goes beyond contract law when compared to the PECL. It encompasses a wider range of legal subjects[182] and new material, including the input of the Acquis Group. Through the DCFR, the PECL was extended in three directions: (a) rules on specific types of contracts; (b) rules on non-contractual obligations (Law of Non-Contractual Liability, Law of Unjustified Enrichment and the Law of Benevolent Intervention in Another's Affairs) and (c) rules for fundamental questions in the law of mobile assets.[183] In comparison to the PECL, the DCFR expanded rules, included definitions, improved the drafting and the structure, and presented a more "transparent" document.[184] The political authority of the DCFR has been called superior to that of the PECL, because the former counted the institutional backing of the EU institutions from the beginning.[185]

There were many justifications[186] for the broader scope of the DCFR than that envisaged by the Commission.

---

[178]For details on the structure of the DCFR, see Schulte-Nölke (2009a), p. 54 ff.; Zoll (2011b), pp. 557–558. In a publication, the Head of the Commission's Internal Working Group said that the DCFR should deal with the same content as contained in the general part of the BGB, and also including contracts in general, as well as special contracts (Staudenmayer 2005, p. 103). It should be noted, however, that the first part of the DCFR does not correspond to the *Allgemeiner Teil* of the BGB and neither can it be said that the DCFR was drafted in the light of the BGB (von Bar 2008d). See also Schmidt (2015), particularly p. 50.

[179]von Bar et al. (2009), Intr. 34 ff., pp. 23–25. See also Schulte-Nölke (2009a), pp. 51–54.

[180]von Bar et al. (2002), p. 213; von Bar (2009d), p. 59.

[181]Heutger and Jeloschek (2004), p. 544.

[182]See MacQueen (2010), p. 181.

[183]von Bar (2002c), p. 139; von Bar (2005), p. 18.

[184]For details, see Clive (2008), pp. 18–26.

[185]Hesselink (2009), pp. 924–925. For further details on the political authority of the DCFR see Tit. § 3, Subtit. II, Secs. 1 and 2 below.

[186]For a thorough description of the main arguments, see von Bar (2008b), pp. 8–9.

It was argued that the DCFR was not subject to the same limitations as the "political" CFR,[187] and that it had to cope with the scope agreed upon with the Commission within the Sixth European Framework Programme on Research.[188]

It was also argued that, even if the CFR were ultimately to become solely an instrument of Contract Law, that the DCFR could always be "re-contractualised", which would be easier than having a smaller DCFR and turning it into a political instrument applicable to all sources of obligations.[189]

It was suggested that the *acquis* related to topics far beyond the law of contracts and that the legal European terminology provided in the DCFR was expected to meet such topics.[190] Finally, the argument to defend a broader scope of the DCFR as compared to the CFR, was that the exact definition of Contract Law is different in each Member State (relating in particular to the demarcation line between Property Law and Contract Law), and thus a narrow definition would exclude large areas of domestic law from the DCFR.[191]

Nevertheless, the DCFR does not have an unlimited scope. It explicitly states (I.–1:101(2)) that it does not extend to certain matters of law, which are, namely, "the status or legal capacity of natural persons, wills and succession, family relationships, negotiable instruments, employment relationships, immovable property law, company law, and the law of civil procedure[192] and enforcement of claims".[193] These are policy-related topics, and less likely to lend themselves to harmonisation throughout Europe.

bb) Structure and Drafting Technique

English was the draft language of the DCFR.[194] It was structured with an introduction, tables, indexes, principles, definitions and model rules. The PECL Series contains comparative introductions to the different books, as well as the translation

---

[187] See von Bar (2007), p. 355; von Bar et al. (2009), Intr. 4, p. 6.

[188] von Bar (2007), pp. 355–356.

[189] Schulte-Nölke (2009a), p. 48.

[190] von Bar (2007), p. 355; von Bar (2008b), p. 8.

[191] von Bar (2011d), pp. 203–204. For a thorough explanation of the difficulty in setting clear boundaries between Contract and Non-Contractual law, see generally von Bar and Drobnig (2004). See also Koziol (1998b), p. 98; von Bar (2002c), p. 140; von Bar (2004b), p. 1223 ff.; von Bar (2008b), p. 8.

[192] According to Brüggemeier, the DCFR included a few aspects on Procedural Law (such as the standard of proof). See Brüggemeier (2009a), p. 189.

[193] von Bar et al. (2009), Intr. 38, p. 24.

[194] The drafters of the DCFR admit that in Latin countries the English language is less widespread than in Northern Europe. However, they consider English to be the only language in which a pan-European debate could take place because of financial constraints which preclude the use of other languages (von Bar 2009a, p. 1858).

of the Principles into several EU Member State languages.[195] Its content complies with the scheme set out in the European Commission's Communications of 2003 (*Action Plan*) and 2004 (*The Way Forward*).

The structure of the DCFR, which has been characterised as "complex and clumsy" by some of its critics,[196] is similar to that of a traditional civil code.[197] It is systematised in 10 books,[198] which are further divided into chapters, sections, subsections and, finally, (model) rules.[199] From these 10 books,[200] Books II and III update former PECL rules. They also revise and adopt materials present in the Acquis Principles.

The most important "tool" provided for by the DCFR are the model rules,[201] which are accompanied by extensive commentaries, including illustrations and national notes. The national notes provide the "essential background information" about the law of each Member State.[202]

In legal areas of greater harmonisation between the EU Member States (and which correspond almost invariably to those subject to more EU legislation), the strategy was to establish "common rules" (rules which display a common legal tradition). In the remaining cases, the drafters opted for rules which were considered by the DCFR's wide expert group of pan-European lawyers as "best solutions" or at least compromise solutions.[203] In the cases considered best solutions, the commentaries set out the decisions for that particular policy choice.[204] As for the compromise solutions, they recognise it is not always possible to come up with a set of model rules for Europe without diverging from the solutions of some legal systems compared to others,[205] but that it is indeed possible for the most reasonable solutions to prevail.

Definitions were developed, closely aligned with the model rules. These are also part of the "toolbox" function[206] and serve as suggestions for the development of a uniform European legal terminology,[207] which was considered a necessity by the

---

[195] See von Bar et al. (2009), Intr. 54, p. 34.

[196] Eidenmüller et al. (2008a), p. 682.

[197] von Bar (2008a), p. 4. See also Zoll (2011b), p. 556. According to Schulte-Nölke, the intention was to facilitate the tasks of individual users and meet their particular needs (Schulte-Nölke 2011, p. 22).

[198] Book IV is longer than the other books and was thus divided into parts.

[199] von Bar (2005), p. 22. For details on the numbering system, see von Bar (2001a), p. 519, fn. 12 and von Bar et al. (2009), Intr. 42, pp. 25–26.

[200] The Interim Outline Edition contains seven books.

[201] von Bar (2012b), p. 8.

[202] Beale (2009), p. 40. Jansen and Zimmermann believe that the comments and illustrations should have offered legal arguments (Jansen and Zimmermann 2010, p. 111).

[203] Schulte-Nölke (2011), pp. 24–25.

[204] Beale (2009), p. 40. For a critique, see Schulze (2011), p. 7.

[205] von Bar (2002a), p. 173.

[206] For details on the "toolbox" function, see Tit. § 3, Subtit. II, Sec. 2 below.

[207] von Bar (2008b), p. 5; von Bar (2008d), p. 41; von Bar (2009a), pp. 1861–1862.

European Commission.[208] The list of definitions aimed to enhance clarity[209] and legal predictability,[210] even though some scholars argue that the definitions should be restricted, for the sake of legal certainty.[211]

The definitions, listed in the appendix to the DCFR, are part of the DCFR[212] and are necessary additions to the model rules. The definitions would be useless without the model rules, and the reverse is equally true.[213]

As far as the principles are concerned, they seem to hold at least two positions within the context of the DCFR: they refer to the DCFR's core aims and underlying values and are sometimes used in the sense of rules without binding force.[214] As for the core aims and underlying values, the principles provided for in the interim outline edition of the DCFR[215] were organised into *underlying* principles (freedom, security, justice and efficiency) and *overriding* principles (protection of human rights, promotion of solidarity and social responsibility, preservation of cultural and linguistic diversity, protection and promotion of the single market).[216,217] The principles are accompanied by an introduction with comparative elements, illustrations and national notes for each of the EU Member States, where the applicable law is summarily described. Here, it can also be ascertained the extent to which the provision of the Principles is already "anchored" within the national laws of the Member States.[218]

This structure does not require incorporation into national legal systems as a single block, which gives it an advantage over a binding instrument.[219] Each

---

208 That need is shown by the unclear use of the word "damage" in the Simone Leitner case (Case C-168/00 *Simone Leitner v TUI Deutschland* [2002] ECR I–2631). See von Bar (2011b), p. 387. The interest of the European Commission in terminology issues can be shown by its financial backing of the research network "Uniform terminology for European Private Law". For details on results of this programme see Weitenberg (2008).

209 For a critical account see Koch (2005), p. 191.

210 Critical of these definitions, considering them "inconsistent", see Eidenmüller et al. (2008b), pp. 547–549.

211 Eidenmüller et al. (2008a), p. 683.

212 See von Bar (2008b), p. 6.

213 von Bar (2004b), p. 1220. See also von Bar et al. (2009), Intr. 65, p. 40; Schulte-Nölke (2010a), p. 615 f.

214 von Bar et al. (2009), Intr. p. 11 ff., p. 10 ff. See also von Bar (2008d), p. 43. For Jansen, the DCFR's "principles" set legal consequences for a set of given conditions and are thus authentic legal rules (Zimmermann 2004, p. 9 f. and Jansen 2007, p. 15, n. 2).

215 von Bar et al. (2008), Intr. 11 ff., p. 10 ff.

216 According to von Bar, "the CFR is for helping SMEs in doing business, in particular doing business abroad, and it is for strengthening the consumer's trust in the good functioning of the Internal Market when buying goods or ordering services from a business situated in another country." (von Bar 2007, p. 350).

217 See, respectively, von Bar et al. (2009), Intr. 15, p. 13 f. and Intr. 16 ff., p. 14 ff.

218 von Bar (2003b), p. 386. For details on the structure of the DCFR see Schulte-Nölke (2009a), p. 54 ff.

219 von Bar et al. (2009), Intr. 74, p. 44. See, however, Jansen and Zimmermann (2010), p. 112.

country has the freedom to implement only parts of the DCFR or even to implement it with amendments (thereby using only one or a few tools from the "box"). A more comprehensive solution might have had the benefit of certainty and uniformity,[220] however, by opting for this solution, the DCFR offers a flexible mechanism for Member States to move towards the harmonisation of Civil Law.[221]

A key aim for the drafters was to provide a clear text which would be all-inclusive in the field of European Patrimonial Law, and which would contain enduring model rules. This demanded the use of a specific drafting technique, which includes abstract language and open-ended concepts,[222] attracting both criticism and praise.

A group of German legal scholars[223] criticised the DCFR, denouncing what they called an "excessive use" of general clauses and open-textured formulations concepts in the DCFR.[224] They argued that these clauses and concepts, in combination with what they saw as a very broad catalogue of values from which to choose in difficult cases, grant excessive law-making powers to the courts,[225] and that only unambiguous and clear rules will relieve the legal system from resolving disputes.[226] According to such critics, "it is difficult to see how an open-ended regime could work satisfactorily in a community of 28 Member States with divergent systems of tort law".[227]

Criticism also came from Austria, in the form of the argument that without concrete rules no harmonisation of European Private Law can take place, and that courts need assessment criteria and not only general clauses.[228]

Other scholars criticised the drafting technique used by the DCFR, arguing that sets of rules and principles that aim to become a European regulation must be self-sufficient and not dependent on judicial realisation. Europe was

[220]Howarth (2011), pp. 872–873.

[221]Cf. Zemanek (1998), p. 861.

[222]See also Sefton-Green (2009), p. 44.

[223]Eidenmüller et al. (2008b).

[224]*ibid.*, p. 536. But see Zoll (2011b), p. 557, who considers that the DCFR is not sufficiently open to legal change.

[225]Hesselink (2008b), p. 27; Schulze (2012), p. 226. It has been stated that "the role model of the DCFR's tort regime is not the autonomous and rational party who may rightly be held responsible for his or her actions, but the paternalistic judge who strives for social improvement and seeks to bring it about by means of his judgments." (Eidenmüller et al. 2008a, p. 687).

[226]Eidenmüller et al. (2008a), p. 677. It should be noted, however, that the "unambiguous" and clear language used in the BGB did not prevent inconsistencies in resolving legal disputes in so far as pure economic loss is concerned, undermining this argument.

[227]Eidenmüller et al. (2008a), p. 685.

[228]Koziol (2009), p. 96. See also Eidenmüller et al. (2008b), p. 537.

characterised as a "low-context"[229] place, where spelling out solutions was required.[230]

However, the DCFR's drafting technique also received much support, with some, for example, arguing that the use of general clauses and open-textured formulations was present in several European national codes[231] as "gateways through which justice and constitutional values enter the legal system",[232] through the decision-making process of courts.[233] These clauses and concepts are considered by some authors to be particularly important should the DCFR lead to a common European regulation in the future.[234]

d) Legal Nature

aa) An Apolitical Set of Rules

The DCFR states in its introduction that it is envisaged as a proposal for legislation.[235] Its drafters and contributors repeatedly highlighted that the DCFR is not a politically authorised text,[236] and that they leave the decision of whether it will give rise to a CFR (and the content, structure and scope that this might have)[237] to the competent institutions.[238] They argue that, at most, one could view the DCFR as a potential "model code".[239]

The legal nature of the DCFR remains, however, a highly contested issue. The debate has been characterised as a "journey where both the route and the destination are unknown".[240] Many have assumed that the main purpose of the DCFR is to

---

[229]Reference to an anthropological category that speaks, on the one hand, of "low-context societies" (societies which prefer expressly set rules) and, on the other hand, of "high-context societies" (societies which prefer tacit rules). See Hall (1976) and Hall (1990) *apud* Howarth (2011), p. 872 and fn. 120.

[230]Howarth (2011), p. 872.

[231]Cf. Schmidt-Kessel (2006), p. 26. This argument is less significant in light of Case C-237/02, *Freiburger Kommunalbauten GmbH Baugesellschaft & Co KG v Ludger Hofstetter and Ulrike Hofstetter* [2004] ECR I-03403. See Hesselink (2008b), pp. 27–28.

[232]Hesselink (2008b), p. 31.

[233]Schmid (2010b), p. 5.

[234]Magnus (2004b), p. 569.

[235]von Bar et al. (2008), Intr. 4, p. 6.

[236]von Bar (2008b), p. 5; Hesselink (2009), p. 925; von Bar (2009b), p. 24. It has been argued, however, that the DCFR would gain credibility if it were associated with an official text, even if the DCFR were to have a more limited content and a more modest purpose. See Clive (2008), p. 15.

[237]von Bar (2008b), p. 5.

[238]Cf. also von Bar (2005), p. 19.

[239]von Bar (2012a), p. 3. See also Röthel (2009), p. 290; Schulte-Nölke (2009a), p. 62.

[240]See Wallis (2006), p. 10.

become a unitary law for Europe in the form of a European Civil Code.[241] This opinion stems from the name of one of its drafting groups ("Study Group on a European Civil Code").[242] Many legal scholars argue that by presenting "best solutions", the DCFR is a political, rather than simply a technical, toolbox.[243] Eidenmüller, Faust, Grigoleit, Jansen, Wagner and Zimmermann consider that the DCFR contains codified rules which would need to be enacted through a legitimised legislature,[244] instead of a group of academic scholars.[245]

This argument has generated overly emotional and fearful responses,[246] in particular in countries with a high regard for their Civil Code,[247] such as Portugal.

bb) A (Re)statement

Due to the way in which the model rules of the DCFR reproduce law, the latter is often seen as a restatement[248] of private law relevant for the single market.[249]

It is recognised that the Restatements of the American Law Institute were an important model for the DCFR and its "predecessors",[250] and thus that they share considerable similarities.[251] Nevertheless, many also highlight the considerable differences between the DCFR and the Restatements,[252] such as the lack of institutional legitimacy and tradition, but also the fact that "the state private law systems to which the US Restatements refer are relatively homogeneous, while the

[241] von Bar et al. (2009), Intr. 19, p. 16. See, *e.g.*, Legrand (2006), p. 14.

[242] See Jansen and Zimmermann (2010), p. 99.

[243] Sefton-Green (2009), p. 45 ff.

[244] Eidenmüller et al. (2008b), p. 533.

[245] Jansen and Zimmermann (2010), pp. 106–107.

[246] von Bar (2003b), p. 48; von Bar (2007), pp. 350–361, especially p. 353; von Bar (2008a), p. 5. For a list of arguments for and against a uniform European Law of Obligations, see Lando (1999), pp. 123–125.

[247] That seems to be the case for France where, in his days in Sainte-Hélène, Napoléon Bonaparte declared: "*Waterloo effacera le souvenir de tant de victoires; ce que rien n'effacera, ce qui vivra é ternellement, c'est mon Code Civil*" ("[The Battle of] Waterloo will erase the memory of many victories; but my Civil Code will never be erased, it will live forever"). More recently, Pierre Legrand has been one of the most tireless critics of civil law harmonisation and of the idea of a European Civil Code in particular, which he considers "backward", "arrogant" and "impracticable". See Legrand (1997a), pp. 44–63, particularly pp. 56–60 and Legrand (2006), pp. 13–40.

[248] von Bar (2005), p. 18; von Bar (2007), p. 354; von Bar (2008a), p. 4; von Bar (2008b), p. 7.

[249] von Bar (2009a), p. 1856.

[250] von Bar and Lando (2001), 183, no. 61 ff.; Schulte-Nölke (2011), p. 11. As for the PECL, some legal scholars deny its nature of restatement. See Jansen (2007), p. 15, fn. 3; Hesselink (2009), p. 924.

[251] von Bar (2002c), p. 139 *passim*; von Bar (2005), p. 22; von Bar (2012a), p. 3.

[252] von Bar (2002f), p. 267; von Bar (2005), p. 22; von Bar (2008d), p. 35; von Bar (2009a), p. 1856.

European jurisdictions have different and quite unhomogeneous traditions",[253] which would call upon a "law of harmonisation" instead of a harmonisation of laws.[254] Other differences which have been stressed are the fact that the DCFR is aimed at fulfilling other tasks besides the restatement of the law and that it creates new harmonised law that does not always align with the pre-existing law, for which reason it would be better termed a "statement".[255]

cc) Soft Law Instrument

The DCFR is sometimes characterised as a soft law instrument,[256] in that it creates a set of rules of conduct which do not have binding force but which aim to have certain (indirect) legal effects.[257]

EU soft law is plentiful and heterogeneous, and has thus been subject to many attempts at categorisation. One of these attempts classifies soft law into: preparatory and informative instruments (where, *inter alia*, Green Papers, White Papers and Action Programmes fall); interpretative and decisional instruments (which include Commission communications, notices, guidelines, codes and frameworks); and steering instruments, which cover instruments aimed at promoting EU objectives and policies, and are presumed to realise harmonisation of national law in a non-formal way (conclusions, declarations, recommendations, resolutions and similar).[258] The last two types of EU soft law are distinguished from the others by their purpose and role: while interpretative and decisional instruments are intended to complement legislation—thereby playing a kind of *post-law* function—the steering documents intend to replace legislation and have thus mostly a *pre*-law role or even *para*-law function.[259] Steering instruments are characterised as involving new, independent rules or provisions which consist of competitive alternatives to

[253]Grigoleit (2015), p. 255.

[254]Joerges (1999), p. 222.

[255]von Bar (2002f), p. 266. See also Schulte-Nölke (2011), p. 30.

[256]See Röthel (2009), p. 288; Miller (2011), p. 205; Lehmann (2015), p. 245. The Council referred to the DCFR as a "set of non-binding guidelines" (Press Release from the 2863rd Council meeting from 18 April 2008, 8397/08, Presse 96, retrieved 31 March 2017 from http://www.consilium.europa.eu/uedocs/cms_data/docs/pressdata/en/jha/99991.pdf), p. 18. Cf. also von Bar et al. (2009), Intr. 19, pp. 15–16. But see Hesselink (2008b), p. 28 where the DCFR is classified as a "pseudo-legislature".

[257]Senden (2004), p. 112. See also Röthel (2009), p. 288.

[258]Senden (2005), pp. 81–82. The ECJ refers to steering soft law instruments as those which are aimed at confirming or supporting an interpretation already reached on the basis of binding EU Law. This is called "confirmatory" interpretation. See Senden (2004), p. 397.

[259]Senden (2005), pp. 81–82; Sefton-Green (2009), p. 47.

legislation due to their more rapid (compared to hard law) adaptation to technological progress. This category includes instruments that aim at a "closer cooperation or even harmonisation between the Member States in a non-binding way".[260] Moreover, they can be considered to share a role with interpretative instruments, for example that of supplementing the law, and may thus have a post-law function as well.[261]

The DCFR has been categorised as a steering soft law instrument.[262] This categorisation may be in recognition of the innovative character of its solutions[263] and, particularly, for its aim of serving as a model for a future CFR,[264] a fact clearly stated within the DCFR[265] and by its main drafters.[266]

2. Purposes of the DCFR: a "Toolbox" for the Development of European Private Law

In contrast to the possible roles of the CFR, which are subject to discussion everywhere,[267] the purpose of the DCFR is clearly stated in the introduction to the Interim Outline Edition of the DCFR. The different purposes have been summarised under the umbrella term, "toolbox function".[268]

---

[260] Senden (2005), p. 81.

[261] Senden and Prechal (2001), p. 192.

[262] Sefton-Green (2009), p. 48. Cf. also Mankowski (2012), no. 112a, p. 174 and Valpuesta Gastaminza (2011), p. 31. See, however, Grigoleit (2015, pp. 254–255), who denies the utility of the concept of "soft law" in the first place, considering law to be either enforceable or unenforceable. For this discussion, see Zemanek (1998).

[263] Schulte-Nölke (2011), p. 25.

[264] Hesselink (2009), p. 923, including further references.

[265] von Bar et al. (2009), Intr. 6, p. 7 ff.

[266] See von Bar and Schulte-Nölke (2005), p. 167; von Bar (2008a), p. 4; von Bar (2009b), p. 25; von Bar (2009a), p. 1854.

[267] von Bar (2009b), pp. 28–33; von Bar (2009d), p. 56 ff.; Clive (2010); Hesselink (2010), pp. 441–469. See also European Union Committee of the House of Lords (UK), "European Contract Law: The Draft Common Frame of Reference", 19 May 2009, Session 2008–09, no. 70, retrieved 31 March 2017 from http://www.publications.parliament.uk/pa/ld200809/ldselect/ldeucom/95/9502.htm.

[268] von Bar (2009a), pp. 1850–1871; von Bar (2009d); Clive (2010); Hesselink (2010), pp. 441–469.

This expression was first used in 2004 by the European Commission[269] to refer to the usage the DCFR could have in drafting and amending legislation at European and national level.[270]

The toolbox function corresponded to option 2 of the Commission's Green Paper, which was sidelined in favour of an optional instrument, albeit with a narrower scope than the DCFR, namely, the CESL. Nevertheless, as described above,[271] this discarded function has recently been rediscovered,[272] bringing renewed legal debate.

a) Preliminary Note. An Academic and Apolitical Tool

As mentioned before, one of the aims of the DCFR is to serve as a draft for the creation of a political Common Frame of Reference. Therefore, although the DCFR and the CFR are linked, they consist of independent realities, with different scopes and aims.[273]

Despite the claims of some legal scholars that the DCFR is not politically neutral,[274] it is assumed to be a purely academic project[275] which was prepared and approved by experts in European and Comparative Private Law, who acted freely and without political influence.[276] On the other hand, the CFR is an instrument of a narrower scope,[277] the destiny of which was intentionally left by its authors to the European institutions,[278] even though the political priorities have never been made entirely clear.[279]

---

[269]The expression was used for the first time in *The Way Forward*: "First a policy choice must be made on the need to modify the existing directives in order to address these problems [for the improvement of the acquis]. If so, the Commission will use the CFR as a *toolbox* [emphasis added], where appropriate, when presenting proposals to improve the quality and coherence of the existing acquis and future legal instruments in the area of contract law. At the same time, it will serve the purpose of simplifying the acquis (. . .). The CFR will provide clear definitions of legal terms, fundamental principles and coherent model rules of contract law, drawing on the EC acquis and on best solutions found in Member States' legal orders." (*The Way Forward*, p. 3).

[270]von Bar and Schulte-Nölke (2005), p. 168. The term "toolbox" comprises a wide variety of meanings (von Bar 2005, p. 22) which will be described in this section. For criticism of the "toolbox" function, see Zimmermann (2008), p. 204.

[271]See Tit. § 3, Subtit. II, Sec. 1, Subsec. a) aa).

[272]Cf. also von Bar (2009a), pp. 1862–1863.

[273]Clive (2008), p. 14; von Bar et al. (2009), Intr. 6–7, pp. 7–9.

[274]See generally Somma (2009), with several contributions. See also Jansen and Zimmermann (2010), pp. 98–112.

[275]Schulte-Nölke (2009b), p. 14.

[276]von Bar (2002e), p. 67; von Bar (2008a), p. 5; von Bar (2008d); von Bar et al. (2008), Intr. 39, p. 23.

[277]von Bar (2009d), p. 59.

[278]von Bar (2008a), p. 3, von Bar et al. (2009), Intr. 39, p. 23; Jansen (2010), p. 3.

[279]von Bar (2003a), p. 100; von Bar (2008a), p. 2; von Bar (2009d), p. 62. For details on the differences between the DCFR and the CFR, see Schulte-Nölke (2009a), pp. 48–51.

The non-binding nature of the DCFR has raised questions on how it should and could be implemented. Nevertheless, it has been argued that it can represent a comparative advantage as well.[280] It is considered more flexible than a CFR,[281] more respectful of the principles of subsidiarity and proportionality (Art. 5 TEU),[282] and less likely to be perceived as a threat to the integrity and prevalence of national law.[283] This perception of the DCFR as benign with respect to national law is based on the realisation that it does not imply an acceptance *in toto* (a "take it or leave it" approach)[284] and also because it would leave sufficient room for courts to flexibly adapt it to local or regional needs.[285]

The drafters of the DCFR repeatedly confirmed that, should a CFR emerge, it would not necessarily have the same scope and contents as the DCFR, even though its scope should not be limited to Contract Law.[286]

b) A Tool for Research, Teaching and Disclosure of a Common Legacy

The "Principles, Definitions and Model Rules of European Private Law" were initially conceived to be a *draft* of a future CFR, but are also recognised as having value *per se*.[287]

The text of the DCFR is aimed at providing European Private Law with a structure[288] (*Systembildungsfunktion*) which could play a particularly important role if the DCFR were to become ultimately a political CFR.[289] It would also hold significance for university teaching throughout Europe.[290]

Indeed, with a code-like division into books, each one corresponding to one source of legal obligations, the DCFR is considered by many to have what it takes to become the "perfect teaching tool".[291] It is already taught in comparative law

---

[280] Hesselink (2009), p. 925.

[281] Any influence which would arise for the national legal systems would be "through *imperio rationis* and not through *ratione imperii*" (von Bar 2011a, pp. 438–439). See also Hesselink (2001), p. 59. It is also said that the DCFR would be *verbindend* (uniting) instead of *verdindlich* (mandatory) (Röthel 2009, p. 291).

[282] Hesselink (2009), p. 947. For details on these principles, see De Búrca (2001).

[283] Hesselink (2009), p. 934.

[284] von Bar (2001b), p. 137; von Bar (2007), p. 357; von Bar (2008a), p. 45; von Bar (2009a), p. 1854. See also von Bar (2012a), p. 5; Grochowski (2013), pp. 101, 103.

[285] von Bar (2002c), p. 144.

[286] von Bar et al. (2008), Intr. 4, p. 6; von Bar et al. (2009), Intr. 6–7, pp. 7–9. For further details on the scope of a future CFR see Tit. § 6 below.

[287] von Bar (2009b), p. 25.

[288] Zoll (2011b), p. 555.

[289] von Bar (2009a), p. 1856. See also von Bar (2009b), p. 27 ff.

[290] von Bar (2003a), p. 100; von Bar (2007), p. 351; Clive (2008), p. 14; von Bar (2008a), p. 2; Hondius (2011).

[291] von Bar (2011c), p. 266.

courses specialising in private law all over Europe, but university courses should ideally amend their titles to "European Private Law" instead of "Comparative Private Law", as it is often the case. Legal scholars endorse the teaching of the DCFR in every Member State and see it as promoting the development of a European legal culture which would empower the new generation of lawyers with the knowledge they need to master private law issues in a pluralistic and competitive work environment.[292]

One of the other main functions of the DCFR[293] consists of highlighting those laws which may be seen as regional manifestations of an overall *acquis commun*.[294] According to one of its most prominent drafters, even though national private systems sometimes provide different answers to the same problems, very often the actual outcomes are similar across systems.[295]

c) A Source of Inspiration: The "Toolbox Function" in the Strict Sense

aa) The DCFR as a Guideline for the Legislature

Legislatures are free to choose their sources of inspiration and are accountable only to their electorate.[296]

National law-making is traditionally influenced by the legal environment, including the *opinio juris communis*,[297] which very often is expressed in academic-based "soft law instruments".[298] In the process of looking beyond one's own borders, the DCFR is often regarded as a template for enacting binding legal provisions both at the European ("top-down approach") and national level ("bottom-up approach").[299]

As far as the European legislature is concerned, the DCFR drafters and supporters propose that the DCFR should serve as a guideline in the improvement of the internal coherence of European legislation on the protection of consumers in aspects of contract law.[300]

---

[292]Rajski (2006), p. 24. See generally Remien (2009).

[293]von Bar (2009d), p. 68.

[294]von Bar et al. (2008), Intr. 7, p. 7; von Bar (2013), pp. 8, 11; Mak (2014), p. 376. See also Hesselink (2008b), p. 29.

[295]von Bar (2002b), p. 67. See examples provided for in von Bar (2004a), p. 134. See also Comisión General de Codificación (2009), pp. 11–12.

[296]Hesselink (2008b), p. 4.

[297]Watson (2000), p. VII.

[298]Zemanek (1998), p. 860. For a critique of the "*Diskurs der Experten*", see Habermas (1992), p. 423.

[299]Schulte-Nölke (2003), p. 143; Clive (2008), p. 14; von Bar (2008a), p. 1; Hesselink (2009), p. 927; von Bar (2009a), p. 1865; Miller (2011), p. 121; von Bar (2012b), p. 8.

[300]von Bar (2007), p. 351; von Bar (2008b), p. 7; Jansen (2010), p. 19. Cf. also von Bar (2005), p. 22. In *Action Plan*, the Commission declared that "[a]n improved *acquis* should enhance the

National lawmakers, on the other hand, should endorse the DCFR as a guiding light in the process of (re)codification or revision of national patrimonial laws.

Without doubt, the PECL has had considerable influence on national legislatures in the EU. They have been considered in the process of modernisation of the Law of Obligations in several Member States[301] in Eastern Europe (in Hungary, Poland, Slovakia and the Czech Republic),[302] Western Europe (in Germany),[303] Southern Europe (in Spain)[304] and Northern Europe (in Scotland).[305] In Spain,[306] the Civil Section of the General Commission of Codification (*Comisión General de Codificación*) approved a proposal of modernisation of the Civil Code in matters of Obligations and Contracts (*Propuesta para la modernización del Derecho de obligaciones y contratos*),[307] which proposed a change to Arts. 1088 to 1314 of the Spanish Civil Code as well as to Arts. 1445 ff. (sales contract). This proposal was clearly inspired by the CISG, the UNIDROIT principles and the PECL.[308] This was also the case in the draft of Book VI of the Civil Code of Catalonia, which has been partially approved, is due to replace the Spanish legislation in this matter. This draft also clearly shows the influences of the PECL and the DCFR.

It could be argued that the DCFR might have an even greater impact than its predecessor. The manifest success of the PECL suggests a desire for a wider and more authoritative instrument.[309] The DCFR consists of a more comprehensive[310]

---

uniform application of community law as well as facilitate the smooth functioning of cross-border transactions and, thereby, the completion of the single market" (no. 57). On the contribution of the DCFR for the revision of the *acquis* see generally Wendehorst (2009).

[301] von Bar (2009a), p. 1865; von Bar et al. (2009), Intr. 8, p. 8; Jansen (2010), p. 3.

[302] See Jurčova (2008); Kisfaludi (2008); Rajski (2008).

[303] The PECL were considered during the process of reform of the German Law of Obligations (*Schuldrechtsreform*). See generally Schulte-Nölke (2001). See also Schulze and Schulte-Nölke (2001); Schulte-Nölke (2002); Schmidt-Kessel (2006); Jansen (2010), p. 3, fnn. 12 and 21. On the process of modernisation of contract law in the Member States of Central and Western Europe, see generally Vékás (2008).

[304] Jansen (2010), p. 3.

[305] The ongoing "Eighth Programme of Law Reform" (2010–2014) includes a law reform project called "Contract Law in Light of the Draft Common Frame of Reference". Professor Hector MacQueen, who integrated the Lando Commission and the Co-ordinating Committee of the SGECC, commissioned this project. According to the Scottish report, "The DCFR represents a welcome opportunity to develop Scots law in a manner that is consistent with the theoretical foundations of Scots law" (Macgregor 2008, p. 4).

[306] Retrieved 31 March 2017 from http://www.mjusticia.gob.es/cs/Satellite/Portal/1292338914438?blobheader=application%2Fpdf&blobheadername1=Content-Disposition&blobheadervalue1=attachment%3B+filename%3DPropuesta_de_Modernizacion_del_Codigo_Civil_en_materia_de_Obligaciones_y_Contratos.PDF.

[307] Ministerio de Justicia, 2009.

[308] *ibid.*, p. 11; Fenoy Picón (2013), p. 400.

[309] Cf. Jansen (2010), pp. 11–12. For details on the "toolbox function" see Clive (2010).

[310] Jansen (2001), p. 64; Grochowski (2013), p. 101. For the importance of a comprehensive document, see Schmidt-Kessel (2006), p. 26.

reformulation of European Private Law and the political context today could be said to seem more favorable to the reception of the DCFR than it was at the time of the PECL.[311]

bb) The DCFR as a Guideline for Courts

(1) The DCFR as a Legal Transplant

Also relevant, both in general and for the purposes of this book, is the influence the DCFR has on the courts,[312] both European[313] and domestic.[314] This aim is particularly relevant because, even though the prevailing view considers meeting new regulatory needs through legislation to be a necessity, it involves a lengthy procedure, as is the case for amendments to national civil codes:[315] "laws do not expire when they *should*, but when they *can*".[316]

A recent decision of the Swedish Supreme Court (*Högsta domstolen*)[317] argues that the DCFR has the potential to serve as a solution to lacunae, supplementing existing and binding European and national legal rules.[318] As such, it could serve as a "legal transplant",[319] i.e. as a non-domestic set of rules[320] brought into domestic law to redress a shortcoming. Classically, such transfer is undertaken by legislation but it has also been proposed that the judiciary (*ad hoc*)[321] and legal scholars[322] should be able to do likewise.[323]

The concept of legal transplants is based on the premise that concepts, rules, structures and institutions have a certain degree of tangibility.[324]

Legal concepts are adopted either as a matter of prestige or as a matter of efficiency.[325] With respect to the first, the greater the prestige of the imported

[311] Clive (2008), p. 1 and nos 1 and 2.

[312] *ibid.*, p. 14; von Bar (2008a), p. 100.

[313] See generally Trstenjak (2009).

[314] von Bar et al. (2009), Intr. 8, p. 8; Jansen (2010), p. 3.

[315] Grochowski (2013), p. 100.

[316] Ranchordás (2014), p. 3.

[317] NJA 2009, 672 [3 November 2009], retrieved 31 March 2017 from https://lagen.nu/dom/nja/2009s672. This decision will be mentioned below in this subsection.

[318] See generally Grochowski (2013), pp. 96–104.

[319] On the concept of "legal transplants" see the seminal study of Watson (1974).

[320] Cf. Watson (2000), p. IV; Mancuso (2009), p. 77; Grochowski (2013), pp. 98–99.

[321] From the perspective of the addressee of the rules, it can be said that the court gives "*ad casum* binding power" to certain rules (Grochowski 2013, p. 100).

[322] Mancuso (2009), p. 76.

[323] Grochowski (2013), p. 99.

[324] Watson (2000), p. I.

[325] It is argued that legal transplants are successful whenever they solve a legal problem (Mancuso 2009, p. 82).

rule, the more authority it is likely to hold.[326] As regards the second, legal transplants are deemed to have the advantage of being "cheaper and quicker" than the design of new legislation,[327] and of being the "most fruitful source of legal change".[328]

Despite previous discussions, there is a section of legal scholarship which questions the admissibility of legal transplants.[329]

Critics invoke the lack of constitutional legitimacy of legal transplants.[330] Indeed, it is generally held that, contrary to the legislature, courts are not free to select their sources of law and methods. In countries like Portugal, the admissible sources of law are expressly set out in Civil Code and the Constitution,[331] which might hinder the application of other legal solutions.[332]

As has been seen previously, the DCFR has an apolitical nature, and thus cannot be considered valid (hard) law in the sense of formal law.[333] Nevertheless, since the DCFR has begun to be used as a solution for lacunae, the discussion of whether or not it is a source of law has intensified.[334]

(2) An Assisting Tool in Legal Interpretation

In addition to filling lacunae, the DCFR is tasked with assisting in the interpretation of existing domestic rules.

The use of the DCFR as an interpretative tool corresponds to the first stage suggested for the gradual evolution of the DCFR into "a comprehensive binding text".[335] In this first stage, "measures towards promoting a non-binding text in the form of a restatement of European patrimonial law" should be taken, namely "measures recommending to superior national courts and to the European courts that they have regard to the Restatement where there is doubt as to the principles of national law or as to their correct application in matters falling within the scope of the Restatement".[336]

---

[326] *ibid.*, pp. 77–78. On the importance of authority, see Watson (1996), pp. 345 ff.

[327] Mancuso (2009), p. 77.

[328] Watson (1996), p. 335.

[329] See, *e.g.*, Legrand (1997b), pp. 111–124.

[330] Criticism also stems from the belief that the diversity of contexts of each legal system would cripple the integration of foreign rules and concepts (Kahn-Freund 1974, p. 27; Legrand 1997b, pp. 111–124, in particular p. 116). According to an intermediary position, legal transplants should be adapted to local reality (Mancuso 2009, p. 77).

[331] Cf. Grochowski (2013), p. 99. See also Kischel (2003), pp. 39–62.

[332] Meyer (2007), p. 122; Hesselink (2008b), p. 4; von Bar (2009a), p. 1854.

[333] Jansen (2010), p. 149.

[334] For a critical account see Leible (2009), p. 233; Giliker (2013), p. 41. See, generally, Hesselink (2009), pp. 919–971. In favour of the use of the DCFR as a *Rechtsgewinnungsquelle* (in the sense used by Canaris 1969, pp. 16 ff. *passim*), see Leible (2009), p. 233. See also Vogenauer (2009), p. 165.

[335] See von Bar et al. (2002), p. 236 and Tit. § 3, Subtit. II, Sec. 1 above.

[336] von Bar et al. (2002), p. 236.

Leible considers the DCFR to have the potential to play an important role in the interpretation of national law, both in the form of binding and non-binding law.[337] This is also in line with case law from the ECJ,[338] in particular the *Antonissen* case,[339] but it is only possible where the result reached through appeal to the DCFR is the same as that which would be reached if traditional interpretation methods were used.[340] This opinion is particularly important for the conclusions that will be reached later in this book.[341]

Interpreting domestic rules based on the DCFR can also enhance the internal coherence of such rules, providing them with "validity and authenticity",[342] as well as their compliance with foreign sources of law. Interpretation can also lead to a non-legislative harmonisation process,[343] which is one of the declared goals of the DCFR, i.e. to contribute to "a harmonious and informal Europeanisation of private law".[344] Ultimately, the interpretation of national laws in the light of the DCFR can lead to the development of EU Law as a whole and to the promotion of the rights and obligations of citizens.[345]

(3) Current Impact

Supreme Courts have progressively accepted the PECL and, more recently, the DCFR, as sources of inspiration.[346]

The PECL have often been referenced in the jurisprudence of the ECJ[347] and several European Supreme Courts. They have been mentioned in judicial decisions

---

[337] Leible (2009), p. 228.

[338] For examples in the case law of the ECJ, see Müller and Christensen (2007), p. 407 ff.

[339] Case C-292/89, *The Queen v Immigration Appeal Tribunal, ex parte Gustaff Desiderius Antonissen*. Reference for a preliminary ruling: High Court of Justice, Queen's Bench, UK, ECR 1991 I, p. 745, retrieved 31 March 2017 from http://eur-lex.europa.eu/legal-content/EN/TXT/?uri=CELEX:61989CJ0292.

[340] Anweiler (1997), p. 198; Müller and Christensen (2007), p. 415; Leible (2009), p. 229. For this reason also, the fact that the DCFR includes fundamental principles would be of crucial importance (Leible 2009, p. 230).

[341] Leible (2009), p. 229.

[342] Kalouta (2015), p. 715.

[343] Grochowski (2013), p. 101 ff. See also Schulze (1997), p. 192 *passim*; von Bar et al. (2009), Intr. 8–10, p. 7 ff.; von Bar (2012b), p. 7.

[344] von Bar et al. (2008), p. 7 ff.

[345] Senden (2004), pp. 394–395.

[346] von Bar (2011c), p. 266.

[347] Several Advocates General have cited the PECL in their Opinions. See Opinion of Advocate General Trstenjak, delivered 15 November 2007, Case C-404/06 *Quelle AG v Bundesverband der Verbraucherzentralen und Verbraucherverbände* [2008] ECR I-02685, retrieved 31 March 2017 from http://eur-lex.europa.eu/legal-content/EN/TXT/HTML/?uri=CELEX:62006CC0404&from=EN, no. 44, fn. 28; Opinion of Advocate General Poiares Maduro, delivered 21 November 2007, Case C-412/06 *Annelore Hamilton v Volksbank Filder eG* [2008] ECR I-02383, retrieved 31 March 2017 from http://curia.europa.eu/juris/celex.jsf?celex=62006CC0412&lang1=de&

as principles enhancing cross-border commercial relationships, which provide for coherent and sensible solutions. They have also been seen to provide general rules with the status of *de lege ferenda*, still not expressly recognised within the Civil Code.[348]

The UK House of Lords was the first European national court to cite the PECL.[349] In Spain, the PECL have also had a remarkable impact, being referred to in more than 20 decisions of the *Tribunal Supremo*.[350]

The acceptance of the DCFR has followed the example of the PECL. Indeed, this set of model rules, principles and definitions has been cited on a regular basis by the ECJ in several Opinions of the Advocates General,[351] and in cases which go beyond Contract Law.[352]

To date[353] there have been twelve decisions[354] by the *Tribunal Supremo* referring to the DCFR. From 2009 to 2012, most were led by the Supreme Court Judge Encarnación Roca Trias, who was a member of the Co-ordinating Group of the Study Group on a European Civil Code. Between 2012 and 2016 there has been a

---

lang2=NL&type=TXT&ancre=, no. 68, fn. 30. For details on the references to the PECL in the jurisprudence of the ECJ see Trstenjak (2009).

[348] Vendrell Cervantes (2008), pp. 546 and 548. It is emphasised, however, that the lack of a higher court at the European level to guarantee the uniform interpretation of the PECL could lead to a *pro domo* interpretation of the PECL, which could differ from the original meaning of the text or from the doctrine of other European national courts (*ibid.*).

[349] *Director General of Fair Trading v First National Bank* [2001] UKHL 52, no. 36 and 45. For a recent reference, see the opinion by Lord Malcolm (*Phil Wills v Strategic Procurement* (UK) Ltd [2013] CSOH p. 26).

[350] See, generally, Roca Trías and Fernández Gregoraci (2009), pp. 45–59. See also Vendrell Cervantes (2008).

[351] Opinion of Advocate General Trstenjak, delivered 6 March 2007, Case C-1/06 *Bonn Fleisch Ex- und Import GmbH v Hauptzollamt Hamburg-Jonas* [2007] ECR I-05609, retrieved 30 August 2015 from http://old.eur-lex.europa.eu/LexUriServ/LexUriServ.do?uri=CELEX:62006CC0001:EN:HTML, no. 68, fn. 30; Opinion of Advocate General Trstenjak, delivered 15 November 2007, Case C-404/06, no. 44, fn. 28; Opinion of Advocate General Poiares Maduro, delivered 21 November 2007, Case C-412/06, nos. 23–24, fn. 9, all these concerning references for a preliminary ruling arising in German courts.

[352] See Opinion of Advocate General Mengozzi, delivered 11 January 2007, Case C-282/05 Holcim (Deutschland) AG v Commission of the European Communities (*Holcim v Commission*) [2007] ECR I-02941, retrieved 31 March 2017 from http://curia.europa.eu/juris/showPdf.jsf;jsessionid=9ea7d2dc30d6983f0df0b42d428482a3f72be2e9a0cb.e34KaxiLc3qMb40Rch0SaxuObhb0?text=&docid=64749&pageIndex=0&doclang=EN&mode=lst&dir=&occ=first&part=1&cid=242055, no. 115, fn. 58.

[353] March 2017.

[354] STS 25 May 2009 366/2009 (E. Roca Trias); STS 20 January 2010 870/2009 (E. Roca Trias); STS 13 May 2010 261/2010 (E. Roca Trias); STS 22 June 2010 380/2010 (E. Roca Trias); STS 8 October 2010 597/2010 (E. Roca Trias); STS 3 December 2010 769/2010 (E. Roca Trias); STS 6 May 2011 306/2011 (E. Roca Trias); STS 12 December 2011 872/2011 (E. Roca Trias); STS 29 February 2012 99/2012 (E. Roca Trias); STS 1 March 2012 103/2012 (E. Roca Trias); STS 15 June 2015 333/2015 (Jesus Souto Prieto); STS 12 February 2016 59/2016 (F. J. Orduña Moreno).

significant reduction in that trend,[355] however, since 2016, the DCFR has been cited again,[356] most likely fostered by the recent publication of its Spanish translation.[357] In most decisions, the *Tribunal Supremo* refers to rules in the DCFR which underline its own internal regulations. However, in at least one of these cases, the Supreme Court judge applied a rule in the DCFR which was contrary to the respective rule in the Spanish Civil Code.[358]

Equally impressive is the citation of the DCFR by the Spanish courts of appeal.[359] To date, 115 cases cite the DCFR, most of them endorsing previous decisions of the Supreme Court.

This refutes the argument that harmonised rules would have "destructive effects on judge-made law" and that new judicial law would take decades, if not centuries, to consolidate.[360]

The Swedish Supreme Court has referred to the rules of the DCFR on distributorship contracts. It has applied a rule of the DCFR (IV.–2:302 (3)) to fill in a gap in its domestic regulations.[361] Since 2009, the Swedish Supreme Court is said to have cited the DCFR in eight cases, although the nature of such references has always been "informative or supportive", and the Court has never treated the DCFR as "a source of binding national law".[362]

Recently, a Swedish Supreme Court judge—and former member of the SGECC—wrote that the Supreme Court may be inspired by the DCFR's rules and principles with which it is familiar.[363] The Swedish Supreme Court judge also wrote that "parties ought to deliberate whether there are arguments to present regarding why the Supreme Court should not apply the same solution in the dispute".[364]

In Portugal, the first decision to reference the DCFR came in January 2015. It was an STJ decision and concerned contractual liability.[365]

In this case, a party to a mortgage loan failed to comply with the payment of all of the instalments. The lender (bank) sued the guarantor (who happened to be a lawyer), who blamed the financial crisis and required a change in the terms of the

[355]This trend can be justified by E. Roca Trias's move to the Spanish Constitutional Court.

[356]See, for example, STS 12 February 2016 9/2010 (F. Oruna Moreno).

[357]Vaquer Aloy et al. (2012).

[358]STS 20 January 2010 870/2009 (E. Roca Trias). This Supreme Court decision related to Art. IV. B—4:103 of the DCFR.

[359]See SAP Las Palmas Section 4 216/2011 10 June; SAP Granada Section 3 143/2011 31 March SAP Pontevedra Section 1 451/2013 4 December.

[360]Grigoleit (2015), p. 253.

[361]See NJA 2009, 672 [3 November 2009], retrieved 31 March 2017 from https://lagen.nu/dom/nja/2009s672.

[362]See Håstad (2015), p. 184.

[363]Håstad (2015), p. 184.

[364]*ibid.*

[365]STJ 27 January 2015, proc. 876/12.9TBBNV-A.L1.S1.

contract, based on Art. 437(1) CC, concerning the possibility of the amendment of contracts following a legally relevant change in the circumstances compared to those in place when the contract was undertaken. While analysing whether or not the change of circumstances was legally relevant, the STJ made its decision based on the opinion of a legal scholar, who expressly followed the reasonableness test suggested by the PECL 1:202 and, after, by the DCFR in I.–1:104.[366] With this decision, albeit through the filter of legal scholarship, Portugal followed the example of its neighbour, Spain.[367]

The role of the DCFR as a mere toolbox has not been generally embraced by legal scholarship. Some argue that a coherent set of rules cannot be both an effective toolbox and yet be hampered by a lack of competence to apply such concepts effectively.[368] Others have pointed out that the DCFR is a "reservoir of legal instruments" (*Normspeicher*), a position incompatible with being, simultaneously, a "toolbox".[369]

However, it seems safe to conclude from events in European courts that the DCFR has been widely accepted as a "reliable pattern for judicial reasoning".[370] It is argued that the toolbox function could be fully implemented if the DCFR was subject to regular updates.[371]

(4) Strategies of Legitimation

(a) Political Legitimation

The DCFR is, by its very nature, a text that is not politically legitimised.[372] Domestic courts wishing to apply the DCFR's solutions face the challenge of justifying their faith in this non-binding document, a choice they may make instead of using politically approved domestic principles, definitions or legal rules. This is even more marked in those legal systems which do not recognise the existence of a unified European Private Law, in other words, those systems which do not accept the European and national private law systems as part of a whole.[373] However, other voices defend the use of the DCFR as politically legitimised through present-day EU regulations and principles.

[366] Sousa Antunes (2014), p. 13.

[367] The last decision where the *Tribunal Supremo* referred to the DCFR was STS 103/2012 of 1 March 2012 (Civil Chamber). It referred to a sale of goods and is available through http://www.poderjudicial.es/search/doAction?action=contentpdf&databasematch=TS&reference=6308183&links=DCFR&optimize=20120316&publicinterface=true (retrieved 31 March 2017).

[368] Wendehorst (2009), pp. 324–325.

[369] Grochowski (2013), p. 103. See also Stürner (2010), p. 192, fn. 34.

[370] It remains to be seen if such influence will extend to the arbitration court system as well. See von Bar (2008a), p. 37. See, generally, Lehmann (2009).

[371] von Bar (2009a), pp. 1862–1863. For the difficulties of this task, see Jansen and Zimmermann (2010), p. 102.

[372] See Tit. § 3, Subtit. II, Sec. 1, Subsec. d).

[373] Möslein (2008). See also Hesselink (2009), pp. 919–971; Hesselink (2010), pp. 441–469.

According to Art. 4(3)TEU, Member States (and respective institutions, including the courts) "assist each other in carrying out tasks which flow from the Treaties" (*effet utile* principle). This would be done through the DCFR,[374] which would minimise the damaging effects of excessive legal diversity in the single market[375] and strengthen consumer trust in the functioning of the single market.[376]

Another source claimed to legitimise the use of the DCFR is the preamble of the TFEU. Within it, the text mentions that Member States are "resolved to ensure the economic and social progress of their States by common action to eliminate the barriers which divide Europe", and which would be achieved through legal convergence.[377] In this context, the DCFR is seen as resulting from long-term European-wide cooperation between legal systems[378] towards a common European Private Law.[379]

Finally, another argument sees the potential for the DCFR to be used in the adjudication of legal disputes because of the primacy of community *lex lata*, if not as primary law then as an additional source of precedent.[380]

These arguments pointing to legitimisation for the DCFR within domestic law are, however, widely criticised. According to such criticism, the *effet utile* doctrine and the resulting principle of consistent interpretation would apply only to a political CFR.[381]

For others, the political legitimation of the DCFR does not arise from EU Law but, rather, from the political endorsement of the institutions and, last but not least, from its substantial quality. For the supporters of this theory, courts are entitled to argue that although the DCFR has not been democratically enacted, it was extended with the support and at the request of political institutions[382] and is currently enjoying support from several Member State governments as well.

Connected to this argument is the view that the authority of the DCFR actually derives from its scientific quality.[383] Several legal scholars—although not the

[374]Odersky (1999), pp. 3–4; Grochowski (2013), p. 101. See also Mayr (2012), pp. 8–21.

[375]Moura Vicente (2008), p. 534. See also Schulte-Nölke (2003), pp. 142–145.

[376]von Bar (2007), p. 350; von Bar (2008a), p. 2; von Bar (2011c), p. 265. The Lando Commission referred to the reinforcement of consumer trust as one of the main reasons for drafting the PECL (Lando and Beale 2000, p. xxi).

[377]Odersky (1999), p. 2 ff.

[378]von Bar (2009d), p. 68. See also von Bar (2009a), p. 1858.

[379]Schulze (1997), p. 197; Röthel (2009), p. 291; Grochowski (2013), p. 100.

[380]Leible (2009), p. 233.

[381]Hesselink (2010), pp. 446–451. Within the international legal order, it should be noted that Art. 38 of the Statute of the International Court of Justice reads that "1. The Court, whose function is to decide in accordance with international law such disputes as are submitted to it, shall apply: (...) d. subject to the provisions of Article 59, judicial decisions and the teachings of the most highly qualified publicists of the various nations, as subsidiary means for the determination of rules of law".

[382]Hesselink (2010), pp. 460–461.

[383]But see Eidenmüller et al. (2008a), p. 660 and Jansen (2010), p. 161 ff.

overwhelming majority, according to the prevailing critical positions described here—have praised the comprehensiveness,[384] modernity,[385] reputation[386] and coherence[387] of the DCFR. It has provided for the "best solutions"[388] the courts can apply, through a narrow interpretation of provisions which would have priority of application under the hierarchy of norms.[389]

It is also argued that courts could justify their recourse to the DCFR by pointing to the pan-European *opinio juris communis*.[390]

(b) Legitimation Through Legal Interpretation

It has been suggested that another means of legitimising recourse to the DCFR is through traditional methods of legal interpretation.[391]

A logical interpretation could call upon the DCFR because it contains a list of definitions intended to serve as a toolbox for legislatures and courts.[392] Following the historical argument, an interpretation based on the DCFR would be particularly justified if the object under interpretation would be a future CFR.[393] Systematic interpretation could be called upon because of the purpose of the DCFR—highlighted in several Commission documents—of promoting a coherent *acquis*.[394] Finally, the teleological interpretation would be called upon when taking into consideration the indication of the ECJ, which stated that when interpreting a provision of EU Law, one must consider "the objects of the rules of which it forms part".[395]

It has also been suggested that the DCFR could be consulted in the context of a "comparative method of legal interpretation".[396] However, it is not only the validity

384 Hesselink (2009), p. 923 *passim*.

385 Grochowski (2013), p. 101.

386 *ibid*. See however Jansen (2010), p. 150, fn. 24, who claims that the major drafting work was delegated to academically burdened young scholars. Jansen (2010), p. 150, fn. 24.

387 Swann (2003), p. 5; Hesselink (2009), p. 923. But see Sefton-Green (2009), p. 50, who considers that only a political or democratic instrument can be "coherent".

388 Hesselink (2010), p. 462; Giliker (2013), p. 27. But see Dannemann (2012), p. 117.

389 Cf. Jansen (2010), p. 158.

390 von Bar (2004a), p. 127; von Bar (2009d), p. 60.

391 The following arguments are used in Hesselink (2010), p. 451 ff. regarding a "forthcoming instrument on European contract law" (*CESL*).

392 Hesselink (2010), pp. 452–453.

393 Giliker (2013), p. 43. Cf. Hesselink (2010), p. 453.

394 Hesselink (2010), p. 454. For further details on the use of systematic interpretation to incorporate the DCFR into national law see Riesenhuber (2009).

395 Joined Cases C-402/07 (*Christopher Sturgeon, Gabriel Sturgeon and Alana Sturgeon v Condor Flugdienst GmbH*) and C-432/07 (*Stefan Böck and Cornelia Lepuschitz v Air France SA*) [2009] ECR I-10923; Case C-156/98 *Federal Republic of Germany v Commission of the European Communities (Germany v Commission)* [2000] ECR I-06857, no. 50; Hesselink (2010), p. 455.

396 But see Hesselink (2010), pp. 458–459.

of the comparative method as an autonomous interpretation method that is being discussed,[397] it also raises both theoretical and practical difficulties. The variety of private law systems in Europe is claimed to be a hindrance in the use of such a method.[398]

It has been proposed, therefore, that it is necessary to go beyond comparative law[399] and embrace a brand new method of legal interpretation in compliance with the DCFR. Within such a method, European courts would be able to consider the proposed solutions in the DCFR where there were doubts about the application of a common European legal rule, or where uncertainty existed about the correct application of national law in subjects within the scope of the DCFR.[400] This method would also serve the purpose of filling those lacunae which occur wherever the national legal system fails to provide a reasonable solution to a legal problem.[401]

This would also be served as a "seismograph for the European 'mainstream'", by giving prevalence to those interpretations more in-line with European Private Law,[402] by having a common legal culture in mind.[403]

It is argued that a pro-DCFR oriented method of interpretation would give courts the responsibility and the power to actively participate in the construction of European Private Law.[404] It would promote the rights of citizens, their equality before the law[405] and legal certainty. The interpretation of law would become more precise and would benefit from the results of fruitful scientific debate.[406] In all likelihood, the quality of the interpreted legislation would itself be improved.[407]

In the following section, this alternative will be tested against one of the concepts used by the DCFR, namely, Book VI's concept of legally relevant damage ("Non-contractual liability arising out of damage caused to another").

---

[397]Vogenauer defends an inclusion of the comparative interpretation within the systematic interpretation (Vogenauer 2001, p. 43).

[398]Schulze (1997), p. 197. See also Hesselink (2010), p. 459.

[399]von Bar (2013), p. 10.

[400]von Bar (2002c), p. 144.

[401]von Bar (2003b), p. 387.

[402]von Bar (2002c), p. 139. This *Vorbildwirkung* (model example) is also referred to in Röthel, *Modellgesetz*, p. 291.

[403]Schulte-Nölke and Schulze (1999), pp. 18–19.

[404]von Bar (2004a), p. 127.

[405]*ibid.* pp. 127, 417 and 418; von Bar et al. (2002), p. 235. See also von Bar (1998a), p. 414; Calvão da Silva (2001–2002), p. 271; Violante (2011), p. 352; van Gerven (1994), p. 40.

[406]von Bar (2013), p. 10.

[407]Schulze (1997), p. 192. It is argued that this method of interpretation would be strengthened if legal commentaries on national codes contained references to the DCFR's provisions in the language of each Member State (*ibid.*, p. 197).

Part II
A Plea for the Informal Acceptance of the Concept of "Legally Relevant Damage" as a Way to Break the Stalemate Created by the Category "Pure Economic Loss"

§ 4 General Remarks on the Non-Contractual Liability Regime Arising Out of Damage Caused to Another in the Portuguese Civil Code

I. *Casum sentit dominus* v the Obligation to Repair Losses

Living implies bearing the general hazards of life, such as suffering a personal loss or a loss of one's assets.[1] This idea is supported by the general principle "let the loss lie where it falls"[2] (*casum sentit dominus, res perit domino*).[3] Every time such a principle applies and the case fulfills certain conditions, the victim may receive aid and achieve relief through social security schemes,[4] private insurance,[5] labour law regulations,[6] etc.

However, the principle *casum sentit dominus* does not apply where the loss goes beyond the general risk of life.[7] In such cases, an individual assumes responsibility for the damaging event (*responsabilidade civil*). This allocation of responsibility

---

[1]Cf. Hörster (1992), p. 70; Brandão Proença (1997), pp. 89–92; Sinde Monteiro (2005), p. 353; Carneiro da Frada and Pestana de Vasconcelos (2006), p. 152; Menezes Leitão (2013), p. 46. In the German legal scholarship, see Larenz and Canaris (1977), p. 351; Deutsch (1996a), p. 1; Esser (2000b), p. 129.

[2]Cf. *Chandler v Webster* [1904] 1 KB 493.

[3]Carneiro da Frada (1997), p. 16; Santos Silva (2009), p. 57. For a critical approach to this principle, see Spier (2000), p. 303.

[4]Hondius (2007), p. 47. It is argued that while civil liability is based on considerations of "individual justice", social security schemes are based on considerations of "collective justice" (Almeida Costa 2006a, p. 553).

[5]For details see Brandão Proença (1997), pp. 89–91. There are several compulsory civil liability insurances, among which is car civil liability insurance. For a complete list of compulsory insurances, see http://www.asf.com.pt/NR/exeres/692AD7DF-8349-400D-999C-697D9F8C485C,frameless.htm?NRMODE=Published (retrieved 31 March 2017).

[6]van Dam (2013), p. 348.

[7]Carneiro da Frada (1994), pp. 120–121.

M. Santos Silva, *The Draft Common Frame of Reference as a "Toolbox" for Domestic Courts*, DOI 10.1007/978-3-319-52923-3_4

(*imputação do dano*)[8] operates through the creation of an obligation to compensate (*obrigação de indemnização*).[9] It comprises the obligation relationship (*vínculo creditório*), which binds the person deemed to have inflicted the harm (debtor) and the victim (creditor).[10] This obligation arises directly from the law[11] (Arts. 483, 798 and 562 CC)[12] and not from the will of the parties, even where the agent causing the harm acted intentionally.[13]

The classic principle *neminem laedere* is the bedrock of civil liability,[14] and it favours the position of the person sustaining the harm over that of the person inflicting it.

Legal scholarship diverges on the aims of non-contractual liability, but it is generally held that its main purpose is the protection of legal positions against every loss and injury caused by another.[15]

The literature speaks of the "principle of full reparation" (*restitutio ad integrum*),[16] according to which reparation should never fall short of the losses sustained: "no less, but also no more",[17] in other words, returning the person who has incurred the loss to the position held prior to the loss, *indemne* (*in+damno*).[18] This principle can be deduced from Art. 562 CC,[19] in conjunction with Art. 564 (1) CC,[20] and is based on the German § 249 BGB.[21] This principle is often regarded

[8]Pessoa Jorge (1995), p. 33 ff.; Hörster (2004a), p. 326. For details on the allocation of responsibility, see Carneiro da Frada (1994), pp. 187–219.

[9]Carneiro da Frada (1997), p. 16; Menezes Cordeiro (2010b), p. 721; Menezes Leitão (2013), p. 46.

[10]Galvão Telles (1997), p. 214. See also Menezes Cordeiro (2010b), p. 721.

[11]Hörster (2004a), p. 326; Menezes Cordeiro (2010b), p. 732.

[12]Mota Pinto (2005), p. 128.

[13]Almeida Costa (2006a), pp. 518–520.

[14]Carneiro da Frada (1994), p. 127. Cf. also Spier (2000), p. 303.

[15]Cf. Santos Silva (2006), p. 831.

[16]According to one classification, the principle of full reparation stems from one of the principles regulating the obligation of compensation, i.e. the "principle of reparation or equivalence between the loss and the reparation". See Pinto Oliveira (2011), p. 590 ff. See, similarly, STJ 14 November 2014, proc. 478/05.6TBMGL.C1.S1; RP 10 April 2014, proc. 1942/12.6TJVNF.P1.

[17]von Bar (2009c), n. B7 to VI–6:101, p. 909.

[18]von Bar (2000a), p. 137; Menezes Cordeiro (2010b), pp. 721 and 726.

[19]Art. 562 ("General principle") reads: "That who is obliged to repair a loss [*dano*] must reinstate the situation which would have existed had the event that leads to reparation [*reparação*] not taken place".

[20]Art. 564(1) CC ("Calculation of compensation") reads: "The duty to compensate encompasses not only the loss [*prejuízo*] caused but also the benefits foregone by the injured person as a consequence of the injury". See also Art. 1(1) of Resolution (75) 7 of the Council of Europe, on compensation for physical injury or death, adopted by the Committee of Ministers on 14 March 1975 at the 243rd meeting of the Ministers' Deputies, retrieved 31 March 2017 from http://www.whiplashinfo.se/Europaradet/resolutioner/75_7/resolution_75_7.htm.

[21]Magnus (2001b), p. 91; Santos Júnior (2003), p. 249; Menezes Cordeiro (2010b), p. 729.

as one of the fundamentals of modern tort law,[22] yet exceptions are expressly provided for in the Portuguese Civil Code.[23]

Although reparation of the losses sustained (*Ausgleich*) is generally seen as the main aim of non-contractual liability, it serves other purposes as well. Those are, *inter alia*, satisfaction or vindication of the law's authority (*Genugtung*),[24] through punishment,[25] as well as prevention, through deterrence.[26] Despite their support in the Portuguese Civil Code,[27] these purposes are not generally accepted.[28]

II. Kinds of Obligations

1. Non-Contractual Liability v Contractual Liability

a) Main Differences

Civil liability is regulated in Book II (Title I, Chapter II, s. V) of the Portuguese Civil Code and, as mentioned before, it applies whenever a person must, by force of statute, repair damage done to another.

[22]Rogers et al. (1996), p. 2.

[23]The exceptions to the principle of full reparation are: graded compensation, in cases of negligence on the part of the person inflicting the harm (Art. 494 CC); contractual exclusion or limitation of liability (Art. 810(1) CC) and the fault of the injured person as grounds for reduction of damages or exclusion of liability (Art. 505 CC).

[24]van Dam (2013), p. 349. For details on the German legal system, see Markesinis and Unberath (2002), p. 981 ff. See also BGHZ 18, 149.

[25]On the punitive function for non-contractual liability, see Gomes (1989), pp. 105–144; Meira Lourenço (2006); Sousa Antunes (2011). See also Ribeiro de Faria (1990), pp. 426–427; Hörster (2004a), pp. 337–338; Sousa Antunes (2009); Menezes Cordeiro 2010b, p. 419 (initially, in Menezes Cordeiro (1986), p. 277. Menezes Cordeiro was against a punitive function for non-contractual liability, taking the position that where no damage was caused, no behaviours should be punished. In Germany, see Stoll (1970), pp. 3–21; Kern (1991), pp. 247–272; Müller (2000), p. 360 ff.; Jansen and Rademacher (2009); Ebert (2011).

[26]See generally Schlobach (2004). See also Steiner (1983), p. 21 ff.; Stoll (1993), p. 147 ff.; Rosengarten (1996), pp. 1935–1938; Möller (2006), p. 329 ff.; Almeida Costa 2006a, p. 590. The DCFR expressly provides for a right to prevention in VI.–1:102.

[27]Arts. 494 CC, 497(2) CC, 570 CC and 829-A CC (for the punitive aim) and Art.70 (for the preventative aim). In the legal scholarship, Antunes Varela defends the punitive function of liability based on the fact that the person inflicting the harm must always compensate the loss, irrespective of the way profit was obtained, the above-mentioned rules in the Portuguese Civil Code and the irrelevance of alternative causes (*causa virtual*) (Antunes Varela (2000), pp. 542–543).

[28]For details on the compensatory, punitive and preventative aims of non-contractual liability, see Pinto Oliveira (2011), pp. 688–692.

The dominant view in academia is that there is a dualist[29] system of civil liability in which the general rules for each kind of liability co-exist in a relationship of autonomy and complementarity.[30] Within civil liability, a distinction is traditionally made between contractual liability (*responsabilidade civil contratual*) and non-contractual liability (*responsabilidade civil extracontratual*).[31] This means that the Portuguese legislature, in line with the remaining European legal orders[32] and the DCFR,[33] provided for a dualist system of liability in the Civil Code.[34]

On the one hand, contractual liability results from the infringement of a right of credit (*direito de crédito*) or an obligation in its technical sense. This means that contractual liability can result: a) from the breach of a contract (*incumprimento contratual*) or from the breach of ancillary duties of conduct (*deveres acessórios de conduta*), b) from the breach of legal acts (*negócios jurídicos*), and c) from the law.[35] On the other hand, non-contractual liability results from the breach of a general duty of abstention (*deveres gerais de abstenção*) or from conduct that,

---

[29] A minority of the legal scholarship denies the existence of these differences and endorses a singular treatment of civil liability. See Gomes da Silva (1944), p. 328; Pessoa Jorge (1995), pp. 41–42; Menezes Leitão (2013), p. 361 ff. (although he endorses a "third" modality of liability, as will be referred to in Tit. § 4, Subtit. II, Sec. 2 below). Against, Pinto Oliveira (2011), pp. 592–593.

[30] Pinto Oliveira (2011), p. 592.

[31] "*Responsabilidade civil extracontratual*" is one of the most commonly-used expressions in Portugal to refer to non-contractual liability arising out of damage caused to another. See for example, Vaz Serra (1959e), pp. 115–342; Pires de Lima and Antunes Varela (1987), n. 1 to Art. 483 CC, p. 470 *passim*; Antunes Varela (2000), pp. 518 ff. Almeida Costa 2006a, pp. 539–554 *passim*. When refering to this kind of liability, some Portuguese legal scholars opt for other expressions: "*responsabilidade aquiliana*" (Menezes Cordeiro 2010b, p. 387 *passim*), "*responsabilidade delitual*" (Trigo 2009), "*responsabilidade extranegocial*" or "*responsabilidade extraobrigacional*" (Sinde Monteiro 2005, p. 350; Almeida Costa 2006a, pp. 539–540, fn. 1). The Portuguese draftsmen apparently preferred the expression "*responsabilidade extracontratual*": it was used in Art. 45 and on the legal regime of non-contractual liability from the State and other public entities (Act 67/2007 of 31 December 2007, DR, 1st Ser., no. 251 2007, pp. 9117–9120). Within the Civil Code, the expression "*responsabilidade civil*" is used to refer to non-contractual liability in the epigraph of Sec. V, Chap. 2, Tit. I, Book II CC and Art. 799(2) CC (Almeida Costa 2006a, p. 540, fn. 1). The courts seem to prefer the expression "*responsabilidade civil extracontratual*" (STJ 20 June 1975, proc. 065043; STJ 30 July 1994, proc. 97A412; STJ 26 May 2015, proc. 1798/09.6TBCSC.L1.S1).

[32] Picker (1987), p. 1041; von Bar and Drobnig (2004), p. 44.

[33] For details on the DCFR's non-contractual liability system see Tit. § 6, Subtit. II below.

[34] See Carneiro da Frada (1994), p. 123. For a comparison between these two kinds of civil liability see generally Vaz Serra (1959e), pp. 115–342.

[35] Galvão Telles (1997); Sinde Monteiro (2005), p. 350; Almeida Costa (2006a), p. 539. As contractual liability can result from sources other than a contract, the expression "*responsabilidade negocial*" or "*responsabilidade obrigacional*" is sometimes used instead (Hörster 2004a, pp. 323 ff.; Almeida Costa 2006a, pp. 539–540, fn. 1). Vaz Serra admitted that the expression "*responsabilidade contratual*" was not accurate. However, he stated that it should be used because it was widespread (Vaz Serra 1959e, pp. 115–116, fn. 1). Antunes Varela follows the same line of thought (Antunes Varela (2000), pp. 519–520, fn. 1).

albeit lawful, causes damage to another.[36] Duties of abstention fall on every person[37] and they require abstaining from interfering in the absolute rights of another[38] (right with *erga omnes* effect),[39] otherwise the agent of the interference has a duty to repair the damage.[40]

The two kinds of liability, therefore, have different starting points. In contractual liability, the starting point is the specific contractual bond that exists between the parties and which confers obligations on both. If the debtor does not perform the obligation to which he or she agreed, he or she must compensate the creditor.[41] In non-contractual liability there is no (relevant)[42] legal bond between the parties prior to the act which gives rise to liability.[43] The starting point of the obligation to compensate is the moment at which the damage is inflicted. This gives rise to a duty to provide remedies provided that all remaining conditions of non-contractual liability are met.[44] The existence (or lack thereof, as the case may be) of a previous bond between the parties is considered one of the main differences between non-contractual and contractual liability.

There are several other structural differences between non-contractual and contractual liability,[45] which reflect different value systems and carry practical implications.[46]

One relates to the burden of proof (*Beweislast*). It is the debtor who must prove that he or she either performed his or her obligation (under Art. 342(2) CC), or had a defence (*causa de justificação*) or valid reason (*causa de excusa*) for failing to

---

[36]Almeida Costa (2006a), p. 494.

[37]Hörster (1992), p. 46; Kegel (2002), p. 119; Santos Silva (2006), p. 831; von Bar (2009c), n. III16 to VI.–1:101, p. 254. According to Heck, the absolute right is similar to "a circular stronghold, which offers defence in every direction", while the credit right (*obligatorisches Recht*) resembles "a barricade, which only defends in one direction", and does not prevent aggressions arising from other directions (Heck 2011, p. 2, nos. 1, 4).

[38]Antunes Varela (2000), p. 520. In the German legal scholarship, see von Bar (1994b), p. 107; Honsell (1990). With further reference on the notion of absolute rights see von Bar (2015), p. 32 ff.

[39]Almeida Costa (2006a), p. 540.

[40]Vaz Serra (1960d), p. 112.

[41]Menezes Leitão (2013), p. 256.

[42]Carneiro da Frada highlights that while there might be a contractual relationship between the victim and the person inflicting the harm, the law of non-contractual liability does not take this into account (Carneiro da Frada 1994, pp. 117 and 125 ff., with reference to the German legal scholarship). See also, highlighting the difficulties of distinguishing between claims, von Bar (1980b).

[43]von Bar (1996a), pp. 12–13. See also Galvão Telles (1997), p. 212; von Bar (1998a), pp. 2–3; Menezes Cordeiro (2010b), p. 391.

[44]Menezes Cordeiro (2010b), p. 391.

[45]See Pessoa Jorge (1995), pp. 40–41; Sinde Monteiro (2005), pp. 351–352; Almeida Costa 2006a, pp. 543–546; Menezes Cordeiro 2010b, pp. 391–394; Menezes Leitão (2013), pp. 254–256.

[46]Menezes Cordeiro (2010b), p. 393.

perform it (Art. 799(1) CC) under contractual liability.[47] The presumption of fault (*presunção de culpa*) in Art. 799(1) CC is thus also a presumption of automatic unlawfulness. Under non-contractual liability, to avoid unnecessary limitations to freedom of action,[48] the legislature decided that it is the injured person (creditor) who must prove that the conditions of non-contractual liability have been met[49] (Art. 342(1) CC).

Another difference between the two kinds of liability in the Portuguese legal system is the fact that contract law protects pure economic interests as a rule, whereas non-contractual liability only does so (as will be seen below in detail)[50] when particular conditions are met.[51]

The Portuguese legislature followed the direction provided by the Seabra's Code in regulating the two civil liability regimes in different places in Book II of the Civil Code.[52] Arts. 483–510 CC, within Chapter II ("Sources of obligations"), provide for non-contractual liability, whereas Arts. 798–800, within Chapter VII ("Performance and non-performance of obligations") provide for contractual liability.

Each of these kinds of legal responsibility has its own set of rules and his own conditions.[53] Similar to the BGB (§§ 249 ff.),[54] but in contrast to the DCFR,[55] the Portuguese legislature gave a singular treatment to the obligation of compensation (Arts. 562 to 572 CC).[56] The purpose of this systematic innovation might have been to reunite, in a single legal institution, the principles concerning the effects of civil liability common to all of its categories.[57]

---

[47]Brüggemeier (1982), p. 418.

[48]Larenz and Canaris (1977), pp. 350–351.

[49]Menezes Cordeiro (2010b), p. 392. In the case law, see STJ 12 November 2013, proc. 874/08.7TCSNT.L1.S1. See also Diederichsen (1965).

[50]See Tit. § 5, Subtit. III below.

[51]Picker (1987), pp. 1041–1042. See also Brüggemeier (1982), p. 418; von Bar and Drobnig (2004), p. 43.

[52]Pires de Lima and Antunes Varela (1981), n. 1 to Art. 483 CC, p. 470.

[53]Almeida Costa (2006a), p. 758.

[54]Röckrath (2001), p. 1197; Kötz and Wagner (2013), p. 265.

[55]The DCFR did not opt for a single regime on remedies for both contractual and non-contractual liability. Such an approach appeared too "Germanic" for some of the members of the SGECC, while others felt that providing for a single regime on remedies would have overburdened Book III with additional provisions (von Bar 2011b, p. 394). Instead of providing for a special set of rules on reparation for non-contractual liability arising out of damage caused to another, the drafters opted to focus on the needs of this regime (von Bar 2001a, p. 530). See, critically, Markesinis and Unberath (2002), p. 263.

[56]Vaz Serra (1960a), p. 5; Pessoa Jorge (1995), p. 41; Antunes Varela (2000), p. 521; Sinde Monteiro and Veloso (2001), p. 178. As Almeida Costa points out, this consists of an important innovation of systematic order introduced in Portuguese law (Almeida Costa 2006a, p. 757).

[57]Sinde Monteiro (1983), p. 351, fn. 7; Sinde Monteiro (2005), p. 351. Critically, see Galvão Telles (1997), p. 217 ff. For the characteristics of the obligation of compensation which justify its autonomousness in the continental literature, see Menezes Cordeiro (2010b), pp. 721–722.

b) Concurrence of Actions in Law on Non-Contractual Liability and the Law of Contract

Whenever a given situation fulfills the conditions of both contractual and non-contractual liability, a concurrence of claims arises.[58]

The Portuguese Civil Code does not set out the system of liability to take precedence in such cases.[59] The legal scholarship is, therefore, divided between a "system of cumulating remedies" and a "system of non-accumulating remedies".

As regards the system of non-accumulating remedies, this implies the absorption of non-contractual liability by contractual liability (*princípio da consunção*[60] or *princípio da subsunção*).[61] The application of the contractual liability regime is justified by the principle of private autonomy of the parties. Its critics, however consider it to lead to a "hypertrophy of contractual liability".[62]

With respect to the system of accumulating remedies, three understandings have been endorsed. One is the "system of the hybrid solution", supported by Vaz Serra in the *travaux préparatoires* of the Portuguese Civil Code[63] and by some contemporary scholars,[64] according to which the injured person may select rules from each of the liability regimes. Another system holds that the injured person has two claims, one under contractual liability and another under non-contractual liability. Finally, there is a third understanding related to the situation in which the injured person is given the option to select the legal regime that shall apply (*teoria da opção*).[65] This last understanding was adopted by the DCFR[66] and is deemed to correspond to the practical outcome in the European legal systems, even where they are based on different theories, such as the theory on non-accumulating remedies.[67]

---

[58]For this topic, see generally Vaz Serra 1959e, p. 208 ff.; Schlechtriem (1972). See also Deutsch (1972), p. 26 ff.; Viney and Ghestin (1982), p. 403 ff. and no. 216; Sacco (1984); Monateri (1989).

[59]Antunes Varela (2000), p. 637.

[60]See Almeida Costa (2006a), pp. 548–553.

[61]RL 27 September 2012, proc. 512/10.8TCFUN.L1-2.

[62]Romano Martinez (2001), p. 242.

[63]Vaz Serra (1959e), p. 230 ff.

[64]Alarcão (1983), pp. 209, pp. 212–214.

[65]Pinto Monteiro (1999), p. 713 ff.; Antunes Varela (2000), p. 637; Pinto Monteiro (2003), p. 425 ff.

[66]von Bar (2009c), Intr. to Chap. 1, D30, p. 240.

[67]von Bar (2004a), p. 134.

2. A Third Kind of Liability?

A recent trend acknowledged in the Portuguese scholarship is that, in addition to contractual and non-contractual liability, a *tertium genus* of liability is identified.[68] This references a theory from German legal scholarship,[69] according to which this kind of liability comprises the violation of specific duties[70] not covered by the other liability regimes.[71]

In the German example, some have argued that reference to the "area 'between' contract and delict"[72] has lost its meaning since the 2001/2002 reform of the BGB[73] (with the addition of § 311(2)).[74] In Portugal, however, the admissibility and convenience of the "*terceira via de responsabilidade*" remains current.

Some academics are sceptical about the viability and relevance of this regime, as the regulation of both modalities of civil liability in the Portuguese Civil Code would be sufficiently broad and flexible to cover every possible constellation of liability.[75]

Other legal scholars endorse this "third way"[76] and include it in the list of legal concepts, such as pre-contractual liability (*culpa in contrahendo*), post-contractual

---

[68]On a third kind of liability, see generally Carneiro da Frada (1997), p. 85 ff. See also Sinde Monteiro (1989), p. 508 ff. *passim*; Carneiro da Frada (1994), pp. 24 ff. *passim*; Sinde Monteiro (2005), p. 350 ff.; Carneiro da Frada (2007b), p. 99 ff. *passim*; Menezes Leitão (2013), pp. 318–320.

[69]As in the case of (Canaris 1983b, pp. 33–34 and 84 ff.), who speaks of "*Haftung aus einer 'Sonderverbindung'*" ("liability arising out of a special relationship") and of "*dritte Spur*" ("a third way"), (Picker 1983, p. 385 ff.).

[70]Menezes Leitão (2013), p. 318. These duties would be particularly related to good faith and fair dealing (Carneiro da Frada and Pestana de Vasconcelos 2006, p. 158).

[71]Picker (1983), p. 437 ff.; Picker (1987), p. 1041 ff.

[72]Picker (1983), p. 386.

[73]Menezes Cordeiro (2010b), pp. 390–391, 402; Münch-Komm-Krüger 2003, § 311, nos. 35 ff. For details on the reform of the Law of Obligations see von Bar (1991); Schulze and Schulte-Nölke (2001); Schulte-Nölke (2002); von Bar 2003c; Schmidt-Kessel (2006).

[74]§ 311 BGB sec. 311 (Obligations created by legal transaction and obligations similar to legal transactions). "(1) In order to create an obligation by legal transaction and to alter the contents of an obligation, a contract between the parties is necessary, unless otherwise provided by statute. (2) An obligation with duties under Section 241 (2) also comes into existence by: 1. the commencement of contract negotiations; 2. the initiation of a contract where one party, with regard to a potential contractual relationship, gives the other party the possibility of affecting his rights, legal interests and other interests, or entrusts these to him; or 3. similar business contacts." Translation provided by the German Federal Ministry of Justice and Consumer Protection in cooperation with juris GmbH, available through http://www.gesetze-im-internet.de/englisch_bgb/german_civil_code.pdf (retrieved March, 31, 2017).

[75]Galvão Telles (1997), p. 75 (associating this concept with the "*direito livre*" or *Freirechtslehre*); Almeida Costa (2006a), pp. 540–541 (recognising, however, the coherence of the concept); Menezes Cordeiro (2010b), pp. 400–403 (recognising, nevertheless, the utility of the concept within the area of the duties of care).

[76]Carneiro da Frada (1997), p. 113.

liability (*culpa post pactum finitum*) and contract with protective efficacy towards third parties (*Vertrag mit Schutzwirkung für Dritte*).[77]

III. Kinds of Non-Contractual Liability

Two distinct schools of thought can be identified in the literature: those who relate non-contractual liability to the idea of *culpa* or fault ("doctrine of subjective liability"), and those who deny such a pre-requisite and focus particularly on the social need to remedy the loss suffered by the injured person ("doctrine of objective liability"). The latter group attempts to provide a solution to situations where loss is inflicted without fault or unlawfulness.[78]

These thoughts have some bearing on the Portuguese Civil Code, which provides for three kinds of imputation of loss: imputation by unlawful behaviour, imputation by risk and imputation by sacrifice.

In imputation by unlawful behaviour (Arts. 483–498 CC), liability stems from an unlawful act or omission of the person inflicting harm. In imputation by risk (Arts. 499–508 CC), liability is grounded in the idea of distributive justice, according to which the person who benefits from a situation that causes risk to another, ought to assume the resulting negative consequences.[79] Finally, in imputation by sacrifice, liability results from the idea that it is fair to compensate a person whose property is sacrificed towards a superior legal value.[80]

Both imputation by risk and imputation by sacrifice are exceptional circumstances.[81] For the former, Art. 483(2) CC provides that strict liability (*responsabilidade pelo risco*) is only admitted in the cases expressly provided for by the law (namely, Arts. 500 to 510 CC and other special rules).[82] For the latter liability, Art. 483(1) CC refers to the condition of unlawfulness. The possible admissible situations are thus expressly provided for in individual provisions.[83]

---

[77]Menezes Leitão (2013), pp. 327–328. For details on this "third way" of liability, see Tit. § 5, Subtit. III, Sec. 3, Subsec. c) below.

[78]Antunes Varela (2000), pp. 523–524, with references in footnote.

[79]Sinde Monteiro (1983), p. 10, fn. 8. See also Vaz Serra 1958a, pp. 259–305.

[80]Hörster (2004a), p. 331; Almeida Costa (2006a), p. 657; Menezes Leitão (2013), p. 359. Those are: exercise of a right or fulfillment of a duty, self-help (*ação direta*), necessity (*estado de necessidade*), self-defence (*legítima defesa*) and consent (*consentimento do lesado*). They are expressly provided for in the Civil Code in Arts. 336, 339, 337 and 340 CC, respectively.

[81]Menezes Cordeiro (2010b), p. 719. Vaz Serra put forward a general rule for liability without a requirement for unlawfulness (Art. 490 of the project of Civil Code), but such a rule was abandoned in the first Ministerial revision by Antunes Varela. See Menezes Cordeiro (2010b), pp. 714–715 *passim*.

[82]Two examples of prominent sets of rules providing for strict liability are: DL 383/89 of 6 November 1989 (liability for damage caused by defective products) and Act 67/2007 of 31 December 2007 (non-contractual liability of the State and remaining public entities).

[83]See Antunes Varela (2000), p. 717. For details see Vaz Serra (1959b), p. 23 ff.

All three types integrate non-contractual liability. However, liability by risk and liability by sacrifice only follow the regime if certain adaptations are made.[84]

Throughout Europe, a fault-based regime more often applies,[85] which is also true in Portugal.

IV. General Principles and Requirements of Non-Contractual Liability Arising Out of Damage Caused to Another

While the principle *neminem laedere* is the rule in contractual liability due to the exclusive and isolated nature of the contractual relationship,[86] in non-contractual liability it applies only when specific conditions are fulfilled, in order to protect the freedom of contracting.[87]

In line with most European systems of non-contractual liability,[88] liability is incurred from a basic rule of law.[89] This basic norm sometimes consists of a general clause, a principle according to which anyone who causes damage to another person as a result of the non-observance of standards of conduct shall compensate the victim for his or her losses.[90]

In Portugal, the general non-contractual liability rule is contained in Art. 483 CC:

Art. 483 (General principle)	Art. 483 (Princípio geral)
1. Whoever, whether by willful misconduct or by negligence, unlawfully infringes the right of another person or any legal provision aimed at safeguarding the interest of others, is obliged to compensate the injured person for the resulting loss. *2. An obligation to compensate only exists independently of fault in the cases specified by the law.*	*1. Aquele que, com dolo ou mera culpa, violar ilicitamente o direito de outrem ou qualquer disposição legal destinada a proteger interesses alheios fica obrigado a indemnizar o lesado pelos danos resultantes da violação.* *2. Só existe obrigação de indemnizar independentemente de culpa nos casos especificados na lei.*

---

84 Menezes Cordeiro (2010b), p. 406.

85 von Bar (2009c), Intr. to Chap. 3, A2, p. 557.

86 Picker (1983), pp. 465–466.

87 Amaral Cabral (2001), p. 1030.

88 See von Bar (1999f), p. 41; von Bar (2010a), pp. 210–211.

89 von Bar (2010a), p. 210.

90 A typical general clause system is the French *Code Civil* (Arts. 1382 and 1383) and the codes which it influenced. According to these codes, intention or negligence (*faute*), damage and causation are required if liability is to be incurred. See Viney and Jourdain (2006), p. 1 ff.

This rule of liability is similar to that of Germany (§ 823(1) and (2) BGB),[91] which directly influenced the wording of this provision. Indeed, a right of action depends on the cumulative fulfillment of every requirement of liability prescribed by at least one of the core elements of non-contractual liability arising out of damage caused to another in the BGB[92] (§ 823(1) and (2) and § 826 BGB).[93] When compared to German law, however, the Portuguese provisions appear more restrictive, as they recognise only the breach of absolute rights, the breach of statutory rights and infringement of protective laws, as giving rise to liability,[94] excluding liability for "wilful damage committed in breach of good morals".[95]

The wording of Art. 483 CC results in a situation where, under the general terms of non-contractual liability, a person only has a claim for compensation against the person who caused the harm when several conditions are present *in concreto* and cumulatively.[96]

Even though there are different opinions on the conditions of liability,[97] the most influential classification is that of Antunes Varela. According to him, the conditions of non-contractual liability are: a voluntary act (*facto voluntário*), unlawfulness

[91]§ 823 BGB ("Liability in damages") reads: "1. A person who, intentionally or negligently, unlawfully injures the life, body, health, freedom, property or another right of another person is liable to make compensation to the other party for the damage arising from this. 2. The same duty is held by a person who commits an infringement of a statute that is intended to protect another person. If, according to the contents of the statute, it may also be infringed without fault, then liability to compensation only exists in the case of fault". Translation provided by the German Federal Ministry of Justice and Consumer Protection in cooperation with juris GmbH, available through http://www.gesetze-im-internet.de/englisch_bgb/german_civil_code.pdf (retrieved 31 March 2017).

[92]The classification is tripartite: *Tatbestand*, *Rechtswidrigkeit* and *Schuld* (Habersack 2013, § 823, no. 1). On the tripartite classification of the requirements of non-contractual liability in Europe, see von Bar (1999c).

[93]von Caemmerer (1968), p. 65 ff.; Canaris (1983b), pp. 30 ss.; von Bar (1999c), p. 4 ff.

[94]von Bar (1999f), p. 42. See also von Bar (2009c), Intr. to Chap. 1, B8, p. 231.

[95]von Bar (1999f), p. 42. For details on the compensation of pure economic loss in Portuguese non-contractual liability law see Tit. § 5, Subtit. III, Sec. 3, Subsec. a).

[96]Menezes Cordeiro (2010b), p. 429.

[97]Menezes Cordeiro puts forward an original classification of the requirements of non-contractual liability: loss (*dano*) and accountability (*imputação*) (Menezes Cordeiro 2010b, pp. 429–434). In this classification, loss is a central element of liability and accountability is the starting point, arising from a series of complex events foreseen by the law (Menezes Leitão 2009, pp. 256–257). The infringement of the law would result from the non-observance of duties to respect the subjective rights of others or the non-observance of other rules aimed at protecting the interests of others. It is imperative that there be a relationship between the infringed rule and the loss caused (Menezes Cordeiro 1994, pp. 342–343). Pessoa Jorge also considers unlawful behaviour to be that which breaches a duty (Menezes Leitão 2009, p. 257). He points to the unlawful act (which would comprise fact, unlawfulness and fault) and the compensable loss as the requirements of non-contractual liability (Pessoa Jorge 1995, pp. 61 ff.). Menezes Leitão (2009, p. 836) distinguishes between unlawfulness, fault and causation: the fact and damage would be mere objects of the allocation to the agent. Pereira Coelho, on the other hand, considers the fact the core of every other legal condition (Pereira Coelho 1950, p. 60).

(*ilicitude*), fault (*culpa*), loss (*dano*) and causation (*nexo de causalidade entre acto e dano*).[98] In order words, there must be an unlawful, voluntary act that is the result of a censurable conduct of the agent and which causes a loss. This position is adopted by an overwhelming majority of academics, who consider it the most comprehensive and best-conceived position, most closely aligned to the letter and the spirit of the Portuguese Civil Code concerning civil liability.[99] Of particular note is the fact that the Portuguese legislature opted to separate the conditions of fault and unlawfulness, a separation which traces its roots to von Jhering (*Schuldmoment*).[100] This distinction, contrary to the views of some commentators, spread "without being fruitful".[101]

1. Voluntary Conduct

The first condition of non-contractual liability is the voluntary conduct of the agent.[102]

Only acts by free human[103] agents can be seen as the expression of a responsible subject and may give rise to non-contractual liability.[104]

The behaviour of the agent that breaches the absolute right of another person or violates protective provisions most often consists of an *action*. Within linguistics, the word "*violar*" (to infringe) seems to refer, tacitly, to actions. However, the behaviour can also consist of an omission,[105] if there was, by force of the law or legal transaction, a duty to practice the omitted act (Art. 468 CC).[106] Art. 486 CC thus complements Art. 483(1) CC. There is an ongoing debate as to whether it is the conduct itself, or its result, that is unlawful.[107]

---

[98] Pires de Lima and Antunes Varela (1987), no. 2 to Art. 483 CC, p. 471; Antunes Varela (2000), pp. 525–527 ff.

[99] See, *e.g.*, Vaz Serra (1960d), p. 39 ff.; Alarcão (1983), p. 238; Almeida Costa (2006a), p. 557.

[100] Von Jhering (1867).

[101] von Caemmerer (1968), p. 127.

[102] Here, "voluntary" is used in the sense of "under the individual's control" and not necessarily "intentionally".

[103] Pereira Coelho (1950), p. 61, fn. 1; von Caemmerer (1968), p. 128; Menezes Cordeiro 2010b, p. 435.

[104] Vaz Serra (1960d), pp. 39–40; Antunes Varela (2000), pp. 527–529. In the German legal scholarship, see Larenz (1963), p. 170; Larenz and Canaris (1977), p. 360.

[105] Alarcão (1983), pp. 238–239; Almeida Costa (2006a), p. 558; Menezes Cordeiro (2010b), pp. 436–437.

[106] For details on Art. 486 CC see Pires de Lima and Antunes Varela (1987), nn. 1–3 to Art. 486 CC, pp. 487–488.

[107] On unlawfulness in Portugal see Tit. § 4, Subtit. IV, Sec. 5 below.

Liability for omissions was specifically regulated in the *travaux préparatoires* to the Portuguese Civil Code,[108] which admitted it extensively.[109]

The present Portuguese Civil Code does not provide for a general rule relating to omissions, but the concept is legally relevant in several instances, including Art. 491 (*culpa in vigilando*), Art. 492 (damage caused by buildings and other works) and Art. 493 (damage caused by things or animals) from the Portuguese Civil Code, as well as other provisions outside of the Civil Code.[110]

Some legal scholars endorse the extension to Portuguese law of the German case-law solution of the duties of care (*deveres de segurança no tráfego,*[111] *Verkehrs(sicherungs)pflichten*)[112] or duties to prevent danger (*deveres de prevenção de perigo*).[113] These duties would have dual utility. Firstly, they would indicate the situations in which omissions are the equivalent of actions for the purposes of liability, and they would provide for a framework of indirect damage to legally protected goods. Secondly, they would indicate that persons should not be exposed to more risks or dangers than those which are, in principle, unavoidable.[114]

---

108 Sinde Monteiro (1989), p. 313, fn. 496. Arts. 738(2), (3) and (4) state that "[he or she] who opens a source of dangers has the duty to take necessary precautionary measures, even if they are not imposed by administrative regulations"; "if, in the sphere of power of someone, a situation which produces risks takes place, risks that only that person may be able to eliminate, must be eliminated by that person"; "[he] who, not having any serious reason to abstain, does not avoid a serious loss unless for someone else, even though he or she is conscious of the danger, in a way that they will not manifestly proceed against social conscience, shall compensate" (Vaz Serra 1960b, p. 254 ff.).

109 Vaz Serra (1959c), p. 108 ff.

110 Some of the rules determining a duty to act are: Art. 491 CC (liability of persons obliged to supervise others); Art. 492 CC (losses caused by buildings or other works); Art. 493 CC (losses caused by things, animals or activities); Art.1878 CC (duties of parents towards their children); Art. 7 (situation of urgency) of the Code of Conduct for practicing doctors; and Art.135(4), b (liability for contraventions) of the Portuguese Street Code. See Almeida Costa (2006a), p. 559, fn. 2. On liability for omissions, see STJ 28 September 2010, proc. 2206/03.1TVPRT.P1.S1; STJ 4 November 2010, proc. 2762/03.4TVLSB.L1. For details on Art.486 CC, see Pires de Lima and Antunes Varela (1987), nn. 1–3 to Art. 486 CC, pp. 487–488. For details on omissions, see generally Nunes de Carvalho (1999), pp. 85–133, and in particular pp. 134–241.

111 Sinde Monteiro (1989), pp. 307–330; Carneiro da Frada (1994), pp. 163 ff.; Menezes Leitão (2009), p. 571 ff.

112 In the German legal scholarship, see Mertens (1980), pp. 397–408; von Bar (1980b), p. 6 ff. *passim*; Canaris (1983b), pp. 77–84; von Bar (1983); von Bar (1986); von Bar (1988),pp. 169–174. See also on von Bar's theses, Carneiro da Frada (2007b), p. 234 ff.; Menezes Leitão (2009), pp. 150–153 and 576 ff.

113 Antunes Varela (1981), pp. 40–41, 72–79; Menezes Cordeiro (1984b), p. 832 ff.; Miranda Barbosa (2006a), pp. 335–379; Menezes Cordeiro (2010b), pp. 571–589.

114 Carneiro da Frada (1994), p. 164. See also Antunes Varela (1981), pp. 35–41, 77–78. It is argued that the need to resort to this theory in Portuguese law is considerably less than in other countries, given that Art. 493 CC provides a solution for loss caused by things, animals and dangerous activities. See Sinde Monteiro et al. (1993), p. 15, fn. 13; Sinde Monteiro (2005), p. 361.

This doctrine of the duty of care was used to expand non-contractual liability arising out of damage caused to another to include omission, beyond the strict typical cases provided for in the BGB.[115] While it is considered "solid case-law doctrine"[116] by some, others see it as *contra legem.*[117] One opinion states that the *ad hoc* creation of duties of care should not be admitted to compensate purely economic interests.[118]

The systematic organisation of these duties within the non-contractual liability legal framework is controversial. The prevailing view in Portugal is that duties of care should be integrated in Art. 483(1) CC.[119] In Germany, duties of care have already been integrated within 823(1),[120] with a minority believing that they should be integrated within 823(2) BGB,[121] or even maintained autonomously.[122] The inclusion into 823(2) BGB is seen as opening the way for extension of the protection of these duties to pure economic loss.[123]

Some legal scholars point out that the question of whether conduct was voluntary often remains unanswered by the analysis of other liability conditions, such as *ilicitude* and fault.[124]

2. Damage

a) A Central But Non-Codified Concept

Another essential condition of non-contractual liability, the "centrepiece of all delict law",[125] is the existence of an identifiable damage having been caused to

---

[115]Honsell (2001), p. 486.

[116]Antunes Varela (1981), pp. 35–41, 77.

[117]See von Bar (1980b), p. 25. See also Larenz and Canaris (1977), p. 399 ff.; Canaris (1983b), p. 77 ff.

[118]Menezes Leitão (2009), p. 835. But cf. Canaris (1983b), p. 81 f.

[119]Carneiro da Frada (1994), p. 164 f.; Carneiro da Frada (2006), p. 72.

[120]Esser (2000a), pp. 472–474; Larenz and Canaris (1977), p. 611 ff.; Canaris (1983b), p. 77 ff.

[121]von Bar (1980b), p. 157 ff. Menezes Leitão believes that these duties should be inserted into every basic constellation of liability to avoid a situation where § 823(2) BGB transforms itself into a "French-like general clause" (Menezes Leitão (2009), p. 660).

[122]von Caemmerer (1968), p. 136; von Bar (1981), pp. 1761, 1763 and 1765 ff. This is, in some ways, the solution endorsed by Mertens (1980), p. 398 ff.

[123]van Dam (2013), p. 86.

[124]Menezes Cordeiro (2010b), p. 440 f. (in particular p. 441) and p. 439 f.

[125]von Bar (1998a), p. 6. See also Galvão Telles (1997), p. 373; Freitas Rangel (2002), p. 14; Almeida Costa (2006a), p. 557; Menezes Leitão (2013), p. 297.

someone.[126] Indeed, the mere breach of a right without resulting loss only leads to liability in exceptional circumstances.[127]

The duty to compensate arises from the *danno-conseguenza*, and not from the so-called *danno-evento* or damage *per se*.[128] A notorious exception is the case of *dano biológico*, which Portuguese case law has recognised as leading to the obligation to compensate.[129]

Damage is a term for which there is no one-size-fits-all definition.[130] This explains why there is no express statutory definition of damage at the EU level and why European codifications[131] rarely put forward a thorough legal definition from a non-contractual point of view.[132] The Portuguese Civil Code is no exception. No general notion of loss can be found, so courts use doctrinal definitions[133] that classify damage into different categories.

b) Classifications of Damage

aa) Factual and Legal Strands of the Concept of Damage

Scholarship traditionally distinguishes between the factual and legal strands of the concept of damage. For the former (*faktischer* or *natürlicher Schadensbegriff*), damage is the suppression or reduction of a favorable situation.[134] According to the

---

[126]The drafter, the legal scholarship and the courts have used several nomenclatures as a synonym of *danos*, namely, *prejuízos* and *perdas e danos*. See Pessoa Jorge (1995), p. 372. For an extensive bibliography on the concept of *dano* in the Portuguese legal scholarship, see Miranda Barbosa (2006a), p. 203, fn. 342. On the nature of the *dano* see Menezes Cordeiro (1999), pp. 527–529; Mota Pinto (2008b). On *Schaden* in the German legal scholarship, see, *e.g.*, Zeuner (1964), pp. 380–400; Lange and Schiemann (2003), pp. 26–49; Hohloch (1981), pp. 395–401; Magnus (1987); Roussos (1992), pp. 101–192; Stoll (1993), pp. 236–286; Schlechtriem (1997), pp. 232–254; von Bar (1999b); von Bar (1999e), pp. 1–57; von Bar 2011b.

[127]von Bar (1999b), p. 30.

[128]von Bar (1998a), pp9 ff.

[129]This might be due to the fact that "[w]here rights of the person are concerned, the law is more ready to find damage, because life, physical integrity (...) are generally considered more important than property rights" (von Bar 1999b, p. 33).

[130]Cf. von Bar (1999f), p. 54. On the difficulties in defining "loss" and "damage" see, in particular, von Bar (1996a), p. 7; von Bar (1999c), p. 5; von Bar (2011b), pp. 387–399.

[131]The same is true for European law, which has decided on the losses to be compensated on an *ad hoc* basis (Winiger et al. 2011, pp. 66–67 and 701). With further reference see Schmid (2010a), pp. 762–763.

[132]von Bar (1999f), p. 4. Only the Austrian Civil Code defines damage as "every detriment which is made to someone's assets, rights or person" (§ 1293 ABGB).

[133]Winiger et al. 2011, p. 35.

[134]Menezes Cordeiro (1994), p. 283; Menezes Leitão (2005a), p. 313; Menezes Cordeiro (2010b), p. 511. On the *natürliche Schadensbegriff* in the German legal scholarship, see, *e.g.*, Lange and Schiemann (2003), pp. 26–29.

latter (*normativer Schadensbegriff*), damage is every injury to goods or alien interests protected by the legal order,[135] thus arising out of an assignation of value under the law.[136]

The factual notion of damage is currently disregarded, as it is considered incapable of effectively solving the problems relating to damages under the law.[137] As for the normative notion (damage as harm leading to civil liability), some scholars suggest that it refers to the harm that only *potentially* leads to civil liability, to include cases of pure economic loss.[138] In any case, the notion of "damage" as it is present in Art. 483 CC, is a factual notion.[139]

Within the normative notion of damage, a distinction can be drawn between actual damage (*dano real, realer Schaden*) and calculable damage (*dano de cálculo, rechnerischer Schaden*).[140] The first is defined as the loss suffered by the person *in natura* in the form of destruction, physical loss or deterioration of a certain corporeal or ideal good,[141] and it relates to the principle of *restitutio ad integrum* (Art. 562 CC) or restoration of the *status quo ante*.[142] The second form of damage consists of the economic expression of actual damage.[143]

bb) Economic Loss, Non-Economic Loss and Damage *per se*

In Portuguese statutory law, legal scholarship and case law, a separation exists between economic loss (*danos patrimoniais, Vermögensschäden*) and

---

[135]Vaz Serra 1959c, pp. 5–303, especially pp. 8–9; Santos Júnior (2003), p. 239; Sinde Monteiro (2005), p. 377; Almeida Costa (2006a), p. 591.

[136]Menezes Cordeiro (1999), pp. 511–512; Menezes Cordeiro (2010b), p. 511.

[137]Larenz (1987), pp. 426–427; Stoll (1993), pp. 240–241.

[138]Menezes Cordeiro (1999), p. 292, fn. 91 and p. 512. Within the German legal scholarship, Stoll endorses a similar position, stating that, "damage in the legal sense is each detriment the legal system regards as damage to be compensated in a specific form according to tort provisions" (Stoll 1993, p. 239). See also von Bar (1999b), p. 29, no. 39. For details on the distinction between factual and normative loss in the Portuguese legal scholarship, see Menezes Cordeiro (1994), p. 253 ff. and Menezes Cordeiro 2010b, pp. 511–513. For similar in the German legal scholarship, see Zeuner (1964), p. 381 ff.; Knobbe-Keuk (1972), pp. 11–12; Deutsch (1976), pp. 419–424; Larenz (1987), pp. 426–428.

[139]Cf. Pires de Lima and Antunes Varela (1987), n. 10 to Art. 483 CC, p. 475.

[140]For an alternative terminology, see Galvão Telles (1997), pp. 375–377 and Almeida Costa (2006a), p. 595, fn. 1.

[141]Pereira Coelho (1955), p. 250; Almeida Costa (2002), p. 296 and Almeida Costa (2006a), p. 595. But see Menezes Cordeiro (1994), p. 285.

[142]von Bar (2009c), n. I9 to VI.–2:101, p. 318.

[143]Freitas Rangel (2002), p. 26; Almeida Costa (2006a), p. 595. In the German legal scholarship, see, among others, Larenz (1987), p. 429.

non-economic loss (*danos não patrimoniais,*[144] *Nichtvermögensschäden*), according to whether or not they may be subjected to economic valuation (Art. 564(1) CC).[145]

(1) Economic Loss

Economic loss is traditionally defined by Portuguese scholars as the harm incurred to assets or legally protected interests that rely on material or economic interests, with repercussions for the assets of the injured party.[146] Harm inflicted to a thing or the loss of its utility to the owner (*entgangene Nutzungsmöglichkeit*)[147] represents economic losses.

Since Roman law, economic loss has been classified[148] into two categories: economic disadvantages (*danos emergentes*)[149] and lost economic advantages (*lucros cessantes*).[150] Both are present in Art. 564(1) CC,[151] even though the law sometimes provides for the repair of only economic disadvantages.[152]

Economic disadvantages are the direct losses suffered by the injured person, which cause a reduction of the respective assets at the time of the injury.[153] Lost economic advantages, on the other hand, consist of those never having been

---

[144]These losses were traditionally called "*danos morais*" (Mota Pinto 2005, p. 129; Menezes Leitão 2013, p. 300). According to Pires de Lima and Antunes Varela, the designation of "*dano moral*" was replaced by "*dano não patrimonial*", because, sometimes, as in the case of physical pain, the loss is not only moral (Pires de Lima and Antunes Varela 1987, n. 1 to Art. 496 CC, p. 499). Some legal scholars, however, still refer to both expressions indiscriminately (see, *e.g.*, Pinto Monteiro 1992, p. 17 ff.; Pessoa Jorge 1995, pp. 373 *passim*; Ferreira Dias 2001). See von Bar (2000a), p. 164, fn. 957.

[145]Vaz Serra (1959d), p. 69; Pessoa Jorge (1995), p. 373; Menezes Cordeiro (1999), p. 515; Menezes Leitão (2013), p. 301.

[146]Almeida Costa (2006a), p. 592. See also Antunes Varela (2000), p. 598. But see Freitas Rangel (2002), pp. 24–27.

[147]For details on loss for impairment of use, see Tit. § 5, Subtit. III, Sec. 3, Subsec. a), dd), (2).

[148]Galvão Telles (1997), p. 376; Menezes Cordeiro (2010b), p. 525 and fn. 1744.

[149]Antunes Varela (2000), p. 599. Based on the Philipine Edicts (*Ordenações Filipinas*), some ancient legal scholars referred to *perdas e interesses*, where *perdas* referred to the *damnum emergens*, and *interesses* to *lucrum cessans*. This expression was considered preferable to the expression *perdas e danos*, corresponding to the French *dommages-intérêts*, which was composed of two synonyms (Coelho da Rocha (1857), § 122, p. 83 ff. *apud* Almeida Costa 2006a, pp. 596–597, fn. 2).

[150]von Bar 2009c, n. V30 to VI.–2:201, p. 376; Menezes Cordeiro (2010b), pp. 525–527. For the distinction in Germany, see Medicus (2007), pp. 95–98.

[151]For criticism to the formulation of this Article, see Pessoa Jorge (1995), p. 378 and Galvão Telles (1997), p. 377.

[152]See Arts. 899 CC (Compensation when there is neither intention nor negligence) and 909 CC (Compensation in the case of simple error).

[153]Pires de Lima and Antunes Varela (1987), n. 1 to Art. 564 CC, p. 579. Cf. also Pessoa Jorge (1995), p. 377; Almeida Costa (2006a), p. 596.

contained in the assets of the injured person, due to the injury he or she sustained,[154] i.e. the frustration of gain (*frustração de um ganho*).[155]

(2) Non-Economic Loss

Non-economic loss results from the injury to goods which do not integrate the assets of the injured person and which are of a merely spiritual nature.[156] This is the case for: loss of social reputation;[157] grievances;[158] pain and suffering (*pretium doloris*);[159] loss of "coping";[160] aesthetic damage;[161] loss of amenities of life (*dano de afirmação pessoal* or *dano à vida de relação*);[162] loss of youth;[163] impairments or loss of anatomical structures or physical functions;[164] loss of expectation of life;[165] and loss of sexual enjoyment (*dano sexual*).[166] These follow a breach of rights, *maxime* personality rights.[167] In contrast to the increasing European trend,[168] Portuguese legal scholarship and case law maintain that loss of life itself (*dano da vida*) amounts to damage capable of monetary valuation and payable to the survivors.[169]

---

[154]Pessoa Jorge (1995), p. 377; Hörster (2004a), p. 326; von Bar (2009c), n. V30 to VI.–2:201, p. 376.

[155]Galvão Telles (1997), p. 374.

[156]Pessoa Jorge (1995), p. 373; Galvão Telles (1997), p. 378; Menezes Cordeiro (2010b), p. 513.

[157]Galvão Telles (1997), p. 378. In the case law, see STJ 15 March 2012, proc. 3976/06.0TBCSC.L1.S1; RP 18 April 2007, proc.0646052.

[158]See RP 26 October 2004, proc.0423773; RL 11 November 2010, proc.1071/08.7TBSCR.L1-8.

[159]Coelho dos Santos (1994), pp. 76–84; Almeida Costa (2006a), pp. 592–593, fn. 1. In the case law, see STJ 17 June 2004, proc. 04B1844; RP 20 April 2010, proc. 5943/06.5TBVFR.P1.

[160]STJ 9 February 2012, proc. 1002/07.1TBSTS.P1.S1; RP 18 February 2014, proc. 82/11.0TBGDM.P1.

[161]STJ 19 February 2015, proc.99/12.7TCGMR.G1.S1; RL 21 March 2012, proc.4129/06.3TBSXL.L2-2. See also Coelho dos Santos (1994), p. 83; Dias (2002), pp. 763–773.

[162]STJ 5 July 2012, proc.1451/07.5TBGRD.C1.S1; RP 20 April 2010, proc. 5943/06.5TBVFR.P1. See also Coelho dos Santos (1994), p. 83; Dias (2002), pp. 774–778; Almeida Costa (2006a), pp. 592–593, fn. 1.

[163]STJ 7 July 2009, proc. 704/09.9TBNF.S1; STJ 18 December 2013, proc. 3186/08.2TBVCT.G1.S1.

[164]Almeida Costa (2006a), pp. 592–593, fn. 1.

[165]*ibid.*

[166]STJ 15 March 2012 proc.870/07.1GTABF.E1.S1; RL 18 September 2014, proc. 3765/03.4PCAD.L1–2; Braga (2005), pp. 97–104. See also Magalhães and Pinto da Costa (2007), pp. 444–445.

[167]Vaz Serra (1959d), pp. 69–111; Mota Pinto (2005), p. 129.

[168]von Bar (2009c), n. I2 toVI.–2:202, pp. 394–395; von Bar (2011b), p. 394, no. 19.

[169]von Bar (2009c), n. I3 to VI.–2:202, p. 395. See, generally, Leite de Campos (1987), pp. 5–20. See also Antunes Varela (2000), pp. 608–617 and Menezes Cordeiro (2010b), pp. 516–525. In the case law, see STJ 5 February 2009; STJ 24 November 2009; STJ 22 June 2010.

Reparation of non-economic loss (*compensação*), which is constructed based on the *aequitas,*[170] has become increasingly significant in recent decades. In Portugal, under Art. 496 CC, only the most serious[171] non-economic loss is compensated.[172] This follows the logic that more than a protected interest is required to lead to reparation of these losses.[173] Art. 496 CC was recently the subject of two settling case law decisions (*acórdãos uniformizadores de jurisprudência*).[174] One[175] responded to the appeal made in the protocol for revision of the Portuguese Civil Code, as described earlier.[176]

The settling case law decision 6/2014 of 22 May 2014 was remarkable for a number of reasons. Firstly, it constitutes an excellent example of the STJ providing for an interpretation of a rule in the Portuguese Civil Code in line with European[177] and international[178] regulations, and the PECL.[179] Secondly, it opened the path to compensation of pure economic loss, including the resulting confusion arising from the distinction between "direct" and "indirect" victims. Thirdly, it openly endorsed a contemporary interpretation (*interpretação atualista*) which is itself endorsed by the rules of interpretation in the Portuguese Civil Code.

The case concerned an individual who, while exercising his professional activity as a street garbage remover, was run over by a car, sustaining serious injuries that made him dependent on the assistance of a third person. The STJ considered that the non-economic loss suffered by his wife should be repaired, even though Art. 496 (2) CC has been interpreted to mean that third persons can only have a claim for

---

[170] Art. 494 CC applies by virtue of Art. 496(3) CC.

[171] Seriousness shall be measured objectively, according to criteria applied by the courts.

[172] For a comparative overview, see von Bar (2000a), p. 20 ff.; Rogers and Bagińska (eds) (2001); von Bar (2009c), n. F24 ff. to VI.–2:201, p. 312 ff.

[173] von Bar (2000a), p. 20.

[174] Arts 732.°-A and 732.°-B CCP, added to the CCP in 1995, provided for the expanded review trial (*julgamento ampliado da revista*) which takes place when there is a need to create uniformity in case law on a specific topic, thereby creating a settling case law decision (*acórdão uniformizador de jurisprudência*). These decisions are not compulsory for the lower courts and they may be appealed. In practice, however, they play a similar role to *assentos*, i.e. to promote uniformity within case law. For details see the description of "*acórdão uniformizador de jurisprudência*" and "*assento*" in Prata (2010), pp. 39 and 173 f.

[175] Settling case law decision 6/2014 of 22 May 2014.

[176] Settling case law decisions are not binding. See Abrantes Geraldes (2014), p. 26. For details on non-economic loss, see Deutsch (1976), pp. 462–482; Larenz (1987), pp. 428–429; von Bar (1999b), pp. 35–38; von Bar (1999g); von Bar (2000a), p. 20 ff. and 163–164. Art. 496 had been subject to amendment by Act 23/2010 of 30 August 2010, DR, 1st Ser., no. 168 (2010), 3764–3768, as amended by the Act 31/2012 of 14 August 2012, DR, 1st Ser., no. 157 (2012), pp. 4411–4452.

[177] Settling case law decision 6/2014 of 22 May 2014, p. 2931 ff.

[178] *ibid.*, p. 2933 ff.

[179] *ibid.*, p. 2933.

non-economic loss following the personal injury of another where such injury resulted in death.[180]

The STJ was receptive to the defendant's argument that the traditional understanding of legal scholarship (i.e. that non-economic loss of third parties should be rejected in case of non-fatal injury)[181] should be rejected as "too formal" and that "the Law should serve life and case law, which has had a leading role in the redesigning of the law of civil liability".[182]

However, the STJ clearly stated that it was moving within a sphere where several interpretations of Art. 483(1) and 496(1) CC were possible and allowed, and that it was not creating "ex novo" a law which would protect the right of the spouse of the injured person. The STJ made it clear that its decision indicated that case law should be made coherent with respect to its interpretation of the rules,[183] i.e. that: "Arts. 483(1) and 496(1) of the [Portuguese] Civil Code shall be interpreted as comprising particularly serious non-economic loss, suffered by the spouse of a surviving victim, affected in a particularly serious way".[184]

(3) Damage per se

Portugal follows the trend (visible in several other countries)[185] of recognising the existence of a third kind of damage in addition to economic and non-economic loss,[186] namely, *dano biologico.*

Dano biologico is traditionally defined as the psychosomatic loss of the injured person, leading to conspicuous and significant repercussions in the personal and professional life of the victim.[187]

---

[180] Further reasons against compensation of non-economic loss suffered by third parties in case of a non-fatal personal injury are provided for at p. 2927 of the settling case law decision 6/2014 of 22 May 2014.

[181] For a thorough list of those authors in favour of, and against, compensation of non-economic loss sustained by third parties following non-personal injuries see *ibid.*, p. 2928. The STJ itself was largely divided on this case. Nine judges voted against the understanding of the court, which eventually prevailed (*ibid.*, p. 2935 ff.). Among them, some considered the spouse of the injured person to have sustained a non-economic loss of her own (and not an "indirect" non-economic loss) and so her claim would fall under Art. 496(1) rather than under 496(2) CC).

[182] *ibid.*, p. 2928. One of the leading supporters of a contemporary-based interpretation of Art. 496 (2) CC was Abrantes Geraldes, himself Justice of the STJ (Abrantes Geraldes 2003).

[183] *ibid.*, p. 2931.

[184] *ibid.*, p. 2935.

[185] For a comparative overview on *dano biologico/dano per se* see von Bar (2009c), IV to VI.–2:201, p. 371 ff.

[186] See, however, STJ 17 December 2009, proc. 340/03.7TBPNH.C1.S1.

[187] von Bar (2009c), n. 7 to VI.–6:204, p. 989. See also STJ 20 May 2010, proc. 103/2002.L1.S1 and generally Trigo (2012). In the Italian scholarship, see Castronovo (1997), p. 61 ff.; Gozzi (2006), pp. 45–46.

In Portugal, the statutory provisions only include *dano biologico* in one set of rules, where it provides for the compensation of victims of road traffic accidents.[188] However, some have argued that its compensation can be based upon Art. 25 Const. ("right to personal integrity") and Art. 70 CC ("general protection of personality").

Courts still struggle with the legal nature of "*dano biologico*".[189] However, following the Italian lead, legal scholars[190] and courts[191] have recognised this damage as actionable *per se* (independent of its concrete framing within the normative categories of economic loss or non-economic loss (*danno-evento*).[192]

3. Causation

Another fundamental condition of non-contractual liability is causation (*nexo de causalidade*).[193]

Art. 483(1) *in fine* CC states that the agent inflicting the harm shall compensate "the losses resulting from the infringement".

In Portuguese case law, similar to damage, there are both factual and legal strands of causation.[194] The first relates to the question of whether a particular conduct led to a given loss, while the second determines if, in general and in abstract, the conduct of the person inflicting the harm was the legal cause of the

[188] Art. 8 of the State Ordinance 377/2008 of 26 May 2008, DR, 1st Ser., no. 100 (2008), pp. 4802–4803.

[189] "*Dano biológico*" has been classified as non-economic loss (STJ 8 March 1979, *BolMinJus* 285 (1979), p. 290; STJ 19 February 2015, proc. 99/12.7TCGMR.G1.S1; RP 7 April 1997, *CJ* 22 (1997-2), p. 204), based partially upon the Civil Code (Sousa Dinis 2001, p. 5). In some decisions, its economic nature is highlighted (STJ 6 May 1999, proc. 99B222; STJ 22 September 2005, proc. 05B2470; STJ 11 December 2012, proc. 269/06.7GARMR.E1.S1); in others, the assessment is made on a case-by-case basis, which decides the characterisation as economic or as non-economic loss (STJ 5 February 1987, *BolMinJus*364 (1987), p. 819; STJ 17 May 1994, *CJ (ST)*, 12 (1994-2), p. 101; STJ 14 July 2010, *CJ (ST)* 18 (2010-3), p. 81). See further Dias (2001b), p. 123.

[190] See Sinde Monteiro (1983), p. 248; Dias (2001b), p. 99; Trigo (2012).

[191] See Corte Cost. 14 July 1986, no. 184, *Foro it.*1986 I2053.

[192] Dias (2000), p. 86; von Bar 2000a, p. 24; Dias 2001a, p. 47. See STJ 27 April 2004, proc. 4A1182; STJ 21 March 2013, proc. 565/10.9TBPVL.S1; STJ 2 December 2013, proc. 1110/07.9TVLSB.L1.S1.

[193] Gomes da Silva (1944), pp. 90–106; Pereira Coelho (1950); Pereira Coelho (1955); Vaz Serra (1959c), p. 21 ff.

[194] von Bar (2009c), n. I10 to VI.–4:101, 760. See STJ 15 May 2003, proc. 03B1314; STJ 27 January 2005, proc. 04B4639.

loss[195] (*haftungsausfüllende Kausalität*).[196] The principle of personal responsibility[197] requires such a causal link to be proven for liability to apply.[198]

Causation is also referred to when determining the scope of liability (*haftungsbegründende Kausalität*).[199] Art. 563 CC reads "[t]he obligation of reparation exists only in relation to the damage that the injured person would not have suffered, if it was not for the injury". However, the prevailing view is that causation is not about determining the scope of the compensation for the damage but, rather, is concerned with determining the damage to be attributed to the agent (imputation).[200]

There are several theoretical constructs that attempt to determine causation.

The so-called naturalistic theories of causation, namely the doctrine of the *conditio sine qua non* (the "but-for" test),[201] the doctrine of the last condition, or proximate cause (*doutrina da última condição* or *doutrina da causa próxima*),[202] and the doctrine of the efficient condition (*doutrina da condição eficiente*),[203] are deemed unsatisfactory in determining causation.[204]

---

[195]Antunes Varela (2000), p. 617; Prata (2007), p. 201; Almeida Costa (2006a), p. 605.

[196]Lange and Schiemann (2003), pp. 77–78.

[197]Banakas (1999), p. 19.

[198]Pessoa Jorge (1995), p. 388; Menezes Cordeiro (1999), 531; Pires de Lima and Antunes Varela (2010), n. 1 to Art. 563 CC, p. 578.

[199]Pereira Coelho (1950), pp. 170–171; Almeida Costa (2006a), pp. 567–578, 605; von Bar (2009c), n. I10 to VI.–4:101, p. 760. On the difference between *haftungsausfüllende Kausalität* and *haftungsbegründete Kausalität*, see von Bar (1999c), p. 25 ff., in particular pp. 28–29; Rönnau [et al.] (2004), pp. 115–116; Medicus (2005), p. 289; von Bar 2009c, n. I7 to VI.–4:101, p. 758 f.; Brox and Walker (2016), pp. 519 and 522; Rosenbaum (2010).

[200]Pereira Coelho (1955), p. 87; Menezes Cordeiro (1994), p. 297. See also von Bar (1999c), p. 29. For a critical account see Pereira Coelho (1950), p. 49.

[201]The doctrine of the last condition, credited to von Buri, is also called "doctrine of equivalence of conditions" (*doutrina da equivalência das condições*)—Menezes Leitão (2013), p. 311—because of its assertion that every condition is even-handed (Pessoa Jorge 1995, p. 389). The theory considers that a loss was caused by a fact in situations where the loss would not have been produced if the fact had not occurred (Santos Júnior 2003, p. 52; Almeida Costa 2006a, p. 761; Menezes Cordeiro 2010b, pp531–532). For details on the doctrine of equivalence of conditions see Pereira Coelho (1950), p. 185 ff. and Deutsch (1976), p. 76 ff.

[202]This theory, like the doctrine of the efficient condition, arose from the need to identify the conditions under which the real and only cause of the loss would occur (Pessoa Jorge 1995, p. 391; Menezes Cordeiro 2010b, p. 532; Menezes Leitão 2013, p. 312). It states that relevance should be given to the last condition. On the description of this theory and related criticism, see Menezes Cordeiro (1994), p. 335; Pessoa Jorge (1995), pp. 391–392.

[203]Pessoa Jorge (1975–1976) (p. 162) names it *doutrina da condição mais eficaz* (doctrine of the most effective condition).

[204]For criticism of the *conditio sine qua non* doctrine, see von Bar (1999c), p. 29; von Bar (2000a), pp. 5 and 30; Almeida Costa (2006a), pp. 761–762; Menezes Leitão (2013), p. 311. For criticism of the doctrine of the last condition and the doctrine of the efficient condition, see Almeida Costa (2006a), p. 762. See also Pereira Coelho (1967), p. 162; Pessoa Jorge (1995), pp. 391–392; Menezes Cordeiro (2010b), p. 532.

The theory dominating legal practice[205] is the doctrine of adequate causation (*doutrina da causalidade adequada, Adäquanzlehre*), developed by von Kries.[206] It attempts to determine which of the possible events leading to the damage was the one *adequate* to produce it.[207] This theory can be found in several variations.[208] Art. 563 CC provides that "the obligation to compensate only exists in relation to the losses which the injured person would probably not have suffered if it was not for the injury". Most Portuguese scholars,[209] as well as case law,[210] consider this article to adopt the adequacy theory in the negative formulation of Ennecerus.[211]

Lately, the adequacy theory has come in for considerable criticism, with many scholars and sitting judges[212] preferring the doctrine of scope of the protection of the legal rule (*doutrina do fim de proteção da norma*).[213] It was uncovered by von Caemmerer, who attempted to substitute it for adequacy theory,[214] or a combination of both.[215] According to this theory, losses can only be compensated if they lie within the scope of the legal rule, or insofar as there is a connection between the conduct of the agent and the loss, if it is unlawful to cause loss in that way (*Rechtswidrigkeitszusammenhang*).[216]

---

205 Sinde Monteiro et al. (1993), p. 14; Pessoa Jorge (1995), p. 392; Almeida Costa (2006a), p. 763; Menezes Cordeiro (2010b), p. 533. See also Banakas (1999), p. 21.

206 von Kries (1886).

207 Menezes Cordeiro (1994), p. 335; Pessoa Jorge (1995), p. 393 ff.; Galvão Telles (1997), p. 404; Almeida Costa (2006a), p. 763. Within the case law, see STJ 5 May 2015, proc. 614/06.5TVLSB.L1.S1; RL 30 November 2010, proc.1198/08.5TVLSB.L1–7. In the German scholarship, see Deutsch (1976), pp. 103–104; Brox and Walker (2016), pp. 537–538; Kötz and Wagner (2013), pp. 84–85.

208 For details on the doctrine of adequate causation see Pereira Coelho (1950); Menezes Cordeiro (1994), pp. 335–336; Pessoa Jorge (1995), p. 392 ff.; Antunes Varela (2000), pp. 887 ff. In the German legal scholarship see Bernert (1969), pp. 421–442; Weitnauer (1969); Larenz (1970); Deutsch (1976), pp. 143–154; Lange (1976), pp. 198–207; Larenz (1987), p. 431 ff., especially p. 435 ff.

209 Sinde Monteiro et al. (1993), p. 14. See also Pires de Lima and Antunes Varela (1987), n. 1 Art. 563 CC, p. 578; Pessoa Jorge (1995), pp. 412–413; Almeida Costa (2006a), p. 766; Menezes Leitão (2013), p. 313. But see Menezes Cordeiro (2010b), pp. 542 and 549.

210 On the analysis of the causal link by the STJ see von Bar (2000a), p. 439 and Menezes Cordeiro (2010b), pp. 542–548.

211 See Menezes Leitão (2009), p. 716 f., with further references. See also Deutsch (1976), p. 93.

212 Brandão Proença (1997), pp. 458–461.

213 Carneiro da Frada (2006), p. 101. This theory is also called *teoria do escopo da norma violada* or *Schutzzweck der Norm* (Menezes Leitão 2013, p. 313) or *doutrina do fim da norma (Normzweck)* (Santos Júnior 2003, p. 251, fn. 849). For details on the doctrine of the scope of protection of the legal rule see Sinde Monteiro (1989), pp. 269–280.

214 von Caemmerer (1970), pp. 283–292.

215 Sinde Monteiro (1989), p. 270; Brandão Proença (1997), p. 454; Antunes Varela (2000), p. 902.

216 Santos Júnior (2003), p. 251, fn. 849, with details and further references. For a discussion of the relevance of alternative causes, see Pereira Coelho (1955), p. 40; Pessoa Jorge (1995), pp. 417–418.

4. Fault

The liability enshrined in Art. 483 CC is a liability for acts (or omissions) committed with fault (*culpa,*[217] *Verschulden*),[218] a subjective liability.[219] The model of von Jhering was thus adopted.[220]

Fault in the broad sense[221]—also called nexus of imputation (*nexo de imputação*) of the fact to the injuring party[222]—is seen as the subjective element of the unlawful act.[223] It is defined as the quality, or combination of qualities, of the act allowing the formulation of a legal-ethical judgment of disapproval, or the placing of blame on the injuring party.[224]

The conditions of fault are accountability (*imputabilidade, Zurechnungsfähigkeit*)[225] and blameworthiness, also called fault in the strict sense.[226]

As regards accountability, Art. 488(1) CC provides that "the person who was, for any reason, incapacitated of understanding or wanting at the time that the fact took place [will not be liable for the consequences of the damage] (...)". This means that, to be culpable (*imputável*), a person must have certain discernment (emotional and intellectual capacity) and a certain freedom of determination (volition, or free will).[227]

With respect to blameworthiness, it consists of the psychological nexus between the undertaken act and the will of the injuring party. Private Law distinguishes between negligence (*negligência* or *mera culpa, Fahrlässigkeit*)[228] and intention (*dolo, Vorsatz*).[229] The former consists of the breach of the duty of care,[230] while

---

[217] Or *culpabilidade* (Pessoa Jorge 1995, p. 315 ff.).

[218] For the differences between civil fault and moral fault, see Almeida Costa 2006a, p. 520.

[219] Alarcão (1983), p. 237; Sinde Monteiro et al. (1993), p. 12; Hörster (2004a), p. 328. In Germany, see Kötz and Wagner (2013), p. 54.

[220] Menezes Cordeiro (1999), p. 377.

[221] For the several uses of "*culpa*" see Menezes Cordeiro 2010b, p. 465.

[222] Antunes Varela (2000), p. 562; Almeida Costa 2006a, pp. 578–579, p. 580, fn. 2.

[223] Cf. Antunes Varela (2000), p. 566.

[224] See Antunes Varela (2000); Menezes Cordeiro (2010b), p. 459 ff.

[225] Pessoa Jorge, however, considers accountability a mere indirect requirement (Pessoa Jorge 1995, p. 319).

[226] See Almeida Costa (2006a), p. 582.

[227] Antunes Varela (2000), p. 563. See also Sinde Monteiro (2005), p. 369; Menezes Cordeiro (2010b), p. 439 (who approaches this subject in the analysis of the requirement of liability "voluntary conduct"). Cf. Pessoa Jorge (1995), p. 331. On the topic see, generally, Miranda Barbosa (2006b), pp. 485–534.

[228] See, generally, Huber (1973).

[229] von Bar (2000a), p. 265. Traditionally, the intentional unlawful acts were called *delitos* (delicts) and the negligent unlawful acts were called *quase-delitos* (almost-delicts). See Almeida Costa (2006a), pp. 198 and 554.

[230] Antunes Varela (2000), p. 573. In the German literature see Deutsch (1987), pp. 505–509; Deutsch (1995). For the classification of negligence see Menezes Leitão (2013), p. 287.

the latter corresponds to "conduct incurring damage with *Wissen und Willen,*[231] in other words, it entails foresight and acceptance of the damaging event".[232]

In principle, both intention and negligence give rise to the obligation to compensate,[233] but a distinction is sometimes reflected in the form of the compensation.[234]

According to Art. 487(2) CC, unless otherwise provided for in the law, fault should be appraised in abstract[235] and objective terms[236] (*objektiver Fahrlässigkeitsmaßstab*).[237] This means that it will be assessed through the diligence of a reasonable, average-person standard (*bonus pater familias*, the man on the *Clapham omnibus*)[238] considering the circumstances of each case (Art. 487 (2) CC),[239] in other words, taking into account the factual relationships and circumstances into which the agent is inserted.[240]

Fault, as for every other requirement of liability, must be proven by the injured party (Art. 342(1) CC), except when there is a legal presumption of fault, such as in Arts. 487, 492 and 493 CC. In these cases, the term *culpa* is said to have been used in the sense of the French *faute*, showing that the current Portuguese Civil Code, in line with its predecessor, was influenced in its drafting by "possibly the most open and liberal system of non-contractual liability in the world".[241]

Art 483(2) CC states that liability without fault exists only in those cases expressly provided for in the law. Those are the cases of strict liability (*responsabilidade pelo risco* or *responsabilidade objetiva*).[242]

---

[231] von Bar (2000a), p. 266.

[232] Galvão Telles (1997), p. 343. For the classifications of "dolo" see Antunes Varela (2000), pp. 569–572. For details on the categories of negligence and intention see Santos Júnior (2003), p. 256 and fn. 867 and 869, and Sinde Monteiro (2005), pp. 370–371.

[233] Almeida Costa (2006a), p. 554.

[234] The Portuguese drafter allows for a limitation to compensation, based on *aequitas,* whenever the liability is based on mere fault, in Art. 494 CC (STJ 30 June 1998, proc. 98A628; STJ 9 February 2011, *CJ (ST)* 9 (2001-1), p. 72), whereas when it is based on intention, it will always be calculated according to Arts. 562 ff. CC. See Pires de Lima and Antunes Varela (1987), n. 1 to Art. 494 CC, p. 497 (admiting, however, a fair limitation of damages for moral losses in cases of deceit, *ibid.*, p. 501. See also STJ 18 December 2013, proc. 3186/08.2TBVCT.G1.S1; Mota Pinto (2005), p. 130; Almeida Costa (2006a), pp. 554–555 *passim.*

[235] Sinde Monteiro and Veloso (2001), p. 14. But see von Bar (1999c), p. 22, who considers the concept of "culpa in abstracto" to be, like fault, a contradiction in terms "*etwas Persönliches und Konkretes*".

[236] Sinde Monteiro et al. (1993), p. 14.

[237] Looschelders (2014), p. 433; Kötz and Wagner (2013), p. 54.

[238] Markesinis and Unberath (2002), p. 84; von Bar (2002d), p. 100.

[239] Sinde Monteiro et al. (1993), p. 14; Hörster (2004a), p. 328.

[240] Kötz and Wagner (2013), p. 54. This means that fault is not assessed according to the usual diligence of the author of the unlawful act (Rodrigues Basto 1988, n. 2 to Art. 487 CC, p. 285). On abstract and concrete fault see Sá e Mello (1989), pp. 525–526.

[241] Banakas (1996), p. 16.

[242] Vaz Serra *Jus* 92 (1960a), pp. 133–134; Antunes Varela (2000), p. 566; Almeida Costa (2006a), p. 579. For details on strict liability see Antunes Varela (2000), p. 629 ff.; Hörster (2004a), pp. 330–332; Almeida Costa (2006a), p. 611 ff.; Menezes Cordeiro (2010b), pp. 405–406 and 591; Menezes Leitão (2013), pp. 329–359.

5. *Unlawfulness*

a) Notion and Function

The regime of non-contractual liability arising out of damage caused to another in the Portuguese Civil Code is largely based on the concept of unlawfulness (*ilicitude*), and is to be distinguished from the conduct from which it stems.[243] Liability for unlawful acts (*responsabilidade por factos ilícitos*) is the rule, as regulated in Arts. 483 to 498 CC.

Ilicitude has been defined in several different ways,[244] but it generally refers to a resistance to the legal order.[245] Its main aim is to define the scope of protection of non-contractual liability arising out of damage caused to another by reference to the legally protected interests[246] and the persons to whom a compensatory right is attributed.[247] This is despite the argument that the restriction of liability[248] is an indirect consequence of its original aim: defining which conducts shall be deemed unlawful.[249]

The demarcation of scope is made by the expression in the law, "*violar ilicitamente*" (infringing unlawfully): "*violar*" demarcates the condition positively (it relates to infringements), whereas "*ilicitamente*" demarcates it negatively, because *lawful* infringements (i.e. where there is a defence) do not create liability.[250]

As far as civil liability for unlawful acts is concerned, Portuguese law combines two general provisions of liability for unlawful acts (*Grundtatbestände*), together with various specific provisions (*Sondertatbestände*), which either embody the two basic provisions or complement them.[251]

---

[243]von Bar (1999b), p. 27. See also Almeida Costa (2006a), p. 557 and Antunes Varela (2000), pp. 526, 597–598.

[244]Rito provided for 12 different definitions of the concept (Rito 1946, p. 52).

[245]Menezes Leitão (2009), p. 648. See also von Bar (1998a), pp. 33–36; Menezes Cordeiro (2010b), p. 444; Menezes Leitão (2013), p. 260. *Ilicitude* is also defined as breach of a legal duty (Almeida Costa 2006a, pp. 561–562, fn. 1).Unlawfulness, however, differs from illegality (*ilegalidade*). In both cases, a legal rule is infringed upon, unlawfulness implies a sanction for the person inflicting the harm, while illegality implies only a disadvantage. For details, see Almeida Costa (2006a), p. 561, fn. 1.

[246]Howarth (2011), p. 845.

[247]Habersack (2013), § 823, no. 2.

[248]Howarth (2011), p. 875. The concern is considered "understandable" to the present day. See von Bar (1981), p. 1719.

[249]Gordley (2003), p. 39.

[250]Ribeiro de Faria (1990), p. 415 ff.; Menezes Leitão (2013), p. 273; Menezes Cordeiro (2010b), pp. 444, 483.

[251]Carneiro da Frada (1994), p. 136. See also Almeida Costa (2006a), p. 564; Menezes Cordeiro (2010b), p. 454.

b) Legislative Background

Unlawfulness is at the centre of non-contractual liability arising out of damage caused to another.[252] However, the formulation of Art. 483(1) CC is attributed to the "historical accident" of the preference of Portuguese legislature for the German solution. With the exception of Vaz Serra (who revealed a clear inclination for the solutions provided for in the BGB), there was little jurisprudence on the topic.[253]

The evolution of the provision had some similarities with the process in the case of the BGB.[254]

The legislature debating the Portuguese Civil Code had to decide whether to include an open value judgment in the general rule on non-contractual liability or to leave such value judgments to the courts, running the risk that unlawfulness would become an element of fault,[255] along the lines of the French model.

In the *travaux préparatoires*, Vaz Serra analysed the Italian, French, Swiss and German solutions.[256] He also analysed Art. 28 of the DL 32171 of 29 July 1942 (regulation on the liability of doctors and medical assistants), which relied heavily on the concept of "*dano injusto*".

Vaz Serra initially considered that "in spite of the merits which have been attributed to the system of the German [Civil] Code", it would be "better to provide for the formulation of a general principle of civil liability, similarly to the French, Italian, Swiss, Portuguese [the previous Civil Code of 1867] etc. codes". That was the case because "the simple statement of special unlawful acts (softened however by a rule such as the § 826 BGB)" would be too inflexible to stretch to "all situations where one could reasonably admit liability".[257]

However, Vaz Serra recognised that the possible infinite nature of the interpretation of the content of a general principle could lead to judicial discretion in determining which conducts were considered unlawful, thus creating legal uncertainty. He also observed that the German solution did not avoid judicial discretion because: (a) it raises a "number of questions"; and (b) because legal scholars have always interpreted the word "rights" in § 823(1) BGB in a very broad sense.[258]

---

[252]von Caemmerer (1960), p. 131.

[253]Menezes Cordeiro (2010b), pp. 444.

[254]For details, see Gordley (2003), pp. 38–46; Menezes Cordeiro (2010b), pp. 331–342.

[255]Sinde Monteiro (2007), p. 455 and fn. 5.

[256]As for the German Code, despite initial suggestions of a formulation close to the *Code Civil*, it was decided to opt for identifying the unlawful conducts leading to liability—namely, that which includes a violation of right, that which includes a violation of a provision and that which involves the intention of causing harm (Prot. of the *Vorkommission* (1891–1893) and Prot. of the *Kommission* (1890–1896), respectively, in Jakobs and Schubert 1983, pp. 969 and 972–973), which were to distinguish it from fault for both dogmatic and pragmatic reasons. This was in line with the doctrine of von Jhering and, before him, Savigny (von Savigny 1841, p. 5) and it was intended to restrict liability (Mugdan 1896, p. 817).

[257]Vaz Serra (1960d), p. 67.

[258]*ibid.*, p. 66.

Vaz Serra proposed that the drawbacks of a general clause could be avoided by requiring "the breach of a right of another or, at least, the violation of a legally protected interest". For the former, he concluded that liability should include the violation of subjective rights interpreted in wider terms than those in the BGB.[259] He therefore proposed a hybrid solution, combining a general clause with a typified rule.

This idea led to Art. 731 (General Rules) of the final draft (*anteprojeto final*) of the Portuguese Civil Code:

> 1. The person who, with intention or negligence, unlawfully [antijuridicamente] infringes the rights of other persons, must compensate the injured person for the loss which results from such violation.
> 2. Also the person who, with intention or negligence, unlawfully infringes a rule aimed at protecting the interests of another, must compensate the latter for the damage which resulted therein in the legal good that such rule was aimed at protecting and following a danger which it was aimed at avoiding.
> 3. It is presumed that the injury of rights or rules aimed at the protection of the interests of other persons is unlawful [antijurídica]. This presumption may be rebutted by some defences, according to the law.[260]

The article showed a systematic mirrorring of the BGB, with Arts. 731(1) and (1) resembling §§ 823(1) and (2) BGB. As for the third paragraph, it referred to the negative demarcation of unlawfulness by reference to possible defences (*causas de justificação*).[261]

The adjective "*antijuridicamente*" referred to the character that the violation must have if it was to lead to reparation. Any such adjective was supressed in the first Ministerial revision, which gave a new wording to the provision (Art. 462 (1) CC):

> The person who, with intention or negligence, infringes the right of other persons or other rules aimed at protecting the interests of individuals, must compensate the latter for the damage which resulted therein.[262]

The provision was amended to the current version in the second Ministerial revision, including once again the qualification of the conduct ("*ilicitamente*", instead of "antijuridicamente") without giving any justification for the change.[263]

---

[259] *ibid.*, p. 78.

[260] Vaz Serra (1960b), p. 598.

[261] Menezes Cordeiro (2010b), p. 444. For details on defences of lawfulness, see *ibid.*, pp. 483–505.

[262] "*Todo aquele que, com dolo ou mera culpa, viola o direito de outrem ou qualquer disposição legal destinada a proteger interesses dos particulares, fica obrigado a indemnizar o lesado pelos danos resultantes da violação cometida*" *BolMinJus* 119 (1962), p. 68.

[263] Menezes Cordeiro (2010b), p. 445.

c) Categories of Unlawfulness (*Grundtatbestände*)

The acts that trigger reparation have traditionally been grouped into two general clauses, or two categories of unlawfulness.[264] The first, described in Art. 483(1), 1st part CC, consists of the harm inflicted to a right held by others ("...*violar ilicitamente o direito de outrem*..."), the second, in Art. 483(1), 2nd part CC, concerns the infringement of legal provision(s) intended to safeguard the interests of others ("...*disposição legal destinada a proteger interesses alheios.*"). The similarity with § 823(1) and (2) BGB, respectively, is thus apparent.

By taking this two-pronged approach to unlawfulness, the legislature distanced itself from the concept of unlawfulness as contained in the Seabra's Code, which was connected only to the breach of a subjective right.

The draftsmen also rejected the criterion of relying upon the negative valuation of the unjust damage. This decision was favourably received by the legal scholarship because the DL 32171 considered unlawfulness a judgment on the loss and not the occurrence, contrary to the prevailing view of legal scholars.[265]

According to Antunes Varela, the establishment of two forms of unlawfulness in the Code both limits the independent judgment of the judge and also assists him or her in selecting those behaviours which may cause damage to others but which are required by law, or which are indifferent to, or tolerated by, the legal order.[266]

aa) "Right of Another"

(1) The Prevailing Thesis of "Absolute Rights"

Portuguese law parted from the German solution in that it did not enumerate legally protected goods.[267] This deliberate decision has two consequences. Firstly, it requires frequent reference to the provisions of the general part of the Portuguese Civil Code, which protects personality rights (Arts. 70 ff. CC).[268] Secondly, an extensive interpretation of this provision[269] is possible, which ensures more adaptability to the reality regulated by the Civil Code.

---

[264] Sinde Monteiro et al. (1993), p. 12; Carneiro da Frada 1997, p. 34; Antunes Varela (2000), pp. 533–544; Sinde Monteiro (2007), p. 454. See, however, Menezes Leitão A., who rejects a single concept composed of these two modalities of unlawfulness and defends a plural concept of unlawfulness (Menezes Leitão 2013, p. 837).

[265] See Menezes Leitão (2013), pp. 260–261. See also Alarcão (1983), pp. 415–416; Pires de Lima and Antunes Varela (1987), n. 6 to Art. 483 CC, p. 474.

[266] Antunes Varela (2000), pp. 532–533.

[267] Sinde Monteiro (1989), p. 175; Sinde Monteiro et al. (1993), p. 12; Amaral Cabral (2001), p. 1040. See also Vaz Serra (1960d), p. 43 ff.

[268] von Bar (1998a), p. 36.

[269] Amaral Cabral (2001), p. 1040. See also Canaris (1983b), pp. 35–39.

There is considerable controversy in respect of the interpretation of "right of another" (*direito de outrem*).[270] Traditional and prevailing legal opinion—which relates to the place in the Civil Code where the provision is to be found[271]—is that it refers only to *erga omnes* rights (*direitos absolutos*),[272] as is the case of property rights (Arts 1251 ff. CC).[273] That was the intention of Vaz Serra,[274] influenced by German law,[275] and it is also the prevailing opinion among legal scholars.[276]

Current opinion holds that *direito de outrem* includes personality rights (Arts. 70 ff. CC).[277] Disagreements remain, however, about whether or not "personal family rights" are included in Art. 483(1) CC.[278] Menezes Leitão upholds the inclusion of *patrimonial* family rights only, and denies the inclusion of personal family rights, as the law would provide other kinds of sanctions for their breach.[279]

From this doctrine, it follows that, in principle, relative rights do not deserve protection under non-contractual law.[280] This position is not, however, unanimous.

---

[270] Fabricius (1961), p. 274.

[271] See, with further arguments, Carneiro da Frada (1994), p. 162, fn. 333.

[272] See Alarcão (1983), p. 242; Pires de Lima and Antunes Varela (1987), n. 5 a to Art. 483 CC, p. 472; Sinde Monteiro et al. (1993), p. 12; Antunes Varela (2000), p. 533; Hörster (2004a), p. 327; Pestana de Vasconcelos (2007), p. 163; Dias Pereira (2008), p. 514.

[273] Pires de Lima and Antunes Varela (1987), n. 5 a to Art. 483 CC, p. 472; Hörster (1992), pp. 46–47; Carneiro da Frada (1997), pp. 34–35, fn. 22; Almeida Costa (2006a), p. 562. Non-contractual liability law arising out of damage caused to another reasonably protects property rights based on Art. 62 Const. (Miranda 2000, p. 467). According to this position, Portugal—unlike Germany (*e.g.* von Caemmerer 1968, p. 81 ff.)—does not discuss if mere possession amounts to protection within non-contractual liability arising out of damage caused to another (see further von Bar 2009c, n. II23 to VI.–2:206, p. 500, with case law references). For more on the ownership right in Germany see Stoll (1973).

[274] See Vaz Serra (1960d), pp. 37 ff. and 112.

[275] In Germany, the expression *sonstiges Recht* has been understood to refer to absolute rights (Deutsch 1976, p. 195; von Bar 2000a, p. 235; Schlechtriem 2003, p. 358).

[276] See von Bar (1998a), p. 34, fn. 83; von Bar (2009c), III16 to VI.–1:101, p. 254.

[277] Vaz Serra (1960d), pp. 82–112; Pires de Lima and Antunes Varela (1987), n. 5 to Art. 483, p. 472; Hörster (1992), p. 46; Sinde Monteiro et al. (1993), p. 13; Carneiro da Frada and Pestana de Vasconcelos (2006), p. 170. In the case law, see *e.g.* STJ 28 April 1977, *BolMinJus* 266 (197), p. 165; STJ 4 July 1978, *BolMinJus* 279 (1978), p. 124. Against the idea that personality rights are included within Art. 483 CC, Antunes Varela (2000), p. 532, fn. 2. But see von Lillienskiold (1975), pp. 34–35.

[278] Some legal scholars hold that personal family rights are not included in Art. 483(1) CC (Pessoa Jorge 1995, p. 284; Antunes Varela (2000), p. 533; Pereira Coelho and Oliveira 2001, p. 37), while others take no position (Prata 2007, p. 198). Cf. Pires de Lima and Antunes Varela (1987), n. 5 to Art. 483 CC, p. 472, instead including only the family rights with efficacy *erga omnes*. In Germany, this is also discussed. See Fuchs and Pauker (2012), p. 36 f.

[279] Menezes Leitão (2013), p. 262. See also Alarcão (1983), p. 417.

[280] Santos Silva (2007), p. 25. Against the so-called *efeito externo das obrigações* (external effect of obligations), see Vaz Serra, *BolMinJus* 85 (1959), p. 345 ff.; Antunes Varela (2000), p. 176, fn. 1; Almeida Costa (2002), p. 132, with several references; Almeida Costa (2006a), p. 93; Menezes Leitão (2013), p. 262. In the case law, see STJ 9 October 2014, 267/12.1TCGMR.G1. S1RL 21 February 1991, proc. 0034522.

A minority of legal scholars holds that *direito de outrem* means *direito subjetivo* (subjective right)[281] and that this would, therefore, also include credit rights under the scope of Art. 483 CC.[282] Others endorse an intermediate position, upholding the external efficacy of obligations[283] within the case of *abus de droit* (*abuso de direito*).[284] Still others view the external efficacy of obligations within a broader context: inducement of breach of a contract; *culpa in contrahendo*;[285] contracts with protective efficacy towards third parties; producer's liability; subrogatory claim (*ação subrogatória*); revocatory action (*ação pauliana*); and the duty of maintenance leading to death or personal injuries.[286]

Another important conclusion drawn from the interpretation of Art. 483 CC to include absolute rights only, is that pure economic loss is, in principle, not compensated in Portuguese law.[287]

Some legal scholars highlight the disadvantages of this approach. It is, for example, criticised for not encompassing all of the arguments used to exclude liability, as is the case in Common Law systems, which considers whether it is "just, fair and reasonable" that there would be a duty of care.[288] This position is also based on the misunderstanding that the unlawfulness results from the absolute nature of a right, when it should perhaps be the other way around, i.e. a right is absolute precisely because its violation is unlawful.[289]

---

[281] Menezes Cordeiro (1986), p. 223; Amaral Cabral (2001), p. 1042; Sinde Monteiro (2007), p. 465. Santos Júnior is apparently inclined to the same position (Santos Júnior 2003, p. 67). In case law, see STJ 25 October 1993, proc. 084098; STJ 14 December 2014, proc. 1376/08.7TBBNV.L1.S1. For Germany, see references in Schlechtriem (1998), p. 10, fn. 25.

[282] von Bar (1998a), p. 34, fn. 83. However, it is argued that "a foreign observer might find it more convincing to interpret the term *direito* in Art. 483(1) CC as including relative rights" (*ibid.*, p. 53). For the discussion see Pestana de Vasconcelos (2007), p. 168 ff.

[283] The recognition of the external effect of obligations objects to the general principle of relativity of the effects of contracts. See generally Almeida Costa (2002), pp. 130–136. See also Vaz Serra (1958b), pp. 333–368; Ferrer Correia and Lobo Xavier (1979); Pinto Oliveira (2005), pp. 251 ff.; Santos Silva (2006), p. 829, fn. 12, with case law references. Portuguese law does not expressly refer to whether or not obligations have external effects under some circumstances, although Antunes Varela considers it is implicit in Arts. 406(2) and 1306(1) CC (Antunes Varela 2000, p. 179 ff.). In Germany see von Bar (1982).

[284] Sinde Monteiro (2007), p. 465 and Menezes Leitão (2013), p. 89. This same position has been adopted by the courts. See RP 1 October 1998, proc. 9830815; RL 16 May 2006, proc. 3834/2006-7.

[285] Gomes (2005), p. 10.

[286] See Ferrer Correia and Lobo Xavier (1979), p. 8 ff.; Almeida Costa (2006a), pp. 95 ff.; Santos Silva (2006), p. 830; Abrantes Geraldes (2007b), pp. 19–22; Sinde Monteiro (2007), p. 465; Dias Pereira (2008), pp. 513–521, especially p. 515.

[287] Carneiro da Frada (1997), p. 37. For details on the exclusionary rule see Tit. § 5, Subtit. III, Sec. 2 below.

[288] Howarth (2011), p. 876.

[289] von Bar (2000a), p. 235; von Bar (2000b), p. 606.

(2) Unlawfulness of the Result and Unlawfulness of the Act

Although *ilicitude* is generally understood as hostility to the legal order, whether such opposition is towards the conduct of the agent (*Handlungsunrechtslehre*) or towards the result of such conduct (*Erfolgsunrechtslehre*),[290] is debatable.

Traditionally (including in the *travaux préparatoires* of Vaz Serra),[291] only the result of an action or omission was legally relevant.[292] However, this theory faced two problems[293] and the majority of the legal scholars now defend a compromise solution.[294] In terms of the direct violations of legal goods, the *Erfolgsunrechtslehre* prevails.[295] The unlawfulness is indicated (*indiziert*) through the infringement or violation of a provision, meaning that normal practice only analyses whether or not the remaining conditions are present and if there is a defence.[296] Indirect violations will be unlawful only when the conduct itself corresponds to the violation of a specific duty of care.[297]

bb) "Legal Provision Intended to Safeguard the Interests of Others"

The second category of unlawfulness is provided for in Art. 483(1), 2nd part CC, whose "direct ancestor" is § 823(2) BGB,[298] and it comprises the infringement of a "legal provision intended to safeguard the interests of others". According to one school of thought, Vaz Serra drew inspiration from the work of Enneccerus in

---

[290] For a critical account see von Bar (1999c), p. 8.

[291] Pinto Oliveira (2002), p. 528. For a critical account see Menezes Leitão (2009), p. 650.

[292] Menezes Cordeiro (2010b), pp. 437–438. See also Pereira Coelho (1950), p. 63 f. In Germany see Larenz (1963), pp. 192–193; von Caemmerer (1968), p. 127 ff.

[293] The conducts which caused the loss despite complying with the duties of care (Wiethölter 1961, p. 53 ff., p. 65 ff.; Menezes Leitão 2013, p. 260) and indirect loss (Larenz and Canaris 1977, p. 364).

[294] Pinto Oliveira (2002), p. 539; Menezes Cordeiro (2010b), p. 438. See also Larenz 1963, p. 193; Hager (1985), p. 137; von Bar (1988), p. 170; Habersack 2013, § 823, no. 7.

[295] von Bar (2000a), p. 235; Fuchs and Pauker (2012), p. 81. For criticism, see von Bar (2000b), pp. 607 and 235 ff., especially p. 237. von Bar (1981), p. 1760, suggests changing the epigraph of § 823 BGB to "direct infringement of a right or legally protected good (...)".

[296] BGHZ 24, 21; Fuchs and Pauker (2012), p. 81. But see von Caemmerer (1960), p. 133. For this discussion, see Menezes Leitão (2009), pp. 648–653.

[297] von Caemmerer (1968), p. 132 ff.; Sinde Monteiro (1989), p. 305; Deutsch (1996a), pp. 160–161; Fuchs and Pauker (2012), p. 81. This is called the "theory of indirect interference" (Markesinis and Unberath 2002, p. 82). For the discussion, see Münzberg (1966), p. 109 ff., p. 201 ff. According to one opinion, the *Handlungsunrechtslehre* is relevant in relation to general clauses and negligent conduct (Menezes Leitão 2009, p. 649). See, however, Carneiro da Frada (1994), pp. 136–137, fn. 273.

[298] Menezes Cordeiro (2010b), pp. 449–450, 536. For details on § 823(2) BGB, see Canaris (1983b), pp. 45–76; Coester-Waltjen (1992), pp. 209–212; Deutsch (2004), pp. 137–142. For more on the topic in the Portuguese legal scholarship see generally Menezes Leitão (2009), pp. 654–660.

introducing the reference to "interests" to Portuguese law, which had no such tradition prior to the current Civil Code.[299]

Some legal scholars call these rules "protective provisions" (*normas de proteção*)[300] because they protect, in the main, private interests. However, they do not confer subjective rights onto individuals. While the law wishes to protect these interests, it does not want the respective subjects to be able to freely dispose of them,[301] so it protects them indirectly through reference to these rules.[302]

In addition to the rules protecting private interests, this category also encompasses the provisions aimed at protection against abstract danger.[303]

"Legal provision intended to safeguard the interests of others" shall thus be understood in the broad sense.[304]

This includes any rule in the material sense (not necessary in the formal sense),[305] that was enacted by a competent legislative authority,[306] namely private and public legal provisions[307] (including criminal law[308] and disciplinary law).[309]

---

[299]Menezes Cordeiro (2010b), pp. 449–450.

[300]Alarcão (1983), p. 243; Sinde Monteiro et al. (1993), p. 12; Dias Pereira (2008), p. 514; Menezes Leitão (2013), p. 265. For such a classification, Menezes Leitão, 2013 p. 265, fn. 642 expressly relies on the notion of *Schutzgesetze* from Canaris (Canaris 1983b, p. 45).

[301]Antunes Varela (2000), p. 536, fn. 2; Menezes Leitão (2013), p. 265.

[302]Cf. Rito (1946), p. 13; Vaz Serra (1960d), p. 72. But see Menezes Leitão 2009, p. 834.

[303]Antunes Varela (2000), p. 536.

[304]Carneiro da Frada (1997), p. 41.

[305]Alarcão (1983), p. 243; Sinde Monteiro (1989), p. 246; Sinde Monteiro (2005), p. 365. See also Bistritzki (1981) ss. 2.1 and 2.2.

[306]Vaz Serra (1960d), p. 77; Pestana de Vasconcelos (2007), p. 177. There is an infringement of laws aimed at protecting the interest of others, for example, whenever a driver parks at a roundabout (Art. 49(1) *lit.* a of the Road Traffic Regulations, DL 114/94 of 3 May 1994, DR, 1st Ser., no. 102 (1994), pp. 2162–2190 as republished by Act 72/2013 of 3 September 2013, DR, 1st Ser., no. 169 (2013), pp. 5446–5499) or when the director of a solarium refrains from carrying out the annual technical evaluation of the tanning beds, or fails to make legally required information available to the users (Art. 12(1) and Art. 19 of DL 205/2005 of 28 November 2005, DR, 1st Ser., no. 228 (2005), pp. 6804–6810, respectively).

[307]Vaz Serra (1960d), pp. 72–74. But see von Bar (1981), p. 1765, where it is considered that, for the purposes of § 823(2) BGB, only civil provisions should be included.

[308]Vaz Serra (1960d), p. 77; Alarcão (1983), pp. 242–243; Sinde Monteiro (1989), p. 256. But see Menezes Cordeiro (2010b), p. 453.

[309]Antunes Varela (2000), pp. 538–539; Menezes Leitão (2009), p. 833; Menezes Leitão (2013), p. 265. An example would be behaviours that infringe competition. See Menezes Leitão (2009), p. 834; Pestana de Vasconcelos (2007), pp. 183–191. A wider concept of protective provisions (Antunes Varela 2000, p. 536, fn. 1) is present in Art. 9 ("Unlawfulness") of the regulation of non-contractual liability arising out of damage caused to another of the State and remaining public entities (Act 67/2007 of 31 December 2007, p. 9118), which reads: "Are unlawful the actions or omissions of the public officers, workers and agents which infringe rules or constitutional, legal or disciplinary principles or infringe technical rules from which result the injury of rights or legally protected interests. 2 There is also unlawfulness when the injury of rights or legally protected interests results from the abnormal functioning of the service (…).".

Some scholars speak of an *Enumerationsprinzip* as far as these provisions are concerned.[310]

Even though it is interpreted broadly, therefore, the unlawfulness category which respects protective rules in the Portuguese Civil Code is deemed narrower than its German equivalent, which includes unwritten customary law.[311] Some authors have held that this would cripple the intended placement of duties of care in this category of unlawfulness,[312] but legal scholars do not share this opinion in general, instead believing that protective provisions do not need to be statutory, and can result from "legal and scientific elaboration".[313] In the face of this debate on the scope of protective rules, some legal scholars argue that the concept must be analysed by reference to the legal system and the intention of the legislature.[314]

Before this second category of unlawfulness was identified in the Portuguese Civil Code, it was the case that if one caused damage to a person, or to his or her assets, as a result of any of the behaviours described,[315] the person sustaining the harm could be entitled to compensation, notwithstanding the fact there was no breach of any of his or her subjective rights.[316]

In contrast to what happens in relation to the first category of unlawfulness, here, compensation for pure economic loss is permitted.[317] Indeed, it became clear that the doctrine of protective provisions could take the protection against unlawful conduct "very far".[318] To limit the number of claims, the scope of this second category of unlawfulness was thus restricted.[319] The person sustaining the harm will only have a right to compensation based on this second category of unlawfulness, in cases where: (a) a protective provision exists; (b) such provision is aimed at protecting private interests worthy of such protection,[320] the infringement of which leads to a loss; (c) the agent inflicting the harm infringes such protective provision; and (d) the conduct

310 Menezes Leitão (2009), p. 839.

311 Canaris (1983b), pp. 45–46; Sinde Monteiro (1989), p. 246, fn. 222; Carneiro da Frada (2007b), 254, fn. 231.

312 Carneiro da Frada (2007b), p. 254, fn. 231; Pestana de Vasconcelos (2007), pp. 177–178, fn. 86.

313 Menezes Cordeiro (2010b), p. 453.

314 Cf. Pestana de Vasconcelos (2007), p. 182.

315 Provided that the remaining conditions of liability are verified and there is no defence (von Bar 2000a, p. 236).

316 Antunes Varela (2000), no. 2, p. 536; Prata (2007), p. 198; Menezes Leitão (2013), p. 265. According to one view (in relation to § 823(1) BGB), the law should expressly provide that unlawfulness is indicated in cases of violation of protective provisions (von Bar 1991, p. 220).

317 Sinde Monteiro et al. (1993), p. 13; Menezes Leitão (2013), p. 266. In the German literature, see Lorenz (1973), p. 575; Canaris (1983b), pp. 58–77. For details on the situations for compensation of pure economic loss see Tit. § 5, Subtit. III, Sec. 3 below.

318 Vaz Serra (1960d), p. 78.

319 von Bar (1999c), p. 19.

320 Some legal scholars suggest that only the injury of interests of individuals would give rise to an *unfair loss* (*prejuízo injusto*) and thus an attainable claim for damages. See Pessoa Jorge (1995), p. 303.

affects the interests protected by the protective provision.[321] When these conditions are not met cumulatively, the harm is indirect and not reparable. Perhaps because of these conditions, the freedom of the court for legal development (*richterliche Rechtsfortbildung*) is considered smaller, compared to the legal rights.[322]

Due to the complexity of the category of protective provisions, some legal scholars maintain that it respects not only the condition of unlawfulness, but also fault and causation,[323] thereby recognising the interlinked nature of non-contractual liability arising out of damage caused to another.

cc) A Third Category of Unlawfulness?

In addition to the two clauses of liability in Art. 483(1) CC, legal scholarship discusses whether Art. 334 CC should be deemed a third category of unlawfulness similarly to § 826 BGB (*clausula doli*).[324] The Portuguese legislature did not include any provision in this direction among its provisions on liability based on fault.

The *travaux préparatoires* of the Portuguese Civil Code included rules providing for the unlawfulness of intentional conducts *contra bonos mores*. They also had a wider scope than § 826 BGB (Arts. 735 and 736).[325] However, such rules did not pass into the present-day Civil Code, dividing legal scholars, with the majority being in favour of its inclusion.[326]

---

[321]Vaz Serra (1960d), pp. 72–73 and fn. 56, p. 75; Pires de Lima and Antunes Varela (1987), nn. to Arts. 539 to 542 CC, p. 549 ff.; Pessoa Jorge (1995); Antunes Varela (2000), pp. 539 ff.; Almeida Costa (2006a), pp. 515–516; Menezes Cordeiro (2010b), pp. 451–452; Menezes Leitão (2013), pp. 265–266.

[322]Canaris (1983b), p. 46.

[323]Menezes Leitão (2009), p. 837 ff.

[324]von Caemmerer (1968), p. 67 ff.; Deutsch (1976), pp. 48–49. The former provides for the compensation of harm caused intentionally *contra bonos mores* (*gegen die guten Sitten*) independent from the nature of the affected goods. It is argued that it aims to allow the judge to avoid unjust results which he or she would reach by a strict application of the law. For details see Doobe (2014), pp. 74–76.

[325]Sinde Monteiro (2007), p. 458. Art. 735(1) reads: "Whoever causes losses to someone by facts which manifestly contrast with the legal conscience dominant in society, or when claiming the exercise of a special right, shall repair them". Art. 736(1) reads: "There is also, exceptionally, abuse of right when, also without the intention mentioned in Art. 735, the act *gravely offends the dominant legal conscience* (emphasis added)". See Vaz Serra, *BolMinJus* 85 (1959), pp. 243–343.

[326]In favor of this identification, see Sinde Monteiro (1989), pp. 545–582, in particular, pp. 546–547 and p. 552; Sinde Monteiro et al. (1993), p. 12; Sinde Monteiro (2005), pp. 366–369; Carneiro da Frada and Pestana de Vasconcelos (2006), p. 158; Miranda Barbosa (2006a), p. 297 ff. *passim*; Sinde Monteiro (2007), p. 464 *passim*; Dias Pereira (2008), p. 514; Menezes Leitão (2013), pp. 267–268. For a critical account see Pires de Lima and Antunes Varela (1987), n. 5 to Art. 483 CC, p. 472; von Bar (1998a), p. 42; von Bar (1999f), p. 42; Carneiro da Frada (2007b), p. 165, fn. 121 (defending it, however, under strict limits, for the case of liability for information at p. 164 ff., n. 121); Menezes Cordeiro (2010b), p. 455.

Art. 334 CC provides a remedy for the "willful damage committed in breach of morality"[327] (*contra os bons costumes, gegen die guten Sitten*). According to this provision, the exercise of a right outside of the fundamental values of the legal system as a whole is illegitimate, even when it formally respects the powers which integrate the right.[328] Thus, if the conduct gives rise to harm, the person inflicting the harm must compensate the person who sustained it.[329]

d) Special Cases of Unlawfulness (*Sondertatbestände*)

In addition to the categories of unlawfulness provided for in Art. 483 CC, there are a few special cases of unlawfulness (*delitos específicos*)[330] (*Sondertatbestände*) in the Portuguese Civil Code.[331] These are the injury to reputation and good name (*Ofensa do crédito ou do bom nome*) in Art. 484 CC[332] and liability for advice, recommendation or information (*Conselhos, recomendações ou informações*) in Art. 485 CC.[333]

---

[327] von Bar (1999f), p. 42; n. II4 to VI.–1:101, p. 250; n. III16 to VI.–1:101, 254; n. IV20 to VI.–1:101, p. 256. With further reference see Vaz Serra, *BolMinJus* 85 (1959b), p. 243 ff.; Vaz Serra (1960d), p. 63 ff.; Ferrer Correia and Lobo Xavier (1979), p. 8; von Bar (1981), pp. 1704–1705; Pires de Lima and Antunes Varela 1987, nn. 1 ff. to Art. 334, pp. 298–300. On the legal matrix of *abus de droit* (*abuso do direito*) in Portugal see Cunha de Sá (1973) and Coutinho de Abreu (2006).

[328] See Menezes Cordeiro (1984b), pp. 886 ff.—if the exercise of the right is to be translated into the practice of a legal act, this act will be void. See also Pires de Lima and Antunes Varela 1987, n. 6 to Art. 334 CC, pp. 299–300.

[329] See Vaz Serra, *BolMinJus* 85 (1959b), p. 243 ff.; Ferrer Correia and Lobo Xavier (1979), p. 8 ff.; Pires de Lima and Antunes Varela (1987), n. 6 to Art. 334 CC, pp. 299–300.

[330] According to Menezes Leitão, these *delitos específicos* are legal or negotial obligations, from which it can be assumed that the regime of contractual liability applies. See Menezes Leitão (2013), pp. 266–272.

[331] For a critical account see Carneiro da Frada (1994), p. 175, fn. 363.

[332] In Art. 484 the situation is protection of personality and moral integrity, good name and reputation (Menezes Cordeiro 2010b, p. 551). *Exceptio veritatis* does not oppose the unlawfulness of the act. Here it diverges from § 824 BGB, which was a clear influence (Menezes Cordeiro 2010b, p. 552).

[333] According to one classification, duties of care shall be included as special delict provisions (Menezes Cordeiro 2010b, p. 551 ff.), while another (which includes those situations provided for in Arts. 484 and 485 CC as well) includes liability for omissions (Art. 491 CC). See Antunes Varela (2000), pp. 551–552; Almeida Costa (2006a), pp. 566–567. For details on liability for advice, recommendation or information see Tit. § 5, Subtit. III, Sec. 3 below.

Although the prevailing legal scholarship does not refer in detail to the liability regime of these provisions in comparison to the general regime, they are considered to have characteristics diverging from it,[334] such as particularities for every requirement of liability,[335] and inclusion of contractual elements.[336]

[334] Almeida Costa (2006a), p. 564; Menezes Cordeiro (2010b), p. 551.

[335] For such reason, they would form "global models of imputation, which go beyond unlawfulness" (Menezes Cordeiro 2010b, p. 454).

[336] Cf. Menezes Cordeiro (2010b), p. 454. For details on these rules see Pessoa Jorge 1995, p. 308 ff. and Menezes Cordeiro (2010b), p. 551 ff.

§ 5 Drawbacks of Unlawfulness and Compensation of Pure Economic Loss

I. An Ambitious Quest for a Definition of Pure Economic Loss

In recent decades, "pure economic loss" and its remedies have been one of the most highly debated topics in Civil Law.[1] This is the case despite the fact that this concept has little legal standing in some European countries, namely France, Belgium and Luxembourg.[2]

Within the legal systems in which the concept is recognised, no unanimously agreed definition exists,[3] with only one European country having drafted a legal definition of "purely financial loss" to date.[4]

---

[1]The first comparative study on the topic in Europe was published in the 1980s and consisted in an analysis of the English, French and German legal systems (Banakas 1989). A recent list of international literature on the topic can be found in Santos Silva (2009), pp. 52–53, fn. 2.

[2]See von Bar (1999c), p. 2; von Bar (1999f), p. 44; von Bar (2002a), p. 31, fn. 149; von Bar and Drobnig (2004), p. 30, fn. 15; Palmer and Bussani (2007), p. 194; von Bar (2009c), Intr. to Chap. 1, B13, p. 234; von Bar (2011d), p. 210. See also Herbots (1985), pp. 7–33; Lapoyade-Deschamps (1996). According to Banakas, different approaches between legal systems arise from the fact that in the French legal family (in contrast to the Anglo-American and Germanic legal families), the foundations of modern law of tort do not lie in the medieval metaphysical view of wealth as (physical) property (Banakas 1996, p. 11). For an overview of the reparation of pure economic loss in Europe see Stapleton (2007) and Voss (1987), for a comparison between German, Anglo-American and Dutch law.

[3]See von Bar (1999e), p. 11; van Boom (2004), pp. 2–4; von Bar and Drobnig (2004), pp. 29–30, p. 119; Palmer and Bussani (2007), p. 194.

[4]According to the Swedish Damages Act (Chap. 1, 2), "... purely financial loss shall mean an economic loss that is entirely unconnected with a person sustaining personal injury or damage to his or her property" (translation: von Bar 1999f, p. 44, fn. 8). See also von Bar (1996b), p. 43, fn. 158; von Bar (1999c), p. 6, fn. 18; von Bar (1999e), p. 36.

M. Santos Silva, *The Draft Common Frame of Reference as a "Toolbox" for Domestic Courts*, DOI 10.1007/978-3-319-52923-3_5

Legal systems traditionally define "pure economic loss" using a "damage-oriented" or "interest-oriented" approach.[5] The former is described as any loss not stemming from damage to a tangible object or the personal injury of a person.[6] According to the latter, pure economic loss corresponds to the harm inflicted without breaching an absolute or statutory right.[7] The latter perspective is adopted in Portugal and Germany,[8] *inter alia*. In both perspectives the loss does not involve either injury or damage to property by the person suffering the economic loss.[9]

In Germany, this category of losses is based on the listing of legal goods in § 823 (1) BGB,[10] the infringement of which is unlawful (*Enumerationsprinzip*).[11] In Portugal, this concept results from the liability condition of *ilicitude*.[12]

Portuguese legal scholars[13] have increasingly recognised the legal category of *danos económicos puros*,[14] developing an interchangeable nomenclature of meaning to describe this loss.[15] Current opinion sees "pure economic loss" as a loss of economic nature not violating the absolute rights of the person sustaining the

---

[5]Banakas (1989), p. 126; von Bar (1999e), p. 31. For criticism of the "interest-oriented" approach see Koziol (2006), p. 872.

[6]von Bar (1999f), p. 44; von Bar (2009c), Intr. to Chap. 1, B13, p. 234. For details see Wilkinson and Forte (1985), pp. 8–9; O'Sullivan (1991), pp. 109–125; Wetterstein (2001), pp. 565–589. This approach prevails in England, Ireland, Scotland, Sweden and Finland. See von Bar and Drobnig (2004), p. 29, n. 46.

[7]von Bar (1999f), p. 44. See also Banakas (1989), p. 126; Sinde Monteiro (1989), p. 153; Carneiro da Frada (1994), p. 174; Carneiro da Frada (1997), p. 37; von Bar and Drobnig (2004), pp. 29–30; Carneiro da Frada (2007b), p. 238; Pestana de Vasconcelos (2007), p. 149; von Bar (2009c), Intr. to Chap. 1, B13, p. 234.

[8]See von Caemmerer (1968), p. 65 ff.; von Bar (1992a), pp. 410–443; Schlechtriem (1998), p. 2; von Bar (2000b), p. 606; Honsell (2001), p. 483.

[9]van Boom (2004), pp. 2–3; Menezes Leitão (2009).

[10]For further information on the rights and interests protected by § 823(1) BGB see Reinhard (1961), pp. 3 ff.; von Bar (1981), p. 1699; Markesinis (1986), pp. 25–40; Coester-Waltjen (1992), p. 210 ff.; von Bar (2009c), n. VII62 to VI.–2:101, p. 338; Kötz and Wagner (2013), p. 46 ff.

[11]See Kötz and Wagner (2013), p. 173. Cf. also Brüggemeier (1982), pp. 385–452; Gursky (2005), p. 207; Palmer and Bussani (2007), p. 224; von Bar (2009c), Intr. Chap. 1, B13, p. 233.

[12]Miranda Barbosa (2006a), p. 216. See also von Bar (2000b), p. 606; Castronovo (2006), p. 109; Menezes Leitão (2009), p. 31 ff.

[13]Sinde Monteiro (1989), p. 187 ff.; Carneiro da Frada and Pestana de Vasconcelos (2006); Miranda Barbosa (2006a), p. 294 ff.; Pestana de Vasconcelos (2007); Santos Silva (2008), pp. 234–252; Menezes Leitão (2009).

[14]See Carneiro da Frada (1997), p. 36 ff.; Miranda Barbosa (2006a), pp. 214–253; Santos Silva (2008), pp. 234–252. The expression *danos económicos puros* is considered to more fully express this reality, as being "more suggestive, more in accordance with the foreign expressions used currently to refer to it and less inclined to create confusion with the economic loss which is usually produced by an infringement of a property or personal right" (Carneiro da Frada and Pestana de Vasconcelos 2006, p. 155, fn. 5). See also Amaral Cabral (2001), pp. 1028–1029, fn. 7.

[15]Some common designations in use are: *danos patrimoniais primários* (França Gouveia 2005, p. 40), *danos meramente patrimoniais* (Sinde Monteiro 1989, p. 187), *danos puramente patrimoniais* (Menezes Leitão 2009), *danos patrimoniais puros* (Pestana de Vasconcelos 2007) and *danos puramente económicos* (Menezes Leitão 2002).

harm.[16] A minority position, however, describes it as a loss inflicted to third parties not engaged in a relevant contractual or near-contractual relationship, and without infringement of any general duty of abstention or omission.[17]

Pure economic loss is distinguished from consequential economic loss[18] (*Folgeschaden,*[19] *danno-conseguenza*),[20] which is, in principle, recoverable in every legal system.[21]

In Portugal, this category finds cautious support in a small number of judicial decisions.[22] The first decision in which the category was applied was a case of state civil liability, and here the reference was merely *en passant.*[23]

II. Categories of Pure Economic Loss

Pure economic loss includes a wide variety of damage, with legal scholars suggesting some means of organising such losses in subcategories, though more for "didactic than scientific reasons".[24]

---

[16]Alarcão (1983), p. 242; Ribeiro de Faria (1990), p. 416; Carneiro da Frada (1994), p. 174; Carneiro da Frada (1997), p. 36; Menezes Leitão (2005a), p. 19; Carneiro da Frada and Pestana de Vasconcelos (2006), p. 155; Pestana de Vasconcelos (2007), p. 149; Almeida Costa (2006a), p. 562.

[17]Antunes Varela (2000), p. 621. This definition seems to be open to criticism, firstly because loss caused to third parties is, by definition, caused outside of a contractual or para-contractual relationship and, secondly, because pure economic loss can also be inflicted on contractual parties (in which case they are, typically, compensated).

[18]Gómez Pomar and Ruiz García (2002), p. 3; Bussani and Palmer (2003c), pp. 5 *passim*; von Bar and Drobnig (2004), p. 119; Witting (2004), p. 103; Menezes Leitão (2005a), p. 19, fn. 1; Santos Silva (2009), p. 55.

[19]Frank (1979), p. 589; Blobel (2004), p. 190.

[20]Castronovo (1997), p. 153 ff.

[21]Banakas (1989), p. 122; von Bar (2000a), p. 40; von Bar and Drobnig (2004), p. 119; Palmer and Bussani (2007), pp. 196–197. The opinion that pure economic loss can be compensated (Koziol 2004, p. 148) when it is consequential therefore seems contradictory.

[22]Within non-contractual liability cases, see: RP 7 June 2004, proc. 0452504 (injury of spectator of car race); RP 10 November 2009, proc. 13579/07.7TBUNG.P1 (product liability); RL 24 January 2013, proc. 31324/09.OT2SNT.L1-2 (deprivation of use); RL 11 March 2014, proc. 13359/02.6TJL.SB.L1-7 (product liability); RL 17 December 2014, proc. 35/13.3TBCSG.L1-2 (road traffic accident).

[23]STJ 11 March 2003, proc. 03A418.

[24]Miranda Barbosa (2006a), p. 220.

There are several categorisations of pure economic loss.[25] The most common,[26] also present in the Portuguese scholarship,[27] corresponds to recurrent situations ("standard cases").[28] These are: "ricochet loss"; "transferred loss"; "loss caused by the closure of public markets, transportation corridors and public infrastructures";[29] and "loss caused by the reliance upon flawed data, advice or professional services".

The first two categories are three-dimensional.

Ricochet loss[30] (*dano reflexo,*[31] *préjudice par ricochet,*[32] *reine Vermögensschäden Dritter*)[33] occurs whenever physical damage is inflicted on the property or person of a primary or direct victim, causing economic harm to a secondary or indirect victim.

A transferred loss takes place when A (a creditor) suffers damage to property caused by B (a debtor) and this damage is transferred to C (a third party) through a contract or statutory-based risk-allocation arrangement[34] ("transfer of risk"

---

[25] See Banakas (1989), pp. 40 ff.; Deutsch (1996b), p. 61; Martín Casals and Ribot Igualada (2003), pp. 901–917; van Boom (2004), p. 4; Koziol (2006), pp. 871–895; Menezes Leitão (2009), pp. 312–314.

[26] van Boom (2004), p. 34; von Bar and Drobnig (2004), p. 122. See generally Bussani and Palmer (2003c), p. 10 ff.; Parisi et al. (2006), p. 16 ff. This systematisation is also referred to in von Bar and Drobnig (2004), pp. 121–123.

[27] Carneiro da Frada and Pestana de Vasconcelos (2006), pp. 159 ff., pp. 219–220. Another classification divides pure economic losses into four categories: reflex losses; cable cases; loss resulting from the exercise of contractual freedom, and competition freedom (Pestana de Vasconcelos (2007), pp. 151–153).

[28] This classification refers to the standard cases referenced in the largest European-wide comparative study in the field of pure economic losses. Those cases are: 1. a cable case: the laid-off workers; 2. the injured key-player; 3. the infected animal; 4. the cancelled cruise; 5. the dutiful spouse; 6. Auditor's liability; 7. ruined credit; 8. evidence spoliation; 9. the pension scheme. See Palmer and Bussani (2007), pp. 272–273. This corresponds, essentially, to the recent classification of Doobe (Doobe 2014, pp. 43–52).

[29] See further, Palmer and Bussani (2007), pp. 202–203; Doobe (2014), pp. 93–100.

[30] Also called "relational economic loss" (Perry 2004, pp. 711–788; van Boom 2004, pp. 24–26; Koziol 2006, p. 880).

[31] Abrantes Geraldes (2007b). In Germany see Marschall von Bieberstein (1967).

[32] Ricochet loss is also called *préjudice réfléchi* (Lapoyade-Deschamps 1996, p. 373; Viney and Jourdain 2006, p. 154 ff.).

[33] Honsell (2001), p. 484. Also called *Reflexschaden* (Marschall von Bieberstein 1967) or "reinen Vermögenschaden Dritter" (Honsell 2001, p. 484).

[34] See generally Unberath (2003). See also von Bar (1980b), pp. 10–15; Banakas (1989), pp. 198–208; von Bar and Drobnig (2004), p. 121 ff.; Miranda Barbosa (2006a), p. 219; Palmer and Bussani (2007), pp. 201–202.

situations).[35] Transferred loss does not require distinct damage to the interests of the "secondary" victim, as is the case with ricochet loss.[36] A typical example is the cluster of so-called "cable cases" (*Kabelbruchfälle*), where cables or conductors are damaged through negligence.[37]

In the case of both transferred loss and ricochet loss, neither the creditor nor the third party has a cause of action against the debtor: the creditor suffered *injuria sine damno* (his or her legal right or legally protected interest has been infringed upon but he or she did not suffer a loss), while the third party suffered *damnum sine injuria*[38] (he or she suffered a loss but none of his or her rights or legally protected interests were infringed upon).[39] In these cases, therefore, the principle *casum sentit dominus* applies.[40]

The category of pure economic loss related to the closure of public services and infrastructures involves situations where, whenever there is physical damage, it is to "'unknown resources' that lie in the public domain".[41] The greatest concern this raises is the question of "liability in an indeterminate amount, for an indeterminate time to an indeterminate class", as Justice Cardozo so concisely put it.[42]

A fourth and final category relates to pure economic loss resulting from advice, data or services,[43] which will be discussed below.

---

[35]Banakas (1989), pp. 198–208. See also von Bar (1980b), p. 10.

[36]See BGHZ 114, 284. See also Palmer and Bussani (2007), p. 201; Miranda Barbosa (2006a), p. 219; von Bar and Drobnig (2004), p. 121.

[37]von Bar (2009c), n. B12 to VI.–2:206, p. 483; n. F34 to VI.–2:206, p. 489; Doobe (2014), pp. 82–83. For a detailed survey of the cable-cases in the Portuguese legal scholarship, see Sinde Monteiro (1989), p. 199 ff. and p. 257 ff.; França Gouveia (2005), pp. 30–48 and Miranda Barbosa (2006a) (who, however, classified these losses as "transferred loss" - *ibid.*, p. 219). In the German legal scholarship see Bürge (1981), pp. 57–72; Honsell (2001), pp. 492–495; Markesinis and Unberath (2002), p. 56 ff.; Brüggemeier (2006), pp. 380–382.

[38]von Bar (1999b), p. 23; Amaral Cabral (2001), p. 1029, fn. 9; Pestana de Vasconcelos (2007), p. 153. See also Brüggemeier, who considers this loss a *per se Schaden* (Brüggemeier 2006, p. 561).

[39]von Bar (1980b), p. 11; Carneiro da Frada (2006), p. 97 *passim*.

[40]Sinde Monteiro (1989), p. 153.

[41]Goldberg (1991), p. 37.

[42]*Ultramares Corp v louche* (1931) 255 NY 170, p. 179. See also von Bar and Drobnig (2004), p. 122.

[43]Bussani et al. (2003), p. 120. *White v Jones* [1995] 2 AC 207 (HL) was a leading English tort law case on professional negligence. For details on this category of damages see generally, within the Portuguese literature, Sinde Monteiro (1989). See also Carneiro da Frada (1997), pp. 65–77. Within the German literature see Lorenz (1973), Mertz (1994), von Bar (1994b), Decku (1997), Honsell (2001), pp. 500–506; Plötner (2003); Büttner (2006), pp. 555–579; Doobe (2014), pp. 100–113.

III. The Compensation of Pure Economic Loss

1. The General Principle of Non-Compensation of Pure Economic Loss in Portuguese Civil Non-Contractual Liability Arising Out of Damage Caused to Another

In Portuguese non-contractual liability, the extent of the penetration of German legal thought is particularly evident[44] in the rejection of the recovery of pure economic loss in general.[45]

As already described, the basic provision of liability (Art. 483 CC) distinguishes between the infringement of a right (*violação de um direito* or *Verletzung*) and the resulting damage (*dano* or *Schaden*), which is thus termed "consequential loss" (*danno-conseguenza*).

The distinction between *Verletzung* and *Schaden*, some have argued, does not work in the case of pure economic loss.[46] Indeed, pure economic loss is excluded from the constellation of liability for the infringement of subjective rights in Art. 483(1), 1st part CC,[47] because the Portuguese Civil Code contains no law (*damnum sine injuria*) generally protecting the right of people to the assets of their estate, a right to assets, as such[48] (*wirtschaftliches Eigentum*).[49] It is argued that in both Portugal and Germany,[50] this exclusion is not a coincidence but, rather, the exercise

[44]See Ranieri (2003), p. 1510. See also von Bar (1981), p. 1698; Deutsch and Weir (1996); Weir (1996); von Bar (1998b); Honsell (2001), p. 486; Markesinis and Unberath (2002), p. 43; von Bar and Drobnig (2004), p. 131; Schäfer and Ott (2005), p. 296; Schweizer (2005).

[45]Carneiro da Frada (1994), p. 153; Antunes Varela (2000), pp. 181–182; Carneiro da Frada and Pestana de Vasconcelos (2006), p. 156.

[46]von Bar (2011b), p. 394.

[47]Sinde Monteiro (1989), p. 187; Carneiro da Frada and Pestana de Vasconcelos (2006), p. 155; Menezes Leitão (2013), p. 261.

[48]Sinde Monteiro (1989), p. 190; Gomes Canotilho and Vital Moreira (1997), n. 10 to art. 62, p. 805; Antunes Varela (2000), p. 621; Almeida Costa (2006a), p. 190; Santos Silva (2006), p. 833; Pestana de Vasconcelos (2007), p. 183; Menezes Leitão (2013), p. 261. See also STJ 25 November 2009, proc. 397/03.0GEBNV.S1. See also, for Germany, von Bar (1981), pp. 1697–1698; Canaris (1983b), p. 36 *passim*; Blobel (2004), p. 190. In this regard, it has been argued that "as the assets consist of the final benchmark of compensation, were it the object of protection, it would not be a new right to add to the catalogue of compensable rights but (. . .) an antagonistic principle capable of undermining the entire system of economic loss" (Castronovo 1997, pp. 110–111). However, it has been pointed out that in Germany § 826 BGB would protect a person's assets, as such (Frank 1979, p. 585).

[49]Junker (1993), pp. 348–363.

[50]Legal commentators add that recoverability of pure economic loss is made difficult through other devices, such as the *Exkulpationsmöglichkeit* (§ 831(1), See. 2 BGB), and the fact that the burden of proof relies with the person who sustains the loss (Schmidt-Kessel 2006, p. 21, fn. 128).

of a carefully considered legislative option,[51] as previously discussed.[52] Had an unconditional protection to a person's assets been admitted, the distinction between the infringement of a right on the one hand, and the violation of a protective rule on the other, would be unnecessary and unjustified.[53]

2. The Exclusionary Rule and the "Floodgates Argument"

The "exclusionary rule", *i.e.* the general rule of no compensation for pure economic loss,[54] exists in many legal systems, including those with general liability clauses.[55]

This rule is based on several arguments, among which are allegations that: (a) pure economic loss would have been traditionally left unprotected by the law;[56] (b) its compensation would affect legal certainty[57] and insurance premiums;[58] and (c) that its compensation would, at best, be neutral within the system and, at worst, be undesirable within a context of a *laissez-faire* market economy.[59]

There is a danger that professionals would be exploited by people not paying for their services. An example would be non-payment for services rendered before payment, as is the case in many instances of advice, recommendation or information.[60]

It has also been argued that a person would have a moral *duty* to purchase insurance covering another's economic negligence to avoid facing personal

[51]Sinde Monteiro (1989), pp. 193–199; Carneiro da Frada (1994), p. 176. For Germany, see Canaris (1983a), pp. 36–38; von Bar (1999f), p. 43; Gordley (2003), pp. 39 ff. Cf. Picker (1987), p. 1041. See further Schlechtriem (1998), pp. 1–2.

[52]See Tit. § 1, Subtit. IV above.

[53]Pestana de Vasconcelos (2007), p. 176.

[54]For details on the arguments for exclusion of compensation of pure economic loss see Dari-Mattiacci and Schäfer (2007), p. 2 ff.; Palmer and Bussani (2007), p. 205 ff.

[55]Koziol (2008), p. 28.

[56]Honsell (2001), p. 484; Palmer and Bussani (2007), p. 219. For details on the historical development of non-contractual liability within Civil Law see Gordley (2003); Ranieri (2003), p. 1409 ff.

[57]Menezes Cordeiro (1986), p. 217; Sinde Monteiro (1989), p. 196 ff.

[58]Schäfer and Ott (2005), p. 327.

[59]von Bar (1991), p. 218; von Bar (1994b), pp. 107–108; Gómez Pomar and Ruiz García (2002), pp. 12–13; Backaus (2003), p. 67; Albuquerque and Pereira (2004), p. 115; Dari-Mattiacci and Schäfer (2007), pp. 3–4 *passim*; Pestana de Vasconcelos (2007), p. 175; Menezes Leitão (2009), p. 267. Cf. also Atiyah (1997), p. 63. Victor Goldberg developed a theory to explain why compensation of pure economic loss outside contract law (in non-contractual law) is not efficient (Goldberg 1991, pp. 249–275). But see Banakas (1996), p. 8; Koziol 2004, p. 152 (for whom the more clearly the person inflicting the harm acted in his or her own economic interest, the more acceptable it is to compensate the resulting pure economic loss).

[60]Banakas (1996), p. 9.

consequences. In this situation, contract law would form an adequate mechanism of protecting against pure economic loss because it would promote self-control.[61]

Also, there would be a problem of non-recovery of these losses as a matter of principle, due to the lack of social standing of the protected goods[62] compared to personality rights.[63]

One of the most common arguments is the so-called "floodgates argument",[64] which is traditionally analysed from three different perspectives.

The first perspective relates to the fear that allowing a general claim for pure economic loss would give rise to "a flood" of claims[65] in the courts, drowning them in administrative chaos.[66] Von Jhering referred to this concern as early as the nineteenth century ("Where would it all lead if everyone could be sued. . .!").[67] It has been claimed that the "elimination of the danger of an indeterminate number of claims (*uferlose Schadensersatzansprüche*) by 'indirect' victims" was, in fact, behind the Second Commission of the BGB's rejection of a "general clause system".[68]

The second perspective is the belief that such claims would put the person inflicting the harm at risk of incurring a liability that is unpredictable and disproportionate to the respective fault.[69] This is considered "the real concern" underlying the objection[70] to compensate for pure economic loss, as it requires that individual freedom be compromised[71] by limiting freedom of movement by implying

[61] *ibid.*, p. 7.

[62] Carneiro da Frada (2007b), p. 167; Pestana de Vasconcelos (2007), p. 166; Menezes Leitão (2009), pp. 266–267.

[63] Koziol (2004), p. 144. But see Jansen (2007), pp. 40–41. Likewise, Miranda Barbosa (2006a), p. 224 ff.

[64] Martín Casals and Ribot Igualada (2003), p. 897 ff. On this argument see Spier and Haazen (1998), p. 6 ff.; Miranda Barbosa (2006a), p. 230 ff.

[65] The floodgate argument is variously referred to as a flood of claims, an avalanche (*Prozeßlawine*) or chain reaction (*Kettenreaktion*) of lawsuits. See von Bar and Markesinis (1981), p. 10. For further policy aspects in the field of pure economic loss see von Bar (1980a), p. 456.

[66] Miranda Barbosa (2006a), p. 232; Carneiro da Frada (2007b), p. 245. See also Dari-Mattiacci and Schäfer (2007), p. 2; Palmer and Bussani (2007), p. 209. van Boom (2004), p. 33; Palmer and Bussani (2007), p. 209. As Lord Denning put it, "[i]f claims for economic loss were permitted for this particular hazard, there would be no end of claims" (*Spartan Steel & Alloys Ltd. v Martin & Co (Contractors) Ltd.* [*1973*] 1 *QB 27,* p. 38).

[67] von Jherings (1861), pp. 12–13 *apud* Palmer and Bussani (2007), p. 208, fn. 58. Menezes Leitão minimises the weight of this argument and considers that the problem of the extension of liability is a problem of all kinds of liability (Menezes Leitão 2009, p. 266).

[68] Banakas (1989), p. 216. See also von Caemmerer (1968), pp. 452, 471–472.

[69] Azevedo de Almeida (2004), p. 52. See also von Bar (2000a), p. 29; Palmer and Bussani (2007), p. 209.

[70] van Boom (2004), pp. 33–34; Koziol (2006), p. 875.

[71] Carneiro da Frada (1994), p. 119; Carneiro da Frada (2007b), p. 250. See also Picker (1983), pp. 470–473; Honsell (2001), p. 484; Schäfer and Ott (2005), pp. 289, 296.

additional duties of care,[72] and generates a risk of over-deterrence that could ultimately affect commercial activity as a whole.[73]

The third and final viewpoint relates to the need to keep the modern trend of expanding tort liability under control.[74] Some legal scholars rely heavily on this concern, arguing that the floodgates must be "kept shut".[75]

3. Situations for Compensation of Pure Economic Loss

Despite the general rule of non-compensation of pure economic loss, compensation has, in some cases, entered the jurisprudence, where it was argued that some pure economic interests deserve protection to some extent and within reasonable limits.[76] The societal movement towards the dematerialisation[77] and unpredictability of economic values creates pressure in this direction.[78]

The law sometimes expressly undertakes the protection of pure economic interests. Other times, it results from case law development, often anchored in legal scholarship, in line with events in recent decades in Germany. Indeed, soon after the BGB entered into force, it was clear that §§ 823(1), (2) and 826 BGB were insufficient to encompass all cases in which it would be just to provide a claim for a pure economic loss.[79]

Among academics, a distinction is generally drawn between situations where pure economic loss is repaired in contract law, near-contract law and non-contractual law, to which it adds some particularities. In continental law, such situations are categorised as contractual liability, near-contractual relationship, statements to guide third parties, consequential loss, intentional infliction of harm, infringement of contracts, and relational loss.[80]

---

[72]Koziol (2004), p. 149.

[73]Carneiro da Frada (1997), p. 32; von Bar (2000a), p. 4 ff.; van Boom et al. (2004b), p. 196. Cf. also Atiyah (1997), p. 65.

[74]Rogers et al. (1996), p. 1; Palmer and Bussani (2007), p. 210. See generally Spier and von Bar (1998).

[75]See Spier and Haazen (1998), Palmer and Bussani (2007), p. 210, fn. 64. See, generally, Spier and von Bar (1998).

[76]Carneiro da Frada (1997), p. 40; Carneiro da Frada and Pestana de Vasconcelos (2006), p. 156; Santos Silva (2006), p. 833 ff.; Carneiro da Frada (2007b), p. 248 ff. See also van Boom et al. (2004a), p. 191. For the difficulties in assessing which pure economic interests shall be protected, see Carneiro da Frada (2007b), pp. 238–251.

[77]The "new property" would comprise intangible goods in particular (Vaz Tomé 1997, p. 145 ff.).

[78]Carneiro da Frada (2007b), p. 251. It is in this context that the scholar defends the autonomy of a liability for trust.

[79]van Dam (2013), p. 211.

[80]Koziol (2004), pp. 145–149. See also Koziol (2006), pp. 878–882.

As for Germany specifically, these situations have also been grouped into supplements to non-contractual liability arising out of damage caused to another, and supplements to contracts. The former consists of the extension of the concept of "rights", more specifically the extension of "injury to property". The latter includes the violation of ancillary duties of care (*positive Vertragsverletzung*); fictitious contracts; "third party beneficiaries of protective duties"; and *culpa in contrahendo*.[81] This last classification is distinct from situations of compensation for third party loss only. Here, it is divided between loss of maintenance, indirect loss arising out of professional contact, cable cases, borderline cases between consequential and pure economic loss in cases of delivery of defective products, construction of defective buildings and liability for advice, liability for supplied information and liability involving wills.[82]

a) Compensation in Non-Contractual Liability

aa) Special Rules in the Portuguese Civil Code

(1) Loss Resulting from Injury to Reputation and Good Name

Art. 484 CC (*ofensa ao crédito e ao bom nome*) provides that the person who affirms or disseminates a fact capable of harming the reputation and good name of another must repair the resulting harm, that is, pure economic loss.

Some argue that there is liability for such injuries even in cases where the person asserted or disseminated true facts.[83] However, liability is exempted where the person was exercising a right, performing a duty or otherwise acting for the protection of legitimate public interests.[84]

Art. 484 CC does not expressly provide for honour, leading to the argument that impugning the reputation but not the honour, would not create an obligation of reparation.[85] However, where there is an injury to credit and honour simultaneously, the claimant is also covered by the general protection of personality rights in Art. 70 CC (which, as mentioned before, are traditionally included in Art. 483(1), 1st part CC). Injury to credit may give rise to the crimes of unfair competition,[86] libel (Art. 180 CCrim), slander (Art. 180 CCrim) or insult (Art. 181 CCrim). In all

[81]Schlechtriem (1998), pp. 6–21.

[82]Honsell (2001), pp. 488–507.

[83]Antunes Varela (2000), p. 548. But see Pessoa Jorge (1995), p. 310. In the case law see RL 21 May 1987 *CJ* 12 (1987–3), p. 88.

[84]Carneiro da Frada and Pestana de Vasconcelos (2006), p. 169; Almeida Costa (2006a), p. 517.

[85]Carneiro da Frada and Pestana de Vasconcelos (2006), p. 170. In the case law, see RP 11 January 2006, proc. 0512088; RP 19 April 2006, proc. 0515927; RG 27 Abril 2006, proc. 358/06–2. But see STJ 26 February 2004, proc. 03B3898.

[86]Arts. 9 ff. of the Act 19/2012 of 8 May 2012, DR, 1st Ser., no. 89 (2012), pp. 2404–2427.

of these cases, the person inflicting the harm would also be liable under Art. 483(1), 2nd part CC.[87]

(2) Loss Resulting from Advice, Recommendation or Information

Art. 485 CC provides for the reparation of harm arising from rendered advice, recommendation or information.[88]

It reads:

1. The simple advice, recommendations or information do not make the respective provider liable, even if the provider acted negligently.
2. The obligation to reparation exists, however, when the provider had assumed the legal duty of giving the advice, recommendation or information and had acted with negligence or intention to cause harm, or when the procedure of the provider is a criminal offence.

The provision, which can benefit both simple and legal persons[89] albeit only the entitled recipient of the information,[90] has a wording similar to § 675(2) BGB.[91] Both start from a general rule of non-reparation for advice, recommendation of information provided (Art. 485(1) CC and § 675(2) BGB, respectively)[92] and then list the circumstances in which such reparation is permitted.[93] In this respect, Art. 485(2) CC allows for reparation each time the provider of the advice, recommendations or information had: assumed liability for any resulting loss; the duty to provide such advice, recommendations or information and acted with fault;[94] or thereby committed a crime.[95] Thus, the person who provided the advice, recommendations or information in the fulfilment of a duty without negligence or intention will not be liable for the loss caused. The provision also apparently withdraws liability for "Kerbstone" advice (such as the DCFR),[96] as provision by a professional seems insufficient.

---

[87]Carneiro da Frada and Pestana de Vasconcelos (2006), p. 171.

[88]The topic was thoroughly analysed by Sinde Monteiro (1989). See also the comparative contributions of Lorenz (1973), von Bar (1994b).

[89]STJ 24 February 1960, *BolMinJus* 94 (1960), 107; STJ 15 June 1994, *BolMinJus* 438 (1994), p. 383.

[90]RL 22 May 1993, *CJ* 18 (1993-3), p. 188; Pires de Lima and Antunes Varela (1987), n. 2 to Art. 485 CC, p. 487.

[91]Liability for advice, recommendations or information is dealt with within non-contractual law almost exclusively through § 826 BGB (Markesinis 1986, p. 148; von Bar 2009c, n. 5 to VI.–2:207, p. 516). But cf. Lorenz (1973), p. 579. On liability for advice see generally Musielak (1974).

[92]von Bar et al. (2008), n. 8, VI.–2:207, p. 517; Menezes Cordeiro (2010b), p. 563. See also von Bar (1994b), p. 99.

[93]Favourably, Antunes Varela (2000), p. 550.

[94]STJ 4 April 2006, proc. 06A222. See also Carneiro da Frada (1997), p. 66.

[95]Pires de Lima and Antunes Varela (1987), n. 1 to Art. 485 CC, pp. 486–487. See generally Sinde Monteiro (1989).

[96]For details see Tit. § 7, Subtit. IV below.

Liability for these acts is provided for in most jurisdictions every time reliance on advice, recommendations or information is justified and should have been foreseen by the respective provider.

This provision, however, is not without its critics. Firstly, the provision is claimed to be "superfluous"[97] because the interests protected were already protected by Arts. 26(1) CC and 70(1) CC.[98] Secondly, this provision was only included after lobbying on its behalf by Vaz Serra, despite its being "against the system" and not a "socially adequate rule of law".[99]

In Germany, opinion holds that one should generally impose a duty of care on experts towards persons relying on their advice,[100] and that the BGB should contain a provision imposing such a duty.[101] In Portugal, legal scholarship relies on near-contractual devices to provide for such liability.[102]

(3) Loss for Close Relations

Loss for close relations is provided for in Art. 495 CC (Compensation to third parties in the case of death or personal injury), which is considered an exceptional provision in comparison to the general regime.[103]

It reads:

1. In the case of injury resulting in death, the person responsible shall compensate the expenses incurred in order to save the injured person, and every other expense, including the funeral expenses.
2. In this case, as in every other case of personal injury, those who rescued the injured person are entitled to damages, as well as hospitals, doctors or other persons or entities who had contributed to the treatment or assistance of the victim.
3. Those who could demand maintenance from the injured person, or those to whom the injured person rendered it in the performance of a natural obligation, are also entitled to damages.

(a) Expenses, Including Funeral Costs

In the first paragraph of this provision, the legislature foresaw the reparation of loss resulting from the treatment of, or the assistance rendered to, a person incurring a

[97] von Bar (2009c), n. I8 to VI.–2:204, p. 450.

[98] Capelo de Sousa (1993), p. 305; Gouveia de Andrade (1996), p. 28.

[99] Menezes Cordeiro (2010b), pp. 563–564.

[100] See von Bar (1981), p. 1771; von Bar (1994b), p. 125 ff. See also BGH *NJW* 1987, p. 1758; BGHZ 166, 84, p. 108; Canaris (1999), pp. 206–245. According to Huber, the duties of care of professionals should be regarded as protective norms (Huber 1978, p. 359 ff.).

[101] von Bar (1981), p. 1761. See Markesinis and Unberath (2002), p. 292.

[102] One example of reliance in near-contractual devices is the case of that which is so far the only systematic legal theory on liability for advice, information and recommendation (Sinde Monteiro 1989).

[103] This would not, however, prevent Art. 495 CC from being susceptible to extensive interpretation (Vaz Serra 1971, p. 16). A similar situation exists in Scotland. See also von Bar (1980b), pp. 11–12.

personal injury (i.e. drugs, medical treatments, etc.). This is also the case if the person incurring a personal injury subsequently died (funeral costs).[104] A recurring point of disagreement exists with respect to transportation costs incurred by visits to the injured person during recovery.[105]

Another disputed point is whether the persons who incurred the expenses have a direct claim over the person who inflicted the harm.

Some argue that, according to the letter of the law, they do have such a claim.[106] The costs incurred are included in the compensation to the injured person only if the persons who paid for them did not claim for them separately.[107] For those in support of this position, the expenses incurred are not a form of pure economic loss but, rather, a consequential loss, which can be repaired under the general principle of liability arising out of damage caused to another.

Others hold that the persons sustaining the expenses are indirectly affected (following the violation of an absolute right of another, namely, injury to health) and thus do not have a claim for compensation. Those who hold this view believe that the persons incurring the expenses suffer a pure economic loss, or more specifically, a *transferred loss*. Nevertheless, as an imperative for justice, it could be argued that the expenses could be assigned to the injured person (through a mechanism of recovery of third party damage or *Drittschadensliquidation*) who, *vis-à-vis* those who paid them, would be liable under benevolent intervention in another's affairs.[108]

---

[104]The legislature intentionally abstained from expressly providing for the precise amount of such expenses, leaving it up to the courts to determine the number based on the uses and socioeconomic conditions of the deceased and his or her family (Abrantes Geraldes 2007b, p. 17).

[105]Viney and Markesinis (1985), p. 66. PEL Liab. Dam. refers to this subject in Art. 2:201. Para. 1 refers to losses sustained by the person who suffers the bodily injury. According to para. 2 a) consequential loss includes "the costs of health care, including expenses reasonably incurred for the care of the injured person by those close to him or her" (von Bar (2009c), n. D18 to VI.–2:201, p. 364). In France, if the injured person is a minor or a dependant, the parents or the person charged with care of the former have the right of claiming compensation for the medical and paramedical expenses incurred by the accident. However, when the victim is an adult, these claims exist only when the life of the victim is in danger, or the presence of the respective spouse or parents is medically justified (Le Roy 2004, p. 69). According to one position, the adequacy between the means of transport used and the journey, the number of people transported, the family habits, the existence of cheaper alternatives of transportation, etc. shall be assessed (Dias 2001b, p. 215, fn. 483).

[106]Carneiro da Frada and Pestana de Vasconcelos (2006), p. 165.

[107]Abrantes Geraldes (2007b), pp. 15–17. The Supreme Court of Justice has considered that the persons included under this provision have a right to compensation even when they do not display the "need" to receive such compensation (STJ 16 April 1974, *RLJ* 108 (1975–1976), p. 180).

[108]von Bar (2009c), n. D18 to VI.–2:201, p. 364.

(b) Losses Arising from Assistance or Treatment

The second paragraph of Art. 495 refers to those who rescued, assisted or otherwise contributed to the recovery of the injured person. It thus includes the costs incurred by personal carers (*terceiras pessoas*,[109] *acompanhantes*),[110] i.e., those who come to the support of the dependent[111] patient, replacing or assisting him or her whenever he or she is unable to carry out, wholly or in part, the activities of daily living, the activities needed for his or her health state, and providing psychological support.[112]

With regard to the provision of personal care and the associated consequences, Art. 495(2) CC raises several questions of interpretation, namely whether it applies to relatives or only to persons or entities who provide professional care, and, assuming that it does, whether it includes unrealised incomes or profits.[113]

As for the question of whether Art. 495(2) CC applies to relatives or only to professional carers, despite the guidance from the *travaux préparatoires* referring only to professional assistants, the prevailing view is that the provision includes any person assisting the injured person, i.e. also "informal" carers (namely, relatives or friends).[114]

With respect to the inclusion of unrealised incomes or profits in Art. 495(2), courts have taken different positions in this regard, with the respective implications in the qualification of these losses. One of the outcomes, in line with a legal

[109]Not only legal literature (Dias 2001b, p. 242 *passim*) refers to the expression "third person". According to the French Federation of the Associations of Medical Experts in Bodily Injury Evaluation (*Féderation Française des Associations de Médecins Conseils Experts en Évaluation du Dommage Corporel, FFAMCE*), made in the respective 29th Congress in 1993 in La Rochelle, there are three types of care providers: a provider of replacement (*tierce personne de remplacement*), who executes or helps to execute acts for the injured person; a provider of surveillance (*tierce personne de surveillance*), who ensures that the injured person stays safe; and a provider of encouragement (*tierce personne de stimulus*), whose role is to help in the execution of acts and the development of skills whenever the injured person lacks motivation. See Muñoz et al. (2000), p. 99 ff.; Braga (2005), pp. 114–115.

[110]Braga (2005), p. 113.

[111]The legal system of social protection of situations of dependency (*Regime da Protecção Social das Situações de Dependência*) approved by the DL 265/99 of 14 July 1999, DR, 1st Ser., no. 162 (1999), pp. 4397–4401, considers in situation of dependency "the individuals who cannot practice with autonomy the acts indispensable to the satisfaction of daily needs, without the assistance of someone else" (Art. 3(1)). These acts are defined in the following number as those which concern the realisation of domestic services, movement and hygiene (Dias 2001b, pp. 231–232, fn. 525). The need of a personal carer must, in any case, be prescribed by a medical expert according to the seriousness of the handicap and the quality of the available technical tools (Dias 2001b, p. 243).

[112]Dias (2001b), pp. 228, 242 *passim*. See also Horsburgh (1992), pp. 423–504.

[113]The STJ has already considered that the patrimonial value of the care provided must be proven by the carer (STJ 17 September 2009, proc. 292/1999-S1).

[114]Abrantes Geraldes (2007b), p. 18; Carneiro da Frada and Pestana de Vasconcelos (2006), p. 165.

position,[115] is that informal carers have a claim for these losses[116] arising from their legal family duties, namely, the duty of aid and assistance between spouses (Art. 1675 CC) and the duty of providing for the security and health of their own children (Art. 1878(1) CC). According to some scholars, the provision is not sufficiently clear on the question. However, if the teleological element is considered, the *ratio* of Art. 495(2) CC is meant to encourage assistance to the injured victim.[117] Accordingly, those providing aid for such a purpose (such as informal carers) are entitled to be fully compensated for the losses incurred.[118]

Others hold that informal carers should be compensated under this provision because their assistance bypassed the need to contract professional assistance, the costs of which would always be charged to the person inflicting the harm.[119] Not granting a claim would thus amount to an unjustified enrichment on the part of the person inflicting the harm.[120]

Opinions in case law are also divided, as it often attributes a direct claim to the carer, but case law bases this choice upon different reasonings, i.e. upon family provisions imposing the protection of children by their parents[121] or upon personality rights.[122] The amount which may be claimed varies, and is adapted in case of

---

[115]Carneiro da Frada and Pestana de Vasconcelos (2006) Pure economic loss: Portuguese report. Unpublished manuscript, pp. 165–166.

[116]Dias (2001b), p. 245; Menezes Leitão (2013), p. 366. The Court of Appeal of Oporto decided that the injured person himself could not claim compensation for the lost income of his wife who assisted him (RP 8 November 2012, proc. 6439/07.3TBMTS.P1). The STJ (STJ 8 March 2005, proc. 05A395) further considered that in relation to the foregone wages of the carer, the injured person suffered an indirect loss. See also von Bar (1980b), p. 12. This shows that the legal matrix as such is not very convincing, nor is the distinction between primary and secondary victim that is often used in the same context (von Bar 2011b, p. 394).

[117]See also Pires de Lima and Antunes Varela (1987), n. 1b to Art. 495, p. 498.

[118]Carneiro da Frada and Pestana de Vasconcelos (2006), pp. 165–167. Such right is limited to the period of absolute incapacity of the injured person (STJ 13 May 2004, proc. 04B1185).

[119]Abrantes Geraldes (2007b), p. 18. In line with this reasoning, the STJ granted compensation to the carer of an injured person until the moment a professional carer was contracted (STJ 2 March 2011, proc. 1639/03.8TBBNV.L1).

[120]See argumentation of the claimants in STJ 26 February 2004, proc. 03B3604.

[121]The STJ provided a right to compensation of the difference in the wage since he assisted his injured child, even though his mother was already assisting the child, based on Art. 1874 CC (STJ 16 December 1993, proc. 084508). In another decision, the STJ recognised the right of the mother to be compensated for the income foregone in the 342 days during which she assisted her son because the support was exceptional and more demanding than that normally expected of parents in respect of their children (STJ 13 May 2004, proc. 04B1185). The Supreme Court also already considered that such excess in the normal support of a patient must be proven by the carer (STJ 17 September 2009, proc. 292/1999-S1). In two dissenting opinions to this ruling (Salreta Pereira; Salazar Casanova), it was held that the added personal sacrifice of the spouse in the performance of her marital duty of assistance should have amounted to the grant of a compensation for moral losses.

[122]The STJ considered that the need to render assistance to the injured husband consisted of a serious limitation to the wife's freedom of action and represented a breach of her personal rights under Art. 70 CC (STJ 8 March 2005, proc. 05A395).

contributory fault.[123] However, case law has already denied the claim of the carer based upon lack of adequate causation between the damage inflicted and the loss sustained by the carer.[124]

In a somewhat isolated and puzzling decision, the Court of Appeal of Oporto held that because husband (injured person) and wife (carer) were married and living together, they were living in a domestic economy, and that it was the domestic economy *itself* that was impaired. For this reason, any of the claimants, or both claimants together, could ask for compensation.[125]

In a dissenting opinion to another decision, the carer was considered to have sustained his own damage (*dano próprio*), which amounts to the sacrifice imposed in the performance of legal duties towards the injured person. Therefore, reparation should be granted not under Art. 495(2) CC, but under 496(1) CC,[126] i.e. as a non-economic loss.[127]

(c) Loss of Maintenance

In Art. 495(3) CC, the Portuguese Civil Code provides for a compensation right integrating a loss of maintenance (*alimentos*).[128] The persons who are legally entitled to such a claim are expressly set out in the law (Art. 2009 CC).[129] Although

---

[123] STJ 3 March 2009, proc.09A0009.

[124] In a 2004 decision (STJ 26 February 2004, proc. 03B3604), the STJ decided that despite the fact that the carer of the victim had abandoned her job and done the work which would otherwise have required three domestic workers, she did not have a claim for reparation. Due to the length of the care and the harsh conditions in which it was provided (due to the need for round-the-clock care, the carer was "forced" to live in a window-less storage room with bad smells from the sores of the injured person) it seems that the Supreme Court relied excessively on the letter of the law, and a more equitable judgment would have been desirable in that instance.

[125] RP 4 April 1991, proc. 0124636.

[126] In the recent settling case law decision 6/2014 of 22 May 2014, the STJ decided that "[A]rticles 483(1) and 496(1) CC shall be interpreted in the sense of comprising non-economic loss, particularly serious loss, suffered by the spouse of a surviving victim, affected in a particularly serious way", as was mentioned above (§ 4 IV).

[127] STJ 17 September 2009, proc. 292/1999-S1.

[128] The customary practice (*gemeinrechtliche Praxis*) since the seventeenth century has been to grant a maintenance claim to the children, the widow or widower, and the parents of the deceased, through a development of the Roman *actio legis Aquiliae* (Ranieri 2003, p. 1465). For further developments, see von Bar (1999e), pp. 192–196. According to some, the spirit of the law also includes those persons who become holders of a right to maintenance after the injury (Antunes Varela 2000, pp. 608 ff.), such as a foetus (Vaz Serra 1959a, p. 123). See also STJ 16 April 1974, *RLJ* 108 (1975–1976), p. 180.

[129] Nevertheless, courts often have difficulty in determining those persons entitled to claims in each specific case. The case law has not been clear about the circumstances for invoking a compensation right. In the decision STJ 29 February 1996, *CJ (ST)* 21 (1996-1), p. 104, the court denied compensation to a woman who lived separately from her husband. In another decision, the Supreme Court denied the claim of a grandson, who "could only distantly invoke the right to support" (STJ 16 March 1999, *BolMinJus* 485 (1999), p. 386).

these people were affected indirectly, the law considered that the circumstance connecting them to the victim through a legal tie—which, moreover, implies the benefit of support—was worthy of a specific compensatory protection, likely to remedy the effects of the reduction or suppression of its source.[130]

The special element in this solution is that, in contrast to the German solution (§ 845 BGB)[131] but in line with several other European systems,[132] it includes those who do not have a claim based upon the law but who were nevertheless receiving maintenance.[133] It equates natural and legal obligations for the purposes of maintenance, in spite of their traditional unenforceability (Art. 402 CC).[134] A real detriment to the right to maintenance must, in any case, be proven by the claimant.[135]

As has been mentioned, the prevailing view argues that credit rights are not accounted for by Art. 483(1) CC. The obligation of maintenance (*obrigação alimentar*) consists of a relative right with which the person inflicting the harm has no connection. Therefore, the person inflicting the harm only has an obligation to compensate due to the existence of this provision.[136]

With Art. 495 CC, the Portuguese Civil Code joins several other systems in admitting the desirability of exceptions to the exclusionary rule in cases of relational loss resulting from personal injury.[137] This would correspond to situations where traditional non-contractual liability law less easily accommodates "'deserving' loss-situations"[138] involving infringement to "high-ranking values" (the right to life or the right to health) and where a risk exists to the livelihood of the person sustaining the harm,[139] to which the law cannot be indifferent.[140] The arguments of the exclusionary rule usually do not apply to pure economic loss suffered by

---

[130] STJ 9 May 1991, *BolMinJus* 407 (1991), p. 141; STJ 11 November 1997, *BolMinJus* 471 (1997), p. 369; STJ 16 March 1999, *BolMinJus* 485 (1999), p. 386.

[131] Honsell (2001), p. 489; Ranieri (2003), p. 1467.

[132] Ranieri (2003), p. 1480.

[133] van Boom et al. (2004a), p. 193. Before the regime of protective measures of non-marital relationships came into force (Act 7/2001 of 11 May 2001, DR, 1st Ser., no. 109 (2001), pp. 2797–2798, republished by Act 23/2010 of 30 August 2010, DR, 1st Ser., no. 168 (2010), pp. 3764–3768), non-marital partners were already potential claimants within Art. 495 (3). See von Lillienskiold (1975), pp. 353–356. See STJ 9 May 1991, *BolMinJus* 407 (1991), p. 141; STJ 11 November 1997, *BolMinJus* 471 (1997), p. 369.

[134] von Lillienskiold (1975), pp. 352–356; Ranieri (2003), p. 1466, fn. 125.

[135] Vaz Serra (1959a), p. 122.

[136] Antunes Varela (2000), pp. 622–623.

[137] van Boom (2004), p. 37 ff.

[138] Banakas (1989), pp. 152, 223. For Banakas, "tort law should show more awareness of the fact that, being a residual loss-allocation system, it may well have to be resorted to, when the secondary loss-allocation system breaks down completely" (*ibid.*, 154). On the characterisation of the law of civil liability as a law of balance (*droit d'équilibre*) and law-function (*droit-function*) see Mekki (2008), pp. 745–755. See also Tunc (1990), p. 22 ff.

[139] van Boom et al. (2004b), p. 199.

[140] Carneiro da Frada and Pestana de Vasconcelos (2006), p. 166.

relatives of victims of personal injury.[141] By definition, families are limited in size and one can easily calculate average family incomes, which means that both the circle of possible claimants and the scope of the claims are determinable.[142] It is, in any case, argued that this positive discrimination is "remarkable" when one compares it to the normal treatment of third party claims in the case of property damage.[143]

bb) Protective Provisions in Art. 483(1) of the Portuguese Civil Code

Pure economic loss is also reparable in Portuguese non-contractual law where there is an infringement of a legal rule intended to protect pure economic interests.[144] A similar situation occurs in Germany, where a claimant can recover pure economic loss under the special provisions governing the breach of a statutory duty (§ 823 (2) BGB).[145]

Protective provisions expand further on the interests that are legally protected, namely, pure economic interests.[146] This is despite the argument that they shall only be compensated when they are connected to the violation of criminal rules as well.[147] An important area of protection in these rules is unfair competition.[148]

---

[141]Bussani and Palmer (2003a), p. 535; Koziol (2004), p. 149; Koziol (2006), p. 882.

[142]Nevertheless, when they sustain ricochet loss and there is no legal protective rule involved, claims are usually denied (Marschall von Bieberstein 1967, p. 128 ff.).

[143]van Boom et al. (2004a), pp. 193–194.

[144]Sinde Monteiro (1989), pp. 254–256; Carneiro da Frada (1994), p. 175; Carneiro da Frada (1997), p. 40 ff.; Pestana de Vasconcelos (2007), pp. 177–182; Palmer and Bussani (2007), pp. 256–257; Menezes Leitão (2009), p. 260; Menezes Leitão (2013), p. 266; Miranda Barbosa (2015), p. 221.

[145]Canaris (1983b), pp. 58–78; Carneiro da Frada (1994), p. 175, fn. 363; von Bar (2004a), p. 134. von Bar defended that the scope of § 823(2) BGB should be understood as comprising not only statutes aimed at protecting individual persons but also case law establishing duties (von Bar 1988, pp. 169–174) but this has not yet been adopted. See von Bar (1994b), p. 103, fn. 23.

[146]Carneiro da Frada and Pestana de Vasconcelos (2006), p. 163. According to the same legal scholar (*ibid.*, p. 167), one of the rules that protects pure economic interests within its particular scope, is Art. 10 (Liability of auditors) of the Portuguese Securities Code, DL 486/99 of 13 November 1999, DR, 1st Ser., no. 265 (1999), 7968–8040, last amended by DL 124/2015 of 7 July 2015, DR, 1st Ser., no. 130 (2015), pp. 4467–4670, which reads: "1. The losses caused to issuers or third persons due to a deficiency in a report or opinion drafted by an auditor must be entirely [*solidariamente*] and in an unlimited way compensated by: (a) Statutory auditors and other persons who had signed the opinion; (b) firms of statutory auditors and other firms of auditors, provided that the audited documents had been signed by one of their members." On this topic see Ganuza and Gómez (2005), pp. 1–25.

[147]Sinde Monteiro (1989), p. 256. It is interesting to note the similarities of this position with Swedish Law and Finnish Law, both of which consider pure economic loss recoverable only when the damage constituted a crime (von Bar 1999c, p. 6).

[148]Pestana de Vasconcelos (2007), pp. 183–191.

Nevertheless, Portuguese case law does not traditionally base claims for "pure economic losses" on this provision, due to some doctrinal variance in the field of protective provisions.[149]

cc) *Abus de droit*

Beyond the situation where a protective provision exists, there is a general approach which takes the view that pure economic loss of relevance in delict[150] occurs every time the conditions listed in Art. 334 CC (*abuso de direito*) are fulfilled,[151] in other words, when damage is committed in breach of good morals. This argument is held both by those who consider this Article to be a general clause of civil liability similar to § 826 BGB, and those who do not.[152]

Art. 334 is said to assume particular importance in the protection of pure economic interests, because it does not require the infringement of an absolute right. Nevertheless, resorting to Art. 334 CC entails practical limitations. Firstly, there must exist an applicable right in the first place (only a right can be abused).[153] Secondly, it requires a particular conduct and a particular degree of fault.[154] Indeed, if someone falls within the respective general freedom of acting (or, as may be the case, freedom of economic initiative),[155] that person cannot be liable for the resulting loss.[156] For this reason, even though some legal scholars support an obligation to compensate loss from market actions not taken in good faith and fair dealing,[157] namely unfair competition rules,[158] it seems difficult to treat them as abusive conduct.[159]

---

[149]Menezes Leitão (2009), pp. 261, 279.

[150]Carneiro da Frada (1997), p. 50.

[151]Santos Silva (2006), p. 834.

[152]See generally Carneiro da Frada (1997), p. 48 ff., in particular 50.

[153]Cf. Carneiro da Frada and Pestana de Vasconcelos (2006), p. 158.

[154]Carneiro da Frada and Pestana de Vasconcelos (2006), p. 158.

[155]Carneiro da Frada (1997), pp. 32–33, fn. 17 and 61 ff. According to Carneiro da Frada, the freedom of economic initiative is not susceptible to individual appropriation and, therefore, it cannot be attributed to individuals in terms of a subjective right (*ibid.*, pp. 61 ff.).

[156]Carneiro da Frada (1997), p. 62; Carneiro da Frada and Pestana de Vasconcelos (2006), p. 158; Carneiro da Frada (2007b), pp. 164–174, fn. 121.

[157]Carneiro da Frada and Pestana de Vasconcelos (2006), p. 158.

[158]On this issue, see generally, Pestana de Vasconcelos (2007), pp. 183–191. For case law see von Bar (2009c), n. 9 to VI–2:208, 527.

[159]Santos Silva (2006), p. 835.

dd) Extension of Absolute Rights

In Germany, the development of liability based upon §§ 823 ff. has been extended by several means.[160]

One such method is the creation of new general clauses within § 823(1) BGB and its extension "*sonstiges Recht*":[161] the right to an established and operative business (*Recht am eingerichteten und ausgeübten Gewerbebetrieb*),[162] the general personality right and duties of care (*Verkehrspflichten*).[163] This extension, which stands in opposition to the *Enumerationsprinzip*,[164] has been largely criticised.[165]

In Portugal, the concept of "*direito de outrem*" (another person's right) has also been reinterpreted,[166] thereby expanding the scope of non-contractual law.

(1) Rights Relating to Personality

The Portuguese Civil Code expressly provides for a general protection of rights relating to personality (*direitos de personalidade*, Art. 70 CC). This would make the recognition of a "general right" to personality unnecessary within the first modality of unlawfulness,[167] a solution Germany has tried to achieve.[168] Nevertheless, in recent decades the judiciary has been at the forefront of the protection of personality rights.[169] They are taking advantage of the general clause (Art. 70 CC), and the fact that personality is also protected by the Constitution.[170] In the settling case law decision 6/2014 of 22 May 2014, two Justices considered that the serious personal injury caused to a man, which led to his spouse assisting him full-time and suffering

[160]According to one theory (Brüggemeier 1982, p. 419, including further references), the expansion would have occurred through admission of prima facie means of proof for causation and fault (*Haftungsverlagerung durch beweisrechtliche Mittel*); the inclusion in § 823(1) BGB of damage caused with organisations, liability *in vigilando* and enlargement of liability of organs; the listing and standardisation of conditions for the classification of a conduct as negligent, which led to a new special category of liability for negligent acts; and the expansion of the scope of § 826 BGB to allow for the protection of economic interests. See also von Bar (1980b), p. 211 ff. and references therein.

[161]Deutsch (1963), pp. 385–390.

[162]For further details see following subsection.

[163]Brüggemeier (1982), p. 419 and references therein for the first case law on each of these novelties.

[164]Deutsch (1963), p. 388; Frank (1979), pp. 586, 589.

[165]See, for example, von Bar (2000b), p. 606.

[166]For the interpretation of the expression in German law, see Schlechtriem (2003), p. 353 ff.

[167]Pires de Lima and Antunes Varela (1987), n. 5 a to Art. 483 CC, p. 472; Menezes Leitão (2009), p. 558 ff.; Menezes Cordeiro (2010b), p. 447.

[168]von Caemmerer (1968), p. 102 ff.; von Bar (1981), p. 1763 *passim*.

[169]On the protection of personality rights, see Capelo de Sousa (1978), Leite de Campos (2009), Capelo de Sousa (1995).

[170]Menezes Cordeiro (2002), pp. 1229 and 1245.

as a result of his condition, consisted of a direct and serious breach of the fundamental right to personality development.[171]

(2) Loss for Impairment of Use

An important expansion to Art. 483(1), 1st part relates the right of property[172] to impairment of use.[173]

The question of the recoverability of harm resulting from impairment of use has long been discussed by legal scholars,[174] and has been variously interpreted by the courts. It seems to be particularly favoured by courts in the case of loss resulting from impairment of use of motor vehicles,[175] where even non-economic loss has been compensated.[176]

(3) Right to Enterprise

As referred to above, one of the most debated general clauses developed from § 823 (1) BGB is the so-called "right to an established and operative business" (*Recht am eingerichteten und ausgeübten Gewerbebetrieb*).[177]

This matrix is said to have come into being[178] at the beginning of the twentieth century through the German *Reichsgericht,* to protect enterprises against unlawful direct interference in the respective business (called *direkt und unmittelbar* and later *betriebsbezogener Eingriff*).[179] As for its scope, the "right to an established and operative business" includes the cases of patent rights, servitudes, house property, trademarks and fishing rights.[180] Some scholars criticise the development

---

[171] Settling case law decision 6/2014 of 22 May 2014, p. 2937, p. 2939.

[172] For Germany see Möschel (1977), pp. 1–4.

[173] Almeida Costa (2006a), pp. 592–594; Menezes Leitão (2013), p. 301. For details on the loss resulting from impairment of use see generally Gomes (1986), pp. 169–239. Within the case law see, *inter alia*, STJ 29 May 2014, proc. 130/09.3TBCBC.G1.S1 and STJ 26 February 2015, proc. 693/10.0TVPRT.C1.P1.S1. See, however, STJ 17 November 1998, proc. 98A977. As for the DCFR, VI.–2:206 ("Loss upon impairment of property or lawful possession") "includes being deprived of the use of property" (2, *lit.* a).

[174] See generally Abrantes Geraldes (2007a).

[175] See, however, STJ 12 January 2006, proc. 05B4176; RP 8 July 1997, *BolMinJus* 469 (1997), p. 663; Miranda Barbosa (2006a), p. 212. In favour, STJ 9 May 1995, *BolMinJus* 457 (1995), p. 325; Menezes Leitão (2013), p. 301.

[176] STJ 23 January 2001, proc.00A3525; RE 26 March 1980, *CJ* 5 (1980–2), p. 96. See however STJ 4 December 2003, proc. 03B3030. In Germany, BGHZ 153, p. 159; BGH *NJW* 1977, p. 2264. For a discussion, see generally von Bar (1992c), p. 28 ff.

[177] Fabricius (1961), p. 304 ff.; Wolf (1967).

[178] Sinde Monteiro (1989), p. 206, fn. 102.

[179] Schlechtriem (1998), p. 11; van Dam (2013), p. 211. For an overview of case law see references in BGHZ 29, p. 65.

[180] Opoku (1972), p. 233.

of this legal concept.[181] Others argue that the expression "*sonstiges Recht*" has been intended by the legislature to comprise only "rights comparable to property".[182]

The right is not expressly protected in the Civil Code,[183] despite the best efforts of the main drafter, Vaz Serra.[184]

The transposition of this legal matrix to the Portuguese legal order has been defended by some academics,[185] particularly where it relates to repairing losses caused to businesses which cannot be integrated either within the scope of Art. 483 (1), 1st part CC or Art. 334.[186] In severe cases,[187] particularly whenever there is an *abus de droit,*[188] an unlawful loss of business could lead to a claim for damages.[189]

With the exception of an isolated decision of the Constitutional Court,[190] the principle has still not been generally recognised.[191] Some scholars consider it an "expendable burden",[192] stating that it is up to Competition Law to decide which conducts are unlawful.[193]

b) Compensation in Contractual Liability

In Portugal, as in Germany, pure economic loss is greatly compensated through contractual or contract-like mechanisms.[194]

In the area of contract law, pure economic loss is a common consequence of the breach of contractual duties[195] and every legal system admits its compensation,[196]

---

181 An autonomous presence in the BGB has been defended (von Bar 1981, p. 1793 *passim*).

182 Schlechtriem (1998), pp. 1 and 9.

183 Santos Silva (2006), p. 836.

184 Vaz Serra (1960a), p. 11.

185 Sinde Monteiro (1989), pp. 206–222; Calvão da Silva (1990), p. 360, no. 4.

186 Menezes Leitão (2009), p. 835.

187 Vaz Serra (1960a), p. 11; Almeida Costa (2006a), p. 83.

188 Carneiro da Frada (1997), p. 50.

189 Vaz Serra (1960a), p. 11; Almeida Costa (2006a), p. 83. In case law, STJ 19 March 2002, *CJ (ST)* 10 (2002–1), p. 138.

190 The Constitutional Court considered the right to form an enterprise to be guaranteed by the Constitution (TC 12 July 1990, proc. 89-0102).

191 Santos Silva (2006), pp. 826–838.

192 Menezes Leitão (2009), p. 569; Menezes Cordeiro (2010b), p. 447.

193 Menezes Leitão (2009), p. 835. On the "right to form and run a business enterprise" see generally Schmidt (1993), pp. 985–992; Schildt (1996), pp. 2261–2266. See also Schlechtriem (1998), pp. 9–13; von Bar (1998a), pp. 64–66; Brüggemeier (2006), pp. 361–375; von Bar (2009c), n. 6 to VI.–2:208, pp. 525–526 (with case law references). For criticism see, in particular, von Caemmerer (1968), p. 89 ff.; Deutsch (1963), p. 387; Frank (1979), p. 586.

194 On contractual solutions for recovery of third party loss see, generally, Mersinis 1999.

195 Schlechtriem (1998), p. 1.

196 Koziol (2004), p. 145. Contract remedies are particularly employed in Germany, not only due to the tight constraints caused by the *Enumerationsprinzip* (Koziol 2006, p. 878 ff.).

independent of fault, or at least without the need for intention on the part of the person inflicting the loss.[197] Contract liability is considered by many to be the best place to protect pure economic interests.[198] Indeed, within contract liability the problem of exclusion—the floodgates argument—is avoided because the circle of claimants is, by its nature, limited,[199] and reparation does not involve additional duties of care. Furthermore, there is a relation of proximity to the affected person[200] and the *pacta sunt servanda* principle,[201] together with the principle of *neminem laedere,* is said to impose compensation anyway.

There are, however, limitations to the recovery of pure economic loss in contract law for those indirectly affected.[202] This is particularly the case because, as described earlier, the Portuguese legal scholarship does not generally accept the doctrine of external efficacy of obligations.[203] Even those who consider credit rights to be protected within non-contractual liability arising out of damage caused to another recognise that it is uncommon, due to the difficulties in fulfilling the remaining conditions of liability that are usually faced in these cases.[204]

c) Compensation in Near-Contractual Liability

The category of *quasi-vertragliche Haftung* (*vertragliche Verkehrssicherungspflichten*)[205] is a borderline case lying between contract and non-contractual liability. A German judicial creation,[206] it has also had an impact on the Portuguese legal scholarship.

---

[197]Koziol (2004), p. 153.

[198]van Boom (2004), p. 37 ff. In a case related to loss sustained by family carers, the STJ expressly recognised that, had the carer (daughter) undertaken a contract of provision of care with the mother, her foregone wages would have been compensated (STJ 26 February 2003, proc. 3B3604).

[199]von Bar and Drobnig (2004), p. 132.

[200]Koziol (2004), p. 153.

[201]Cf. *ibid.*, p. 146, with further arguments.

[202]Carneiro da Frada and Pestana de Vasconcelos (2006), p. 158.

[203]For a detailed account, see Koziol (2004), pp. 145–146; Koziol (2006), p. 879. On the extension of contractual liability for protection of pure economic interests in Germany, see Schlechtriem (1998), pp. 16–19.

[204]Menezes Cordeiro (2010b), p. 448.

[205]von Bar (1982), pp. 637–654. For a classification of the cases which integrate this "*tertium genus* of liability", see Brüggemeier (1982), p. 420 (including further references). For a detailed account see Schlechtriem (1998), pp. 20–21; Schäfer and Ott (2005), pp. 291–295 *passim*, critical on p. 297. In the case law see BGH *NJW* 1962, p. 31; BGH *NJW* 1977, p. 376; BGH *NJW* 1979, p. 643; BGHZ 66, p. 51.

[206]Most of these "tort-like" instruments of liability have been included in the Act on the Modernisation of the Law of Obligations (*Gesetz zur Modernisierung des Schuldrechts*) of 29 November 2001, published in BGBl I, no. 61, p. 3138 ff. See von Bar and Drobnig (2004), pp. 132–133.

The category resulted from stretching the limits of contractual liability, as provided for in the Portuguese Civil Code, to encompass liability for breach of ("implied") duties of care.[207] The emergence of near-contractual liability[208] was due to the lacunae in the reparation of pure economic loss in contractual and non-contractual liability.[209] This "third kind of liability" permits the reparation of pure economic loss in cases where there was no duty to act towards the protection of such a loss,[210] but where there was nonetheless some reliance on such protection.[211] As a result, there have been attempts to classify these cases under a general "theory for liability based upon reliance" (*teoria da confiança, Vertrauenshaftung*).[212]

The nature of near-contractual liability has also been debated. While some legal scholars highlight its contractual nature[213] and classify it as a "*Sonder-Deliktsrecht*",[214] others hold that it is of a non-contractual nature[215] and only comes close to contract law in its effects.[216] Still others say it is both contractual and non-contractual.[217]

Despite having some strong supporters, near-contractual liability is heavily criticised, particularly in Germany[218] but also in Portugal. This trend of near-contractual liability gave *momentum* to a current, sustained "hypertrophy" of contract law,[219] of which these pseudo-mechanisms are a sort of "illegitimate children".[220]

---

[207]von Bar and Drobnig (2004), pp. 132–133.

[208]For the areas that non-contractual liability took from contracts see Brüggemeier (1982), p. 419 f.

[209]Markesinis and Unberath (2002), p. 59. The reason for extending the protection to the field of near contracts is related to other weaknesses of non-contractual liability, namely the exculpation possibility in § 823(1), 2nd part BGB, and the fact that the burden of proof lies with the person who suffered the loss (Schmidt-Kessel 2006, p. 21).

[210]Carneiro da Frada and Pestana de Vasconcelos (2006), p. 158.

[211]van Boom (2004), p. 22.

[212]In Germany, Canaris is considered the *caput scholae* of liability based on reliance (Carneiro da Frada 1994, p. 249). See Canaris (1965), pp. 475–482; Canaris (1971) and Canaris (1983b), pp. 85 ff. In Portugal, this theory is particularly endorsed by Carneiro da Frada. See Carneiro da Frada (1997), Carneiro da Frada (2007a), Carneiro da Frada (2007b).

[213]Conduct which affects recognised economic interests is considered "contractual duties of care", firstly because of its closeness to contractual relationships and secondly because the scope of liability is increased, in these cases, to that provided for contractual liability within the BGB. For details see Brüggemeier (1982), pp. 422 ff.

[214]Brüggemeier (1982), p. 424.

[215]ibid., pp. 423–424.

[216]According to Canaris, this liability would involve not a contractual interest but, rather, the interest of the "integrity of the remaining legal goods" (*Integrität der übrigen Rechtsgüter*) and thus the difference would be in degree but not in principle (Canaris 1983b, p. 90).

[217]Jansen (2007), p. 39.

[218]For criticism of near-contracts see von Bar (2001c), p. 219 *passim*.

[219]von Caemmerer (1968), p. 56 ff.; Schlechtriem (1981), p. 1600.

[220]von Bar (1982), pp. 637 and 643.

aa) Pre-Contractual Liability

One of the institutions called upon to repair pure economic loss is pre-contractual liability (*culpa in contrahendo*),[221] i.e. liability occurring during the negotiation of a contract[222] (*responsabilidade pré-contratual*).[223] This is despite the fact that the condition can only be drawn from the law de *lege lata* (Art. 227 CC),[224] and the scope of the nature of this cause of action remains disputed.[225]

bb) Loss for Inducement to Breach a Contractual Obligation

According to Art. 734 of the Preliminary Draft of the Civil Code, if someone fails to perform a contractual duty through enticement by a third party, that third party is liable under *abus de droit*.[226] The provision, however, did not pass into the Civil Code.[227]

Art. 490 CC provides that where several authors, instigators or auxiliaries commit an unlawful act, all are liable, although this does not necessarily involve the breach of a contractual obligation.[228] According to Art. 406(2) CC (principle of relativity of contractual obligations), a contract cannot affect persons other than the parties to whom it refers and, as outlined, the doctrine of external efficacy of obligations is generally not accepted. According to the general rule, therefore, only the person induced to breach the contract is liable under contract law (and not the person inducing the breach of contract under non-contractual liability arising out of damage caused to another).[229] The person sustaining the harm must rely on a contractual mechanism, such as an attachment to the rights of the person induced to breach the contract, as against the person inducing the breach of contract (*"commodum" de representação*), to see his or her loss repaired.

---

[221] Menezes Cordeiro (1984a), p. 585; Carneiro da Frada (1997), p. 38; Carneiro da Frada and Pestana de Vasconcelos (2006), p. 175. In the German legal scholarship see Canaris (1983b), p. 90.

[222] Almeida Costa (2006a), pp. 298–312.

[223] Almeida Costa (2006a), p. 301. See also von Bar (1998c), p. 3.

[224] This provision reads: "the person who negotiates with another for the conclusion of a contract shall, in the preparation of such contract and its formation, act according to good faith, or otherwise must compensate the loss it culpably causes to the other party". For an analysis see Antunes Varela (2000), pp. 269 ff.

[225] Schlechtriem (1998), p. 8; Palmer and Bussani (2007), p. 257. It is considered that *culpa in contrahendo* should be dealt with within non-contractual liability law (BGH *NJW* 1982, p. 2431; von Bar 1982, p. 645), where the law would provide for a "satisfactory basic regulation". See Almeida Costa (2006a), p. 301.

[226] Vaz Serra, *BolMinJus* 85 (1959c), p. 345 f.

[227] Sinde Monteiro (2007), p. 457.

[228] In this section, von Bar (2009c), n. 10 to VI.–2:211, pp. 553–554 is closely followed.

[229] Antunes Varela (2000), p. 179.

Inducement to breach of contract is particularly relevant in competition law.[230] Due to the lack of express regulation, the courts have used some creative techniques to grant a claim for reparation, e.g. basing the claim on offence to credit, in Art. 484 CC.[231] Legal scholars have also defended exceptions to the principle of relativity of contractual obligations to accommodate claims based on inducement to breach of contract,[232] but this does not correspond to the prevailing opinion, either in academic scholarship, or in case law.[233]

cc) Contract with Protective Efficacy Towards Third Parties

The fact that no non-contractual consequences arise to the debtor who did not perform his or her contractual duty (at least according to the prevailing opinion) does not mean that contractual parties do not have duties of care towards third parties.[234]

A contract for the benefit of third parties (*contrato com eficácia de proteção para terceiros,*[235] *Vertrag mit Schutzwirkung für Dritte*) is an example of a device that leads to "contractual liability without a contract".[236]

It consists of a judicially created[237] variation to the contract in favour of third parties (*contrato a favor de terceiros, Vertrag zugunsten Dritter*),[238] provided for in Art. 443 CC. In this case, the third party is in a relationship of such proximity to the creditor that the circle of protection of the contract is justifiably extended to him or her. However, the third party does not acquire a right to performance, but is protected only by the duties of good faith and fair dealing that the law imposes in relation to the parties, the infringement of which give rise to a claim for damages for losses incurred.[239]

---

[230]STJ 29 September 1995, *BolMinJus* 449 (1995), p. 374; Alarcão (1983), p. 84; Antunes Varela (2000), p. 177.

[231]STJ 18 December 2013, proc. 6479/09.8TBBRG.G1.S1.

[232]Menezes Cordeiro (1986), p. 251; Galvão Telles (1997), p. 554.

[233]STJ 25 October 1993, *BolMinJus* 430 (1993), p. 455; STJ 19 March 2002 *CJ (ST)* 10 (2002-1), p. 138; Vaz Serra, *BolMinJus* 85 (1959), pp. 345–360; Antunes Varela (2000), p. 176; Almeida Costa (2006a), p. 81. With further reference see Santos Silva (2006), pp. 826–838.

[234]Carneiro da Frada (1997), p. 88.

[235]*ibid.* This institution is also called "*contrato de proteção em relação a terceiros*". See Menezes Cordeiro (1984b), p. 619 ff.; Sinde Monteiro (1989), pp. 518 ff.; Carneiro da Frada (1994), pp. 43–44; pp. 71–72, 143; Carneiro da Frada (2007b), p. 103 ff.

[236]von Bar (1998c), p. 3.

[237]*ibid.*, p. 4. This doctrine arose in 1917 (RGZ 91, p. 21 ff.).

[238]Markesinis and Unberath (2002), p. 59; Medicus and Petersen (2011), pp. 423–424. For an analysis of contracts in favour of third parties, see generally Leite de Campos (2009).

[239]Menezes Leitão (2013), p. 341.

Despite not being party to the contract, a third person could be granted a claim for reparation of harm due to the infringement of secondary contractual obligations (*deveres acessórios*).[240]

This principle is thus neither purely contractual nor exactly aligned with non-contractual liability arising out of damage caused to another,[241] as it does not involve a general duty of abstention.[242] Still, it has been considered "a tortious safety valve: the greater the pressure, the more legal competence is transferred to contract law".[243]

This principle seems applicable in theory to the reparation of ricochet loss and opens up a path for the recognition of the external efficacy of obligations.[244] Within it, the proximity of a third person to the creditor would justify the extension of the circle of protection.[245] However, this position has been considered too narrow.[246]

dd) Recovery of a Third Party Loss

As described earlier, the case of transferred loss involves a debtor, a creditor and a person who sustained the loss, who is, at the same time, a third party to the contractual relationship. On the one hand, the party to the contractual relationship does not have a cause of action under the law for an infringement of his or her rights, as he or she did not sustain any harm. On the other hand, however, the third party sustained harm, despite no infringement of his or her rights. The problem in this situation, apart from the disadvantage for the person sustaining the loss, is that the debtor is exonerated by this unfortunate combination of events.[247] One of these mechanisms for repairing pure economic loss has, therefore, been developed.

(1) Subrogation

One of these mechanisms is subrogation. Art. 593(1) CC provides for its effects through the substitution of the third party into the legal position of the original

[240]Carneiro da Frada (1994), p. 89; Markesinis and Unberath (2002), p. 59; Menezes Leitão (2013), p. 328.

[241]But see Luther (2013), p. 575.

[242]See von Bar and Drobnig (2004), p. 132.

[243]von Bar (1998c), p. 5. See also von Bar (1982), pp. 641–642.

[244]von Bar (1998c), pp. 4–5.

[245]Menezes Leitão (2013), p. 328.

[246]Carneiro da Frada (1994), p. 91. For the consideration that the protected third party need not be in a close personal relationship with the creditor see von Bar and Drobnig (2004), p. 132. For details see Gomes (2011).

[247]von Bar (1998c), pp. 10–11 *passim*.

creditor[248] or direct victim".[249] There are two kinds of subrogation: contractual subrogation (which results from an agreement between the third person and the original creditor) and statutory subrogation.

This legal principle is frequently referred to in practice as it allows recovery of the loss without affecting the position of the original creditor or the debtor.[250]

*(2) Recovery of a Third Party Loss (*Drittschadensliquidation*)*

(a) A German-Based Judicial Device

Recovery of a third party loss (*Drittschadensliquidation*)[251] is a judge-made doctrine[252] which allows a creditor to a contract to claim for loss resulting from the non-performance or defective performance of the contracted act to a third party, due to a shift of responsibility (*Schadensverlagerung*).[253]

The legal concept, which involves an exception to the principle of parallel injury and loss (*Parallelität von Verletzung und Schaden*)[254] is considered one of the principles which the legislature encouraged the courts to develop to fill lacunae.[255]

---

[248] Almeida Costa (2006a), p. 825.

[249] *ibid.*, pp. 821–822, fn. 3. See also Vaz Serra (1960a), pp. 23–24.

[250] Almeida Costa (2006a), pp. 821–822.

[251] The forerunner of the development of the liquidation of third party loss was a case in the second half of the nineteenth century which, curiously, involved Portugal and Germany. For a description of the case see von Caemmerer (1965), pp. 241–242; Carneiro da Frada (2006), p. 98, fn. 114; Oliveira e Sá (2007), p. 210; Mota Pinto (2008b), p. 805, fn. 2263.

[252] von Caemmerer (1965), p. 243; Hagen (1971), p. 102; Berg (1977), p. 365 ff.; Lange and Schiemann (2003), p. 462. The *Drittschadensliquidation* is considered a "rare species of judicial creativity" the development of which is achieved by means of reliance on judicial precedent (von Caemmerer 1965, p. 245).

[253] See Santos Silva (2007), p. 25; Mota Pinto (2008b), p. 804, fn. 2263; Medicus and Petersen (2011), p. 423. According to Medicus, the transfer of what was obtained to the third person is a matter of internal relations, and in case of need one may resort to § 281 BGB (Medicus 2003, p. 616). Banakas (1989), p. 201.

[254] Deutsch (1996b), p. 69.

[255] Markesinis (2000), p. 298, fn. 24. In Germany, and despite the fact that some commissioners in the draft of the BGB (Mugdan 1899, pp. 517–518) proposed rules prescribing when a third party loss would be recoverable, the question was ultimately unanswered and left to the courts to develop a solution outside of the BGB (Unberath 2003, p. 85).

(b) Characteristics and Categories

This mechanism is recognised as a "trick" to ensure reparation because the person who would have a claim for reparation could recover the loss sustained by another had it been sustained by him or herself.[256]

The principle thus involves an exception to the so-called "doctrine of the creditor's interest" (*dogma do interesse do credor, Dogma vom Gläubigerinteresse*),[257] according to which a creditor can claim, as a rule, for his or her own loss only[258] and not for the loss of indirect victims.[259]

Unlike the contracts with protective efficacy towards third parties, the mechanism of recovery of a third party loss does not affect the notion of relativity of contract (*Relativität der Rechtspflichten*)[260] as it does not enable the third party to sue directly.[261] This makes this legal solution inappropriate for third parties who have suffered consequential loss or pure economic loss which is reparable by a protective provision or in the context of *abus de droit*.[262] Moreover, by not enabling a direct claim by the person who sustained the loss, this type of contract plays an important role in risk limitation (*Risikobegrenzung*).[263]

---

[256]Medicus and Petersen (2011), p. 423. The problem of the divergence between the formal title to claim compensation and the substantial loss exists as long as "loss" is considered to be a patrimonial subtraction (von Caemmerer 1965, p. 241 ff.); Canaris (1983a), p. 148; Junker (1991), p. 23 ff., p. 47 ff.; Junker 1993, pp. 348–368). Academic proponents of an objective concept of damage deny that there is a liquidation of a third party loss, affirming instead that the loss is suffered by the owner of the object or the claimant seeking compensation (Larenz 1987, p. 463 ff.; Würthwein 2001, pp. 422–423; Medicus and Petersen 2011, p. 423). Some legal scholars suggest resorting to "compensation of advantages" (*Vorteilsausgleichung*) to solve cases of recovery of a third party loss (Knobbe-Keuk 1972, pp. 196–198; Büdenbender 1995, pp. 920–921).

[257]Lange and Schiemann (2003), p. 456; Oliveira e Sá (2007), p. 209.

[258]Vaz Serra (1959a) in particular, p. 103; Mota Pinto (2008b), p. 803, fn. 2263. In the German literature, see von Caemmerer (1965), pp. 241–279; Neuner (1999), pp. 126–127; Staudinger-Schiemann (2005), § 249, no. 62 ff.

[259]Rebmann and Krüger (2016), § 249, no. 281.

[260]Carneiro da Frada (1997), p. 24; Traugott (1997), pp. 16–18. For a critical account see Luther (2013), p. 574. Luther criticises the principle as such, as he considers "absolute rights" to be relative, because the person infringing them is liable only for the person affected.

[261]Markesinis and Unberath (2002), p. 64; Unberath (2003), p. 85; Mota Pinto (2008b), p. 804, fn. 2263. For further differences, see Windelen (1996), pp. 19–27, in particular pp. 26–27; Traugott (1997); Medicus (2003), pp. 616–621, in particular pp. 618 and 619; Carneiro da Frada (2006), pp. 97–100; Carneiro da Frada (2007b), p. 140, fn. 108. For a detailed account of the differences between the contracts with protective efficacy towards third parties and the mechanism of recovery of third party loss, see Doobe (2014), pp. 76–82, in particular pp. 81–82. In addition to the liquidation of losses of third parties and the contract of protection of third parties, Medicus says that another exception to the doctrine of the interest of the creditor can be achieved through the extension of non-contractual law, either through the duties of care (*Verkehrspflichten*); the "other right" (sonstigesRecht) at § 823(1) BGB; protective laws (*Schutzgesetze*) at § 823(3) BGB; or the extensive interpretation of § 826 BGB (Medicus 2003, p. 613).

[262]von Bar (1998c), p. 12.

[263]Oliveira e Sá (2007), p. 210.

A few common elements unite the significant variety of cases that are brought under the banner of *Drittschadensliquidation*.[264]

Firstly, the floodgates argument cannot be invoked here. Only one person sustains the harm[265] thus liability is not extended beyond the level calculable by the debtor.[266]

Secondly, in all of these cases the person who has suffered the loss has no remedy while the person who has the remedy has suffered no loss. If such a situation remains unchallenged, the defaulting party would never face the consequences of the negligent conduct.[267] He or she would benefit from the risk transfer (*Gefahrverlagerung*), contravening the basic principles of the law of damages.[268] This is magnified by the fact that the party inflicting the harm usually knows nothing about the relationship between the owner of the interest and the third party.[269] Furthermore, the insurer of the party inflicting the harm may receive an undeserved windfall and, finally, and more particularly, the person who sustained the loss would be left without redress, opening up a "legal black hole".[270] In cases where the third party does not wish to recover the loss, the claim of the owner of the right collapses,[271] which would avoid a potentially unjustified enrichment at the expense of the debtor. This legal mechanism thus not only provides an effective solution to the relationship between the contracting parties, but also to the relationship between the third party and the owner of the right.[272] For all of these reasons, there is a trend towards admitting reparation of transferred loss.[273]

The loss to be remedied cannot, however, go beyond that which would have been compensated had it occurred to the creditor.[274] The risk of the debtor must remain the same (*Schadensidentität*).[275] An increase in the amount of the loss would only be justified if the conditions of a contract for the benefit of a third party were

[264]Markesinis and Unberath (2002), pp. 214, 216. Tägert was likely the first author to identify these common features (Tägert 1938, p. 35 ff.).

[265]Medicus (2003), p. 614.

[266]Cf. Banakas (1989), p. 206.

[267]von Bar (1998c), p. 11. See also Carneiro da Frada (2006), p. 98; Mota Pinto (2008b), p. 804, fn. 2263.

[268]See BGH *NJW* 1977, p. 1283; BGHZ 7, p. 30; BGHZ 21, p. 112. Although admitting that the removal of responsibility from the person inflicting the harm could lead to problems with the preventative aim of liability (Luther 2013, p. 582), others argue that this must be grounded within the law of damages (*ibid.*, pp. 574–575).

[269]Büttner (2006), p. 10; Münch-Komm (2016), §249, no. 289.

[270]Markesinis and Unberath (2002), pp. 66–67.

[271]RGZ 115, 419, 426; BGH *WM* 1987, 581, p. 582.

[272]Unberath (2003), pp. 89–90.

[273]Banakas (1989), pp. 201–202; Unberath (2003).

[274]Decku (1997), p. 10; Doobe (2014), p. 80. See also Unberath (2003), p. 89. See also BGH *NJW* 1963, 2071, p. 2076.

[275]Medicus (2003), pp. 616–617 and 621.

satisfied.[276] This mechanism is thus inappropriate to repair ricochet loss, which is usually of a different order than the financial loss suffered by the creditor.

In addition to the cases where the recovery of a third party loss is agreed upon between the parties (*Drittschadensliquidation kraft Vereinbarung*)[277]—and although there is no unanimously accepted classification[278]—there are, traditionally, four clusters of cases encountered in the recovery of a third party loss.[279] These are: cases of indirect agency (*mittelbare Stellvertretung*);[280] the so-called *obligatorische Gefahrentlastung*;[281] the guardianship of an item of a third party (*Obhutspflichten für Sachen eines Dritten*);[282] and trusteeship (*Treuhandverhältnisse*).[283] The courts have been reluctant to extend the scope of the institution and the BGH dismissed its application to the facts of the "cable cases" and situations of product liability.[284]

While some German legal scholars are in favour of extending the concept of *Drittschadensliquidation,*[285] others remain extremely critical. Recently, it has been argued that only when the system has lacunae are the courts entitled to develop the law, and that there is no such gap filled by the mechanism of recovery of third party loss.[286] The developed concept should not, therefore, be admissible.[287] Some scholars endorse its replacement by other legal principles,[288] such as *Vertretung im Vertrauen*, the contract with protective efficacy towards third parties and aids in performance of duties.

---

[276]Knobbe-Keuk (1972), p. 197; Heck (2011), p. 53; Larenz (1987), p. 464; Büdenbender (2000), pp. 986–992, especially p. 987. In the Portuguese legal scholarship see Vaz Serra (1959a), pp. 112–113.

[277]See Medicus (2000), p. 611 ff.; Medicus (2003), p. 617; Staudinger-Schiemann (2005), § 249, no. 68.

[278]Banakas (1989), p. 206. Banakas includes the cases of loss caused by a statutory transfer of risk of a particular transaction (such as in the context of the *Versendungskauf*). See von Caemmerer (1965), p. 235; Esser (2000a), pp. 266–268; Banakas (1989), p. 206. Fikentscher suggests the following alternative classification: indirect representation (*mittelbare Stellvertretung*), transferred loss (*schuldrechtlicher Schadensverlagerung*), *legatee* (*Vermächtnisnehmer*). See Fikentscher (2006), p. 308.

[279]Vaz Serra (1959a); Mattamouros (2006), pp. 303–333; Mota Pinto (2008b), p. 804, fn. 2263. Among the German legal scholars, see Lange and Schiemann (2003), pp. 471–473.

[280]Lange and Schiemann (2003), pp. 466–469.

[281]For details see Mota Pinto (2008b), pp. 804 ff., fn. 2263. See also Lange and Schiemann (2003), pp. 464–465; Medicus (2003), p. 616.

[282]Mota Pinto (2008b), p. 804, fn. 2263.

[283]Doobe (2014), p. 81. See also Banakas (1989), p. 206; Oliveira e Sá (2007), pp. 212–213.

[284]Markesinis and Unberath (2002), pp. 65–65.

[285]See, for example, Traugott (1997).

[286]Luther (2013), pp. 575 and 583. The author argues that this institution is "superfluous" (ibid., p. 603).

[287]Luther (2013), p. 600.

[288]Hagen (1971), p. 137; Larenz (1987), p. 466. For details see Oliveira e Sá (2007), pp. 225–234.

The BGH seems open to the creation of a contractual duty on the owner of the right to assign the right of action to the third party[289] or to account for the damages recovered.

(c) Recovery of a Third Party Loss in Portugal

The recovery of third party loss has spread from Germany to several other legal systems, including the English[290] and the Portuguese.[291]

According to Art. 575(2) of the summarised version of the preliminary draft of the Civil Code proposed by Vaz Serra: "if, at the date of the injury, by virtue of a specific statutory provision or pre-existing legal relationship between the creditor of compensation and a third party, the loss, which should affect the former, is produced in the sphere of the latter or is transferred to him or her later, that creditor may seek reparation of the loss suffered". The third party would then be entitled to receive reparation from the creditor of compensation, irrespective of whether or not a statutory provision granted him or her such right.[292]

The present-day Civil Code does not contain the provisions proposed by Vaz Serra. The creditor's interest theory is implicitly enshrined in the Portuguese Civil Code, meaning that only the person whose right or interest was directly harmed has a right to compensation. Nevertheless, there are exceptions to this principle,[293] such as those described earlier. One of these is provided for in Art. 496(2) CC and in Art. 495(2) CC.[294] The extent to which an exception shall be made in this case remains to be seen. According to one opinion, however, the rules which, in German Law, may justify the recovery of a third party loss in most situations of "obligational liberation" of the risk (as is the case of § 447 BGB) do not apply in the Portuguese legal system, where the creation and transmission of property rights is achieved *solo consensus* (Art. 408(1) CC).[295]

Some authors endorse the view that situations of transfer of risk between the creditor and the third party sustaining the loss should be treated as one entity for compensation purposes, which would imply that situations which involved the creditor (such as contributory fault) would rebound in the outcome of the claim.[296]

---

[289]See BGH *ZIP* 1998, pp. 511, 512. The legal basis could be an implied term or an analogy to § 285(1) BGB. See Unberath (2003), p. 90.

[290]The trend in English law seems to be to apply reasoning similar to *Drittschadensliquidation* instead of extending recoverability of pure economic loss in tort (Markesinis and Unberath 2002, p. 66). See, *inter alia*, *Ross v Caunters* [1980] Ch. 297 and *Leigh and Sillavan v Aliakmon Shipping Co. Ltd. (The Aliakmon)* [1986] AC 785. For a similar approach, see Lord Clyde's speech in *Alfred McAlpine Construction Ltd. v Panatown Ltd.* (No. 1) [2001] 1 AC 518, p. 529. For a detailed account see Banakas (1989), pp. 207–208; Doobe (2014), p. 140 ff.

[291]Mota Pinto (2008b), p. 809. See also Oliveira e Sá (2007), pp. 244–245.

[292]Vaz Serra (1960c), p. 131.

[293]Antunes Varela (2000), pp. 620 ff., fn. 177; Almeida Costa (2006a), pp. 608 ff.

[294]Mattamouros (2006), pp. 325 and 330. But see Mota Pinto (2008b), p. 809, fn. 2263.

[295]Mota Pinto (2008b), p. 808, fn. 2263.

[296]Banakas (1989), p. 206. For a detailed account see Deutsch (1976), p. 485.

4. The Arguable Conservativism of Portuguese Non-Contractual Law Towards Pure Economic Loss

Within the discussion and consideration of the process of harmonisation or possible unification of European Private Law,[297] the legal systems of Europe were classified according to their openness to compensate for pure economic loss. The various systems were described as *liberal*, *pragmatic* or *conservative*.[298]

The main characteristic of liberal systems is their inclusion of a general clause of liability in the codified law which does not exclude the possibility of compensating pure economic loss, and thereby deal with the reparation of this loss strictly in non-contractual liability arising out of damage caused to another. The French system would clearly be a liberal system in this categorisation. It allows compensation of loss in general (provided that one proves *faute*) and thereby also of "pure economic loss" which, it has been seen, is not recognised as a category on its own.[299] A limitation of liability would be through other mechanisms, such as rules of causation for example,[300] to avoid a flood of claims.[301]

As for the pragmatic systems, they are characterised by the case-by-case nature of their decisions on the compensation of pure economic loss, where they openly take policy considerations into account. Compensation for pure economic loss would be excluded from non-contractual liability through the "duty of care concept", and an example of this legal system is that of England.[302]

Finally, the conservative regimes are those where pure economic interests are excluded from the absolute rights protected by their laws on non-contractual liability arising out of damage caused to another. In these systems, compensation for pure economic loss often occurs through other means, either through specific provisions or by the application of contractual mechanisms. As a result of this, such "conservative" systems would be, in practice, "liberal" or "pragmatic" systems by another name.[303]

The authors of this system of categorisation classified both Portugal and Germany as conservative legal regimes.[304]

The "conservative" character of the Portuguese and the German systems of non-contractual liability arising out of damage caused to another creates some "optical illusions".[305] On the one hand, they deliberately exclude reparation of pure

[297]Parisi (2003), p. 75.

[298]Palmer and Bussani (2007), pp. 222–260.

[299]See Deschamps (1998), p. 367.

[300]Bussani and Palmer n.d, p. 697 ff.; Miranda Barbosa (2015), p. 256, fn. 23 and p. 221.

[301]Palmer and Bussani (2007), pp. 222–223.

[302]*ibid.*, pp. 223–224.

[303]*ibid.*, p. 224. For this reason, some legal commentators consider there to be few differences in terms of outcome (Howarth 2011, p. 863). For this discussion see generally Bussani and Palmer (2003b).

[304]Palmer and Bussani (2007), pp. 252–260.

[305]Sacco (1991), p. 27 ff.

economic loss in their respective civil codes. On the other hand, they progressively tried to find ways to compensate the insufficiencies of the general provisions of liability in protecting pure economic loss.[306] They achieved reparation of pure economic loss through extension of the categories of unlawfulness and their concepts,[307] i.e. through the extension of the category of absolute rights,[308] but also through the extension of the scope of protective provisions,[309] which traditionally already protects pure economic interests.[310] In the case of the Portuguese system, in addition to the special provisions in the Portuguese Civil Code and Art. 483(1), 2nd part CC, which provide for reparation of pure economic loss as a rule, reparation for this loss has been grounded in Art. 334 CC, similar to § 826 BGB. In addition, contract[311] or near-contractual devices have been applied.[312] These mechanisms work in practise as "tortious safety valves",[313] which allow the judge to "pull through the window [through granting of a claim of reparation] what they pushed out the door [through *ilicitude* or *Rechtswidrigkeit*]".

Therefore, and even though financial interests are not as comprehensively protected as other interests, there is indeed a considerable frame of protection[314] in contract law, near-contract law and non-contractual law.[315]

[306]von Bar (2000a), p. 38; van Dam (2013), p. 213.

[307]Huber (1978), pp. 359–360; von Bar (1994b), p. 103; Schlechtriem (1998), p. 4 ff.; von Bar (2000a), p. 54; von Bar (2000b), p. 606.

[308]See von Bar (1999c). See also von Bar (1982), p. 645. For the extension of the concept of "*Eigentum*", see Schlechtriem (1998), pp. 7–9. (For criticism of such extension, see von Bar (1999c), p. 13, fn. 34; von Bar 2000b, p. 605 ff.).

[309]Schäfer and Ott (2005), p. 300. The BGH also believed that pure economic loss ought to be protected through the diffusion of the subjective conditions of § 826 BGB (BGH *NJW* 1993, p. 2931, p. 2934. See also von Bar 1982, p. 645), bringing it closer to the "objectified liability for negligence" (*objektivierte Fahrlässigkeitshaftung*). See Schäfer and Ott (2005), p. 297; Habersack (2013), § 826, nos. 3 ff. For criticism of this approach, see von Bar (1981), pp. 1696–1697.

[310]The number of these laws is said to be the determinant of the true liability risk (von Bar 2000a, p. 54).

[311]von Bar (1994b), p. 110, p. 120 *passim*; von Bar (2000a), pp. 52–53; Schäfer and Ott (2005), p. 290; Schmidt-Kessel (2006), pp. 20–21. An indication of the possible reasons for these developments is available in von Bar (1994a), p. 108.

[312]Schmidt-Kessel (2006), p. 21, fn. 128. On the role of near-contractual liability as a means of tricking the limits of non-contractual liability, see von Bar (1982), pp. 637–654. For criticism see von Bar (2000b), pp. 606–607.

[313]von Bar (1998c), p. 5.

[314]Palmer and Bussani (2007), p. 271.

[315]Honsell (2001), p. 487.Cf. Schäfer and Ott (2005), p. 300. For underlying reasons see von Bar (1994b), p. 108. For Banakas, however "the German non-liability presumption in the area of pure economic loss has, in general, survived the judicial activism around the established exceptions" (Banakas 1989, p. 117).

This is a departure from the legal foundations,[316] and it may have repercussions in the characterisation of the Portuguese non-contractual liability system as a whole.

According to the dominant view, this forms a mixed model[317] as, in drafting the Civil Code, the legislature avoided both the very broad, virtually unlimited scope of Arts. 1382 and 1393 of the *Code Civil*[318] and the compartmentalised model of the BGB.[319]

While the positions highlighting the similarities between Art. 483 CC and the French general clause of liability—either as a "strict general clause" (*cláusula geral restrita*),[320] or as a real general clause[321]—have always been in a minority, they are now in a position to become more widespread. This is based on the argument that these "conservative" systems have, in their practical application, come close to the general-clause ones.[322]

In this context, legal scholars put forward an alternative system of categorisation concerning liability for pure economic loss, according to which a distinction should be made between the "systems of general clause" (*sistemas de cláusula general*), such as France, Italy and Spain, and the "typical systems" (*sistemas típicos*), such as Germany and England.[323] It remains to be seen which category will be applied to Portugal.

---

[316]von Bar (1981), p. 1693. Scholars and courts have significantly changed the "rigid" complexion of the enumerative system in § 823(1) BGB (Banakas 1989, p. 116). For an analysis of § 823 (1) BGB see Fränkel (1979); Jansen (2002), pp. 517–554.

[317]At the time of enactment of the BGB, by providing for three general clauses the BGB found a mid-point solution between Roman law and the French civil code (Kuhlenbeck 1903, p. 670).

[318]von Bar (1998a), pp. 22 and 23.

[319]On the fragmentary approach of the English law of torts, see Dias Pereira (2008), p. 515. In the early development of Common Law, a certain parallel between tort and *delictum* could be drawn (von Bar 2009d, p. 56). However, while the *delictum* suffered from the confluent processes of abstraction and generalisation until it led to general formulae such as Art. 483 CC, tort has remained unsystematic (Hedley 2011, p. 2), except for concrete situations of liability (Markesinis 1986, pp. 1056 ff.; Wagner 2006, pp. 1005–1012). Nevertheless, it is argued that the current formulation of the tort of negligence in English tort law may be comparable to a general clause of model liability (von Bar 2010a, p. 210). For details see Clerk and Lindsell (2011), Winfield et al. (2014). For criticism of the *Rechtskreislehre* see von Bar (2014a), p. 477 f.

[320]See Trigo (2012), p. 644.

[321]The separation between unlawfulness and fault, already described, was inspired by the German model (Santos Júnior 2003, p. 260 and pp. 264–265). For a critical account see Menezes Leitão 2009, p. 258, fn. 703. But see Carneiro da Frada (1994), p. 138; von Bar (1998a), p. 34; Ranieri (2003), 1443, no. 70; Palmer and Bussani (2007), p. 256.

[322]Stoll (1984), p. 30.

[323]Martín Casals and Ribot Igualada (2003). See also von Bar (1999f), p. 43. Bussani and Palmer arrived at a similar conclusion from the results of their comparative study, saying that from the perspective of compensation of pure economic loss, "the Civil Law countries are themselves divided, not *from* the Common Law but *along with* the Common Law" (Bussani and Palmer 2003a, p. 530).

5. The Drawbacks of the Category of Unlawfulness Before the Compensation of Pure Economic Loss

Irrespective of the system of categorisation chosen, it seems clear that unlawfulness is a concept at the core of the Portuguese Civil Code provisions of non-contractual liability arising out of damage caused to another. However, in light of the transformation it has undergone, some scholars question if this categorisation is justified.[324]

In Germany, some consider categorisation into three clauses to be "too ambitious from a theoretical point of view and too restrictive in practical terms".[325] Indeed, the concept of *Rechtswidrigkeit* would be "*inutile, illusoire* [and] *dangereuse*".[326] "*Useless*", because it would be a mere tautology (by not specifying the presence of a misconduct)[327] and because the indication of unlawfulness in the case of absolute rights would hinder the harmonisation of systems on non-contractual liability arising out of damage caused to another.[328] The concept would be "*illusory*" because it could never list every possible breach leading to unlawfulness.[329] Finally, it would be "*dangerous*" because it assumes that the duty to return the claimant to the original state should exist where neither a right nor statute have been violated,[330] which would have implications in cases of compensation of pure economic interests.

As regards the concept of *ilicitude*, a similar criticism was offered even before the present-day Civil Code had passed through Parliament, with the concept considered either "extremely useless" or "extremely dangerous".[331] For the former, it will remain useless as long as it is anchored in the idea of unlawfulness of conduct.[332] The danger, on the other hand, arises from the fact that it appeals to a repressive function of liability that it does not have,[333] as well as its effect on legal certainty: citizens would not know exactly what constitutes *ilicitude*.[334]

---

[324]von Bar (2000b), p. 606. Cf. also von Bar (1999f), p. 43.

[325]von Bar (2000a), p. 239. Cf. Also Frank (1979), p. 589.

[326]von Bar (1999c), p. 9.

[327]*ibid.*; von Bar (2000a), pp. 242–243. The concept of "*Rechtswidrigkeit*" would serve only to indicate the lack of defence (von Bar 1999c, p. 15).

[328]von Bar (1999c), pp. 3, 9–10.

[329]Debate on the arguments suitable for the determination of the interests that shall be considered legally relevant divides academia (Miranda Barbosa 2015, p. 225).

[330]von Bar (1999c), p. 10; von Bar (2000a), pp. 242–243.

[331]Pereira Coelho (1950), p. 47.

[332]*ibid.*, p. 68. Critical of the *Unrechtlehre* in general, see Stoll (1984), p. 25. For criticism of the *Erfolgsunrechtslehre* see von Bar (2000a), pp. 237–238.

[333]Pereira Coelho (1950), *passim*.

[334]*ibid.*, p. 69.

This position does not correspond with the prevailing view, which continues to list unlawfulness as a condition of non-contractual liability arising out of damage caused to another, often without discussing its usefulness.[335] It is argued that unlawfulness does not necessarily identify the violation of the right or infringement of the interest. Furthermore, many consider that non-contractual liability arising out of damage caused to another should be recognised as a repressive function.[336] The claim that unlawfulness lacks the flexibility to adapt to the situation in question assumes that the law is the positivist law as provided for the legislator. If the same logic is to be followed, then the argument of unlawfulness leading to creative interpretations also fails.[337] The concept of *ilicitude* seems to hold its importance, however, in the case of omissions, where only those who would have a duty of care can be liable.[338]

Irrespective of the position that is taken on the concept of unlawfulness, it is apparent that the requirements of liability have not avoided liability for pure economic loss.[339] The expanded use of the concept has undermined the original will of the legislature,[340] it is argued, which aimed to avoid a general liability by the negligent causation of pure economic loss.[341] The concept is thus inefficient.[342]

The rule against pure economic loss has been claimed to be a "historical accident", attributed to a developing theoretical chasm between absolute and relative rights[343] (where only the infringement of the first would lead to liability)[344] adopted by the courts. The liability clauses had the effect of limiting harm, even though that was not their initial purpose.[345]

Some scholars have lobbied for legal change to accommodate the new developments.[346] However, it seems that there is no political will to take action on the judicial development or to discuss the transformation of the typical system into a general clause.[347] In Germany, the most recent reform of the Law of Obligations

[335] Antunes Varela (2000), pp. 530 ff.; Menezes Leitão (2013), pp. 259–279; Sinde Monteiro (2007), p. 454; Almeida Costa (2006a), pp. 561 ff.

[336] Cf. Miranda Barbosa (2015), p. 226.

[337] Miranda Barbosa (2015), pp. 224–225.

[338] Antunes Varela (2000), p. 543.

[339] Carneiro da Frada (2006), pp. 72–73. For a similar situation in Germany to the BGB see von Bar (2000b), pp. 596–597.

[340] Carneiro da Frada (1994), p. 138, fn. 275. See also Stoll (1984), p. 25.

[341] Mertens (1978), p. 229; Howarth (2011), p. 875.

[342] von Bar (2000a), p. 239.

[343] See also von Bar (2000b), p. 606. Before the nineteenth century, judges did not identify pure economic losses but, rather, losses the claimant could recover (Gordley 2003, p. 29).

[344] The value judgment was thus over actions and not over the damage itself (see *Prot. I*, pp. 969–972; Gordley 2003, p. 39 f.).

[345] See, however, Brüggemeier (2006), p. 1553.

[346] von Bar (1981), p. 1694; von Bar (1991).

[347] Reinhardt (1943), p 187. Cf. Stoll (1984), p. 31.

left §§ 823 and 826 unchanged,[348] nor did the last agreement between the Portuguese Ministry of Justice and Portuguese faculties address the issue.

6. The Alternatives as Suggested by Legal Scholarship

It has been argued that the concept of unlawfulness is based on the definition of a protected right, and that these rights were defined heteronomously, i.e. outside of, and independently from, non-contractual liability damage (*heteronom begründetes Unrecht*). Unlawfulness, which the courts must consider in their decision, would be oriented to the needs of Civil Law and not towards considerations of material justice.[349]

In this context, there is a view that judges should be allowed to decide cases based on "the laws, the principle of *neminem laedere* and the general duty of care"[350] and not, as it is currently the case in Germany and Portugal, based on specific rights and legally protected interests.[351]

The entitlement of the judges to render judgments based on their personal sense of justice[352] could arise from this legal development, as would the need to ensure that the system would be efficient and lasting.[353]

Legal scholars have taken the lead in attempts to change this perspective.

An increasing number of academics[354] embrace Wilburg's idea of a "flexible" approach to law (*bewegliches System*), as opposed to the rigid approach of traditional legal theories.[355] This consists of a comprehensive, unitary system of non-contractual law,[356] which assumes that legal provisions are based on a plurality of interacting legal values (*Elemente*).[357] The decision-making process would have to take such elements into account, as well as their different weights within the decision framework and the overall socio-legal setting.[358] This respective weight would be assessed through the "basic values" (*Basiswertungen*).[359]

---

348 von Bar (2003c), p. 11; Menezes Cordeiro (2010b), p. 334, fn. 1198.

349 Cf. Stoll (1984), pp. 26–27. Cf. also von Bar (1981), p. 1693.

350 von Bar (1999c), pp. 11–12; von Bar (2000a), p. 239.

351 von Bar (2000a), p. 239.

352 Bussani and Palmer (2003d), p. 126; Palmer and Bussani (2007), p. 256; Dias Pereira (2008), p. 514, fn. 7.

353 von Bar (1999c), p. 10.

354 Miranda Barbosa (2015), p. 261, fn. 17.

355 Koch (2002), p. 545. See generally Wilburg (1941). See also Wilburg (1964), pp. 346–379; Canaris (1969), von Bar (1986), Koch (2002). For a critical view, which believes that it results in a fragmented understanding of the law of non-contractual liability arising out of damage caused to another, see Jansen (2003), pp. 565–569, 595.

356 Canaris (1969), p. 76.

357 Wilburg (1941), p. 26; Miranda Barbosa (2015), p. 261.

358 Koch (2002), p. 545; Jansen (2007), p. 33.

359 Koch (2002), p. 546; Koziol (2004), p. 153 ff.

Such a system would reject the idea that non-contractual liability arising out of damage caused to another could be traced to one single condition (for example, *faute*), or that legal arguments could be applicable in an all-or-nothing manner.[360] Instead, it would favour the systematic and teleological interpretation.[361] Those who endorse this view hold that it would provide for equal treatment under the law and allow for the adaptation of the system to real life.[362] A more sceptical section of the legal scholarship, however, argues that it should be kept to a minimum, as it has a negative effect on legal certainty.[363]

There seems to be some sympathy for a more flexible solution within the Portuguese legal scholarship. There is a view that the damages that should be compensated for should be selected through criteria of material justice and not simply excluded from the system.[364]

The SGECC is said to defend a similar model,[365] i.e. a model of the *alternative* interaction, due to the interconnectedness of the elements of liability.[366] In taking a position on this qualification, it is useful to examine the way in which it deals with the reparation of pure economic interests, as a way of informing the decision.

[360] Jansen (2007), p. 33.

[361] Kling (2008), p. 233 f.

[362] Koch (2002), p. 545.

[363] Jansen (2007), p. 33.

[364] Menezes Leitão (2009), p. 274.

[365] von Bar (2001a), p. 521.

[366] Cf. Jansen (2003), pp. 594–595. The difference could be a possible admission of a certain hierarchy of values (Canaris 1969, pp. 77–78).

§ 6 General Remarks on the Non-Contractual Liability Regime Arising Out of Damage Caused to Another in the Draft Common Frame of Reference (PEL. Liab. Dam.)

I. Brief Remarks on the Europeanisation of the Non-Contractual Liability Regime Arising Out of Damage Caused to Another

1. The Need for Harmonisation

The first academic initiatives aiming at comparing and harmonising European Private Law arose in the field of Contract Law. However, attention soon shifted to other areas of Private Law, such as non-contractual liability arising out of damage caused to another.

Significant European legislation was enacted, case law followed[1] and a considerable amount of comparative research was published.[2] European legal systems were analysed and compared, sparking a discussion about the feasibility and desirability of common European Law in the field of non-contractual liability arising out of damage caused to another.[3]

---

[1]See generally Schmidt-Kessel (2006), p 28 ff., where the *acquis communautaire* in the field of non-contractual liability arising out of damage caused to another is divided into three groups: liability for defective products and services; liability for illegitimate business practices; and liability for installations. For an overview of fault liability until 2009, see Lukas (2008), pp. 83–99. On the role of EU institutions in the process of harmonisation of private law see Antoniolli and Fiorentini (2011), p. 7 ff.

[2]von Bar (1994d), Brüggemeier (1999) (of which Brüggemeier (2004) is a revised and updated version); von Bar (1996b, 1999e) (English transls.: von Bar 1998a and von Bar 2000a, respectively); Wurmnest (2003b). See also the textbooks van Gerven et al. (2000) and Ranieri (2003). The term "binding European tort law" is used to refer to legislation, Treaty provisions, Regulations, Directives and ECHR and ECJ case law. As for the latter, the case of Francovich (Joined cases C-6/90 and C-9/90 (Andrea Francovich and Danila Bonifaci and others v Italian Republic) [1991] ECR I-05357) was one of the most significant in the field of state liability.

[3]van Dam (2013), p. 5.

M. Santos Silva, *The Draft Common Frame of Reference as a "Toolbox" for Domestic Courts*, DOI 10.1007/978-3-319-52923-3_6

The desirability of a non-contractual harmonised regime for Europe is the subject of much debate among academics and legal officials alike. The opponents of such a regime consider it unnecessary, even inconvenient, in light of the principle of subsidiarity.[4]

Several reasons are given in favour of harmonisation of this field of law.[5] Firstly, the diversity of legal systems may lead to distortions in the area of competition, affecting the free movement of people and services and thus the overall European Economic Area.[6] Secondly, as was explained through the example of Portuguese law, it is argued that non-contractual and contract law interact and are actually converging.[7] It is not possible, therefore, to harmonise one without the other. Thirdly, harmonisation would ensure equality among the legal systems.[8] Finally, European primary law contains no systematic regime of non-contractual liability arising out of damage caused to another,[9] as the expansion of the field was created piecemeal at the European (secondary) level,[10] resulting in substantial and formal inconsistencies.[11]

2. *Academic Initiatives Towards a European Framework: The European Group on Tort Law and the Study Group on a European Civil Code*

In recent decades, research groups have undertaken comparative studies aimed at providing a pan-European common framework for non-contractual liability arising out of damage caused to another, made up of common principles and rules.[12] These were the Principles of European Tort Law (PETL),[13] drafted by the European Group on Tort Law (EGTL),[14] and the Principles of European Law on

---

[4]Sinde Monteiro (2002), p. 51; Menezes Leitão (2009), p. 354.

[5]von Bar (1999a), p. 208; Kellner (2009), pp. 133–154.

[6]von Bar (2011d), p. 203 f.

[7]Such as in the Portuguese Civil Code. The PECL also had chapters common to both regimes.

[8]Hondius (2007), pp. 48–49. For further arguments, see f. Sec.

[9]Wissink (2008), p. 344. This is in spite of the existence of several Treaty provisions that cover aspects of Private Law and the references to Private Law by the EU Charter of Fundamental Rights. See Schulze (2011), pp. 4–5.

[10]Koziol (2008), p. 589 *passim*. According to Magnus, non-contractual liability arising out of damage caused to another has been treated "negligently" by the EU (Magnus 2004b, p. 562).

[11]See generally von Bar (1994c), pp. 221–232. See also von Bar (2011e). For further details on non-contractual liability arising out of damage caused to another at the EU level see von Bar (1992b).

[12]Colombi Ciacchi (2009), p. 157; van Dam (2013), p. 5; Miranda Barbosa (2015), p. 219.

[13]European Group on Tort Law (2005).

[14]Once called "Tilburg Group". For details on the Tilburg Group's work see Koch (2005), pp. 189–205.

Non-Contractual Liability Arising out of Damage Caused to Another, drafted by the Working team on Extra-Contractual Obligations[15] of the Study Group on a European Civil Code.[16]

Some similarities exist between these two groups.[17]

Firstly, both groups acknowledge that were the harmonisation of contract law to occur without non-contractual liability arising out of damage caused to another, this would result in a set of "mutually uncoordinated, overlapping legal layers".[18] They also admit that the lines between contract and non-contract law are unclear and, further, that they also differ between the legal systems.[19] In addition, the harmonisation of non-contractual liability arising out of damage caused to another could serve as a fundamental protection for the activity covered by Contract Law, namely, the exchange and growth of assets.[20]

Secondly, both groups consider that harmonisation of Private Law should be carried out through the creation of a modern set of European black letter rules[21] and that a uniform terminology in this legal field must be developed and used comprehensively at European and national level.[22]

---

[15]The remaining teams were the Working Team on Sales, Services and Long-Term Contracts; the Working Team on Trusts; the Working Team on Credit Securities; the Working Team on Transfer of Movable Property; the Working Team on Rental of Movable Property; the Working Team on Loan Agreements; and the Working Team on Gratuitous Contracts.

[16]Both academic groups included Portuguese scholars. The EGTL currently features Sinde Monteiro (Coimbra) as a member and Rangel Mesquita as a guest in one of the projects. For the Portuguese scholars and researchers participating in the SGECC see Tit. § 1, Subtit. IV, Sec. 4, Subsec. B above.

[17]A significant number of preparatory materials (Kellner 2009, p. 153) preceded both groups. For a list, see Koziol (2008), p. 609, n. 93; von Bar (2010a), p. 209, fn. 7. Several other groups of academics carried out pan-European comparative research in the field of Private Law. Rooted in the belief that legal science was not ready to embark on a legislative journey in the field, they drafted research guides that highlighted academic input instead. That was the case of the Common Core of European Private Law, the Academy of European Private Lawyers, the Society of European Contract Law (SECOLA) and the Social Justice Group. For a detailed account, see Antoniolli and Fiorentini (2011), p. 7 f. Infantino classified the European research groups in the field of European Private Law into two groups: the "striving for harmonisation research groups" (including the SGECC and the ETLG) and the "knowledge-building research groups" (including, among others, the Common Core Group). See Infantino (2009), p. 60 ff.

[18]von Bar (2011d), p. 202. See also Koziol (2008), p. 608 and Moura Vicente (2008), pp. 68–69. Also, in favour of the extension of harmonisation to the field of non-contractual liability arising out of damage caused to another, Magnus (2004b), pp. 562–563.

[19]Howarth (2011), p. 848. On this matter see generally von Bar and Drobnig (2004).

[20]von Bar (2010a), p. 208. Howarth mentions other arguments in favour of harmonisation of the law of non-contractual obligations, namely its influence on the viability of investment projects, the creation of a single insurance market, the promotion of free circulation of legal practitioners and European citizenship (Howarth 2011, pp. 848–849). Also in favour of the harmonisation of tort law see Rogers and Bagińska (2001), p. V.

[21]von Bar (2001a), p. 532; Antoniolli and Fiorentini (2011), pp. 4–5. See also von Bar (2010a), p. 224.

[22]von Bar and Drobnig (2004), p. 13 ff. and p. 457 f.; Koziol (2008), pp. 600–601.

Thirdly, both groups make suggestions for a flexible system, similar to those mentioned before.[23] They attempted to provide for "best solutions",[24] and rejected the unification of every aspect of non-contractual liability arising out of damage caused to another.[25]

However, differences are also visible between the groups, with, arguably, diverging perspectives on the future of the European framework of non-contractual liability arising out of damage caused to another,[26] as well as differences in substance and system.[27] From these perspectives, two main sets of fundamental differences arise, with implications for the working methods and set aims of the EGTL and the SGECC.

Firstly, both groups attribute different importance to comparative law studies. The leader of the SGECC plays down the importance of comparative law[28] and prefers to speak of "European Private Law" (European non-contractual liability arising out of damage caused by another).[29] The differences between legal systems do not stop cases in different jurisdictions from reaching the same outcomes.[30] The drafters of the PETL, on the other hand, support exactly the opposite approach, believing that the similarities between legal systems do not stop them from being fundamentally different.[31] The commentaries thus seem to play the leading role in their sets of rules, whereas that place is occupied by the model rules in the DCFR.[32]

Secondly, the drafters of the PETL intended to remain close to the traditional terminology,[33] while the drafters of the DCFR, by contrast, developed a list of definitions to end the lack of uniformity in the use of concepts within the EU.

Thirdly, while the EGTL merely aims to provide guidelines for the national and European legislature to achieve an improvement in the drafting of legislation,[34] as

---

[23]Jansen (2006), pp. 752–753. See also von Bar (1986), p. 63 ff.; von Bar (2001a), pp. 515–532; Miranda Barbosa (2015), p. 224. See, however, Oliphant (2011), p. 310, according to whom only the PETL is a flexible system, while "the DCFR approach is to identify eleven paradigm instances of non-contractual liability for damage".

[24]Colombi Ciacchi (2009), p. 160.

[25]See, for example, the case of the regulation of wrongful birth and wrongful life claims (Hondius 2007, p. 55). These are, however, the subject of a very useful comparative description in the DCFR (von Bar 2009c, VI.–2:101, p. 347 ff.).

[26]For a comparison between the aims and methodology of both groups see Wurmnest (2003a), pp. 714–744.

[27]von Bar (2010a), p. 209. For a general overview see Magnus (2004b), pp. 562–580. See also Schmidt-Kessel (2006), p. 74 ff.

[28]See foreword of von Bar (1996a).

[29]For a critical account see Brüggemeier (2009b), p. 5, even though the author revealed a significant preference for "best solution" model rules in the study Brüggemeier and Yan (2009).

[30]See also Zweigert and Kötz (1996), p. 38.

[31]Spier (2005), p. 16 f.; van Dam (2013), p. 210. The focus on the differences is evident. See Koziol (2008).

[32]Jansen (2006), p. 735, fn. 15.

[33]Martín-Casals (2005), p. 6 ff.

[34]Koch, *AJCL* 53 (2005), p. 191.

well as providing guidelines for doctrine and courts,[35] the aims of the SGECC go beyond this. The intention of the drafters was, *inter alia*, to provide academic material which could form a basis for a future, political instrument of private patrimonial law.[36]

The main drafter of the PETL believes that an "approximation from within" would prevent the "destruction of legal cultures".[37] However, he also states that the political institutions should draw up an overall framework for non-contractual liability arising out of damage caused to another to ensure homogeneity, consistency and justice. If the Commission were to adopt such a framework, it would be left with two choices: either adopting the PETL, which admittedly was never conceived of becoming binding law,[38] or drafting a new set of principles or model rules with the purpose of forming such a framework.[39]

Although the strategy of the SGECC is seen as more plausible in this context, its work has received significant criticism from one section of legal scholarship. This criticism ranges from allegations of lack of scientific maturity, over-ambition[40] and personal attacks on its authors.[41]

II. Towards a European Non-Contractual Liability with the DCFR

1. Preliminary Terminological Considerations

Contrary to what happens in the Rome II Regulation,[42] Book VI of the DCFR does not refer either to "tort law" or the "law of delict", as its drafters considered both

---

[35]Koziol (2008), p. 609; Miranda Barbosa (2015), p. 219.

[36]See Tit. § 3, Subtit. II, Sec. 2 above.

[37]Koziol (2008), p. 609. See also Kellner (2009), p. 154.

[38]Spier (2005), pp. 16 ff.

[39]Even the choice of numbering of the provisions reveals the intention of forming a framework for non-contractual liability: the numbering system followed the "Usages of the Commission on European Contract Law" to avoid great editorial changes were the DCFR to become a CFR. See von Bar (2010a), p. 208, n. 5. See, however, Magnus (2004a), pp. 141–162. Magnus considers that both groups came up with sufficiently materialised general principles that could become binding. See Magnus (2004b), p. 564.

[40]Widmer (1999), p. 99; Faure et al. (2002), pp. 205–230; Antoniolli and Fiorentini (2011), p. 34 ff. See, however, the contribution of Magnus in the same work (Magnus 2002); as well as Jansen (2001), p. 64. See also Banakas (2002), p. 374, who sees the possible outcomes of the SGECC's initiative with more optimism.

[41]Legrand (2006).

[42]See epigraph of Chap. III ("Torts/Delicts") of the Regulation (EC) no. 864/2007 of the European Parliament and of the Council of 11 July 2007 on the law applicable to non-contractual obligations (Rome II).

terms inappropriate and even incorrect.[43] While "tort law"—despite being extensively referenced in comparative literature[44]—is inextricably bound up with Common Law,[45] "law of delict" (which is used in most jurisdictions outside Common Law)[46] is too close to the Latin tradition and may lead to associations with criminal law.[47] The term is also not entirely accurate, given the widespread forms of liability without *dolus* or negligence.[48] The DCFR's drafters chose the longer and predominantly descriptive ("cumbersome")[49] expression[50] of "non-contractual liability arising out of damage caused to another", which allows for a "neutral" approach, separated from preconceptions based on either Civil Law or Common Law systems.[51] This expression is also suitable, as wrongful conduct is not a requirement of liability, as it is in the law of delict, nor is a list of torts proposed.[52] The designation of "non-contractual liability" is not accurate, as it encompasses both liability arising from the law of benevolent intervention in another's affairs and unjustified enrichment.[53] As a result, the term "non-contractual liability arising out of damage caused to another" was chosen.

[43]von Bar (2008c), p. 34; von Bar (2009c), p. xiii and n. A3 to VI.–1:101, p. 244. Swann admits there is no "ideal short description that encapsulates the full remit of that area of non-contractual liability which focuses on the reparation of harm done" (Swann 2003, p. 3).

[44]See van Dam (2013).

[45]With further references see von Bar (1998a), p. 7; von Bar (2009c), n. A3 to VI.–1:101, p. 244. Opoku also argues that "the area covered by the law of torts in the Common Law systems is much wider than that covered by delicts in the Civil Law systems". See Opoku (1972), p. 230, fn. 1. Also, to avoid unintended common law baggage, instead of using the expressions "wrongdoer" and "tortfeasor", which are often found in non-contractual law literature, it was opted to refer to the descriptive form of "person inflicting the harm".

[46]von Bar (2009c), Intr. to Chap. 1, A1, p. 229.

[47]von Bar (2009c), n. A2 to VI.–1:101, pp. 243–244.

[48]Opoku (1972), p. 230; von Bar (1998a), p. 2, fn. 1; von Bar (2009c), p. xiii; Introduction to Chapter 1, C14; n. A3 to VI.–1:101, p. 244; von Bar (2010a), p. 209; von Bar (2011b), p. 391; Schulze (2012), p. 223. Cf. also Swann (2003), p. 3; Menezes Cordeiro (2010b), p. 429 ff.

[49]Brüggemeier (2009a), p. 197.

[50]On the descriptive language see von Bar (2011b), p. 391. Legal scholarship is said to generally support descriptive expressions (van Dam 2013, p. 5).

[51]Schulze (2012), p. 223.

[52]von Bar (2001a), p. 525; von Bar (2010a), p. 209. See, however, Menezes Cordeiro, who considers the list to resemble a list of torts (Menezes Cordeiro 2010b, p. 352).

[53]Schulze (2012), p. 223.

2. *Drafting Method of the Working Team on Extra-Contractual Obligations of the Study Group on a European Civil Code*

The Osnabrück team of the SGECC undertook the work on non-contractual liability arising out of damage caused to another. This team, together with the Advisory Council, developed a concept and structure for the principles and model rules that were subsequently approved by the Co-ordinating Group.[54]

When developing the text that would become Book VI of the DCFR, the drafters stated that they did not attempt to come up with (as is sometimes suggested)[55] a compromise between legal systems, nor had they a particular legal system in mind when they chose their solutions.[56] Instead, they aimed to provide a solution which could potentially be adopted by all European Member States.[57] For this reason, the drafters conceived, discussed and passed model rules in English[58] and solved difficulties in definitions by creating a list of terms.

Each chapter of Book VI contains principles, model rules, comments and notes.

The notes consist of short texts setting out limits and deadlines for the European national systems to follow, either expressly or implicitly. In the "Principles of European Law (PEL)" series of the SGECC, introductions containing comparative policy considerations precede the national notes.[59] This series also includes translations of the principles into the 16 European languages.[60]

3. *The Overall Structure of Book VI*

a) Kinds of Obligations and Their Relationship in the DCFR

As described earlier, the DCFR contains rules on private patrimonial law, which go beyond Contract Law principles and the rules provided for in the PECL.

The DCFR contains two kinds of obligations: contractual and non-contractual, with a third form of obligation intentionally excluded. According to its drafters, such an obligation would not be in line with some national statutory provisions and

---

[54]von Bar (2001a), p. 516.

[55]Jansen (2006), pp. 752–753. Antoniolli & Fiorentini, *e.g.* speak of "distillation of best rules" (Antoniolli and Fiorentini 2011, p. 5).

[56]von Bar (2002a), p. 169.

[57]*ibid.*, p. 168. See also von Bar (2001a), p. 517.

[58]von Bar (2002a), p. 167.

[59]See Chapters 1 and 2 (von Bar 2009c, p. 229 ff. and von Bar 2009c, p. 299 ff., respectively).

[60]von Bar (2009c), p. 16 ff.

would confuse those legal systems in which it is not recognised. It would also raise further questions of demarcation and definition.[61] The absence of a *tertium genus* of liability was deemed to avoid a situation in which pure economic loss would be "artificially included in the field of contract law".[62] This is why the DCFR excludes a liability system for reliance and contains only two provisions relating to *culpa in contrahendo*.[63]

Both kinds of obligations are treated separately.[64] While Books II ("Contracts and other juridical acts") and IV ("Specific contracts and the rights and obligations arising from them") apply to contractual obligations only, Books V ("Benevolent intervention in another's affairs"), VI ("Non-contractual liability arising out of damage caused to another") and VII ("Unjustified enrichment") concern only non-contractual obligations.

Nevertheless, the DCFR acknowledges the overlap and interdependency of contractual and non-contractual obligations.[65] The drafters created a set of rules that apply to both kinds of obligations[66] (Book III, "Obligations and corresponding rights"), as provided for in III.–1:101.[67] To that end, the drafters framed the model rules in Book III in general terms, avoiding repetitions or cross-references and allowing for the possibility that, "if a CFR were to be confined to contracts and contractual obligations it would be a very easy matter to use the model rules in Book III for that purpose. Most of them would need no alteration."[68] The drafters of the DCFR also recognised the potential to cross-use some of the concepts (such as "economic loss" and "reparation") and thus decided to draft a list of terms applicable to all 10 books.[69]

With respect to the concurrence problems between contractual and non-contractual liability, the DCFR adopted the principle of free concurrence of actions.[70] This means that the injured person can select the most advantageous from among several bases of claim.

---

[61] von Bar (2009c), Introduction to Chapter 1, n. D29, pp. 239–240.

[62] Cf. von Bar (2002a), p. 178.

[63] See II.–3:301 and II.–3:302 (both former PECL provisions). Should there be an enlargement of the concept of *culpa in contrahendo* in the future, the DCFR would not be opposed to such. See von Bar (2002a), p. 178.

[64] Menezes Cordeiro (2010b), p. 351.

[65] See generally von Bar and Drobnig (2004).

[66] von Bar (2008c), pp. 32–33.

[67] III.–1:101 reads: "This Book applies, except as otherwise provided, to all obligations within the scope of these rules, whether they are contractual or not, and to corresponding rights to performance".

[68] von Bar et al. (2009), Intr. 46, p. 28.

[69] von Bar (2008c), pp. 33–34. For points of contact with the Law of Benevolent Intervention in Another's Affairs and Unjustified Enrichment, see von Bar (2009c), Intr. to Chap. 1, nn. D31 and D32 to VI.–1:101, pp. 240–241.

[70] von Bar (2011b), p. 399. See also von Bar (2009c), n. C7 to VI.–1:103, p. 276.

b) The Seven Chapters of Book VI

Book VI, together with Book VII and Book VIII, contains the principles and model rules on non-contractual obligations in the DCFR.

Its more than 50 model rules are divided into seven chapters.

Chapter 1 ("Fundamental provisions") contains the basic principle of liability (VI.–1:101) and a rule on preventing impending legally relevant damage (VI.–1:102, which shall be read in conjunction with VI.–6:301),[71] as well as the scope of application of both, including the issue of the concurrence between non-contractual and contractual liability (VI.–1:103).[72] This initial chapter provides for the internal coherence of Private Law in general, and for the foundation of, and framework for, non-contractual liability arising out of damage caused to another in particular.[73]

Chapters 2 to 4 list the specific instances of liability, namely: "legally relevant damage" (Chapter 2), "accountability" (Chapter 3) and "causation" (Chapter 4). Chapter 5 ("Defences") deals with particular claimants and those inflicting harm, as well as covering exclusion and mitigation of liability. Chapter 6 ("Remedies") deals with reparation in general, while Chapter 7 includes ancillary rules, comprising those matters that the SGECC left out of the DCFR, either because it was impossible to reach an agreement or because they could not be analysed from the perspective of purely non-contractual liability arising out of damage caused to another.[74]

III. The Basic Rule

1. Structure

When analysing the structure of European regimes on non-contractual liability arising out of damage caused to another, at least four groups can be identified. Common law systems are based on torts. Romano systems deal with a general clause of liability,[75] *i.e.* a principle providing that those whose conduct deviates from the required standards of care must compensate for the resulting losses,[76] and contain rules on strict liability. Germanic systems opted for rules that specifically indicate the conditions of liability, including unlawfulness. Finally, the Nordic

[71]For details see von Bar (2001a), p. 522.

[72]For a detailed account see von Bar (2009c), nn. C7 and C8 to VI.–1:103, pp. 276–277.

[73]von Bar (2009c), Intr. to Chap. 1, n. C19, p. 236; von Bar (2010a), p. 205.

[74]von Bar (2010a), p. 208.

[75]Also, in Common Law systems, negligence may be considered the functional equivalent to a basic rule. For details see von Bar (2001a), pp. 519–520. Cf. also von Bar (1999b), p. 205.

[76]von Bar (1999f), p. 42.

systems rely on *culpa*[77] and include specific statutory provisions in the field of pure economic loss and interference with personality rights.[78]

The SGECC had to find a solution that was comprehensible and acceptable to all countries, while also providing both certainty and flexibility in all systems.[79] It started by adopting a basic rule comprising different conditions leading to liability, in the same fashion as Continental European and Scandinavian countries:

VI.–1:101: Basic rule

(1) A person who suffers legally relevant damage has a right to reparation from a person who caused the damage intentionally or negligently or is otherwise accountable for the causation of the damage.
(2) Where a person has not caused legally relevant damage intentionally or negligently that person is accountable for the causation of legally relevant damage only if Chapter 3 so provides.

2. *Main Features*

The basic rule of liability in Book VI of the DCFR has three functions: (a) it lists the grounds of liability;[80] (b) it indicates the aims of liability: and (c) it clarifies the relationship between the basic rule and the subsequent specific provisions.[81] It also shows that damage, causation (VI.–1:101(1)) and accountability (VI.–1:101(2)) are deeply intertwined.[82]

This legal rule resembles a general clause of liability, but VI.–1:103[83] *lit.* a clarifies that in reality it is not one[84] as it does not stand independently.[85] This holds true even if it is the only basis for a claim under Book VI.[86]

---

[77]*ibid.*

[78]See von Bar (2008c), p. 35. Miranda Rodrigues also suggests a four-system classification. Instead of the Nordic fault system, she recognises the Italian model (Miranda Barbosa 2006a, pp. 19–29).

[79]See Blackie (2005), p. 145.

[80]von Bar (2010a), p. 205; von Bar (2011b), p. 396.

[81]von Bar (2001a), p. 518.

[82]See examples in von Bar (2011b), p. 392, although the first example given still seems to discuss the condition of damage rather than any of the remaining conditions for there to be a claim in damages.

[83]VI.–1:103 (Scope of application) reads: "VI.–1:101 (Basic rule) and VI.–1:102 (Prevention): (a) apply only in accordance with the following provisions of this Book; (b) apply to both legal and natural persons, unless otherwise stated; (c) do not apply insofar as their application would contradict the purpose of other Private Law rules; and (d) do not affect remedies available on other legal grounds".

[84]Schmidt-Kessel (2006), p. 85. Cf. also Blackie (2007), p. 65 ff.

[85]von Bar (2009c), n. A16 to VI.–1:101, p. 247. See also von Bar (2010a), p. 213.

[86]von Bar (2008c), p. 35.

In fact, this rule must be read in conjunction with the provisions of Chapters 2 to 4. These provisions give concrete content to each rule by describing what should be understood under each condition of liability. A person will thus only have a claim for damages (under the rules of Chapter 6) if: (a) he or she suffered a damage which is legally relevant (according to rules on Chapter 2); (b) the damage can be *attributed* to the person responsible (according to the provisions on Chapters 3 and 4); and (c) the person responsible does not have a legally relevant defence against liability (Chapter 7).[87] At the same time, each specific provision only carries weight insofar as it is in accordance with the basic rule.[88]

Another important feature of the basic rule is that it deliberately takes the injured party as a subject, rather than being formulated from the perspective of the person inflicting the harm, as is the case of Portuguese Civil Code ("*Whoever (...) unlawfully infringes...*") and several other legal systems.[89]

Several reasons are behind this choice of formulation. Firstly, the concept of remedies is at the core of this legal area[90] (in contrast to other legal fields, such as the law of unjustified enrichment).[91] Secondly, the drafters intended to reflect the link between legally relevant damage and the remaining conditions of liability.[92] It also makes it clear that the burden of proof rests with the injured person.[93]

A third important feature of the basic rule is that it comprises both liability with, and liability without, negligence and intention. The issue is considered one of accountability, which explains its inclusion in Chapter 3.[94]

This provision was systematised in a manner similar to that of Art. 483 CC. Both provide, in a separate paragraph to the basic rule, that liability without negligence and intention is also accepted under specific circumstances.[95] It is because of this that the DCFR kept the rule of primacy of fault as the foundation of civil liability.[96]

A fourth aspect relates to the fact that the basic rule—like the overall DCFR—does not contain an express distinction between actions and omissions as contained

[87]von Bar (2001a), pp. 520–521; von Bar (2002a), p. 169; Swann (2003), p. 6; von Bar (2008c), p. 35; von Bar (2009c), nn. A9 and B14 to VI.–1:101, pp. 245–246, respectively; von Bar (2010a), p. 213.

[88]von Bar (2009c), n. A16 to VI.–1:101, p. 247.

[89]von Bar (2002a), p. 175; von Bar (2010a), p. 212.

[90]von Bar (2002a), p. 175; von Bar (2008c), p. 35.

[91]von Bar (2010a), p. 212.

[92]von Bar (2002a), p. 175.

[93]von Bar (2009c), nn. A4 and A10 to VI.–1:101, pp. 244 and 245. There is no express rule in the provisions of Book VI on the burden of proof, as the principle is one of general application (see von Bar (2009c), nn. A4 and A10 to VI.–1:101, pp. 244 and 246). As the burden of proof still rests with the injured person, it has been argued that the shift of perspective lacks utility (Brüggemeier 2009a, p. 180).

[94]von Bar (2002a), p. 176.

[95]Brüggemeier (2009a), p. 181.

[96]Wagner 2009, pp. 243–244; Menezes Cordeiro (2010b), p. 600.

in Art. 483(1) CC. This was not deemed necessary[97] because they follow the same rules.[98]

Finally, the word "reparation" is used as an umbrella term, which includes both reparation in kind and in money (VI.–6:101(2)).[99] Again, it arises from the rule that both forms of reparation are on an equal footing, whereas Art. 566 of the Portuguese Civil Code states that reparation in kind shall prevail.

3. Conditions of Liability

As has been set out before,[100] civil liability meets the need to offset a loss caused in the sphere of the person inflicting the harm based upon uniform legal criteria. The difficulties created by this legal instrument are defining these uniform legal criteria and setting acceptable boundaries on the liability of the responsible party.[101]

The basic rule sets out that every claim for reparation depends on the existence of the following three essential conditions.

a) Accountability

A person can be held *accountable* for damage arising out of damage caused to another on three grounds: intention (VI.–3:101), negligence (VI.–3:102)[102] and a source of danger specifically addressed in Chapter 3, Sec. 2. (VI.–1:101(2)).

The drafters avoided the concepts of "fault"[103] and "strict liability",[104] as these were deemed to have conceptual baggage.[105] For the former, they considered that a person might act negligently, *i.e.* without the required standard of care, without

---

[97]von Bar (2009c), n. A10 to VI.–1:101, pp. 245–246.

[98]von Bar (2002a), p. 175.

[99]von Bar (2008c), p. 35.

[100]See Tit. § 4, Subtit. I above.

[101]von Bar (1998a), p. 525 f.

[102]Liability with intention or negligence may be also called "liability for incorrect conduct". See von Bar (2009c), Intr. to Chap. 1, C17, p. 235.

[103]The concept appears only exceptionally in Book VI, always meaning "*culpa in concreto*" (von Bar (2009c), Intr. to Chap. 1, n. D28, p. 239). VI.–5:102 (Contributory fault and accountability), influenced by French law, to highlight the questions of moral responsibility arising in this context (Blackie 2007, p. 75).

[104]von Bar (2009c), Introduction to Chapter 3, n. A2, p. 557.

[105]*ibid.* "Strict liability" would mean different things in the different European legal systems. See von Bar (2009c), Introduction to Chapter 1, n. C25, p. 238; Blackie (2007), p. 75. See also van Dam (2013), p. 306.

having acted with fault.[106] The latter was rejected in favour of a more descriptive expression.[107]

aa) Liability with Intention and Liability with Negligence

Chapter 3 starts by defining intention[108] (VI.–3:101) and negligence (VI.–3:102). This was considered innovative, as European codifications usually define intention and negligence by legal scholars.[109] This departure stemmed from the extensive differences between Common Law and Civil Law in their conception of terms and definitions, making a more inclusive formulation necessary.[110]

The section of liability with intention or negligence includes rules on liability of minors (VI.–3:103)[111] and liability of supervisors (VI.–3:104).

The drafters opted to distinguish between parents and supervisors on the one hand, and employers on the other (VI.–3:201). According to the DCFR, the latter *wrong* cannot be liable without intention or negligence. Some legal scholars consider this a lost opportunity, as a regime of strict liability would have promoted a more proactive approach to the education of children and the supervision of disabled persons.[112]

bb) Liability Without Intention or Negligence

Section 2 of the chapter on accountability provides for "accountability without intention or negligence".

The drafters did not envisage this section as a separate chapter dealing comprehensively with every strict liability claim. No clear distinction was seen between strict liability and liability based on intention or negligence, and the focus of the liability rests on whether or not a legally relevant damage occurred, irrespective of the intention or negligence of the person inflicting the harm.[113]

---

[106] von Bar (2010a), p. 211.

[107] von Bar (2008c), p. 35.

[108] During the *travaux préparatoires*, breach of duty was used in place of intention (former VI.–3:303). It was defined as "behaviour which does not meet the condition of a statutory provision which aims to protect the other from the damage he or she suffered, or which does not amount to such care as is reasonable in all the circumstances of the case". In short, breach of duty was defined as the failure to reach the required duties of care. Such duties were to be drawn from the subsequent rules or from the circumstances of the case at hand (von Bar 2001a, pp. 526–527).

[109] Wagner (2009), p. 241.

[110] von Bar (2010a), p. 219.

[111] After initial hesitation, it was decided to provide for a rule on the liability of minors. See von Bar (2001a), p. 528.

[112] Wagner (2009), pp. 251–252.

[113] Blackie (2005), p. 144. Cf. also von Bar (2009c), Intr. to Chap. 1, n. C25, p. 238.

The cases of liability without intention or negligence are cases of objective responsibility for a source of danger,[114] because they refer to cases where an appropriate level of care may be insufficient to avoid damage. The system therefore introduces an additional control.[115]

Similar to the Portuguese Civil Code, the DCFR does not provide for a general theory on liability without intention or negligence.[116] The drafters did not deem it possible to gather "in a single mould" all possible manifestations of this theory.[117]

Instead, it provides for a list of situations where such liability is imposed.[118] These are: "accountability for damage caused by employees and representatives" (VI.–3:201); "accountability for damage caused by the unsafe state of an immovable object" (VI.–3:202); "accountability for damage caused by animals" (VI.–3:203); "accountability for damage caused by defective products" (VI.–3:204); "accountability for damage caused by motor vehicles" (VI.–3:205); and "accountability by damage caused by dangerous substances or emissions" (VI.–3:206). Here, too, there are similarities with the Portuguese Civil Code, where the greatest part of strict liability (*responsabilidade objetiva*) corresponds to liability of risk (*responsabilidade pelo risco*).[119]

In the DCFR, the drafters opted for a list of constellations of liability without intention or negligence, both for reasons of public policy and the need to achieve a balance between the different positions of European systems. This task sat uneasily with the drafters, particularly because most of the rules involving this kind of liability stem from national—and not European—regulations.[120] The result is a significant difference between legal systems in the way the provision is formulated and realised.[121]

Section 2 of Chapter 3 starts with a provision on vicarious liability, such as damage caused by employees and representatives (VI.–3:201).[122] In a modern European regime of non-contractual liability arising out of damage caused to another, employers cannot simply be discharged from liability, even where the employees acted with intention.[123] This decision is in line with the prevailing view

[114]von Bar (2009c), Intr. to Chap. 3, n. A1, p. 557.

[115]Wagner (2009), pp. 243–244.

[116]Although it seems like it was initially planned. See von Bar (2001a), p. 527.

[117]von Bar (2009c), Intr. to Chap. 3, n. E24, p. 565.

[118]Magnus (2004b), p. 571.

[119]Antunes Varela (2000), p. 629 ff.; Almeida Costa (2006a), p. 611 ff.; Menezes Cordeiro (2010b), p. 505. The cases of objective liability in Portugal are: liability of the agent (Art. 500); liability of the State and other public legal persons (Art. 501); losses caused by animals (Art. 502); accidents caused by vehicles (Art. 503); collision of vehicles (Art. 506); and losses caused by electrical or gas facilities (Art. 509).

[120]von Bar (1999f), p. 52.

[121]Wagner (2009), pp. 244–245.

[122]For details see von Bar (1998d).

[123]von Bar (2001a), p. 529. The current version highlights the fact that employees can never be discharged from liability in (1) *lit.* b (compare with former version, von Bar 2001a, p. 529, n. 22).

in the European legal systems.[124] The provision is similar to Art. 500 CC, differing only in that the labour relationship is not expressly mentioned and the person who employs another has a right of reimbursement (*direito de regresso*) in cases where the representative acted with fault (Art. 493(3) CC). Some commentators argue that VI.–3:201(1) *lit*. b provides for general rules of accountability and is not a separate form of loss.[125]

The subsequent rules in Section 2 were divided into three categories.

The first category comprises the rule on damage caused by dangerous substances or emissions (VI.–3:206),[126] based on the concept of danger. The second category includes the rule on damage caused by animals (VI.–3:203)[127] and damage caused by motor vehicles (VI.–3:205),[128] and it implies a special connection with a particular type of object. Finally, the third and last category includes the rule on damage caused by the unsafe state of an immovable object (VI.–3:202)[129] and that of damage caused by defective products (VI.–3:204).[130] It involves a special connection with a particular type of object that does not meet expectations of safety. Again, the structure of this section resembles the structure of the Portuguese Code (as well as the German one), which has special laws dealing with particular risks.[131]

---

[124]von Bar (2009c), n. A1 to VI.–3:201, p. 632.

[125]Schmidt-Kessel (2006), p. 89.

[126]The Portuguese Civil Code does not have a provision which corresponds to VI.–3:206. However, it provides for strict liability of the effective direction of an electric or gas driving installation (Art. 509 CC). In Book III (Law of Things), the Portuguese Civil Code contains a rule on liability in respect of relations between neighbours, independent of fault of the owner of a harmful installation, i.e. works, installations or deposits of corrosive or dangerous deposits (Art. 1347 CC). For details see von Bar (2009c), n. 10 to VI.–3:206, p. 730.

[127]The equivalent to VI.– 3:206 would be Art. 502 CC. As compared to VI.–3:203, Art. 502 CC is more demanding, as it requires from the keeper of the animal that he or she uses the animal in his or her own interest and that the loss results from the special danger involved in its use.

[128]Art. 503 CC is the equivalent to VI.–3:205 in the Portuguese Civil Code. However, it has wider scope than this provision. Firstly, it applies to the keeper of vehicles of overland transfer, both motorised and non-motorised. Secondly, it includes every damage that results from the usual risks of the vehicle (*riscos próprios do veículo*); finally, such liability also exists when the vehicle is not in use.

[129]In the Portuguese Civil Code, liability for damages caused by an immovable which suffers full or partial destruction following a defect in construction or conservation, lies with the owner or keeper of the immovable only when he or she acted with fault. The DCFR makes the "person who independently exercises control over an immovable" liable, independent of fault. This formulation is a fitting umbrella term to include owners and keepers of immovables alike, as well as those that are contractually or legally responsible for its state. Therefore, paras (2) and (3) seem to be expendable.

[130]In Portugal, liability for defective products is provided for in special legislation (DL 383/89 of 6 November 1989, DR, 1st Ser., no. 255 (1989), pp. 4880–4882, as amended by the DL 131/2001 of 24 April 2001, DR, 1st Ser., no. 96 (2001), p. 2337).

[131]von Bar (1999f), p. 52.

These categories represent the usual instances of strict liability in European legal systems, with two exceptions: VI.–3:204 ("accountability for damage caused by defective products") and VI.–3:206 ("accountability for damage caused by dangerous substances or emissions"), which some have claimed was included to open the door to liability for environmental damage.[132]

As for VI.–3:204, its detailed regulation is said to have incorporated the "European secondary law practically word for word".[133] However, it is also seen as falling short of including the regime established by the Directive[134] and to diverge significantly in certain respects.[135] Indeed, the DCFR is claimed not to have continued the two-track system of product liability based on both fault and defective products without fault.[136]

As for VI.–3:206, this section deals with "pure ecological damage"[137] and was included at the suggestion of the French members of the SGECC.[138] It is accompanied by VI.–2:209, which explains what constitutes legally relevant damage in the circumstances set out in the provision. It also expands the scope of protection of VI.–3:206.

The rule did not remain without criticism.[139] For once, the 2004 Directive on Environmental Law[140] showed that the EU trend was directed towards including this topic under Administrative Law. However, the drafters believe that most EU Member States include liability for harm sustained as a result of impairment to the environment under the rules of strict liability.[141]

VI.–3:208 is entitled "abandonment" and it is a transversal rule, applying in conjunction with other rules in the same section.[142]

To avoid the shortcomings that could arise from this list, VI.–3:207 refers to "other grounds of accountability". This provision allows judges to decide a case based on other provisions on strict liability,[143] reaffirming the victim-friendly tone of the

---

[132]Wagner (2009), p. 246. For details see Brüggemeier (2009a), pp. 193–195.

[133]Brüggemeier (2009a), p. 193. See also von Bar (2009c), n. A1 to VI.–3:204, p. 687.

[134]Council Directive 85/374/EEC of 25 July 1985 on the approximation of the laws, regulations and administrative provisions of the Member States concerning liability for defective products, OJ L 210, 29–33, as amended by Directive 1999/34/EC of the European Parliament and of the Council of 10 May 1999, OJ L 141, pp. 20–21.

[135]See von Bar (2008c), p. 37.

[136]Wagner (2009), pp. 247–248.

[137]von Bar (2009c), n. A3 to VI.–3:206, p. 719.

[138]See von Bar (2002a), p. 177.

[139]For Wagner, the drafters acted as "environmental activists" (Wagner 2009, p. 248).

[140]Directive 2004/35/CE of the European Parliament and of the Council of 21 April 2004 on environmental liability with regard to the prevention and remedying of environmental damage, p. 56 ff.

[141]von Bar (2009c), n. A4 to VI.– 3:206, p. 719.

[142]VI.–3:208 is applied in conjunction with VI.–3:202, VI.–3:205, VI.–3:206 and VI.–3:207.

[143]Blackie (2005), p. 146; Wagner (2009), p. 245.

DCFR regulation.[144] Nevertheless, some authors have claimed that the drafters should not have transferred the responsibility of strict liability to national systems and that they could have taken the opportunity to Europeanise "strict liability".[145]

As the area of liability without intention or negligence is a particularly sensitive one (especially motor vehicle liability, which has a close connection to insurance policies), the SGECC opted to provide fundamental concepts while still leaving judges room to manoeuvre.[146] Some critics argue that the drafters of the DCFR should have provided only for the basic provisions. Judges would, in all probability, have been able to hold on to those whilst ignoring the specific instances of liability. Nevertheless, the list was drafted with the aim to permit keepers or operators of sources of danger to contract insurance policies in advance, thereby reinforcing legal certainty and foreseeability.[147]

The length of this list is claimed by some to show a trend towards extending strict liability "to every dangerous circumstance that the beneficiary or author is not able to control".[148]

b) Causation

The drafters subdivided the section dealing with the requirement of liability "causation" into two sections. The first contains definitions, while the second is concerned with situations of responsibility being assigned to the damage.

VI.–4:101(1) provides that "[a] person causes legally relevant damage to another if the damage is to be *regarded as a consequence* of that person's conduct or the source of danger for which that person is responsible".[149] This is a shorter formulation of a previously existing version[150] and a clearer one,[151] as it expressly states the source of danger as a trigger of liability. The DCFR is among the first legal rules that attempt to define causation.[152] Indeed, in most cases causation is defined as the relationship between two conditions that are subject to a negative evaluation: the breach of duty or source of danger and legally relevant damage.[153]

---

[144]Wagner (2009), pp. 245–246.

[145]Schulze (2012), p. 227.

[146]For details see Blackie (2007), p. 77.

[147]Wagner (2009), p. 245.

[148]Menezes Cordeiro (2010b), p. 600.

[149]von Bar (2008c), p. 37.

[150]"A person causes damage to another if, having regard to the type and extent of the damage, the basis on which he or she is accountable, the conduct of the injured party and all other circumstances of the particular case, the damage is to be regarded as the consequence of the act for which liability is incurred" (stand: 2001). See von Bar (1999a), p. 221.

[151]But see Brüggemeier (2009a), p. 186.

[152]von Bar (2000a), p. 437.

[153]von Bar (2010a), p. 222.

However, the understanding developed by the DCFR has attracted some criticism from legal scholars,[154] who argue that it adopted a normative concept of causation only.[155] They hold that it poses questions which go beyond the scope of causation and which contain problems of responsibility.[156]

The general rule and the related sub-clauses reveal that the SGECC opted for a minimalist regulation of this requirement of liability.[157] Indeed, the DCFR did not follow the two-pronged approach regarding causation found at both EU and national level. It therefore did not set out the *conditio sine qua non* rule (factual causation) followed by a further legal criterion aimed at determining the legal cause of the damage (normative causation).[158]

There are few rules on causation within the DCFR, with the drafters believing that these problems should be solved on a case-by-case basis.[159] The formulation of this rule aspires to provide an alternative to overcome the shortcomings identified in the *conditio sine qua non* doctrine[160] across Europe, including in Portugal.[161] The drafters recognised that an assessment of causation is also motivated by value judgements and policy considerations,[162] rather than natural connections.[163] It thereby intentionally left room for the judge to determine whether or not the conditions were fulfilled in a given case.[164] The DCFR considers that causation, damage and accountability are "tightly interwoven",[165] with meanings that are fundamentally interdependent.[166]

VI.–4:101(2) deals with a special situation, namely the so-called "egg-shell skull" principle. According to this rule, the person who inflicts an unforeseeable substantial loss cannot relieve him or herself from liability by proving that the special health condition of the person contributed to the damage. This solution is in force in Portugal, but contained within Labour Law and it is, in principle, less

---

[154] Blackie (2007), p. 78; Kellner (2009), pp. 143–144; Wagner (2009), p. 253.

[155] Wagner (2009), p. 252. See also von Bar (2009c), nn. A2 to VI.–4:101, p. 746 and A3 to VI.–4:101, p. 747.

[156] Howarth (2011), p. 882.

[157] Blackie (2007), p. 78.

[158] Brüggemeier (2009a), p. 186.

[159] von Bar (2010a), p. 221.

[160] For details see von Bar (2000a), p. 440 ff.

[161] See Tit. § 4, Subtit. IV, Sec. 3 above. For details on the comparative analysis of causation in the DCFR and in the Portuguese Civil Code see generally Miranda Barbosa (2015), p. 235 ff.

[162] Blackie (2005), p. 145.

[163] von Bar (2000a), pp. 437, 440; Jansen (2001), p. 41; von Bar (2001a), p. 528. The epigraph of the chapter devoted to causation reads "Causation or Attribution". This suggests that some factual considerations are also present (von Bar 2000a, p. 43). See Wagner (2009), p. 252, fn. 63.

[164] Blackie (2007), p. 79. For a critical approach see Kellner (2009), p. 143.

[165] von Bar (2009c), Intr. to Chap. 1, n. C23, p. 238.

[166] von Bar (2000a), p. 461. Cf. also von Bar (2010a), p. 222.

protective of the victim, as it does not grant a right of reparation for those situations where the victim concealed the predisposition.[167] Under Art. 570(1) CC, the previously existing health condition of the claimant may be seen as "an act that the injured person practiced with fault and which contributed to the production or increase of the damage". As such, it can lead to reduction or exclusion of liability[168] because, in such cases, the conduct of the agent may not be considered an adequate cause of the damage.[169]

As for the alternative causation rule (VI.–4:103), it is said to resemble the BGB provisions,[170] as it "paves the way towards joint liability in cases where the relationship between cause and effect remains in the open".[171] In Portugal, Vaz Serra suggested a rule equivalent to VI.–4:103 in the *travaux préparatoires*.[172] This was not included in the text, despite its support from legal scholarship.[173] The solidarity principle regarding all possible persons inflicting the harm is a generally accepted rule in the present Civil Code.[174]

c) Legally Relevant Damage

Legally relevant damage is the remaining condition leading to reparation within non-contractual liability arising out of damage caused to another. This requirement is analysed in the following chapter, highlighting the central importance of legally relevant damage and its role in the stalemate mentioned.

---

[167] Art. 11(1) of Law 98/2009 of 4 September 2009, DR, 1st Ser., no. 172 (2009), pp. 5894–5920, by remission of Art. 284 CT.

[168] Galvão Telles (1997), p. 404; Almeida Costa (2006a), p. 764. For details and case law references see von Bar (2009c), n. IV47 to VI.–4:101, pp. 771–772.

[169] Brandão Proença (1997), p. 192 ff.

[170] For a detailed account on relevant case law on causation see von Bar (2009c), n. 7 to VI.–4:103, pp. 785–786.

[171] Wagner (2009), p. 255.

[172] Vaz Serra (1959c), p. 138.

[173] Pereira Coelho (1955), p. 24, fn. 5. For details see von Bar (2009c), n. 9 to VI.–4:102, p. 779.

[174] von Bar (2010a), p. 222.

§ 7 Reception of the DCFR's Concept of "Legally Relevant Damage" and Its Potential for the Protection of Pure Economic Interests

I. The Concept of Legally Relevant Damage

1. Factual and Normative Concept of Damage in the DCFR

The contents of the DCFR comply with the scheme set out by the European Commission, which asked for the development of a uniform European legal terminology. Indeed, the DCFR includes a list of definitions which are part of the "toolbox" function[1] and serve as suggestions for European legislators.

One of the concepts giving rise to more doubts in European case law (particularly in the Simone Leitner case) was the concept of damage,[2] which is a very difficult concept to define.[3] The DCFR contains two concepts of damage: a factual (*beschreibend-tatsächliches*) one, which it includes in the list of definitions ("damage means any type of detrimental effect")[4] and a normative (*normativ rechtliches*) concept of damage.[5] The drafters of the DCFR believed that the factual notion of damage should be restricted for legal purposes,[6] with the important issue being an understanding of the particular damage leading to a claim for reparation.[7]

---

[1]For details see Tit. § 3, Subtit. II, Sec. 2 above.

[2]von Bar (2011b), p. 387.

[3]Cf. von Bar (2010a), p. 214. See generally von Bar (2011b).

[4]von Bar (1999a), p. 214.

[5]von Bar (2010a), p. 214. That is the case for the concept of *Schade* in § 1293(1) ABGB and the concept present in several other European legal systems as well (von Bar 1999b, p. 23, with comparative reference in the footnote).

[6]von Bar (2010a), p. 214; von Bar (2011b), p. 392.

[7]von Bar (2008c), p. 36; von Bar (2011b), pp. 389–390. See also Carneiro da Frada (2006), p. 89 ff.; Hollander (2012), p. 256.

M. Santos Silva, *The Draft Common Frame of Reference as a "Toolbox" for Domestic Courts*, DOI 10.1007/978-3-319-52923-3_7

From this consideration the drafters developed the notion of "legally relevant damage", defined as damage determined on a case-by-case basis and taking account of the remaining conditions of liability, and which will lead to a claim within non-contractual liability arising out of damage caused to another.[8]

2. Meaning of Legally Relevant Damage

VI.–2.101 provides for the meaning of "legally relevant damage". It reads:

(1) Loss, whether economic or non-economic, or injury is legally relevant damage if:

(a) one of the following rules of this Chapter so provides;
(b) the loss or injury results from a violation of a right otherwise conferred by the law; or
(c) the loss or injury results from a violation of an interest worthy of legal protection.

(2) In any case covered only by sub-paragraphs (b) or (c) of paragraph (1), loss or injury constitutes legally relevant damage only if it would be fair and reasonable for there to be a right to reparation or prevention, as the case may be, under VI.–1:101 (Basic rule) or VI.–1:102 (Prevention).
(3) In considering whether it would be fair and reasonable for there to be a right to reparation or prevention, regard is to be had to the ground of accountability, to the nature and proximity of the damage or impending damage, to the reasonable expectations of the person who suffers or would suffer the damage, and to considerations of public policy.
(4) In this Book:

(a) economic loss includes loss of income or profit, burdens incurred and a reduction in the value of property.

(5) non-economic loss includes pain and suffering and impairment of the quality of life.

II. Categories of Legally Relevant Damage

"Legally relevant damage" is a flexible concept, which is able to encompass different kinds of harm.[9] "Legally relevant" means it carries a right to reparation.[10]

Legally relevant damage can involve, in turn, a loss (economic or non-economic loss), a loss *and* an injury or an injury only.[11] This was particularly clear in the interim outline edition of the DCFR, which expressly included "loss" and "injury" in the concept of damage.[12] Both VI.–2:201(2) *lit.* b and VI.–2:203(1) require an

[8]von Bar (2009c), n. III35 to VI.–1.103, p. 299; von Bar (2010a), p. 214 f.

[9]von Bar (2008c), p. 36. For details see von Bar (1999c), p. 25 ff., in particular p. 27.

[10]von Bar (2002b), p. 70.

[11]von Bar (2001a), p. 523; von Bar (2002a), p. 176; Schmidt-Kessel (2006), p. 86; von Bar (2011b), p. 389.

[12]von Bar (2011b), p. 388.

injury and a loss for the requirement of a legally relevant damage to be met (in which case the solution is similar to that provided for in the Portuguese Civil Code). VI.–2:101(1) *lits.* b and c admit other cases as well.

1. Loss

Throughout the DCFR, legally relevant damage consists of a "loss *consequential upon* a certain injury, infringement or destruction".[13] Legally relevant damage in the form of loss is particularly prevalent in liability involving accountability with intention or negligence.[14]

According to the definition of "loss", as set out in the DCFR (both in the list of definitions and VI.–2:101(4)),[15] "economic loss" and "non-economic loss" are included and recognised as categories of loss.[16] The drafters followed the example of the PECL[17] by allowing for the compensation of both at the level of liability without intention or negligence. For reparation purposes, the DCFR makes no distinction between the two kinds of loss.[18] By avoiding references to the nature of "loss" the drafters refrained from defining "loss" at all. Instead, the "definition" of loss in the list of definitions and in Art. VI.–2:101 is a description of the categories it encompasses. Art. VI.–2:102(4) was drafted to avoid unnecessary repetitions in the remaining Articles of Sec. 2.,[19] the drafters stated. In any case, there seems to be no reason justifying the presence of "loss" in the list of definitions.

a) Economic Loss

The concept of reparation in the list of definitions of the DCFR makes it clear that where the Draft refers to "economic loss", it means "*inter esse*" *i.e.* the economic difference between the actual state of affairs and the state of affairs which would have existed had the damage not been inflicted.[20] This appeals to the so-called difference theory (*Differenztheorie, Differenzhypothese*),[21] developed from the

---

[13]*ibid.*, p. 389. See also von Bar and Drobnig (2004), p. 29, n. 46.

[14]von Bar (2011b), p. 396.

[15]Some legal commentators highlight the lack of concrete utility of the definitions in VI.–2:101.

[16]Brüggemeier (2009a), p. 181.

[17]VI.–9:501(2), *lit.* a.

[18]See von Bar (2009c), n. F25 to VI.–2:101, p. 313.

[19]von Bar (2009c), n. F24 to VI.–2:101, p. 312.

[20]Brüggemeier (2009a), p. 188; von Bar (2011b), p. 396.VI.–6:101(1) reads: "Reparation is to reinstate the person suffering the legally relevant damage to the position that person would have been in had the legally relevant damage not occurred".

[21]Schlechtriem (1997), p. 244; Wagner (2009), p. 263. See also Winiger et al. (2011), pp. 35–36. For details see Menezes Leitão (2013), pp. 363–364.

works of Friedrich Mommsen[22] in the nineteenth century.[23] This theory is also accepted in Portugal, in the direct assessment of "calculable damage".[24]

As for its scope, VI.–2:101(4), *lit.*b (and the definition of loss in the list of definitions) provides that "economic loss includes loss of income or profit, burdens incurred and a reduction in the value of property".

The word "includes" shows that this provision lists examples of economic loss, namely the most important forms that such losses can assume.[25] It would not be possible to include an exhaustive list of recoverable economic loss.[26] The drafters did not distinguish economic loss from pure economic loss.[27]

Apart from the examples listed, other recoverable economic losses are also included in the DCFR,[28] such as health care expenses (VI.–2:201(2) *lit.* a) and the loss resulting from deprivation of the use of property (VI.–2:206(2), *lit.* a).

Both VI.–2:201(2), *lit.* a and VI.–2:206(2), *lit.* a address legal issues which are the subject of much lively debate in Portugal.

VI.–2:201(2), *lit.* a resembles Art. 495(2) CC in its statement that the "expenses reasonably incurred for the care of the injured person by those close to him or her" constitute legally relevant damage.

There are, however, two fundamental differences between both provisions. Firstly, while Art. 495(2) CC gives the persons who incurred the expenditure an independent claim, the DCFR assigns such expenditure of "close persons" to the damage that the injured person sustained.[29] Secondly, while scholars and courts have debated if the foregone wages or profits can be considered "expenses" for the

---

[22]Hohloch (1981), p. 395.

[23]According to difference theory, while assessing damage, courts must calculate the "difference" or *id quod interest* (as the legal scholars of the *Corpus Iuris Civilis* called it) or *Interesse* (Hohloch 1981, p. 395) between the *real* situation (*realer Zustand*) and the *hypothetical* situation (*hypothetischer Zustand*) of the assets (*património*) of the person on whom the harm was inflicted, *i.e.* the situation which would exist if it was not changed by the event giving rise to liability, at the point just before the event (Mommsen 1855, p. 4 *apud* Escher-Weingart 1993, p. 34). See also Lange and Schiemann (2003), pp. 27–28 and 43–44; Hohloch (1981), p. 395; Magnus (2001a), p. 191; Magnus (2001b), pp. 94 and 96. Many legal scholars seem to refer to this theory while attempting to define "damage". See Deutsch (1976), p. 419; Larenz (1987), p. 426; Schlechtriem (1997), p. 244. Others, however, see it more as a method of assessing damage rather than defining it. See Magnus (2001a), p. 191. The relationship between this theory and the definition of *Schaden* thus remains unclear (Escher-Weingart 1993, p. 40). § 249 BGB is considered to allude to the *Differenzhypothese* (Hohloch 1981, p. 396), although it is also mentioned that "Mommsen's 'differential' concept of damage has been seriously damaged by the more modern theory of 'normative' damage" (Banakas 1996, p. 20). In the Portuguese legal scholarship, see Coelho dos Santos, *RPDC* 3 (1994), p. 75; Antunes Varela (2000), p. 599 and Sinde Monteiro and Veloso (2001), p. 179.

[24]Almeida Costa (2006a), pp. 595–596.

[25]von Bar (2009c), n. F24 to VI.–2:101, p. 312.

[26]For this discussion, with examples, see von Bar (2011b), p. 396.

[27]von Bar (2008c), p. 36.

[28]von Bar (2011b), p. 390.

[29]von Bar (2009c), n. A18 to VI.–2:201, p. 364.

purpose of reparation of persons who informally cared for the injured person, the DCFR openly refers to that issue. It states that "expenses" of carers only include foregone wages or profits if these are identical to the costs that the injured person would incur making use of professional help. This corresponds to situations where the person caring for the injured person provided care on a professional basis (nurse, social worker, etc.). In this case, the carer would still have no claim of his or her own: the foregone wages or profit would be recovered as damage of the injured person. Nevertheless, the persons close to the injured person will be able to recover such costs through the mechanisms of benevolent intervention or unjustified enrichment.[30]

As far as VI.–2:206(2) is concerned, *lit.* a and *lit.* b refer to different dimensions of impairment of use. *Lit.* a states that deprivation of use amounts to a loss; *lit.* b states that impairment of use is a form of infringement of property rights. Within this model, legally relevant damage amounts to a loss in *lit.* a, and an injury in *lit.* b. In Portugal, legal scholarship and courts have only taken impairment of use to be a loss.[31]

b) Non-economic Loss

According to the list of definitions of the DCFR, "non-economic loss includes pain and suffering and impairment of the quality of life. (III.–3:701(3) and VI.–2:101(4))". Similar to the definition of "economic loss", the definition of "non-economic loss"[32] is also illuminating, as it includes only the most significant cases of non-economic loss.[33] The drafters considered the legal traditions of some European countries and the prevailing ECJ jurisprudence before deciding that compensable non-economic loss should go beyond "pain and suffering and impairment of the quality of life".[34]

The drafters admit that they provided for a relatively wide compensation of non-economic losses in some instances, such as in the case of non-economic loss as a result of another's personal injury or death (in VI.–2:202). Some scholars view this as a positive development.[35]

VI.–2:202 (which will be analysed below)[36] is quite similar to Art. 496 CC. Both provide for a claim for non-economic losses in case of both fatal and non-fatal injury (in the case of Portugal, in line with the recent settlements in case law) and

[30] von Bar (2009c), nn. A18 and A19 to VI.–2:201, p. 364.

[31] See Tit. § 5, Subtit. III, Sec. 3, Subsec. dd (2) above.

[32] "Non-economic loss" is defined in the annex to the DCFR (von Bar et al. 2008, p. 559). For a discussion of the terminology see von Bar (2011b), p. 397.

[33] von Bar (2009c), n. F30 to VI.–2:101, p. 314.

[34] The drafters recognise that this option may be criticised in respect of policy matters. For details see von Bar (2011b), pp. 390–391.

[35] Pinkel (2008), p. 27.

[36] See Tit. § 7, Subtit. III, Sec. 1.

both take account of the loss of maintenance of those without a legal claim.[37] However, the DCFR adheres to the prevailing view in Europe that "death as such" is not a legally relevant damage.[38] Portugal is one of the few countries that considers "life" to have a monetary value that can be transmitted to the deceased person's heirs.[39]

There is no model rule refering specifically to the compensation of non-economic loss in the DCFR, in a similar fashion to Art. 496(1) CC or § 253 BGB. The DCFR does not limit compensation of pure economic loss according to its seriousness, as Art. 496 CC does. However, the drafters appear to have provided for a regime where the reparation of non-economic loss is subject to more requirements than the reparation of economic loss.[40]

2. *Injury*

Legally relevant damage includes loss, but also injury. VI.–6:204 reads that "[i] njury as such is to be compensated independent of compensation for economic or non-economic loss".

The understanding of injury is said to be in line with "recent developments" in several legal systems in Europe,[41] even though several critics oppose this third category of loss.[42]

The definition of "injury" is absent from VI.–2:101(2),[43] nor can it be found anywhere else in the DCFR. This has sparked a discussion of its meaning, and whether or not it is synonymous with "injury as such"[44] and to "personal injury". Some legal scholars argue that VI.–6:204, which refers to "injury as such", is an unnecessary expression, because the recoverability of "injury" could be extrapolated from VI.–2:101(1) and (2).

On foot of the DCFR itself, as well as other documents written by its drafters, injury and "injury as such" are interpreted as being one and the same.[45]

As for "personal injury", which is found in several provisions of the DCFR,[46] it is apparently an additional qualifier of the term, to distinguish it from the few cases

---

[37]See von Bar (2009c), n. V49 to VI.–2:202, p. 411.

[38]*ibid.*, n. C9 to VI.–2:202, pp. 391–392.

[39]von Bar (2001a), p. 524; von Bar (2011b), p. 394. For details see von Bar (2009c), n. I3 to VI.–2:202, 395. See generally Leite de Campos (1987), pp. 5–20.

[40]von Bar (2001a), p. 524; von Bar (2010a), p. 215.

[41]von Bar (2011b), p. 395 and fn. 20.

[42]Koziol (2009), p. 99; Eidenmüller et al. (2008b), p. 539 f.

[43]Brüggemeier (2009a), p. 181, fn. 10.

[44]*ibid.*, p. 181, fn. 9.

[45]von Bar (2011b), p. 389.

[46]VI.–2:201(2) *lit.* b; VI.–3:104(2) *lit.* a; VI.–3:202(1); VI.–3:203; VI.–3:204(1); VI.–3:205(1); VI.–3:206(1); VI.–4:101(2); VI.–5:401(2) *lit.* a; VI.–5:501; VI.–6:203(2).

where injury is used without connection to damage to the physical integrity or health of a person. That is the case of VI.–2:203 ("Infringement of dignity, liberty and privacy"). Following feedback on the interim outline version, the final version of the DCFR uses the expression "the person suffering the damage" throughout the text and refers to "injured person" only "where the damage is caused by or consists of 'personal injury' and infringement of an incorporeal personality right".[47]

The concept of "injury as such" has been identified by the Italian legal scholars,[48] which has begun to spread to several other jurisdictions, including Portugal, as described earlier.[49]

Some critics of the DCFR point out that the reason for the use of *danno biologico* in Italy had to do with the very narrow limits within which the compensation of non-economic loss was possible.[50] As the DCFR provides for compensation of non-economic loss in broad terms, this "third category of loss" would potentially lead to duplication of compensations.[51] While for some scholars, "injury" is unnecessary because economic and non-economic loss already comprise every possible kind of harm,[52] for others "injury as such" is conceptually different within non-economic loss.[53]

In the DCFR, "injury" does not align with *danno biologico* and it also includes pure ecological damage (VI.–2:209).[54]

In summary, therefore, "injury as such" can be defined for the purposes of the DCFR as the harm which consists of legally relevant damage *per se*, *i.e.* without a (consequential) loss being required.[55] The difference between "injury" and *Verletzung/violação* would be that "injury" for the purposes of the DCFR does not necessarily involve a right or a protective rule. The fact that legally relevant damage sometimes identifies with an injury and does not involve consequential loss[56] has particular relevance in the legal protection of pure economic interests, as will be explained below.

[47] von Bar (2011b), p. 389.

[48] Brüggemeier (2009a), p. 182.

[49] For further details see Tit. § 4, Subtit. IV, Sec. 2, Subsec. bb (3) above.

[50] Brüggemeier (2009a), p. 195, with references.

[51] Eidenmüller et al. (2008a), pp. 683–684.

[52] *ibid.*, p. 684.

[53] Brüggemeier (2009a), p. 196.

[54] Schmidt-Kessel (2006), pp. 60–68; Brüggemeier (2009a), pp. 193–195. For criticism of this provision, which holds that it goes well beyond the EU Directive on environmental liability see Eidenmüller et al. (2008a), p. 685.

[55] von Bar (2011b), p. 390.

[56] Magnus (2004b), p. 576, fn. 87.

III. Circumstances Leading to Legally Relevant Damage

According to VI.–2:101(1), for there to be legally relevant damage, one of three conditions must be met: it is expressly regulated in Section 2 of Chapter 2 (para. 1, *lit.* a); it results from a violation of a right that the law confers (para. 1, *lit.* b); or it results from a violation of an interest which the law protects (para. 1, *lit.* c).[57]

1. Typical Situations of Legally Relevant Damage

a) Purposes and Scope

According to VI.–2:201, *lit.* a, legally relevant damage is, first of all, the loss for which the provisions in Chapter 2 (VI.–2:201 to VI.–2:211)[58] provide.[59]

Legally relevant damage can arise from its own outcomes (*e.g.* personal injury and property damage), from legal circumstances (*e.g.* injury to personality rights) and from factual circumstances (*e.g.* liability for false information).[60]

Some academics commend the "wide and elegant approach" of Section 2 of Chapter 2.[61] Others see striking similarities between the individual listing of instances of legally relevant damage and the English "torticles".[62]

However, the drafters highlight that legally relevant damage is not in itself sufficient to lead to compensation and thus the DCFR does not provide for self-standing "torts".[63] That condition is only met "when every requirement of liability is present and there is no defence that would exclude liability".[64]

---

[57] For details on the structure of the rule in the overall Book see von Bar (2001a), p. 526.

[58] Such provisions are: VI.–2:201 (Personal injury and consequential loss); VI.–2:202 (Loss suffered by third persons as a result of another's personal injury or death); VI.–2:203 (Infringement of dignity, liberty and privacy); VI.–2:204 (Loss upon communication of incorrect information about another); VI.–2:205 (Loss upon breach of confidence); VI.–2:206 (Loss upon infringement of property or lawful possession); VI.–2:207 (Loss upon reliance on incorrect advice or information); VI.–2:208 (Loss upon unlawful impairment of business); VI.–2:209 (Burdens incurred by the state upon environmental impairment); VI.–2.210 (Loss upon fraudulent misrepresentation); VI.–2:211 (Loss upon inducement of non-performance of obligation).

[59] von Bar (2008c), p. 36; von Bar (2010a), p. 217.

[60] von Bar (2001a), p. 524; von Bar (2010a), p. 216. See also von Bar (2009c), Introduction to Chapter 3, n. A7, p. 300.

[61] Menezes Cordeiro (2010b), p. 351; von Bar (2010a), p. 215.

[62] See Brüggemeier (2009a), p. 182; Oliphant (2011), p. 310. See, for a full list of "torticles", Rudden (1991–1992), pp. 105–129.

[63] von Bar (2001a), p. 525.

[64] von Bar (2009c), Introduction to Chapter 2, A2, p. 299. Chapter 5 deals with possible defences. It contains cases traditionally present in the European legal systems under the rubric "grounds for justification" (*Rechtfertigungsgründe*): "consent [of the victim] and acting at own risk" (VI.–5:101); "damage caused by a criminal to a collaborator" (VI.–5:103); "authority conferred by law"

Section 2 of Chapter 2 has three main purposes. Firstly, it singles out individual factual situations where the presence of damage is certain[65] thereby precluding the need for satisfying further tests or hearing of the parties.[66] Secondly, it grants a claim for compensation whenever the person inflicting the loss acted in a particular capacity.[67] That is the case of VI.–2:210(2) on "Loss upon fraudulent misrepresentation". Thirdly, it indicates that some kinds of damage are only legally relevant when provided for by European or national law.[68] That is the case of VI.–2:208 (2) concerning loss upon unlawful impairment of business, as will be set out below.

From another perspective, this means that Section 2 provides for a list of cases where there is no legally relevant damage for the purposes of the DCFR.[69] This list of cases (contrary to Section 2 itself) is exhaustive and shows that legally relevant damage is only present when the damage fulfills particular requirements.[70] Trivial damage, for example, is not enough to qualify as "legally relevant damage" (VI.– 6:102).[71]

The chapter on legally relevant damage includes situations for which there is prevailing support from the EU Member States (also called "unity *de lege lata*")[72] and which involve negligent or intentional behaviours.[73] In many instances of liability without negligence or intention, the concept of legally relevant damage is narrower,[74] as Section 3 describes.[75]

(VI.–5:201); "self-defence, benevolent intervention and necessity" (VI.–5:202); "protection of public interest" (VI.–5:203). To this list the DCFR adds: "Contributory fault and accountability" (VI.–5:102); "mental incompetence" (VI.–5:301); "event beyond control" (VI.–5:302) and "contractual exclusion and restriction of liability" (VI.–5:401). Further defences may result from Book III (particularly Chap. 7, "Prescription") and from rules of national law, because "these model rules are silent on issues that permeate the law on extra-contractual liability from other legal quarters". For possibly applicable defences see von Bar (2009c), n. A3 to VI.–5:101, p. 790. See also von Bar (2008c), p. 37. As for VI.–5:101, it recognises the European-wide legal tradition of reducing or excluding the liability of the person who inflicted the loss whenever the person who sustained the loss contributed with his or her fault to the damage (Magnus 2004b, p. 575).

[65]von Bar (2001a), p. 524; von Bar (2009c), Intr. to Chap. 2, A3, p. 299.

[66]von Bar (2010a), p. 215.

[67]Cf. Claeys (2012), pp. 232–233.

[68]*ibid.*, p. 233.

[69]von Bar (2001a), p. 524; von Bar (2010a), p. 215. For other reasons for this list of particular instances of legally relevant damage see Blackie (2007), pp. 67–68.

[70]von Bar (2010a), p. 215.

[71]This provision (*de minimis rule*) translates the solution of the EU systems (von Bar 1999b, p. 30). Some legal commentators argue it would have been better placed in VI.–2:101 (Brüggemeier 2009a, p. 188). Given that "trivial" damage is still "damage" but is irrelevant for the purposes of reparation, its current placement under the chapter related to "Remedies" thus seems fitting.

[72]von Bar (2009c), Introduction to Chapter 2, B9, p. 301.

[73]von Bar (2010a), p. 215.

[74]*ibid.*

[75]Whenever no restriction is expressly stated, the concept of legally relevant damage maintains the same scope as if it had been caused by negligence or intention (von Bar 2010a, p. 215).

Instances of legally relevant damage "taken with the provisions of accountability without intention or negligence (...) reflect the view of the group that in these situations it is possible to state in detail what the requirements for liability are".[76] Nevertheless, for legally relevant damage (as listed in Section 2) to be recoverable, the remaining conditions in the basic rule must be met.[77]

Whenever there are overlaps between the instances of legally relevant damage, the claimant will have several grounds for action but only one claim to reparation or prevention.[78]

b) Legally Relevant Damage Resulting from Personal Injury

The first particular instance of legally relevant damage is VI.–2:201.[79]

This provides that the injury to the body or health of a person is a form of legally relevant damage independent from the loss resulting from it. Legal commentators consider this to be an autonomisation of the concept of *danno biologico*, according to which physical injuries or injury to health represents damage *per se*.[80] The drafters justified such inclusion by referring to the increasing general acceptance of the concept in several EU legal systems.[81]

The denial of an injury to body and health of the victim as legally relevant does not necessarily mean that no protection is granted to the affected person by the law governing liability. The affected person can have a claim in relation to an interest worthy of legal protection. The DCFR gives the example of a spouse who is affected by the impotence of a partner as a result of an accident.[82] This loss is recognised by case law in Portugal, where the right of the spouse who is indirectly affected is compensated as a non-economic loss or under personality rights.[83]

The losses indicated in VI.–2:201 are not exhaustive, meaning that there are other losses which may be compensated besides those included in the provision. That is the case for the inability to provide domestic services at home,[84] the value of

---

[76]Blackie (2007), p. 65.

[77]von Bar (2010a), pp. 215 and 217.

[78]von Bar (2009c), Intr. to Chap. 2, n. A5, p. 300. However, if the conduct of the person inflicting the harm gives rise to more than one legally relevant damage, the claimant will have several claims to reparation or prevention (von Bar 2009c, Intr. to Chap. 2, n. A6, p. 300).

[79]VI.–2:201 ("Personal injury and consequential loss") provides that: (1) Loss caused to a natural person as a result of injury to his or her body or health and the injury as such are legally relevant damage. (2) In this Book: (a) such loss includes the costs of health care, including expenses reasonably incurred for the care of the injured person by those close to him or her, and (b) personal injury includes injury to mental health only if it amounts to a medical condition.

[80]Brüggemeier (2009a), p. 182.

[81]von Bar (2009c), n. B12 to VI.–2:201, p. 362.

[82]*ibid.*, n. E23 to VI.–2:101, 312 and n. B10 to VI.–2:201, p. 361 f.

[83]STJ 8 September 2009, proc. 2733/06.9TBBCL.S1 and STJ 1 July 2014, proc.6607/09.3TVLSB.L1.S1., respectively.

[84]von Bar (2009c), n. C13 to VI.–2:201, p. 363.

which has been recognised by the Portuguese courts.[85] This recognition[86] led to the addition of a new sub-clause to Art. 1676 CC ("Duty of contributing to the [economic] burdens of the life of the family"), which expressly recognises the right of a spouse to be compensated by the other spouse for having contributed significantly more towards the burdens of family life, or for having sacrificed excessively his or her professional interests in favour of family life.

VI.–2:201 does not distinguish between "primary" and "secondary" victims. The drafters attach importance, rather, to determining whether or not the person suffered an injury to health or body, thus making him or her a victim.[87] The drafters recognised the difficulty of identifying if the damage was suffered by the victim or by other persons, such as where expenses are incurred for the assistance or treatment of the victim. The DCFR opted to assign the expenses of those close to the victim to the damage sustained by the claimant, "a case at the boundary of transferred loss (*Drittschadensliquidation*)".[88] The persons close to the victim would be afterwards entitled to recover such expenses through benevolent intervention in another's affairs or unjustified enrichment.[89] As for the costs of lost wages incurred by informal carers, as mentioned above,[90] the DCFR opted to compensate them only insofar as the carer actually holds a profession within the caring industry. In that case, the recovery of his or her loss would amount to the loss which the person inflicting the loss would always have had to pay to the victim.[91] Whatever their nature may be, expenses must be reasonable to "protect the liable person".[92]

VI.–2:202 ("Loss suffered by third persons as a result of another's personal injury or death")[93] indicates that third parties can sustain both economic and

---

[85]See generally Araújo Dias (2010)

[86]STJ 21 June 1988, proc. JSTJ00011490; STJ 15 May 2004, proc. 04A1549, but see STJ 29 April 2010, proc. 344/04.2GTSTR.S1. Cases where relatives ask for compensation for the value of the domestic work rendered to the victim is different. This has been provided for STJ 4 February 1986, proc. 073433 but the current position held is that no compensation is granted (STJ 10 July 2008, proc. 08A1853).

[87]von Bar (2009c), D16 to VI.–2:201, p. 363.

[88]*ibid.*, D18 to VI.–2:201, p. 364.

[89]*ibid.* The DCFR provides that claims based upon legal grounds other than non-contractual liability damage remain unaffected and respects the supremacy of other legal fields in such claims (VI.–1:103, *lits.* a and d, respectively). See von Bar (2001a), p. 531.

[90]See § Tit. 5 Subtit. III, Sec. 3, Subsec. aa (3).

[91]von Bar (2009c), n. D19 to VI.–2:201, pp. 364–365.

[92]*ibid.*, n. D19 to VI.–2:201, p. 364.

[93]The Article reads: "(1) Non-economic loss caused to a natural person as a result of another's personal injury or death is legally relevant damage if at the time of injury that person is in a particular close personal relationship to the injured person. (2) Where a person has been fatally injured: (a) legally relevant damage caused to the deceased on account of the injury at the time of death becomes legally relevant damage to the deceased's successors; (b) reasonable funeral expenses are legally relevant damage to the person incurring them; and (c) loss of maintenance is legally relevant damage to a natural person whom the deceased maintained or, had death not occurred, would have maintained under statutory provisions, or to whom the deceased provided care and financial support".

non-economic loss following the fatal or non-fatal injury of another. As for non-economic loss, VI.–2:202(1) is an exception to VI.–2:201(1) and is in line with the prevailing view in EU Member States.[94]

The DCFR's approach here is broader than the corresponding provision in the Portuguese Civil Code (Art. 496(2) CC) in two ways. Firstly, a right of reparation does not depend on the gravity of the damage but only on a "close relationship"[95] with the person on whom personal injury was inflicted; secondly, it extends explicitly to cases of non-fatal personal injuries, whereas Art. 496 CC refers only to fatal injuries.[96] On the other hand, the DCFR does not recognise "loss of life" as damage incurring compensation.[97] This follows the mainstream European view, in which Portugal is the only legal system providing for a right of reparation for death.

As for economic loss, it follows that it is both consequential (VI.–2:202(2), *lit.* a) and pure economic loss (VI.–2:202(2), *lits.* b and c). Loss of maintenance may be classified as a consequential loss.[98] Reasonable funeral expenses, on the other hand, may be considered an example of pure economic loss.[99]

2. *Default Rules*

a) Release Valves and Flexibility for the Courts

As stated, the list of particular instances of legally relevant damage in Section 2 of Chapter 2 is not exhaustive, *i.e.* the SGECC did not draft it in the light of a *numerus clausus* principle. It simply comprises the most flagrant cases of legally relevant damage.

Therefore, and contrary to what some legal commentators claim,[100] the fact that Chapter 2 does not provide specifically for damage, does not mean that damage is not legally relevant for the purposes of the DCFR.[101]

Indeed, damage can be compensated within VI.–2:201(1) *lits.* b and c. The drafters call it a "default rule"[102] and they offer a number of justifications.

---

[94]von Bar (2009c), n. B6 to VI.–2:202, p. 391.

[95]*ibid.*

[96]The STJ recently extended reparation to cases of non-fatal injuries. See Tit. § 4, Subtit. IV, Sec. 2, Subsec. bb (2) above.

[97]von Bar (2002a), p. 176; von Bar (2009c), n. C9 to VI.–2:202, pp. 391–392.

[98]Brüggemeier (2009a), p. 182, fn. 15; von Bar (2009c), n. B8 to VI.–2:202, p. 391.

[99]The relationship of DCFR with the category of pure economic loss will be explained under Tit. § 7, Subtit. IV below.

[100]See Magnus (2004b), pp. 576–577.

[101]von Bar (2001a), p. 524; von Bar (2010a), p. 216. For details on the non-exhaustive character of the list of legally relevant damage see Swann (2003), pp. 8–9.

[102]von Bar (2001a), p. 526; von Bar (2010a), p. 217. Other authors consider that *lits.* b and c are default rules, instead of VI.–2:201 itself. See Brüggemeier (2009a), p. 181.

Firstly, the default rule would recognise that in present-day jurisprudence it is not possible to identify every situation leading to liability.[103] Secondly, the default rule is an "open clause" (similar to other clauses in other legal systems)[104] that provides guidelines to courts for resolving cases, particularly those which involve constitutional issues.[105] The default rule provides criteria to aid courts in recognising the presence or absence of legally relevant damage[106] and thereby allows judge-made development of the law and adaptation of the law to the changing social and legal reality.[107] Finally, the default rule is justified by the fact that there are areas where it is not possible to reach a general agreement on some issues, and which must thus be left to each individual Member State. One such area, the drafters claim, is liability for the infringement of "absolute" subjective rights.[108]

aa) Violation of Rights Conferred by Laws

VI.–2:101(1), *lits.* b and c distinguishes between "violation of a right otherwise conferred by the law" and "violation of an interest worthy of legal protection". Paras. 2 and 3 apply equally to both. The drafters provided for the separation in two different *litteras* because the concept of infringement of a right is familiar to some EU legal systems, and because the drafters expect the judge to be more demanding with *lit.* c.

As for VI.-2:101(1) *lit.* b, all of the rights defined as "absolute rights" will be included in this provision.[109] "Bilateral" subjective rights, such as contractual rights, are excluded.[110] This chimes with the prevailing view in both Portugal[111] and Germany.[112] Moreover, "right otherwise conferred by the law" is also understood as rights from areas outside of Private Law.

bb) Violation of Interests Worthy of Legal Protection

As for VI.–2.101(1), *lit.* c illustrates the idea that within the DCFR the interests protected by non-contractual liability are not pre-determined or determined

[103]von Bar (2009c), n. B7 to VI.–2:101, p. 305.

[104]*ibid.*, n. D15 to VI.–2:101, p. 308.

[105]For examples, see von Bar (2009c), B8 to VI.–2:101, p. 305.

[106]Blackie (2007), p. 70.

[107]von Bar (2009c), Introduction to Chapter 2, n. A3, p. 299 and n. D15 to VI.–2:101, p. 308.

[108]*ibid.*, n. B9 to VI.–2:101, pp. 305–306; n. C11 to VI.–2:101, p. 307.

[109]von Bar (2009c), n. C12 to VI.–2:101, p. 307 f.

[110]Blackie (2007), pp. 72–73. An exception of VI.–2:211 (von Bar 2009c, n. C13 to VI.–2:101, p. 308).

[111]See Tit. § 4, Subtit. IV, Sec. 5, Subsec. c, aa) above.

[112]Frank (1979), p. 585.

heteronomously[113] but are instead determined by non-contractual liability itself.[114] This means that those interests are traditionally characterised as "absolute", but that they can protect "relative" interests as well, i.e. those relating to only one party or to a restricted number of parties (*e.g.*, VI.–2:211).[115]

The drafters considered non-contractual liability damage to be a legal field with its own values.[116] As a result, it should be non-contractual liability arising out of damage caused to another that itself decides the legally relevant losses and the conditions under which they constitute such.[117] This type of analysis is based on a multiplicity of factors, such as factual results or the circumstances where the loss was inflicted[118] and should thus be assessed on a case-by-case basis[119] (*ius in causa positum*). The drafters claim to have taken a less dogmatic and more pragmatic approach to liability.[120]

b) The Process of Determination Based Upon Fairness and Reasonableness

VI.–2:101(1) *lits.* b and c must be read in conjunction with VI.–2:101(2), as loss will only be legally relevant if it is "fair and reasonable for there to be a right of reparation or prevention, as the case may be".

This is further explained in VI.–2:101(3). According to this paragraph, while evaluating the fairness and reasonableness of compensating losses which result from the violation of a right or the infringement of an interest, the DCFR provides the court with factors which it must consider in its decision.

An element that the court shall consider is the *ground of accountability*. The decision on whether it will be fair and reasonable to consider a damage legally relevant depends on whether the case at hand is one of liability for intentional inflicted damage, liability for negligently inflicted damage or strict liability (VI.–2:101(3)). The connection between a given form of strict liability and legally relevant damage is set out in most of the provisions of Chapter 2, Section 2, and para. 3 has practical significance only as far as vicarious liability under Art. VI.–3:201 is concerned.[121] The court may decide that there will only be legally relevant damage where intention can be found,[122] such as in cases for the loss upon

[113]Stoll (1984), p. 26.
[114]von Bar (2009c), n. D15 to VI.–2:101, p. 308.
[115]Miranda Barbosa (2015), p. 230.
[116]von Bar (2010a), p. 212.
[117]von Bar (2002a), p. 173. See also von Bar (2010a), p. 212.
[118]von Bar (2002a), pp. 173–174.
[119]von Bar (2010a), p. 214.
[120]On the need for non-dogmatic tort law see von Bar (1996a), p. 15 *passim*.
[121]For details see von Bar (2009c), n. E17 to VI.–2:101, p. 309. See also von Bar (1999a), p. 215.
[122]Blackie (2007), p. 72; von Bar (2010a), p. 211.

inducement to non-performance of obligation, which is only legally relevant damage as long as "the person inducing the non-performance intended the third to fail to perform the obligation" (VI.–2:210, *lits.* a, i).[123] This element shows a particular relationship between legally relevant damage and accountability.

Among such elements is the *nature of the damage* and the considerations involved in causation:[124] the more serious the loss, the less strong the causation has to be and vice versa.[125]

Another element is the *proximity of the damage* or impending damage, which means that there will be legally relevant damage only when there is sufficient connection between the conduct of the person inflicting the harm and the damage caused,[126] further underlining that legally relevant damage and causation are deeply intertwined.[127]

Yet another element listed in VI.–2:201(3) is the *reasonable expectations* of the person who suffers, or who would suffer, the damage. This corresponds to a consideration of distributive justice[128] and is connected to the capacity of a given legal system to provide the injured person with legal redress.[129]

Finally, VI.–2:201(3) *in fine* refers to *considerations of public policy*, *i.e.* based on the good of society and the internal balance of the private law system as a whole.[130]

Some scholars argue that VI.–2:201(3) addresses the Common Law "relational torts" (an expression which is sometimes used as an equivalent to pure economic loss), where legal culpability is accomplished through the duty of care.[131] Its aim would be a removal of indirect harm[132] from liability (including situations of pure economic loss),[133] which in Germany is often achieved through the *Verkehrspflichten*.[134]

The default rule is only called upon whenever the provisions of Section 2 do not apply.[135] It is thus argued that the whole of VI.–2:101 has a "catch-all" function. For this reason, some legal commentators argue that it should have remained in its

---

[123] von Bar (2009c), n. E18 to VI.–2:101, p. 309 f.

[124] *ibid.*, n. E19 to VI.–2:101, p. 310.

[125] von Bar (2001a), p. 522. Cf. also Magnus (2004b), p. 566.

[126] Blackie (2007), p. 72.

[127] von Bar (2009c), n. E21 to VI.–2:101, p. 311, with illustrative examples.

[128] Blackie (2007), p. 72.

[129] von Bar (2009c), n. E22 to VI.–2:101, p. 311 f.

[130] von Bar (1996a), p. 15; von Bar (2009c), n. E23 to VI.–2:101, p. 312.

[131] Blackie (2005), p. 137 f.; Blackie (2007), p. 72; Brüggemeier (2009a), p. 181; Claeys (2012), pp. 234–235. Legal commentators have noticed the absence of any mention of the category of duty (Brüggemeier 2009a, p. 182). The fact that "duty of care" is associated with liability for negligent behaviour may be why this concept was not adopted in the DCFR (Blackie 2007, p. 63).

[132] Cf. Weir (1999), p. 644; Schulze (2012), p. 226.

[133] Lipstein (1963), p. 91; Howarth (2011), p. 846; Claeys (2012), p. 234.

[134] Brüggemeier (2009a), p. 181.

[135] von Bar (2009c), Intr. to Chap. 2, n. A3, p. 299.

original location at the end of Section 2, Chapter 2.[136] The drafters explain that they placed VI.–2:201 at the beginning of the section to counter the possible interpretation that the text contains an exhaustive list of protective interests.[137]

3. Legally Relevant Damage and Danno ingiusto

The DCFR did not follow the German and Portuguese approach of separating the injury of a legally protected good or interest from the consequence of such injury (*danno conseguenza*).[138] The "legally relevant damage" is defined as damage with a certain *quid*, a damage which includes the negative repercussions of the injury and the injury as such.[139]

For this reason, legally relevant damage presents similarities with *danno ingiusto*[140] in Art. 2043 (Reparation for unlawful conducts) of the Italian Civil Code,[141] which reads: "The person who causes unjust damage to another person due to intentional or negligent conduct must repair the damage inflicted".

Both legally relevant damage and *danno ingiusto* imply that "the concept of damage must be viewed in relation to the type of liability and the legal consequences which give it concrete form and, secondly, that there are no methods of defining damage which apply to all situations relevant to liability".[142] Accordingly, both concepts also acknowledge that identifying damage is an evaluation inextricably linked to the remaining conditions of liability.[143]

Italian legal scholarship and courts define *danno ingiusto* as the injury of a legally protected status[144] or as the breach of a protected interest.[145]

---

[136]von Bar (2001a), p. 526; Schmidt-Kessel (2006), p. 87.

[137]von Bar (2009c), Intr. to Chap. 2, n. B11, p. 301.

[138]Brüggemeier (2009a), p. 197.

[139]*ibid.*; Miranda Barbosa (2015), pp. 226–227. This understanding is reinforced by VI.–6:204 (Miranda Barbosa 2015, pp. 226–227).

[140]von Bar (1999f), p. 55; von Bar (2001a), p. 522; von Bar (2011b), p. 393.

[141]Royal Edict 16 March 1942, no. 262, which approved the text of the Civil Code (G.U. no. 79 e 79-bis of 4 April 1942, General Ser.).

[142]von Bar (2009c), Intr. to Chap. 2, n. A4, p. 299. Originally, *danno ingiusto* was interpreted along similar lines to § 823(1) BGB (von Bar 2002b, p. 68), and it still is by some authors. See Ranieri (2003), p. 1480.

[143]von Bar (1999a), p. 214; von Bar (2001a), p. 522; Menezes Cordeiro (2010b), p. 597. Cf. also von Bar (2009c), Intr. to Chap. 2, n. A4, pp. 299–300.

[144]Alpa et al. (1995), p. 135.

[145]Franzoni (1993), p. 183 ff. See Gozzi (2006), pp. 22–23, with case law references in footnote. There used to be a discussion on the meaning of the concept of *danno ingiusto*. It was argued, for example, that there would be *ingiustizia* whenever there was no applicable defence (Schlesinger 1960, p. 336 ff.). In cases where there is no defence, the *antigiuridicità* would be present, but not as a requirement of liability (Castronovo 2006, p. 13 ff.). It was also argued that there would be *ingiustizia* whenever the infringement of an interest is protected by the legal order (Sacco, *Foro Pad.*, I (1960), p. 1420 ff.; Gozzi 2006, p. 24) or determined in each case by the court (Rodotà

According to the *Corte Suprema di Cassazione*, the court has the task of deciding which interest is legally relevant (*interesse legittimo*) and it must decide if it should protect the interest of the person who sustained the harm[146] (*neminem laedere*). The courts assess the interests in question according to criteria which take account of values of society[147] and principles such as the principle of public interest,[148] solidarity[149] and *abus de droit*.[150] The Coordinating Group considered *danno ingiusto* to be too complex to translate into the European languages.[151]

4. Legally Relevant Damage and the Absence of Unlawfulness

It has already been discussed how the DCFR does not work with a closed and "abstract" catalogue of non-contractual protected interests,[152] which it considers unnecessary and, in any case, impossible to achieve.[153]

For this reason, the DCFR does not follow the example of the BGB and the Portuguese Civil Code in providing for "unlawfulness" as a requirement of liability.[154]

The DCFR leaves unlawfulness out of its draft for three main reasons.

Firstly, because they believe that the concept serves the protection of a pre-defined set of rights which are in opposition to other people ("absolute" rights)[155] and which are considered by the legal order, without reason, to be

1964, p. 183 ff.). Traditionally, legal scholars understood it to refer to the infringement of subjective rights (Cian 1966, p. 109) but there was no unanimity on this (Sacco, *Foro Pad.*, I (1960), p. 1429 ff.). Other authors considered that *danno ingiusto* concerned an assessment of the interests present (Trimarchi 2007, pp. 107–109) or even that it was a synonym for *antigiuridicità oggetiva* (unlawfulness) and *antigiuridicità soggetiva* (fault). See Cian (1966), p. 109.

[146]Cass., Sez. Un. 22 July 1999, no. 500, Foro it. 2000 III, 481; Cass. 17 May 2004, no. 9345, Giust. Civ. Mass. 2004, fasc 5. For details see Gozzi (2006), p. 24.

[147]De Cupis (1979), p. 11; Gozzi (2006), pp. 24–25.

[148]Trimarchi (2007), p. 109.

[149]Rodotà (1964), p. 108.

[150]Gozzi (2006), p. 25, with references in footnote. Compared to Art. 483(1) CC, the scope of protection of the *danno ingiusto* is wider, because, according to the prevailing view, for there to be *ingiustizia* there is no need for a violation of a subjective right (Castronovo 2006, p. 128) nor for violation of a protective rule (cf. Gozzi 2006, p. 22).

[151]von Bar (2001a), p. 522; Blackie (2007), p. 63; von Bar (2002a), p. 175.

[152]von Bar (2001a), p. 524; Blackie (2005), p. 142; von Bar (2009c), Introduction to Chapter 2, A1, p. 299; von Bar (2010a), p. 215.

[153]von Bar (2010a), p. 215.

[154]von Bar (1999b), p. 205; Schmidt-Kessel (2006), p. 16; von Bar (2010a), p. 212. Thus, the understanding of Menezes Cordeiro—that the category is displaced to here—is unjustified (Menezes Cordeiro 2010b, p. 352).

[155]Schulze (2012), p. 224.

hierarchically superior to other values.[156] Secondly, because unlawfulness presupposes a clear distinction from negligence which, according to the drafters, has been shown to be impossible.[157] Thirdly, because unlawfulness introduced distinctions which give rise to problems, such as the distinction between foundation of liability (*Haftungsbegründung*) and its consequences (*Haftungsausfüllung*),[158] the difference between "pure" economic loss and "consequential" economic loss, and the assumption that a person whose conduct infringes the law may act without negligence.[159] Overall, the drafters considered the category not "Europeanisable".[160]

The concept of violation of rights present in Art. 483 CC (as in § 823(1) BGB) was thus not adopted for policy reasons.[161] It may be found in some rules of the DCFR, namely in VI.–2:101(1) *lit.* b. However: a) immediately after, *lit.* c places interests worthy of legal protection on an equal footing;[162] b) the violation of rights is not considered damage as such, as the drafters always require "a detrimental effect" to exist before attributing a right to reparation;[163] c) it is subject to the filter provided for in (2) and (3).

As for the concept of infringement of provisions aimed at protecting the interests of others, this was left out of both the basic rule and the provision for the "meaning of legally relevant damage". The drafters claimed that statutory duties may have different content from country to country or even from place to place.[164]

Some legal commentators highlighted the flexibility of the concept of legally relevant damage and applauded the abandonment of the requirement of unlawfulness.[165]

In Portugal, where the condition of unlawfulness is firmly rooted in the legal jurisprudence,[166] it is argued that the problems of a hierarchy of values and the selection of legally relevant damage persist, because the DCFR speaks of "interest

---

[156] von Bar (2002b), p. 70; von Bar (2010a), p. 212. For Lipstein, "where formerly the preservation of physical integrity and the protection of land and movable objects against direct interference ranked foremost, today the law of tort is more concerned with (1) indirect violations of the economic potential of the individual and of commercial and industrial enterprises and (2) with the creation of responsibility in respect of an increasing area of dangerous or potentially dangerous activities" (Lipstein 1963, p. 101). Sinde Monteiro, however, considers that the "interests worthy of legal protection" correspond essentially to absolute subjective rights (Sinde Monteiro 2007, p. 477).

[157] von Bar (1999b), pp. 212–213; von Bar (2010a), p. 212 f.

[158] For further details on this distinction, see Kötz and Wagner (2013), pp. 55–56.

[159] von Bar (2010a), p. 213.

[160] von Bar (2000b), p. 612. See also Weir (1999), p. 644. Cf. also von Bar (2009c), n. B9 to VI.–2:101, p. 306.

[161] von Bar (2011b), p. 395.

[162] von Bar (2002a), p. 173.

[163] von Bar (2011b), p. 395.

[164] von Bar (2009c), n. B9 to VI.–2:101, p. 306. According to one view, however, the DCFR recognises the violation of statutory provisions as a basis for non-contractual liability in Articles VI.–3:102 and VI.–3:207 (Hollander 2012, p. 252 ff.).

[165] Brüggemeier (2009a), p. 183; Hollander (2012), p. 256.

[166] See Tit. § 4, Subtit. IV, Sec. 5 above.

worthy of legal protection" (VI.–2:201(1) *lit.* c), albeit through another frame. It is also argued that the formulation in VI–2:201 involves a particularly complex task requiring consideration of several factors, namely, those in VI.–2:201(2) and (3). For this reason, some hold that the DCFR did not abandon the concept of unlawfulness but, rather, added elements to it.[167] Such positions do not sufficiently consider, however, the fact that the loss must be "fair and reasonable" in order to be the object of reparation. This creates a filter of liability, which the judges can use in each case to determine whether or not the damage is legally relevant.

IV. The Protection of Pure Economic Interests in the DCFR

1. No Recognition of "Pure Economic Loss" as a Category of Loss

The DCFR does not set apart the category of "pure economic loss" as "a free-standing type of damage",[168] which goes hand-in-hand with its denial of "unlawfulness" as a condition for non-contractual liability.

The drafters believed that the category of pure economic loss,[169] like unlawfulness, cannot be "Europeanised".[170] Firstly, several legal systems do not recognise the category of pure economic loss. Secondly, the category has different meanings and differing scopes in the countries in which it is recognised.[171] Therefore, a rule dealing specifically with liability for pure economic loss would conflict with present-day interpretations in some EU Member States and would be unable to encompass every feature of this category of loss.[172] The drafters did not explicitly refer to the category of pure economic loss, stating that its existence is an unnecessary *topos*,[173] which resulted in a "false development" and gave rise to "strenuous amendments".[174]

[167] Cf. Sinde Monteiro (2007), p. 477.

[168] von Bar (2001a), p. 522; von Bar (2008c), p. 36.

[169] "Consequential loss" is not found in Book VI because a *Verletzung* is not a requirement of liability on its own. See von Bar (2002b), p. 70.

[170] von Bar (2001a), p. 523. In the same sense, van Boom et al. (2004a), p. 202 *passim*. But see VI.–2:102 PETL, which provides expressly for liability for pure economic loss, although "they occupy a subordinate place in the hierarchy of protected interests" (Oliphant 2011, p. 310).

[171] Schmidt-Kessel (2006), p. 120.

[172] van Boom et al. (2004a), p. 202 ff.

[173] von Bar (1994b), p. 111; von Bar (2001a), p. 523; von Bar and Drobnig (2004), p. 119; Schmidt-Kessel (2006), p. 21. Cf. also von Bar (2000b), p. 606.

[174] Cf. von Bar (2001a), p. 523. See also Gordley (2003).

By refraining from providing for an autonomous category of pure economic loss, the DCFR follows the example of the PECL. Both dismiss a *tertium genus* of liability between contractual and non-contractual liability,[175] namely liability based upon reliance.[176] The DCFR deals with the reparation of pure economic interests in non-contractual liability arising out of damage caused to another through the concept of legally relevant damage.[177]

2. *Instances of Recovery of Pure Economic Loss*

Although not including the category of pure economic loss as such, the DCFR includes several provisions from which compensation of harmed pure economic interests may be derived,[178] provided that the remaining conditions of liability are met.[179] Among such provisions[180] are VI.–2:207 (Loss upon reliance on incorrect advice or information); VI.–2:208 (Loss upon unlawful impairment of business); and VI.–2:211 (Loss upon inducement of non-performance of obligation). Some legal commentators have claimed that the DCFR went too far in such protections.[181]

a) Reliance on Incorrect Advice or Information

Loss upon reliance on incorrect advice or information is provided for in VI.–2:207. It reads:

> Loss caused to a person as a result of making a decision in reasonable reliance on incorrect advice or information is legally relevant damage if:
>
> (a) the advice or information is provided by a person in pursuit of a profession or in the course of trade; and
> (b) the provider knew, or could reasonably be expected to have known, that the recipient would rely on the advice or information in making a decision of the kind made.

---

[175] The only exception to the non-recognition by the PECL of "pure economic loss" as an autonomous category is a rule on the integration of *culpa in contrahendo* in the overall system.

[176] von Bar (2001a), p. 523. See also von Bar (2002a), p. 178.

[177] von Bar (2011b), p. 394.

[178] Schmidt-Kessel (2006), p. 121.

[179] Brüggemeier (2009a), p. 182.

[180] According to a classification, the full list of provisions is: VI.–2:204 (Loss upon communication of incorrect information about another); VI.–2:205 (Loss upon breach of confidence); VI.–2:207 (Loss upon reliance on incorrect advice or information); VI.–2:208 (Loss upon unlawful impairment of business); VI.–2:209 (Burdens incurred by the state upon environmental impairment); VI.–2:210 (Loss upon fraudulent misrepresentation) and VI.–2:211 (Loss upon inducement of non-performance of obligation). Some legal scholars classify these losses as "economic torts" (Brüggemeier 2009a, p. 182).

[181] Schmidt-Kessel (2006), p. 121.

"Advice or information" may be defined as a single output combining an assertion of fact (and not a mere value judgment) and a recommendation to act accordingly.[182]

The DCFR does not provide for a general principle of liability for advice, recommendation and information, which would overburden professional persons with a risk of liability.[183] The same idea is present in several European legal systems, among them Portugal (Art. 495 CC) and Germany (§ 675 BGB), which do not provide for liability for advice or information in general terms.[184]

However, a person will be liable under VI.–2:207 where someone reasonably relied on advice or information provided during the exercise of a profession or in the course of trade (*lit.* a), or the provider knew or could reasonably be expected to have known that the recipient would rely on said advice when taking a decision based upon such advice or information (*lit.* b).[185] The rule is designed for cases concerning information provided by banks and evaluators.[186] The circumstances where liability is admitted meet the reasonable expectations of the person who suffers or would suffer the damage. The provision thus attends to some of the aspects mentioned in VI.–2:201(2) and (3), even if, by being a particular instance of liability, it was not necessary.[187]

Similar to the Portuguese Civil Code, only the direct recipient is entitled to a claim for damages.[188] If a person receives the advice or information from the original recipient and sustains loss, such loss would probably not pass the filter of *lit.* b and would also be withdrawn in general terms under VI.–2:101(3). Moreover, the condition of causation, which must be filled in the general terms of VI.–1:101, is required at two levels in this provision: firstly, the action of the recipient must be the result of the information or advice and, secondly, the damage must have resulted from such action.[189] This is considered by some scholars as an overly restrictive provision.[190]

Compared to VI.–2:207, the corresponding provision in the Portuguese Civil Code (Art. 485 CC) requires, on the one hand, that the provider that acted within a duty must have acted with fault[191] thus restricting the liability of the provider. On the other hand, Art. 485 CC also admits liability where the provision of information, advice or recommendation amounted to a criminal offence.

---

[182]von Bar (2009c), n. D9 to VI.–2:207, p. 513.In the Portuguese Civil Code, the expression used is "information, recommendation or advice", which means that the rule comprises the transmission of an assertion of fact and advice alone.

[183]von Bar (2009c), n. A1 to VI.–2:207, p. 510.

[184]*ibid.*

[185]*ibid.*, nn. B5, B6, C7, C8 and C9 to VI.–2:207, pp. 512 and 513.

[186]*ibid.*, n. A1 to VI.–2:207, p. 510. See also Carneiro da Frada (1997).

[187]For details see *ibid.*, nn. C7 and C8 to VI.–2:207, pp. 512 and 513.

[188]*ibid.*, n. B6 to VI.–2:207, p. 512.

[189]von Bar (2009c), n. D10 to VI.–2:207, p. 513 f.

[190]Koziol (2009), p. 102.

[191]See Pires de Lima and Antunes Varela (1987), n. 1 *lit.* b to Art. 485 CC, p. 487.

Provided that the conditions of VI.–2:207 are fulfilled, it remains to be seen whether the remaining conditions of the basic rule are present. It is also necessary that the provider of advice or information acted with fault[192] and the presence of contributory fault from the recipient must also be assessed (VI.–5:102).

VI.–2:207 relates to non-contractual liability, although in some cases a liability in contract may also arise. In such cases, the drafters admit that contract law may have preferential application.[193]

b) Unlawful Impairment of Business

According to VI.–2:208, a person will suffer legally relevant damage whenever his or her business has been unlawfully impaired. It reads:

1. Loss caused to a person as a result of an unlawful impairment of that person's exercise of a profession or conduct of a trade is legally relevant damage.
2. Loss caused to a consumer as a result of unfair competition is also legally relevant damage if Community or national law so provides.

This provision reflects the German concept of "right to form and operate a business enterprise", although with a different scope. While VI.–2:208 does not refer to liability arising from unauthorised forms of labour disputes, it does, however, refer to liability arising from unauthorised forms of competitive behaviour.[194]

VI.–2.208(1) is one of the rare provisions where the word "unlawful" is used in the draft. "Unlawful" in this context means against statutory provisions or established practice (including in the courts).[195] This is considered to be the adoption of the requirement of unlawfulness in the draft.[196]

The impairment must be directed against the person who sustained the loss, an accidental impairment would not suffice. However, the complete destruction or obstruction of the business is not required.[197]

According to VI.–2:208(2), a loss suffered by a consumer due to the unfair competition of a business is only a legally relevant damage if European or national law so provides, i.e. if the consumer is encompassed within the scope of protection of the law on unfair competition.[198] The DCFR therefore takes into consideration

---

[192]It is apparent that fault is relevant only when the circumstances in *lits.* a and b are present. The provision of advice or information negligently will not lead to liability on its own, as is the case in Art. 485(1) CC.

[193]von Bar (2009c), n. A3 to VI.–2:207,511; Volens (2010), p. 181.

[194]See von Bar (2009c), n. A1 to VI.–2:208, 520; n. A3 to VI.–2:208, 520 f. and n. B10 to VI.–2:208, p. 522 f. See also Brüggemeier (2009a), p. 182.

[195]von Bar (2009c), n. B9 to VI.–2:208, p. 522.

[196]Koziol (2009), p. 103.

[197]*ibid.*, n. B8 to VI.–2:208, p. 522

[198]*ibid.*, n. B11 to VI.–2:208, p. 523.

the developments in the *acquis communautaire* when considering the right of the consumer to bring a claim.

c) Inducement of Non-performance of Obligation

Loss upon inducement of non-performance of obligation is provided for in VI.–2:211. It reads:

> Without prejudice to the other provisions of this section, loss caused to a person as a result of another's inducement of the non-performance of an obligation by a third person is legally relevant damage only if:
>
> a) the obligation was owed to the person sustaining the loss; and
> b) the person inducing the non-performance:
>
> i) intended the third person to fail to perform the obligation, and
> ii) did not act in legitimate protection of the inducing person's own interest.

This provision corresponds to a common state of affairs throughout the EU, as inducing non-performance of an obligation is considered legally relevant damage in every EU Member State, although sometimes under the form of "intentional causation of damage contrary to good morals".[199]

Indeed, this loss is only legally relevant if the person inflicting the harm intended the third person not to perform his or her obligation.[200] He or she does not need to have wanted to cause the loss.[201] Under such circumstances, the DCFR accepts that a "relative" right has effects outside a relationship regulated by the Law of Obligations (among which are contractual obligations).[202] For that reason, the drafters highlight that this particular instance of legally relevant damage is connected to VI.–2:101(1) *lits.* b and c.[203]

Although the expression "loss" in VI.–2:211 includes non-economic loss as well, the drafters admit that this provision relates particularly to the compensation of "pure economic loss".[204] However, the provision places some limits on that compensation, namely in *lit.* a, according to which only the creditor suffers legally relevant damage.[205]

---

199 von Bar (2009c), n. A1 to VI.–2:211, p. 546.

200 Schmidt-Kessel (2006), p. 121; von Bar (2009c), n. A3 to VI.–2:211, p. 547.

201 von Bar (2009c), n. C10 to VI.–2:211, p. 549.

202 *ibid.*, n. B6 to VI.–2:211, p. 548.

203 *ibid.*, n. A2 to VI.–2:211, p. 546.

204 *ibid.*, n. A4 to VI.–2:211, p. 547.

205 *ibid.*, n. A5 to VI.–2:211, p. 547 and n. B7 to VI.–2:211, p. 548.

d) Default Rule and Pure Economic Interests

Apart from the particular instances of legally relevant damage, pure economic interests are protected in general terms within VI.–2:101(2) and (3). The drafters considered that the necessary limitation of liability for "pure economic loss" can and should be made using the same techniques available for every other loss.[206] A separate category of "pure economic loss" would not therefore be necessary.

[206] von Bar (2001a), p. 523; von Bar (2002a), p. 174. For alternative techniques, see Koziol (2004), pp. 149–152 and Koziol (2006), pp. 882–885.

Part III
Critical Remarks: Cutting the Gordian Knot with the DCFR

§ 8 The Deadlock of Pure Economic Loss and the Quest for a Solution

The German system of Private Law has had a significant and long lasting influence on the Portuguese legal system. This is particularly evident in respect of non-contractual liability arising out of damage caused to another.

The concept of unlawfulness (*ilicitude*) forms the core of the Portuguese Civil Code's general rule on non-contractual liability arising out of damage caused to another (Art. 483 CC), and it is differentiated from fault (*culpa*) in the wake of von Jhering's distinction between *Rechtswidrigkeit* and *Verschulden*.

Art. 483 CC comprises two categories of unlawfulness. One relates to the infringement of "the right of another" (Art. 483(1), 1st part CC), which the prevailing view interprets as an *absolute* subjective right and which has been a category of unlawfulness since the Seabra's Code (1867). The other relates to the infringement of "any legal provision aimed at protecting the interests of others" (Art. 483(1), 2nd part CC). The Portuguese Civil Code does not contain an express provision for the reparation of loss caused intentionally against good morals and fair dealing, as is the case in § 826 BGB. In addition to the cases provided for in Art. 483 CC, a person can be liable within the special cases of unlawfulness provided for in the Portuguese Civil Code.

Although Art. 483 CC does not contain an enumeration of the legally protected rights in the way § 823(1) BGB does, it is safe to say that *ilicitude* has a (even) stricter scope that *Rechtswidrigkeit*.

The Portuguese legislature opted for this strict scope liability model over the general clause model because it limits claims for the reparation of "pure economic loss". In Portugal, this legal matrix is traditionally referred to as economic loss that does not result from the infringement of an "absolute" right.[1] The prevailing view thus holds that the first category of unlawfulness excludes the reparation of pure economic loss.

[1]See Tit. § 5, Subtit. III, Sec. 1 above.

M. Santos Silva, *The Draft Common Frame of Reference as a "Toolbox" for Domestic Courts*, DOI 10.1007/978-3-319-52923-3_8

In theory, such reparation is only possible within the second category of unlawfulness (i.e. involving the infringement of a legal provision aimed at protecting pure economic interests) or within one of the special provisions on unlawfulness in the Portuguese Civil Code. However, given the limited nature of these cases, it can be said that the general principle of non-contractual liability in the Civil Code has prevented reparation of pure economic loss.

Consequently, Portuguese legal scholars and courts—similarly to their German peers—have attempted to stretch the boundaries of the concept of unlawfulness through a more creative interpretation of the expression "right". This resulted in the emergence of new rights, such as the "right to enterprise". It also led to the extension of the protective scope of rights that are generally recognised as absolute subjective rights, such as the recognition that impairment of use equates to an infringement of a property right.

Portuguese courts have also expanded the limits of the special cases of unlawfulness provided for by the Portuguese Civil Code, as in the case of Art. 495 CC (Reparation of third persons' losses in case of death or personal injury). The courts have been innovative in compensating pure economic loss arising out of personal injury caused to another in the form of lost economic advantages (*lucros cessantes*), which is not expressly provided for in that legal rule. These courts have, for example, granted claims for the profits and wages foregone by informal carers, based on the Family Law duties of assistance towards the victims of personal injury. In such cases, no right has been infringed, even where arguments are made that the duty of assistance would necessarily lead to the conversion of spouses to carers, or where legal scholars talk of the "power-duty" (*poder-dever*) of parents in respect of caring for the health and safety of their children. If it is admitted that such family law rules have the nature of protective rules for the purposes of Art. 483(1), 2nd part, their scope of protection would still always encompass solely the interests of the personal aggrieved parties (the spouses and children) rather than the interests of their informal carers. The recent settling case law decision of 2014, which recognised a claim of relatives of non-fatally injured persons to the non-economic loss they suffered in consequence, provides courts with another opportunity to repair pure economic loss in another guise.

However, again following the precedent set by several of their German counterparts, Portuguese legal scholars and courts have moved beyond the boundaries of non-contractual law and appealed to near-contractual remedies, which allow for the reparation of pure economic loss as a rule. Portugal has imported such near-contractual remedies from Germany since the beginning of the twentieth century. For an increasingly large section of the legal scholarship, these remedies form a third kind of liability based upon reliance and the duties of care. The appeal to these near-contractual devices has resulted in a situation which has been called both a progressive dissolution of the border between contractual and non-contractual liability, and, from the opposite perspective, an expansion of the scope of non-contractual liability.

By expanding the limits within which pure economic loss is subject to reparation, Portuguese legal scholars and courts have "pulled through the window" what the legislature "threw out of the door".

Indeed, courts often repair pure economic loss without foreseeable, uniform or coherent legal criteria. As a result of these ad-hoc interpretations, the requirement of unlawfulness as provided by the Portuguese legislature has been unfit for repairing pure economic loss worthy of legal protection. Courts have dealt with the consequences of unlawfulness by bringing in non-contractual and near-contractual solutions. The secondary effects that may arise from diverse decisions are seemingly overlooked, including the potentially significant opening up of litigation concerning pure economic loss claims, as well as undermining legal safety and limiting the freedom of action of persons. By repairing pure economic loss outside of the legislative framework, courts go against the will of the legislature, whose intention was to limit compensation for pure economic loss. This deviation has the potential to affect the reputation of a code which has influenced the civil codes of several nations across the world over the past 50 years.

In view of this, there is a clear and pressing need for a legal solution.

To date, the Portuguese legislature has not addressed this issue. In 2003, the Portuguese Ministry of Justice signed an agreement with Portuguese universities for the revision of the Portuguese Civil Code, but this agreement left non-contractual liability arising out of damage caused to another practically unchanged. Present-day Portuguese legal scholars place considerable emphasis on the Civil Code as a "monument of national reputation",[2] much like their predecessors' pride in the Seabra's Code, with a persistent belief that the time has not yet come for reflective reform.

In eschewing a hands-on approach, the legislature delegated the solution to the legal scholarship and the courts. Such a solution lies, however, in cooperative working between both institutions, with the involvement of the legislature at a later stage, in the following terms.

Chapter 1 outlined Portugal's long history of looking to foreign sources, dating back to the pre-codification period in the eighteenth century. The "Act of Good Reason" (1769) had already encouraged Portuguese courts to apply the law in force in "civilised nations" and the Seabra's Code limited such appeal to foreign sources only for political (not substantial) reasons.

Traditionally, Portuguese legal scholars have looked to German jurisprudence, whose influence can be seen in the Portuguese Law of Obligations in the present-day Civil Code. This is due to the *travaux préparatoires* of Vaz Serra, which showed his staunch support for German legal solutions.

The BGB is 70 years older than the Portuguese Civil Code, and has recently undergone a general reform of its own Law of Obligations. However, the clean-cut conservative approach of German non-contractual liability arising out of damage caused to another is less visible in respect of the reparation of pure economic loss,

[2]See, with references, Schmid (2011), p. 11 and n. 27.

which it protects only within the scope of § 823(2) and § 826 BGB. The courts have opened the floodgates as far as pure economic loss is concerned, choosing either to repair it through the development of new rights based on the expression "*sonstiges Recht*" in § 823(1) BGB, or calling upon legal matrices such as the *Vertrag mit Schutzwirkung für Dritte*, taking advantage of the liberal approach of German contract law to the protection of pure economic interests. German non-contractual liability arising out damage caused to another is more liberal than its Portuguese counterpart in the reparation of pure economic loss, in that it expressly admits such reparation when the loss was intentionally inflicted against good morals and fair dealing. The existing *status quo* in Germany does not provide for a solution to the stalemate inherent in the reparation of pure economic loss.

German jurisprudence has had a lasting influence on the Portuguese Law of Obligations, particularly as far as non-contractual liability is concerned. However, the Portuguese system was influenced by a number of other sources, ranging from the French *Code Civil,* the Italian *Codice Civile* and the Swiss Civil Code. Portuguese legal works make frequent reference to such foreign laws, as do Portuguese courts, to a remarkable extent compared to other European courts. To find an effective and coherent method of dealing with pure economic loss outside of the Portuguese legal system, it would be useful to look to a legal system that acknowledges and synthesises several European experiences (including that of Portugal). The DCFR has the potential to provide these solutions. This book's proposal consists of looking for solutions within the DCFR.

Chapter 2 detailed the structure of the DCFR, explaining how its set of principles, definitions and model rules resulted from sustained pan-European academic effort and agreement. Its model rules present either compromise solutions or those considered "best solutions" by drafters. Such rules, together with the definitions, lend themselves to flexible rather than system-specific use by European legislatures and judicatures. In its rules on non-contractual liability arising out of damage caused to another, the DCFR acknowledges the need to protect some pure economic interests and deals with this need in an innovative way.

§ 9 *Could* Portuguese Courts Use the DCFR over National Sources of Law?

Before analysing any such solutions, the question of whether or not the Portuguese courts are entitled to fall back on the DCFR in judicial practice for the solution of purely domestic cases must first be addressed.

As described in Chapter 2, the Portuguese system of sources of law is a rigid one. It binds courts, in the first instance, to apply statutory law (of both national and European origin) and, with it, the Portuguese Civil Code as the general law applicable in Civil Law cases.

Nevertheless, mindful of present day challenges, Private Law theorists have put forward justifications for the use of non-domestic and non-statutory law by national courts. In this context, some authors propose the DCFR as a systematic, coherent and institutionally endorsed set of principles, definitions and model rules.

At its core, the DCFR aspires to become a Common Frame of Reference that would harmonise European patrimonial law, as described in Chapter 3. This gives it the nature of a steering soft law instrument, *i.e.* a non-binding legal system that is embedded in a particular "persuasive authority".[1]

Indeed, if a binding CFR is ever to become a reality, the DCFR must play its *pre*-law function and take the place of a *travaux préparatoires*. If no such CFR develops, the DCFR will be left with the *post*-law function of an interpretative soft law instrument.[2] Although it lacks democratic legitimacy—being drafted by a non-elected group—it is nonetheless an instrument with a qualified authority, comprising a flexible and realistic alternative to enacted laws.

Yet it seems unfeasible to justify the application of the DCFR rules by Portuguese courts, in preference to Portuguese law. Respect must be maintained for the system of sources as provided for in the Portuguese Civil Code, which the legislature bestowed and the judicial system cannot take away.

---

[1] von Bar (1996a), p. 2.

[2] See Tit. § 3, Subtit. II, Sec. 2, Subsec. c, bb) (2) above.

M. Santos Silva, *The Draft Common Frame of Reference as a "Toolbox" for Domestic Courts*, DOI 10.1007/978-3-319-52923-3_9

Legal integration methods could be used as communication vessels in the dialogue between the Portuguese Civil Code and the DCFR. This is particularly relevant for those situations in which the Portuguese Civil Code lacks a rule for the resolution of a specific legal problem, and where it recommends analogical reasoning or, failing that, a solution according to the rule that the court itself would have created, if it had to legislate within the spirit of the system.

It is less easy to argue, given the current Portuguese legal mindset, that integration methods could also be used whenever there *is* an applicable provision in Portuguese law but it is not the most *effective* solution.

It seems that the legitimation strategy most likely to succeed involves the method of legal interpretation. Undoubtedly, a pro-European method of legal interpretation—using the DCFR—has compelling potential in the convergence of private legal systems and the development of European Private Law. This remains an ambitious undertaking, which seems feasible in the short term only in those systems which have repeatedly looked to the rules in the PECL and the DCFR as interpretative tools or loophole fillers (such as Spain), and where judges have given clear indications of their intention to continue to do so (such as Sweden). It might yet be too soon for Portugal, where reference to the pro-harmonisation set of rules and principles is still infrequent. The solution to the pure economic loss problem in the Portuguese Civil Code might better involve an appeal to more traditional methods of legal interpretation.

As discussed in Chapter 2, the systematic criterion of legal interpretation requires courts to consider the external context of the rule. "External context" of a rule in the Portuguese Civil Code is, firstly, the remaining rules within the Civil Code and then the remaining rules of the Portuguese system. Nevertheless, Zweigert's argument is legitimate,[3] i.e. that "context of a rule" also comprises the non-domestic Private Law rules that offer the courts innovative and workable solutions.

The DCFR rules could also be applied through teleological interpretation. This is particularly relevant because the objective component of teleological interpretation requires a legal rule (in this case, Art. 483(1) CC) to be interpreted according to the intention of the legislature at the time of interpretation. If such interpretation was to translate the current intention of the legislature, it could be argued that there would be a wider rule, going beyond the requirement of the violation of an absolute right and the infringement of a legal provision aimed at protecting the interests of another. This argument is strengthened by the fact that Art. 9(1) CC itself expressly refers the interpreter to "specific conditions of the time where it [the statute] is applied". Updating the interpretation would allow for the rule's meaning to be adjusted in line with the evolution since its enactment and would be in line with the guidelines of foreseeability and reasonableness provided for in VI.–2:101. The STJ itself recognised, in the settling case law decision 6/2014 of 22 May 2014 where it made a contemporary-based interpretation of the general rule on non-contractual

[3]Cf. Zweigert (1949), pp. 9, 10.

liability, that Portugal is "an open country, which closely interacts with other countries" and that what happens "within the internal legal order of each country shall not be followed without prior critical assessment", but it will look to cases abroad because "times had changed".[4]

[4]Settling case law decision 6/2014 of 22 May 2014, p. 2935.

§ 10 *Should* the Portuguese Courts Use the DCFR Concept of "Legally Relevant Damage"?

At this point, it has been argued that the Portuguese courts *can* use the DCFR where the domestic legal provisions do not provide an *effective* solution to a given legal dispute. The question thus follows if, among its 56 rules on non-contractual liability arising from damage caused to another, the DCFR contains a workable solution for the protection of pure economic interests considered worthy of legal protection by the courts.

Chapter 5 explained that Book VI of the DCFR revolves around the basic rule that compensation is only possible if there has been: a) legally relevant damage; b) accountability; and c) causation. Legally relevant damage is an original concept and one which is not present by that name in any of the national legal systems of the EU Member States. Nevertheless, both drafters and commentators agree that legally relevant damage has clear similarities with the concept of *danno ingiusto* in the Italian *Codice Civile*. Both consist of a normative notion of damage, which incorporates both the detrimental effect and/or the injury (*Verletzung*) leading to it.

Legally relevant damage is both endogenously and exogenously determined: endogenously, *i.e.* determined within the DCFR itself, specifically in Section 2 of Chapter 2 (of Book VI), which lists instances of legally relevant damage; and exogenously determined because VI.–2.201(1) *lits.* b and c provide for two additional instances of legally relevant damage which apply thereafter, i.e. whenever no legally relevant damage is found in Section 2 of Chapter 2 and which must go through the legal filters provided for VI.–2.201(2) and (3).

The instances of legally relevant damage included in the Section 2 list correspond partly to situations subject to reparation in *most* of the EU Member States, and partly to situations subject to reparation in only *some* of the EU Member States, but where such reparation is seen by the drafters as good practice, with the possibility of being "Europeanised".

Those instances of damage provide for the types of loss and/or injury, which, in a given factual and legal context, the court shall consider legally relevant for the purpose of reparation. They are one of three necessary conditions for the court to assess whether or not a loss and/or injury should be the object of reparation.

M. Santos Silva, *The Draft Common Frame of Reference as a "Toolbox" for Domestic Courts*, DOI 10.1007/978-3-319-52923-3_10

However, such instances of legally relevant damage often also point to the remaining requirements for reparation and the circumstances in which reparation shall occur. This has led some legal scholars to fall into the trap of arguing that, at times, legally relevant damage refers to one of the three requirements of liability, while at other times it refers solely to the requirement leading to reparation. In fact, the list in Chapter 2, Section 2 does not consist of a list of "torts" in the Common Law sense, but must be read in the light of the basic rule in VI.–1:101.[1]

By listing the most crucial instances of legally relevant damage and the circumstances in which reparation should be granted, the drafters opted for a typical system approach that favours legal certainty and takes a restrictive view of reparation of loss in respect of non-contractual liability arising out of damage caused to another.

However, by admitting that a damage may be legally relevant when it results from a violation of a legally protected right of an interest which shall be legally protected, the DCFR meets, to a large extent, the solution provided by the Portuguese Civil Code, while also remaining flexible in respect of the protection of pure economic loss, which may, in certain circumstances, be considered legally relevant, despite not being expressly included by the categories of unlawfulness provided for in Art. 483 CC.

The default rule allows for the consideration of two other grounds for liability in addition to those provided for and specifically described in the DCFR. The default rule works as a "release valve", which might have created a *de facto* general clause of liability were it not for the fact that the DCFR submits those additional instances of legally relevant damage to filters of "fairness" and "reasonableness". These filters form the bottom-line of the default rule. Given the open-ended nature of the concepts of "fairness" and "reasonableness", the drafters opted to detail the circumstances which must be determined by the court in deciding if "it would be fair and reasonable for there to be a right to reparation".

VI.–2:101 has at least four important virtues.

Firstly, it respects the legal *status quo* of each of the EU Member States. The DCFR protects, to a large extent, the same interests that are worthy of legal protection under individual Member States' domestic regulations. This respectful approach to the legal estate of the EU Member States also shines through VI.–1:103 (Scope of application), which states that the DCFR only applies in a relationship of cooperation with "other Private Law rules" and "remedies available on other legal grounds".

Secondly, VI.–2:101 holds that in a world that is in a permanent state of flux, the interests that are deemed worthy of legal protection today (i.e. pure economic interests) might be replaced by other interests in the future.

Thirdly, VI.–2:101 allows for relevant policy considerations, such as the protection of the most vulnerable.

---

[1]See Tit. § 7, Subtit. III, Sec. 1.

Finally, VI.–2:101 dams the growing *tertium genus* that leads, ultimately, to legal uncertainty and unnecessary limitations on the freedom of action of legal subjects.

These positives highlight the compelling potential of the concept of legally relevant damage as a solution to cases of pure economic loss, in particular in the regime of non-contractual liability arising out of damage caused to another in the Portuguese Civil Code.

Chapter 2 of Book VI, and VI.–2:101 in particular, gives several indications of the legal reasoning used to determine a European system of non-contractual liability arising out of damage caused to another. Even though it does not refer to the category of pure economic loss as such, it provides a roadmap for the structured and reasonable protection of legally relevant pure economic interests.

As described in Chapter 4, the general non-contractual liability rule in the Portuguese Civil Code (Art. 483(1)), reads:

1. Whoever, whether by willful misconduct or by negligence, unlawfully infringes the right of another person or any legal provision aimed at safeguarding the interest of others is obliged to compensate the injured person for the resulting loss.
2. An obligation to compensate only exists independently of fault in the cases specified by the law.

This rule should be subject to a contemporary-based interpretation from the DCFR, more specifically VI.–2:101, according to which it would instead read:

1. Whoever, whether by willful misconduct or by negligence, causes legally relevant damage to another person is obliged to compensate the injured person for the resulting loss, provided that, given the relevant circumstances of the case, it would be fair and reasonable for there to be a right to reparation.
2. Legally relevant damage shall be determined in accordance with the rules of this Code. It shall also be determined according with the rules and principles provided for in Book VI of the Draft Common Frame of Reference. Legally relevant damage may namely result from the infringement of the right of another person or any legal provision aimed at safeguarding the interest of other parties.
3. An obligation to compensate only exists where a person has not caused legally relevant damage intentionally or negligently, in the cases specified by the law.

This suggested interpretation has a number of advantages. It acknowledges that, currently, the damage that is worthy of reparation cannot be reached from a static interpretation of the law, but must instead result from a combination of elements assessed by the court in the resolution of the case *sub judice*. This approach allows for a continuous adaptation to the changing reality of non-contractual liability and it has the potential to end the "need" to appeal to contract and near-contractual devices to repair pure economic loss.

The suggested interpretation should serve as a tool for the inspiration of courts (and legislature). By providing that legally relevant damage "*shall also be determined in accordance with the rules and principles provided for in Book VI of the Draft Common Frame of Reference*", the proposed rule would encompass the cases provided for in Chapter 2, Section 2 of Book VI in the DCFR, thereby reflecting the overall understanding of Portuguese law, legal scholarship and case law on those subjects. It would also allow for a restricted compensation of pure economic loss, in that it would apply the "filters" of fairness and reasonableness to the infringement of a right of another and the infringement of a legal provision aimed at safeguarding the interest of others (as provided for in present-day by Art. 483(1) CC).

While the general use of the DCFR rules can be based on the systematic criterion of legal interpretation, the interpretation of Art. 483 CC in line with the DCFR, and the concept of legally relevant damage in particular, can be anchored in the teleological criterion of legal interpretation.

According to this criterion, legal rules shall be interpreted according to the will of the legislature, both at the time when the rule was enacted *and* in the time when the rule is applied. The will of the legislature was, and still is, for the law to protect (only) the interests deemed worthy of legal protection, irrespective of whether they are "pure economic loss" or simply "economic loss". The updated interpretation associated with this criterion, and to which Art. 9(1) CC expressly refers, allows an adjustment of the meaning of the rule in line with its evolution since enactment. This is in line with the guidelines of foreseeability and reasonableness provided for in VI.–2:101. In the settling case law decision 6/2014 of 22 May 2014, the STJ made a contemporary-based interpretation of the general rule on non-contractual liability, recognising that Portugal is "an open country, which closely interacts with other countries". It also recognised that what happens "within the internal legal order of each country shall not be followed without prior critical assessment", but will look to cases abroad because "times have changed".[2]

It is ultimately up to the judge to decide if a pure economic interest is worthy of protection. The judge's task is to *adapt* enacted law to the reality in which it is applied, taking into account the will of the domestic legislature, but also the context of its application. As Diana Wallis mentioned in the Opening Speech of the ELI 2016 Annual Conference and General Assembly,[3] *"[w]e meet at a challenging time for Europe, but in a way that has always been the case; Europe and its law, which is central to its construct, has to move with the times"*. The present times, it is clear from the considerations discussed here, are the times of European Private Law.

[2]Settling case law decision 6/2014 of 22 May 2014, p. 2935.

[3]Wallis (2016).

Bibliography

Abrantes Geraldes AS (2003) Ressarcibilidade dos danos não patrimoniais de terceiros em caso de lesão corporal. In: Menezes Cordeiro A, Menezes Leitão L, Costa Gomes J (eds) Estudos em homenagem ao Professor Doutor Inocêncio Galvão Telles, vol IV: Novos estudos de Direito Privado. Almedina, Coimbra, pp. 263–289

Abrantes Geraldes AS (2007a) Temas da Responsabilidade Civil, vol I-Indemnização do dano da privação do uso, 3rd edn. Almedina, Coimbra

Abrantes Geraldes AS (2007b). Temas da Responsabilidade Civil, vol II-Indemnização dos danos reflexos, 2nd edn. Almedina, Coimbra

Abrantes Geraldes AS (2014) Sentença cível. Available via the website of the Portuguese Supreme Court of Justice. http://www.stj.pt/documentacao/estudos/civil. Accessed 31 Mar 2017

Aguiar e Silva JM (2011) Para uma teoria hermenêutica da justiça. Repercussões jusliterárias no eixo problemático das fontes e da interpretação jurídicas. Almedina, Coimbra

Alarcão R (1983) Direito das Obrigações. Coimbra, photocopied

Albuquerque P, Lurdes Pereira M (2004) A responsabilidade civil das autoridades reguladoras e de supervisão. Dir 136(1):89–130

Alexy R (1995) Juristische interpretation. In: Alexy R (ed) Recht, Vernunft, Diskurs. Studien zur Rechtsphilosophie. Suhrkamp, Frankfurt am Main, pp. 71–92

Alexy R (2006) Theorie der Grundrechte, 5th edn. Suhrkamp, Frankfurt am Main

Almeida Costa MJ (2002) Reflexões sobre a obrigação de indemnização. Confrontos luso-brasileiros. RLJ 134(3931–3932, February–March):290–299

Almeida Costa MJ (2006a) Direito das Obrigações, 10th edn. Almedina, Coimbra

Almeida Costa MJ (2006b) A eficácia externa das obrigações. Entendimento da doutrina clássica. RLJ 135(3936, January–February):130–136

Almeida Costa MJ (2008) Direito das Obrigações, 11th edn. Almedina, Coimbra

Almeida Costa MJ (2012) História do Direito Português, 5th edn. Almedina, Coimbra

Alpa G (2005) Tradition and Europeanization in Italian law. British Institute of International and Comparative Law, London

Alpa G (2007) Manuale di Diritto Privato. CEDAM, Padova

Alpa G, Bessone M, Zeno-Zencovich V (1995) I fatti illeciti. In: Rescigno R (ed) Trattato di diritto privato, vol XIV. Utet, Turin

Alves Moreira G (1907) Instituições do direito civil Português, vol 1. Imprensa da Universidade, Coimbra

Amaral Cabral R (2001) A tutela delitual do direito de crédito. In: Estudos em homenagem ao Professor Doutor Manuel Gomes da Silva. Coimbra Editora, Lisbon, pp. 1025–1053

Andrade M (1946) Sobre a recente evolução do Direito Privado Português. BFD 22(1):284–343

M. Santos Silva, *The Draft Common Frame of Reference as a "Toolbox" for Domestic Courts*, DOI 10.1007/978-3-319-52923-3

Andrade M (1961) Fontes de direito, vigência, interpretação e aplicação da lei. BolMinJus 102(1): 141–152
Andrade MA (1963) Ensaio sobre a teoria da interpretação das leis. Arménio Amado, Coimbra
Antoniolli L, Fiorentini F (2011) Introduction. In: Antoniolli L, Fiorentini F (eds) A factual assessment of the DCFR. Sellier, Munich, pp. 1–49
Antunes Varela J (1966) Do projecto ao Código Civil. Comunicação feita na Assembleia Nacional no dia 26 de novembro de 1966. Imprensa Nacional de Lisboa, Lisbon
Antunes Varela J (1981) Anotação ao acórdão de 26 de março de 1980. RLJ 114(3683–3684): 35–41 and 72–79
Antunes Varela J (2000) Das obrigações em geral, vol 1, 10th edn. Almedina, Coimbra
Anweiler J (1997) Die Auslegungsmethoden des Gerichtshofs der Europäische Gemeinschaft. Peter Lang, Frankfurt am Main
Araújo Dias CM (2010) O crédito pela compensação do trabalho doméstico prestado na constância do matrimónio (a contribuição consideravelmente superior de um dos cônjuges para os encargos da vida familiar - O art. 1676 do Código Civil). In: Sottomayor M C, Féria de Almeida M T (coords) E foram felizes para sempre? Uma análise crítica do novo regime jurídico do divórcio. Wolters Kluwer/Coimbra Editora, Coimbra, pp. 199–226
Atiyah PS (1997) The damages lottery. Hart, Oxford
Azevedo de Almeida M (2004) A responsabilidade civil do banqueiro perante os credores da empresa financiada - Studia Juridica 75. Coimbra Editora, Coimbra
Backaus JG (2003) Pure economic loss: an economic analysis. In: Bussani M, Valentine Palmer V (eds) Pure economic loss in Europe. Cambridge University Press, Cambridge, pp. 57–74
Bailey SH, Ching JPL, Taylor NW (2007) Smith, Bailey & Gunn on the modern English legal system, 5th edn. Sweet & Maxwell, London
Baldus C (2012) Europäischer Süden und Europäisches Privatrecht. GPR 9(3, June):105
Banakas EK (1989) Tortious liability for pure economic loss. A comparative study. Institut Hellénique de Droit International et Étranger, Athens
Banakas EK (1996) Tender is the night: economic loss - The issues. In: Banakas EK (ed) Civil liability for pure economic loss. Kluwer Law International, London, pp. 1–25
Banakas S (1999) Thoughts on a new European tort law. In: Ahrens H-J, von Bar C, Fischer G, Taupitz J (eds) Festschrift für Erwin Deutsch zum 70. Geburtstag. Carl Heymanns, Cologne, pp. 11–25
Banakas S (2002) European tort law: is it possible? ERPL 10(3):363–375
Baptista Machado J (1999) Introdução ao direito e ao discurso legitimador, 11th repr. Almedina, Coimbra
Barak A (2005) Purposive interpretation in law. Princeton University Press, Princeton
Bargagna M, Busnelli FD (2001) La valutazione del danno alla salute. CEDAM, Padova
Bartman SM (2009) EU law-making and its impact on national company law. In: Snijders H, Vogenauer S (eds) Content and meaning of national law in the context of transnational law. Sellier, Munich, pp. 101–112
Beale H (2009) The drafting of the academic Common Frame of Reference. In: Schmidt-Kessel M (ed) Der Gemeinsame Referenzrahmen. Entstehung, Inhalte, Anwendung. Sellier, Munich, pp. 35–47
Berg H (1977) Verträge mit Drittschutzwirkung und Drittschadensliquidation. JuS 17(1):363–367
Bernert G (1969) Die Leerformel von der "Adäquanz". AcP 169:421–442
Betti E (1971) Interpretazione della legge e degli atti giuridici. Teoria generale e dogmatica. Giuffrè, Milan
Bistritzki W (1981) Voraussetzungen für die Qualifikation einer Norm als Schutzgesetz im Sinne des § 823 Abs. 2 BGB. Universität Munich, Munich
Blackie J (2005) Tort/Delict in the work of the European Civil Code project of the Study Group on a European Civil Code. In: Zimmermann R (ed) Grundstrukturen eines Europäischen Bereicherungsrechts. Mohr Siebeck, Tübingen, pp. 133–146

Blackie J (2007) The torts provisions of the Study Group on a European Civil Code. In: Bussani M (ed) European tort law. Eastern and western perspectives, European private law 5. Stämpfli, Bern, pp. 55–80
Bleckmann A (1993) Die Rechtsquellen des Europäischen Gemeinschaftsrechts. NVwZ 12(9): 824–828
Blobel F (2004) Der europäische Deliktsgerichtsstand und reine Vermögensschäden. Eine Anmerkung zur Entscheidung des EuGH vom 10.06.2004, Kronhofer/Maier et al. ELF 3(1): 187–191
Bobbio N (1995) O positivismo jurídico. Lições de Filosofia do Direito. Ícone Editora, S. Paulo
Bork R (2016) Allgemeiner Teil des Bürgerlichen Gesetzbuches, 4th edn. Mohr Siebeck, Tübingen
Braga A (2005) A reparação do dano corporal na responsabilidade civil extracontratual. Almedina, Coimbra
Brandão Proença JC (1997) A conduta do lesado como pressuposto e critério de imputação do dano extracontratual. Almedina, Coimbra
Brox H, Walker W-D (2016) Besonderes Schuldrecht, 39th edn. Beck, Munich
Brüggemeier G (1982) Gesellschaftliche Schadensverteilung und Deliktsrecht. AcP 182(1): 385–452
Brüggemeier G (1999) Prinzipien des Haftungsrechts. Eine systematische Darstellung auf rechtsvergleichender Grundlage. Nomos, Baden-Baden
Brüggemeier G (2004) Common principles of tort law. A pre-statement of law. The British Institute of International and Comparative Law, London
Brüggemeier G (2006) Haftungsrecht. Struktur, Prinzipien, Schutzbereich. Ein Beitrag zur Europäisierung des Privatrechts. Springer, Berlin/Heidelberg
Brüggemeier G (2009a) Non-contractual liability arising out of damage caused to another: the making of a hybrid. In: Somma A (ed) The politics of the Draft Common Frame of Reference, pp. 179–198. Kluwer Law International, The Hague
Brüggemeier G (2009b) Protection of personality rights in the law of delict/torts in Europe: mapping out paradigms. In: Brüggemeier G, Colombi Ciacchi A, O'Callaghan P (eds) Personality rights in European tort law. Cambridge University Press, Cambridge
Brüggemeier G, Yan Z (2009) Entwurf für ein chinesisches Haftungsgesetz. Text und Begründung. Ein Beitrag zur internationalen Diskussion um die Reform des Haftungsrechts. Mohr Siebeck, Tübingen
Brugger W (1994) Konkretisierung des Rechts und Auslegung der Gesetze. AöR 119:1–34
Bucher E (2004) Zu Europa gehört auch Lateinamerika! ZEuP 12:515–547
Büdenbender U (1995) Wechselwirkungen zwischen Vorteilsausgleichung und Drittschadensliquidation. JZ 50(1):920–928
Büdenbender U (2000) Drittschadensliquidation bei obligatorischer Gefahrentlastung - eine notwendige oder überflüssige Rechtsfigur? NJW 53(1):986–992
Bürge A (1981) Die Kabelbruchfälle. Eine rechtsvergleichende Untersuchung zum schweizerischen, österreichischen und deutschen Haftpflichtrecht. JBl:57–72
Büttner B (2006) Umfang und Grenzen der Dritthaftung von Experten: eine rechtsvergleichende Untersuchung. Mohr Siebeck, Tübingen
Busnelli FD (1993) Einführung in das italienische Deliktsrecht. In: von Bar C (ed) Deliktsrecht in Europa, Landesbericht Italien. Carl Heymanns, Cologne/Berlin/Bonn/Munich
Bussani M, Palmer V (n.d.) The frontiers of tort liability: pure economic loss in Europe. In: Bussani M, Palmer V (eds) Liability for pure economic loss: frontiers of tort law. Cambridge University Press, Cambridge
Bussani M, Palmer VV (2003a) General conclusions of the study. In: Bussani M, Palmer VV (eds) Pure economic loss in Europe. Cambridge University Press, Cambridge, pp. 530–536
Bussani M, Palmer VV (2003b) The liability regimes of Europe - Their façades and interiors. In: Bussani M, Palmer VV (eds) Pure economic loss in Europe. Cambridge University Press, Cambridge, pp. 120–159

Bussani M, Palmer VV (2003c) The notion of pure economic loss and its setting. In: Bussani M, Palmer VV (eds) Pure economic loss in Europe. Cambridge University Press, Cambridge, pp. 3–24

Bussani M, Palmer VV (2003d) Pure economic loss in Europe. Cambridge University Press, Cambridge

Bussani M, Palmer VV, Parisi F (2003) Liability for pure financial loss in Europe: an economic restatement. AmJCL 51(1):113–162

Bydlinski F, Bylinski P (2012) Grundzüge der juristischen Methodenlehre, 2nd edn. Facultas, Vienna

Cabral de Moncada L (1995) Lições de Direito Civil: Parte Geral. Almedina, Coimbra

Caetano M (1941) História do Direito Português. Súmula das lições proferidas ao curso do 1.° ano jurídico de 1940-1 na Faculdade de Direito de Lisboa coligidas por Ernesto Fernandes e Aníbal Rêgo. FDUL, Lisbon

Calliess G-P, Zumbansen P (2010) Rough consensus and running code. A theory of transnational private law. Hart, Oxford and Portland, Oregon

Calvão da Silva J (1990) A responsabilidade civil do produtor. Almedina, Coimbra

Calvão da Silva J (2001–2002) Bicentenário do Code Civil (o Código Civil e a Europa: influências e modernidade). RLJ 134(3930):267–275

Canaris C-W (1965) Ansprüche wegen "positiver Vertragsverletzung" und "Schutzwirkung für Dritte" bei nichtigen Verträgen. JZ 15/16(20):475–482

Canaris C-W (1969) Systemdenken und Systembegriff in der Jurisprudenz entwickelt am Beispiel des deutschen Privatrechts. Duncker & Humblot, Berlin

Canaris C-W (1971) Die Vertrauenshaftung im deutschen Privatrecht. Beck, Munich

Canaris C-W (1983a) Die Feststellung von Lücken im Gesetz, 2nd edn. Duncker & Humblot, Berlin

Canaris C-W (1983b) Schutzgesetze-Verkehrspflichten-Schutzpflichten. In: Canaris C-W, Diederichsen U (eds) Festschrift für Karl Larenz zum 80. Geburstag, Beck, Munich, pp. 27–110

Canaris C-W (1999) Die Reichweite der Expertenhaftung gegenüber Dritten. ZHR 163 (1):206–245

Canaris C-W (2006) Funções da parte geral de um código civil e limites da sua prestabilidade. In: Faculdade de Direito da Universidade de Coimbra (ed) Comemorações dos 35 anos do Código Civil e dos 25 anos da Reforma de 1977, vol II-A Parte Geral do Código e a Teoria Geral do Direito Civil. Coimbra Editora, Coimbra, pp. 23–42

Capelo de Sousa R (1978) A Constituição e direitos de personalidade. In: Miranda J (coord.) Estudos sobre a Constituição, vol 2. Livraria Petrony, Lisbon, pp. 93–196

Capelo de Sousa RV (1993) O direito geral de personalidade. Coimbra Editora, Coimbra

Capelo de Sousa RV (1995) O direito geral de personalidade, 2nd edn. Coimbra Editora, Coimbra

Cappelletti M (1981) The doctrine of stare decisis and the civil law: a fundamental difference or no difference at all. In: Bernstein H, Drobnig U, Kötz H (eds) Festschrift für Konrad Zweigert zum 70. Geburstag. Mohr Siebeck, Tübingen, pp. 381–393

Caramelo Gomes J, Medeiros Nóbrega JC (2011) National report on the transfer of movables in Portugal. In: Faber W, Lurger B (eds) National reports on the transfer of movables in Europe. Sellier, Munich, pp. 581–722

Carneiro da Frada MA (1994) Contrato e deveres de protecção. Coimbra Editora, Coimbra

Carneiro da Frada MA (1997) Uma "terceira via" no Direito da responsabilidade civil? O problema da imputação dos danos causados a terceiros por auditores de sociedades. Almedina, Coimbra

Carneiro da Frada MA (2006) Direito Civil, responsabilidade civil: o método do caso. Almedina, Coimbra

Carneiro da Frada MA (2007a) A responsabilidade pela confiança nos 35 anos do Código Civil: Balanço e perspectivas. In: Aa. Vv. Comemorações dos 35 anos do Código Civil e dos 25 anos da Reforma de 1977, vol III-Direito das Obrigações. Coimbra Editora, Coimbra, pp. 285–307

Carneiro da Frada MA (2007b) Teoria da confiança e responsabilidade civil. Almedina, Coimbra
Carneiro da Frada M (2012) A equidade (ou a justiça com coração). A propósito da decisão arbitral segundo a equidade. In: Otero P, de Quadros F, Rebelo de Sousa M (orgs.) Estudos de homenagem ao Professor Doutor Jorge Miranda, vol 6. Coimbra Editora, Coimbra, pp. 295–322
Carneiro da Frada MA, Pestana de Vasconcelos MJ (2006) Danos económicos puros: Ilustração de uma problemática. In: Miranda J (coord.) Estudos em homenagem ao Professor Doutor Marcello Caetano, vol 2, pp. 151–176. Coimbra Editora, Coimbra
Carvalho Fernandes LA (2009) Teoria Geral do Direito Civil, vol 1, 5th edn. Universidade Católica, Lisbon
Carvalho Fernandes L, Brandão Proença J (2014) Comentário ao Código Civil: Parte Geral. Universidade Católica Editora, Lisbon (cited here with the commentaries of Fontaine de Campos)
Castanheira Neves A (1972) O instituto dos "assentos" e a função jurídica dos Supremos Tribunais. RLJ 105(3472–3473):133–139
Castanheira Neves A (2010) O actual problema metodológico da interpretação jurídica, I. Coimbra Editora, Coimbra
Castro Mendes J (1982–1983) Direito Comparado. AAFDL, Lisbon
Castronovo C (1997) La nuova responsabilità civile. Giuffrè, Milan
Castronovo C (2006) La nuova responsabilità civile, 3rd edn. Giuffrè, Milan
Cian G (1966) Antigiuridicità e colpevolezza: saggio per una teoria dell'illecito civile. CEDAM, Padua
Cian G (2014) Commentario breve al codice civile. CEDAM, Padua
Claeys I (2012) The draft tort rules of the DCFR: a Belgian law perspective. In: Sagaert V, Storme M, Terryn E (eds) The Draft Common Frame of Reference: national and comparative perspectives. Intersentia, Cambridge/Antwerp/Portland, pp. 231–239
Clerk JF, Lindsell WHB (2011) Clerk & Lindsell on torts, 20th edn. Sweet & Maxwell, London
Clive E (2008) An introduction to the academic Draft Common Frame of Reference. ERA Forum 9(1):13–31
Clive E (2010, March) How a Common Frame of Reference might be used as a "toolbox" when drafting EU law. Available via ERA. https://www.era.int/upload/dokumente/10976.pdf. Accessed 31 Mar 2017
Clive E (2015, May) Rebirth of EU contract law proposal. Available via the European Private Law News. http://www.epln.law.ed.ac.uk/2015/05/11/rebirth-of-eu-contract-law-proposal/. Accessed 31 Mar 2017
Codigo Civil Portuguez (1868, 2nd edn.). Imprensa Nacional, Lisbon. Available via the University of Lisbon website. http://www.fd.ulisboa.pt/wp-content/uploads/2014/12/Codigo-Civil-Portugues-de-1867.pdf. Accessed 31 Mar 2017
Coelho da Rocha MA (1857) Instituições de direito civil portuguez, vol 1, 4th edn. J A Orcel, Coimbra. Available via Google books. https://books.google.de/books?id=J6cWAAAAYAAJ&pg=PA12&hl=pt-PT&source=gbs_toc_r&cad=4#v=onepage&q&f=false. Accessed 31 Mar 2017
Coelho dos Santos J (1994) A reparação civil do dano corporal: reflexão jurídica sobre a perícia médico-legal e o dano dor. RPDC 3(4):73–90
Coester-Waltjen D (1992) Rechtsgüter und Rechte i.S.d. § 823 I BGB. Jura:209–212
Colombi Ciacchi A (2009) Alte und neue Paradigmen in der Fahrlässigleitshaftung. In: Colombi Ciacchi A, Godt C, Rott P, Smith LJ (eds) Haftungsrecht im dritten Millenium. Liber Amicorum Gert Brüggemeier. Nomos, Baden-Baden
Colombi Ciacchi A (2014) Judicial governance in private law through the application of fundamental rights. ALJ 1:120–134
Comisión General de Codificación (2009) Propuesta de Anteproyecto de Ley de Modernización del Derecho de Obligaciones y Contratos. Boletín de Información del Ministerio de Justicia, vol 63. Imprenta Nacional, Madrid, pp. 1–73

Conway G (2012) The limits of legal reasoning and the European Court of Justice. Cambridge University Press, Cambridge

Correia de Jesus (1968) Alguns aspectos da responsabilidade obrigacional no Código Civil 1966. Comunicação ao Instituto da Conferência de Lisboa da Ordem dos Advogados, na sessão de 11 de janeiro de 1968. Available via the website of the Instituto Politécnico de Beja. http://portal.oa.pt/upl:%7bf8164fe3-2be4-44e3-8b2b-b250b3849e77%7d.pdf. Accessed 31 Mar 2017

Correia de Mendonça L (1982) As origens do Código Civil de 1966: esboço para uma contribuição. AS 18(72-74, 3°-5°):829–867

Corrêa de Telles JH (1845) Digesto Portuguez ou tratado dos direitos e obrigações civis accommodado às leis e costumes da Nação Portugueza para servir de subsidio ao novo Codigo Civil, vols 1 and 2, 3rd edn. 1845. Imprensa da Universidade, Coimbra. Available via Google books. https://books.google.de/books?id=LfEyAQAAMAAJ&pg=PA165&dq=digesto+portuguez+corr%C3%AAa+telles&hl=pt-PT&sa=X&ei=xZ-BVZPaFYSpsgG7u4GQBQ&ved=0CCUQ6AEwAQ#v=onepage&q=457&f=false. Accessed 31 Mar 2017

Coutinho de Abreu JM (2006) Do abuso de direito - Ensaio de um critério em Direito Civil e nas deliberações sociais, repr. 1999. Almedina, Coimbra

Cruz Villaça J, Pais Antunes L, Piçarra N (1991) Droit constitutionnel et droit communautaire. Le cas portugais. Riv.dir.eur. 21(2):301–310

Cunha P (1966) Do Código Civil (meditações sobre a lei mais importante do país). Dir 98 (1):313–320

Cunha de Sá FA (1973) Abuso do Direito. Centro de Estudos Fiscais do Ministério das Finanças, Lisbon

Dannemann G (2012) In search of system neutrality: methodological issues in the drafting of European contract law rules. In: Adams M, Bonhoff J (eds) Practice and theory in comparative law. Cambridge University Press, Cambridge, pp. 96–119

Dari-Mattiacci G, Schäfer H-B (2007) The core of pure economic loss. IrLE 27(1):8–28

David R (2002) Os grandes sistemas do Direito Contemporâneo. Martins Fontes, São Paulo

De Búrca G (2001) Legal principles as an instrument of differentiation? The principles of proportionality and subsidiarity. In: de Witte B, Hanf D, Vos E (eds) The many faces of differentiation in EU law. Intersentia, Antwerpen/Oxford/New York, pp. 131–199

De Cupis A (1979) Il Danno. Teoria generale della responsabilità civile. Giuffrè, Milan

Decku GW (1997) Zwischen Vertrag und Delikt: Grenzfälle vertraglicher und deliktischer Haftung, dargestellt am Beispiel der Berufs- und Expertenhaftung zum Schutze des Vermögens Dritter im deutschen und englischen Recht. Lang, Frankfurt am Main

Deschamps CL (1998) La réparation du préjudice économique pur en droit français. Rev.int.dr. comp. 50(2):367–381

Deutsch E (1963) Entwicklung und Entwicklungsfunktion der Deliktstabestände. JZ 18(13): 385–390

Deutsch E (1972) Zum Verhältnis von vertraglicher und deliktischer Haftung. In: Pawlowski H-M (ed) Festschrift für Karl Michaelis. V&R Unipress, Göttingen, pp. 26–34

Deutsch E (1976) Haftungsrecht, vol I-Allgemeine Lehren. Carl Heymanns, Cologne/Berlin/Bonn/Munich

Deutsch E (1987) Der Begriff der Fahrlässigkeit im Zivilrecht. Jura:505–509

Deutsch E (1995) Fahrlässigkeit und erforderliche Sorgfalt. Eine privatrechtliche Untersuchung, 2nd edn. Carl Heymanns, Cologne/Berlin/Bonn/Munich

Deutsch E (1996a) Allgemeines Haftungsrecht, 2nd edn. Carl Heymanns, Cologne/Berlin/Bonn/Munich

Deutsch E (1996b) Der Ersatz reiner Vermögensschäden nach deutschem Recht. In: Banakas EK (ed) Civil liability for pure economic loss. Kluwer Law International, London, pp. 55–71

Deutsch E (2004) Schutzgesetze aus dem Strafrecht in § 823 Abs. 2 BGB. VersRAI:137–142

Deutsch E, Weir T (trans.) (1996) Compensation for pure economic loss in German law. In: Banakas EK (ed) Civil liability for pure economic loss. Kluwer Law International, London, pp. 73–87

Dias JA (2000) Dano corporal: uma realidade não subsumível à perda (ou diminuição) da capacidade de ganho. RPDC 9(10, November):71–98

Dias JA (2001a) Algumas considerações sobre o chamado dano corporal. RPDC 10 (11, November):37–75

Dias JA (2001b) Dano corporal. Quadro epistemológico e aspectos ressarcitórios. Almedina, Coimbra

Dias JA (2002) Consequências não pecuniárias de lesões não letais - Algumas considerações. In: Gomes J (coord., ed) Estudos dedicados ao Professor Doutor Mário Júlio Brito de Almeida Costa. Universidade Católica, Lisbon, pp. 753–778

Dias JP, Almeida J (2007) A influência das condições organizativas para a independência do poder judicial em Portugal. Centro de Estudos Sociais, Coimbra

Dias Pereira AG (2005) Portuguese tort law: a comparison with the principles of European tort law. In: Koziol H, Steininger BC (eds) European Tort law 2004. Springer, Vienna, pp. 623–648

Dias Pereira AG (2008) Portuguese case note. ERPL 16(3):513–521

Dias Pereira AL (2015) "Ius est ars boni et aequi": da equidade e da arte de bem interpretar toda a regra jurídica. RJLB 1(3):85–146

Dicey AV (1915) Introduction to the study of the law of the constitution, 8th edn. Macmillan, London. Available via Gale Cengage Learning. http://galenet.galegroup.com/servlet/MOML?dd=0&locID=suub&d1=20001071500&srchtp=a&c=1&an=20001071500&d2=3&docNum=F3753346497&h2=1&af=RN&d6=3&ste=10&dc=tiPG&stp=Author&d4=0.33&d5=d6&ae=F153346495. Accessed 31 Mar 2017

Diederichsen U (1965) Zur Beweislastverteilung bei Schadensersatzansprüchen aus Vertrag, Delikt und Gefährdungshaftung. In: Klingmüller E (ed) Karlsruher Forum 1965: Haftung und Freizeichnung. Versicherungswirtschaft, Karlsruhe, pp. 21–28

Doobe C (2014) Der Ersatz fahrlässig verursachter reiner Vermögensschäden Dritter in Deutschland und England unter besonderer Berücksichtigung der ökonomischen Analyse des Rechts. Versicherungswirtschaft, Karlsruhe

Drobnig U (1999a) The use of comparative law by courts. In: Drobnig U, van Erp S (eds) The use of comparative law by courts. Kluwer Law International, Great Britain, pp. 3–21

Drobnig U (1999b) The use of foreign law by German courts. In: Drobnig U, van Erp S (eds) The use of comparative law by courts. Kluwer Law International, The Hague/London/Boston, pp. 127-147

Ebert KH (1978) Rechtsvergleichung. Stämpfli, Bern

Ebert I (2011) Pönale Elemente im deutschen Privatrecht. Von der Renaissance der Privatstrafe im deutschen Recht. Mohr Siebeck, Tübingen

Eidenmüller H, Faust F, Grigoleit HC, Jansen N, Wagner G, Zimmermann R (2008a) The common frame of reference for European private law - Policy choices and codification problems. OJLS 28(1):659–708

Eidenmüller H, Faust F, Grigoleit HC, Jansen N, Wagner G, Zimmermann R (2008b) Ungesteuerte Richtermacht; ist die Zeit schon reif für ein europäisches Zivilgesetzbuch? Frankfurter Allgemeine Zeitung, 5 June 2008

Escher-Weingart C (1993) Nutzungsausfall als Schaden und sein Ersatz. Lang, Frankfurt am Main

Esser J (2000a) Schuldrecht, vol I-Allgemeiner Teil, 2, continued by E. Schmidt, 8th edn. Müller, Heidelberg

Esser J (2000b) Schuldrecht, vol II-Besonderer Teil, 2, continued by H.L. Weyers, 8th edn. Müller, Heidelberg

European Group on Tort Law (2005) Principles of European Tort law: text and commentary. Springer, Vienna/New York

Fabricius F (1961) Zur Dogmatik des "sonstigen Rechts" gemäß § 823 Abs. I BGB. AcP 160(4/5): 273–336

Faure M, Schneider H, Smits J (2002) Towards a European ius commune in legal education and research. Intersentia, Antwerpen

Fenoy Picón N (2013) The Spanish Obligation and Contract Law and the proposal for its modernisation. In: Schulze R, Zoll F (eds) The law of obligations in Europe: a new wave of codifications. Sellier, Munich, pp. 395–430

Ferreira da Cunha P (1991) Pensar o direito, II. Da modernidade à pós-modernidade. Almedina, Coimbra

Ferreira de Almeida C (2008) Código Civil: atear a chama da reforma. In: Aa. Vv. Código Civil Português. Evolução e perspectivas actuais. Themis. Ed. especial. Almedina, Coimbra, pp. 345–347

Ferreira de Almeida C, Morais Carvalho J (2013) Introdução ao Direito Comparado. Almedina, Coimbra

Ferreira Dias PB (2001) O dano moral na doutrina e na jurisprudência. Almedina, Coimbra

Ferrer Correia A, Lobo Xavier V (1979) Efeito externo das obrigações, abuso do direito; Concorrência desleal. RDE 5(1, January–June):3–19

Fikentscher W (1975) Methoden des Rechts, vol I-Frühe und religiöse Rechte. Romanischer Rechtskreis. Mohr Siebeck, Tübingen

Fikentscher W (2006) Schuldrecht, 10th edn. De Gruyter, Berlin/New York

Fon V, Parisi F (2006) Judicial precedents in Civil Law systems: a dynamic analysis. IrLE 26(4): 519–535

Forster VW (1613) Interpres sive de interpretatione juris, libri duo. Berger, Wittenberg

Fränkel M (1979) Tatbestand und Zurechnung bei § 823 Abs. 1 BGB. Duncker & Humblot, Berlin

França Gouveia M (2005) Cable cases e intervenção de terceiros. CDP 10:30–48

Frank R (1979) Die Schutzobjekte des § 823 Abs. 1 BGB und ihre Bedeutung für die Systematik der Deliktstatbestände. JA 11(10):583–590

Franzoni M (1993) Fatti illeciti. In: Galgano F (ed) Commentario del Codice Civile Scialoja-Branca, libro IV: Obbligazioni, Arts. 2043–2059. Zanichelli, Il foro Italiano, Bologna/Roma

Frasheri E (2010) The power of national courts in interpreting domestic and EU Law. The indeterminacy of choice. In: Jemielniak J, Mikłaszewicz P (eds) Interpretation of law in the global world: from particularism to a universal approach. Springer, Heidelberg

Freitas do Amaral D (2000) A crise da justiça. AS 34(154–155):247–257

Freitas Rangel RM (2002) A reparação judicial dos danos na responsabilidade civil (Um olhar sobre a jurisprudência). Almedina, Coimbra

Fuchs M, Pauker W (2012) Delikts- und Schadensersatzrecht, 8th edn. Springer, Heidelberg/Dordrecht/London/New York

Gabinete do Ministério da Justiça (2005) Reforma do direito civil. Relatórios preliminares elaborados ao abrigo do protocolo celebrado entre o Gabinete de Política Legislativa e Planeamento do Ministério da Justiça e as faculdades de Direito da Universidade de Coimbra, da Universidade de Lisboa, da Universidade Católica Portuguesa e da Universidade Nova. Almedina, Coimbra

Galvão Telles I (1997) Direito das Obrigações, 7th edn. Coimbra Editora, Coimbra

Ganuza JJ, Gómez F (2005) Should we trust the gatekeepers? Auditors' and lawyers' liability for clients' misconduct. InDret 310:1–25

Garapon A (1998) O guardador de promessas. Justiça e Democracia. Instituto Piaget, Lisbon

Gaspar Martinho H (2011) CLS/TJUE-Indeterminação do direito e activismo judicial. In: Manuel Hespanha A, Pizarro Beleza T (coord.) Teoria da Argumentação e Neoconstitucionalismo. Um conjunto de perspectivas. Almedina, Coimbra, pp. 57–77

Gernhuber J (1977) Die integrierte Billigkeit. Eine Skizze zur Billigkeit als Tatbestandselement von Normen. In: Gernhuber J (ed) Tradition und Fortschritt im Recht. Mohr Siebeck, Tübingen

Giliker P (2013) The Draft Common Frame of Reference and European contract law: moving from the "academic" to the "political" text. In: Devenney J, Kenny M (eds) The transformation of European private law: harmonisation, consolidation, codification or chaos? Cambridge University Press, Cambridge, pp. 23–44

Goldberg V (1991) Recovery for pure economic loss in tort: another look at Robins Dry Dock v. Flint. JLS 20(2):249–275

Gomes J (1986) O dano da privação do uso. RDE 12(1):169–239

Gomes J (1989) Uma função punitiva para a responsabilidade civil e uma função reparatória para a responsabilidade penal? RDE 15(1):105–144

Gomes JV (2005) Sobre o dano da perda de chance. Dir.just. 19(2):9–47
Gomes J (2011) A violação do contrato com prejuízo de terceiro - Uma análise comparativa. In: Araújo F, Otero P, Taborda da Gama J (orgs.) Estudos em memória do Professor Doutor J. L. Saldanha Sanchez, vol 2. Coimbra Editora, Coimbra, pp. 601–627
Gomes Canotilho JJ (2001) Direito Constitucional e Teoria da Constituição. Almedina, Coimbra
Gomes Canotilho JJ, Moreira V (1997) Constituição da República Portuguesa anotada, vol 1, 4th edn. Coimbra Editora, Coimbra
Gomes Canotilho JJ, Moreira V (2010) Constituição da República Portuguesa anotada, vol 2, 4th edn. Coimbra Editora, Coimbra
Gomes da Silva MD (1944) O dever de prestar e o dever de indemnizar, vol 1. Tip. Ramos, Lisbon
Goodhart AI (1934) Precedent in English and continental law. LQR 50(1):40–65
Gordley J (2003) The rule against recovery in negligence for pure economic loss: an historical accident? In: Bussani M, Palmer VV (eds) Pure economic loss in Europe. Cambridge University Press, Cambridge, pp. 25–56
Gordley J (2006) Foundations of private law, property, tort, contract, unjust enrichment, vol I. Oxford University Press, Oxford
Gordon M (2015) Parliamentary sovereignty in the UK constitution. Process, politics and democracy. Hart, Oxford
Gouveia de Andrade MP (1996) Da ofensa do crédito e do bom nome: contributo para o estudo do art. 484 do Código Civil. Tempus, Lisbon
Gozzi C (2006) Der Anspruch iure proprio auf Ersatz des Nichtvermögensschadens wegen der Tötung eines nahen Angehörigen in Deutschland und Italien. V&R Unipress, Göttingen
Gómez Pomar F, Ruiz JA (2002) The plural - and misleading - notion of economic loss in tort. A law and economics perspective. InDret (102):1–28
Gridel J-P (2003) Sur l'hypothèse d'un code européen des contrats: les propositions de l'Académie des Privatistes Européens (Pavie). Gazette du Palais. Available via http://www.institut-idef.org/IMG/pdf/Gridel1.pdf. Accessed 31 Mar 2017
Grigoleit HC (2015) Against the background of DCFR and CESL: developing quality standards for future harmonisation of European contract law. In: Afonso AI (ed) Um Direito Europeu das Obrigações? A influência do DCFR. Universidade Católica Editora, Porto, pp. 33–51
Grochowski M (2013) The practical potential of the DCFR: judgment of the Swedish Supreme Court (Högsta domstolen) of 3 November 2009, Case T 3-08. ERCL 9(1):96–104
Groppi T (2013) The use of foreign precedents by constitutional judges. Hart, Oxford
Grosche N (2011) Rechtsfortbildung im Unionsrecht. Eine Untersuchung zum Phänomen richterlicher Rechtsfortbildung durch den Gerichtshof der Europäischen Union. Mohr Siebeck, Tübingen
Guimarães E (1986) A mulher portuguesa na legislação civil. AS 22(92–93, 3.°–4.°):557–577
Gursky K-H (2005) Schuldrecht: Besonderer Teil. Müller, Heidelberg
Habermas J (1992) Faktizität und Geltung-Beiträge zur Diskurstheorie des Rechts und des demokratischen Rechtsstaats. Suhrkamp, Frankfurt am Main
Habersack M (2013) Münchener Kommentar zum Bürgerlichen Gesetzbuch, vol II-Schuldrecht Besonderer Teil III, §§ 705–853, 6th edn. (cited here with the commentaries of G. Wagner). Beck, Berlin
Hall E (1976) Beyond culture. Doubleday, New York
Hall E (1990) Understanding cultural differences. Intercultural Press, Yarmouth
Hager G (1985) Zum Begriff der Rechtswidrigkeit im Zivilrecht. In: Bickel D, Hadding W, Jahnke V, Lüke G (eds) Recht und Rechtserkenntnis. Festschrift für Ernst Wolff zum 70. Geburstag. Carl Heymanns, Cologne/Berlin/Bonn/Munich
Hagen H (1971) Die Drittschadensliquidation im Wandel der Rechtsdogmatik. Athenäum, Frankfurt am Main
Håstad T (2015) DCFR rules in the Swedish Supreme Court. In: Håstad T (ed) The Nordic Contracts Act: essays in celebration of its one hundredth anniversary. DJOF Publishing, Copenhagen, pp. 179–184

Heck P (1974) Grundriß des Schuldrechts, 2nd repr. Scientia, Aalen
Hedley S (2011) Tort, 7th edn. Oxford University Press, Oxford
Henriques da Graça AP (2008) Aspectos metodológicos do discurso judiciário. Intervenção do CEJ, Lisbon. Available via Supremo Tribunal de Justiça. http://www.stj.pt/ficheiros/estudos/apiresgraca_discursojudiciario.pdf. Accessed 31 Mar 2017
Herbots J (1985) Le "duty of care" et le dommage purement financier en droit comparé. Rev.int.dr. comp. 62(1):7–33
Hespanha AM (1986a) Discours juridique et changement politique. In: Heyen EV (ed) Historische Soziologie der Rechtswissenschaft. Klostermann, Frankfurt am Main, pp. 107–131
Hespanha AM (1986b) As transformações revolucionárias e o discurso dos juristas. RCCS (18/19/20, February):311–341
Hespanha AM (2012) Cultura jurídica Europeia. Síntese de um milénio. Almedina, Coimbra
Hesselink MW (2001) The new European legal culture. Kluwer, Deventer
Hesselink MW (2008a) A European legal science? On European private and scientific method. CSECL Working Paper Series (2008/02):1–36. Available via the Social Science Research Network. http://www.ssrn.com/abstract=1113450. Accessed 31 Mar 2017
Hesselink MW (2008b) CFR & social justice. Sellier, Munich
Hesselink MW (2009) The Common Frame of Reference as a source of European private law. TulLRev 83(4):919–971
Hesselink M (2010) A toolbox for European judges. ELJ 17(4):441–469. Available via the Social Science Research Network. http://ssrn.com/abstract=1725783. Accessed 31 Mar 2017
Hesselink MW (2012) How many systems of private law are there in Europe? On plural legal sources, multiple identities and the unity of law. ALSLS 59:1–41
Hesselink MW (2013) The general principles of civil law: their nature, roles and legitimacy. In: Leczykiewicz D, Weatheril S (eds) The involvement of EU Law in private law relationships. Hart, Oxford, pp. 131–180
Heusinger B (1975) Rechtsfindung und Rechtsfortbildung. Carl Heymanns, Cologne
Hériter A (2015) Covert integration in the EU. In: Richardson J, Mazey S (eds) European Union, power and policy-making. Routledge Cavendish, London/New York
Heutger V, Jeloschek C (2004) Towards Principles of European Sales Law. In: Hartkamp AS, Hesselink MW, Hondius E, Mak C, du Perron E (eds) Towards a European civil code, 3rd edn. Kluwer Law International, Nijmegen, pp. 533–550
Höpfner C (2008) Die systemkonforme Auslegung. Zur Auflösung einfachgesetzlicher, verfassungsrechtlicher und europarechtlicher Widersprüche im Recht. Mohr Siebeck, Tübingen
Hörster HE (1992) A parte geral do Código Civil Português. Teoria Geral do Direito Civil. Almedina, Coimbra
Hörster HE (2004a) Esboço esquemático sobre a responsabilidade civil de acordo com as regras do Código Civil. In: Cândido de Oliveira A (coord.) Estudos em comemoração do décimo aniversário da licenciatura em Direito da Universidade do Minho. Almedina, Coimbra, pp. 323–338
Hörster HE (2004b) Evoluções legislativas no Direito da Família depois da reforma de 1977. In: Comemorações dos 35 anos do Código Civil e dos 25 anos da Reforma de 1977, vol I-Direito da Família e das Sucessões. Coimbra Editora, Coimbra, pp. 59–74
Hohloch G (1981) Allgemeines Schadensrecht: empfiehlt sich eine Neufassung der gesetztlichen Regelung des Schadensrechts (§§ 249–255 BGB)? In: Bundesminister der Justiz, Gutachten und Vorschläge zur Überarbeitung des Schuldrechts, vol 1. Bundesanzeiger, Cologne, pp. 375–478
Hollander W (2012) Tort law and the violation of statutory provisions. In: Sagaert V, Storme ME, Terryn E (eds) The Draft Common Frame of Reference: national and comparative perspectives. Intersentia, Cambridge/Antwerp/Portland, pp. 241–260
Hondius E (1997) Towards a European civil code: the debate has started. ERPL 5(4):455–464
Hondius E (2007) Towards a European tort law. In: Bussani M (ed) European tort law: eastern and western perspectives, European private law 5. Stämpfli, Bern, pp. 47–54

Hondius E (2011) From "toolbox" to academic standard. The current and future status of the Draft Common Frame of Reference. In: Brownsword R, Micklitz H-W, Niglia L, Weatherill S (eds) The foundations of European private law. Hart, Oxford and Portland, pp. 531–554
Honsell H (1990) Die Haftung für Gutachten und Auskunft unter besonderer Berücksichtigung von Drittinteressen. In: Beuthien V (ed) Festschrift für Dieter Medicus zum 70. Geburtstag. Carl Heymanns, Cologne/Berlin/Bonn/Munich, pp. 211–234
Honsell H (2001) Der Ersatz reiner Vermögensschäden in Rechtsgeschichte und Rechtsvergleichung. In: Rauscher TM-P, Mansel HP (eds) Festschrift für Werner Lorenz zum 80. Geburtstag. Sellier, Munich, pp. 483–508
Horsburgh B (1992) Redefining the family. Recognising the altruistic caretaker and the importance of relational needs. UMJLR 25(2):423–504
Howarth D (2011) The general conditions of unlawfulness. In: Hartkamp A, Hesselink MW, Hondius EH, Mak C, du Perron CE (eds) Towards a European civil code, 4th edn. Kluwer Law International/Ars Aequi Libri, Alphen aan den Rijn, pp. 845–887
Huber U (1973) Zivilrechtliche Fahrlässigkeit. In: Forsthoff E, Weber W, Wieacker F (eds) Festschrift für Ernst Rudolf Huber zum 70. Geburtstag. Otto Schwartz, Göttingen, pp. 253–289
Huber K (1978) Verkehrspflichten zum Schutz fremden Vermögens. In: Ficker HC, König D, Kreuzer KF, Leser HG, von Bieberstein M, von Caemmerer E (eds) Festschrift von Caemmerer zum 70. Geburstag. Mohr Siebeck, Tübingen, pp. 359–388
Infantino M (2009) Making European tort law: the game and its players. CJICL 20(1):45–87
Jakobs HH, Schubert W (1983) Die Beratung des Bürgerlichen Gesetzbuchs in systematischer Zusammenstellung der unveröffentlichten Quellen. Recht der Schuldverhältnisse III, §§ 652 bis 853. de Gruyter, Berlin/New York
Jansen N (2001) Auf dem Weg zu einem europäischen Haftungsrecht. ZEup 9:30–65
Jansen N (2002) Das Problem der Rechtswidrigkeit bei § 823 Abs. 1 BGB. AcP (202):517–554
Jansen N (2003) Die Struktur des Haftungsrechts. Geschichte, Theorie und Dogmatik außervertraglicher Ansprüche auf Schadensersatz. Mohr Siebeck, Tübingen
Jansen N (2006) Principles of European tort law? Grundwertungen und Systembildung im europäischen Haftungsrecht. RabelsZ 70(1):732–770
Jansen N (2007) The state of the art of European tort law. Present problems and proposed principles. In: Bussani M (ed) East and West in the European tort law perspective. Stämpfli, Bern, pp. 15–45
Jansen N (2010) The authority of an academic "Draft Common Frame of Reference". In: Micklitz H-W, Cafaggi F (eds) European private law after the Common Frame of Reference. Edward Elgar, Chettenham/Northhampton, pp. 147–172
Jansen N, Rademacher L (2009) Punitive damages in Germany. In: Koziol H, Wilcox V (eds) Punitive damages: common law and civil law perspectives. Springer, Vienna, pp. 75–86
Jansen N, Zimmermann R (2010) A European civil code in all but name: discussing the nature and purposes of the Draft Common Frame of Reference. CLJ 69(1):98–112
Jayme E (1993) Luís Cabral de Moncada (1888-1974) e as suas relações com a Alemanha. BFD 69 (1):233–258
Jesus Cunha LM (1994) A Nação nas malhas da sua identidade. O Estado Novo e a construção da identidade nacional. Braga: Universidade do Minho. Available via Universidade do Minho. https://repositorium.sdum.uminho.pt/bitstream/1822/6440/1/1994%20Provas%20APCC%20Tese.pdf. Accessed 31 Mar 2017
Jian M (1995) Da tradição continental e a sua relação com os sistemas do continente (RPC), Taiwan e Macau. Admin 8(28):319–341
Joerges C (1999) Desintegrative Folgen legislativer Harmonisierung: ein komplexes Problem und ein unscheinbares Exempel. In: Schulte-Nölke H, Schulze R (eds) Europäische Rechtsangleichung und Nationale Privatrechte. Nomos, Baden-Baden, pp. 205–222
Joint Brussels Office (2015) The Common European Sales Law - The meaning of "modify". Brussels Agenda 3(1):1–12. Available via The Law Society of Scotland. http://www.lawscot.org.uk/media/455103/brusselsagenda-march2015.pdf. Accessed 31 Mar 2017

Józon M (2008) Integration of the European developments in private law into domestic civil law: factors framing the reception of the DCFR in Romania. JI 14(1):156–165

Junker M (1991) Die Vertretung im Vertrauen im Schadensrecht: ein Beitrag zum Problem des Drittschadensersatzes. Beck, Munich

Junker M (1993) Das "wirtschaftliche Eigentum" als sonstiges Recht im Sinne des § 823 Abs. 1 BGB. AcP (193):348–363

Jurčova M (2008) The influence of harmonisation on civil law in the Slovak Republic. JI 14 (1):166–172

Kahn-Freund O (1974) On uses and misuses of comparative law. MLR 37(1):1–27

Kalouta G (2015) The Draft Common Frame of Reference in the courts. The remaking of comparative law. In: Andenas M, Fairgrieve D (eds) Courts and comparative law. Oxford University Press, Oxford, pp. 696–718

Kapteyn PJ (1997) Europe's expectations of its judges. In: Jansen RH, Koster D, van Zutphen RF (eds) European ambitions of the national judiciary. Kluwer Law International, The Hague/London/Boston, pp. 181–189

Kegel G (2002) Vertrag und Delikt. Carl Heymanns, Cologne/Berlin/Bonn/Munich

Kellner M (2009) Tort law of the European community: a plea for an overarching pan-European framework. ERPL 17(2):133–154

Kennedy D (1996) Strategising strategic behaviour in legal interpretation. ULR 4(1):785–825

Kern B-R (1991) Die Genugtuungsfunktion des Schmerzensgeldes - ein pönales Element im Schadensersatzrecht? AcP 191:247–272

Kern G (2010) Portugal. In: Brüggemeier G, Colombi Ciacchi A, Comandé G (eds) Fundamental rights and private law in the European Union: comparative analysis of selected case patterns. Cambridge University Press, Cambridge, pp. 547–609

Kirchhof P (1976) Rechtsquellen und Grundgesetz. In: Starck C (ed) Bundesverfassungsgericht und Grundgesetz. Festgabe aus Anlaß des 25-jährigen Bestehens des Bundesverfassungsgerichts. Mohr Siebeck, Tübingen, pp. 50–107

Kischel U (2003) Die Begründung zur Erläuterung staatlicher Entscheidungen gegenüber dem Bürger. Mohr Siebeck, Tübingen

Kisfaludi A (2008) The influence of the harmonisation on the development of the civil law in Hungary. JI 14(1):130–136

Kling M (2008) Sprachrisiken im Privatrechtsverkehr. Die wertende Verteilung sprachenbedingter Verständnisrisiken im Vertragsrecht. Mohr Siebeck, Tübingen

Knobbe-Keuk B (1972) Vermögensschaden und Interesse. Röhrscheid, Bonn

Koch BA (2002) Wilburg's flexible system in a nutshell. In: Koziol H, Steininger BC (eds) European tort law 2011. Springer, Vienna/New York

Koch BA (2005) The "European Group on Tort Law" and its "Principles of European Tort Law". AJCL 53(1):189–205. Available via JSTOR. http://www.jstor.org/stable/30038691. Accessed 31 Mar 2017

Kötz H, Wagner G (2013) Deliktsrecht, 12th edn. Vahlen, Munich

Koziol H (2004) Compensation for pure economic loss from a continental lawyer's perspective. In: van Boom WH, Koziol H, Witting CA (eds), Bloch B (contrib.) Pure economic loss, tort and insurance law, vol 9. Springer, Vienna, pp. 141–161

Koziol H (1998a) The "auditor-case". In: Spier J (ed) The limits of expanding liability. Eight fundamental cases in a comparative perspective. Kluwer Law International, The Hague/London/Boston, pp. 25–36

Koziol H (1998b) The borderline between tort liability and contract. In: Koziol H (ed) Unification of tort law: wrongfulness. Kluwer Law International, The Hague/London/Boston, pp. 25–28

Koziol H (2006) Recovery for economic loss in the European Union. Ariz Law Rev 48(4):871–895

Koziol H (2008) Conclusion. In: Koziol H, Schulze R (eds) Tort law of the European community. Springer, Vienna/New York, pp. 589–610

Koziol H (2009) Außervertragliche Schuldverhältnisse im CFR. In: Schmidt-Kessel M (ed) Der Gemeinsame Referenzrahmen. Entstehung, Inhalte, Anwendung. Sellier, Munich, pp. 93–112

Kriele M (1979) Recht und praktische Vernunft. V&R Unipress, Göttingen
Kropholler J (1975) Gleichberechtigung durch Richterrecht. Gieseking, Bielefeld
Kropholler J (2004) Internationales Einheitsrecht. Allgemeine Lehren, 5th edn. Mohr Siebeck, Tübingen
Kuhlenbeck L (1903) Das Bürgerliche Gesetzbuch für das Deutsche Reich nebst dem Einführungsgesetze, 2nd edn. Carl Heymanns, Berlin
Laborinho Lúcio Á (1986) O magistrado hoje. Actuação e formação. RCCS (18/19/20):291–309
Lambert-Faivre Y, Porchy-Simon S (2011) Droit du dommage corporel, 7th edn. Dalloz, Paris
Lamy Pimenta M (2011) "Positivismo jurídico inclusivo": afinamento ou afastamento do positivismo jurídico? In: Manuel Hespanha A, Pizarro Beleza T (coord.) Teoria da Argumentação e Neoconstitucionalismo. Um conjunto de perspectivas. Almedina, Coimbra, pp. 263–289
Lando O (1999) The rules of European contract law. In: von Bar C, Barendrecht M, Basedow J, Drobnig U, van Gerven W, Hondius E, Kerameus K, Koussoulis S, Lando O, Loos M, Tilmann W (eds) The private law systems in the EU: discrimination on grounds of nationality and the need for a European civil code. European Parliament, Luxembourg, pp. 123–132
Lando O, Beale H (eds) (2000) Principles of European Contract Law, parts 1/2. Kluwer Law International, The Hague
Lange H (1976) Adäquanztheorie, Rechtswidrigkeitszusammenhang, Schutzzwecklehre und selbständige Zurechnungsmomente. JZ 31(7):198–207
Lange H, Schiemann G (2003) Schadensersatz. In: Gernhuber J (ed) Handbuch des Schuldrechts, 3rd edn. Mohr Siebeck, Tübingen
Lapoyade-Deschamps C (1996) La réparation du préjudice économique pur en droit français. In: Banakas EK (ed) Civil liability for pure economic loss. Kluwer Law International, London, pp. 89–101
Larenz K (1963) Rechtswidrigkeit und Handlungsbegriff im Zivilrecht. In: von Caemmerer E, Nikisch A, Zweigert K (eds) Vom deutschen zum europäischen Recht, Festschrift für Hans Dölle, vol II-Internationales Recht, Kollisionsrecht und internationales Zivilprozessrecht, Europäisches Recht. Mohr Siebeck, Tübingen, pp. 169–200
Larenz K (1970) Zum heutigen Stand der Lehre von der objektiven Zurechnung im Schadensersatzrecht. In: Barth E (ed) Festschrift für Richard M. Honig. Schwartz, Göttingen, pp. 79–90
Larenz K (1987) Lehrbuch des Schuldrechts, vol I-Allgemeiner Teil, 14th edn. Beck, Munich
Larenz K (1995) Methodenlehre der Rechtswissenschaft, 3rd edn. Springer, Berlin/Heidelberg/New York/Barcelona/Budapest/Hong Kong/London/Milan/Paris/Tokyo
Larenz K, Canaris C-W (1977) Lehrbuch des Schuldrechts, vol II-Besonderer Teil, 11th edn. Beck, Munich
Larenz K, Canaris C-W (1995) Methodenlehre der Rechtswissenschaft, 3rd revised edn. Springer, Berlin/Heidelberg/New York
Le Roy M (2004) L'évaluation du préjudice corporel, expertises, principes, indemnités. Juris-Classeur, Paris
Lebre de Freitas J (2008) Nota de abertura. In: Aa. Vv. Código Civil Português. Evolução e perspectivas actuais. Themis. Ed. especial. Almedina, Coimbra, pp. 7–11
Legrand P (1997a) Against a European civil code. MLR 60(1):44–63
Legrand P (1997b) The impossibility of "legal transplants". MJ 4(2):111–124
Legrand P (2006) Antivonbar. JCL 13(1):13–40
Lehmann M (2009) Anwendung des CFR in Schiedsverfahren. In: Schmidt-Kessel M (ed) Der Gemeinsame Referenzrahmen: Entstehung, Inhalte, Anwendung. Sellier, Munich, pp. 433–455
Lehmann M (2015) Damages and interests. In: Plaza Penadés J, Martínez Velensoso LM (eds) European perspectives on the Common European Sales Law. Springer, Heidelberg/New York/Dordrecht/London, pp. 243–261

Leible S (2009) Auswirkungen des CFR auf eine gemeinschaftsrechtskonforme Auslegung. In: Schmidt-Kessel M (ed) Der Gemeinsame Referenzrahmen. Entstehung, Inhalte, Anwendung. Sellier, Munich, pp. 217–233

Leitão H (2008) O Código Civil Português de 1966 nos PALOP e as tendências de reforma. In: Aa. Vv. Código Civil Português. Evolução e perspectivas actuais. Themis. Ed. especial. Almedina, Coimbra, pp. 129–161

Leite de Campos D (1987) A vida, a morte e a sua indemnização. BolMinJus 365(1):5–20

Leite de Campos D (2009) O contrato a favor de terceiros. Almedina, Lisbon

Leite de Campos D (1993) Lições de Direitos de Personalidade, 2nd edn. N.n, Coimbra

Łętowska E (2010) Transformations in law interpretation: Towards a universal approach - The phenomenon, causes and symptoms. In: Jemielniak J, Mikłaszewicz P (eds) Interpretation of law in the global world. From particularism to a universal approach. Springer, Berlin/Heidelberg, pp. 31–52

Lipstein K (1963) Protected interests in the law of torts. CLJ 21(1):85–103

Lollini A (2007) Legal argumentation based on foreign law. An example from case law of the South African Constitutional Court. UtrLR 3(1, June):60–74

Looschelders D (2014) Schuldrecht: Besonderer Teil, 9th edn. Vahlen, Munich

Lopes Navarro L (1948) A responsabilidade civil do Estado. BolMinJus 4(1):27–43

López Medina DE (2009) El derecho de los jueces. Obligatoriedad del precedente constitucional, análisis de sentencias y líneas jurisprudenciales y teoría. Legis, Bogotá

Lorenz W (1973) Das Problem der Haftung für primäre Vermögensschäden bei der Erteilung einer unrichtigen Auskunft. In: Paulus G, Diederichsen U, Canaris C-W (eds) Festschrift für Karl Larenz zum 70. Geburstag. Beck, Munich, pp. 575–620

Lukas M (2008) Fault liability. In: Koziol H, Schulze R (eds) Tort law of the European community. Springer, Vienna/New York, pp. 81–102

Luther C (2013) Kompensationschadenersatz statt Drittschadensliquidation. AcP 213(4):572–603

Macgregor L (2008, September) Report on the Draft Common Frame of Reference: a report prepared for the Scottish Government by Laura Macgregor, University of Edinburgh, on the document known as "Principles, Definitions and Model Rules of European Private Law". Available via the Scottish Government. http://www.gov.scot/Resource/Doc/262952/0078639.pdf. Accessed 31 Mar 2017

Machado Cabral GC (2010) A Lei da Boa Razão e as fontes do direito: investigações sobre as mudanças no Direito Português do final do antigo regime. Aa. Vv. Anais do XIX Encontro Nacional do CONPEDI. Fundação Boiteux, Florianópolis, pp. 6114–6126

MacQueen HL (2010) The Common Frame of Reference. TulLRev 84(25):177–195

Magalhães Collaço I (2004) A reforma de 1977 do Código Civil de 1966. Um olhar vinte e cinco anos depois. In: Comemorações dos 35 anos do Código Civil e dos 25 anos da Reforma de 1977, vol I-Direito da Família e das Sucessões. Coimbra Editora, Coimbra, pp. 17–40

Magalhães T, Pinto da Costa D (2007) Avaliação do dano na pessoa em sede de Direito Civil. Perspectivas actuais. RFDUL (4):419–454

Magnus U (1987) Schaden und Ersatz: eine rechtsvergleichende Untersuchung zur Ersatzfähigkeit von Einbußen. Mohr Siebeck, Tübingen

Magnus U (2001a) Comparative report on the law of damages. In: Magnus U (ed) Unification of tort law: damages. Kluwer Law International, The Hague/London/New York, pp. 185–217

Magnus U (2001b) Damages under German law. In: Magnus U (ed) Unification of tort law: damages. Kluwer Law International, The Hague/London/New York, pp. 89–107

Magnus U (2002) Towards European civil liability. In: Faure M, Schneider H, Smits J (eds) Towards a European ius commune in legal education and research. Intersentia, Antwerpen/Gröningen, pp. 205–224

Magnus U (2004a) Ein einheitliches Deliktsrecht für Europe? In: Kieninger E-M, Remien O (eds) Privat- und Wirtschaftsrecht im Zeichen der Europäischen Integration. Nomos, Baden-Baden, pp. 141–162

Magnus U (2004b) Vergleich der Vorschläge zum europäischen Deliktsrecht. ZEuP (3):562–580

Magri G, Medeiros Nóbrega JC (2014) Alcune osservazioni sull'influenza del modello italiano in Portogallo. CDCT working paper 27–2014. Eur Leg Cult 16(1):1–23. Available via Centro di Diritto Comparato e Transnazionale. http://www.cdct.it/wp-content/uploads/2014/06/303_11.pdf. Accessed 30 Aug 2015

Mak C (2014) Judges in Utopia: fundamental rights as constitutive elements of a European private culture. In: Helleringer G, Purnhagen K (eds) Towards a European legal culture. Beck/Hart, Munich/Oxford, pp. 375–395

Mancuso S (2009) Legal transplants and economic development: Civil Law vs. Common Law. In: Oliveira J, Cardinal P (eds) One country, two systems, three legal orders: perspectives of evolution. Springer, Heidelberg, pp. 75–89

Mankowski P (2012) Comment to art. 5. In: Magnus U, Mankowski P (eds) Brussels I Regulation, 2nd edn. Sellier, Munich

Markesinis BS (1986) A comparative introduction to the German law of torts. Clarendon Press, Oxford

Markesinis B (2000) Judicial style and judicial reasoning in England and Germany. CLJ 59 (2, July):249–309

Markesinis B (2006) Judicial mentality: mental disposition or outlook as a factor impeding recourse to foreign law. TulLRev 80(4):1325–1375

Markesinis BS, Fedtke J (2005–2006) The judge as comparatist. TulLRev 80(11):11–167

Markesinis BS, Unberath H (2002) The German law of torts. Hart, Oregon

Marschall von Bieberstein W (1967) Reflexschäden und Regreßrechte. Kohlhammer, Stuttgart

Martín-Casals M (2005) Una primera aproximación a los Principios de Derecho Europeo de la Responsabilidad Civil. InDret 284:1–25

Martín Casals M, Ribot Igualada J (2003) "Pure economic loss": la indemnización de los daños patrimoniales puros. In: Cámara Lapuente S (coord.) Derecho Privado Europeo. Colex, Madrid, pp. 883–920

Martins A (2006) Size and composition of highest courts. Selection of judges. In: Pernice I, Kokott J, Saunders C (eds) The future of the European judicial system in a comparative perspective. Nomos, Baden-Baden, pp. 203–210

Mattamouros J (2006) A liquidação do dano de terceiro no Direito Civil Português. RFDUL 3:303–332

Mayr S (2012) Putting a leash on the Court of Justice? Preconceptions in national methodology v effet utile as a meta-rule. EJLS 5(2):8–21

Medeiros Nóbrega C (2015) Die Entwicklung des portugiesischen Sachenrechts. V&R Unipress, Göttingen

Medicus D (2000) Schuldrecht: Allgemeiner Teil, 12th edn. Beck, Munich

Medicus D (2003) Die "Identität des Schadens" als Argument für den Ersatz von Drittschäden. In: Schwenzer I, Hager G (eds) Festschrift für Peter Schlechtriem zum 70. Geburtstag. Mohr Siebeck, Tübingen, pp. 613–628

Medicus D (2005) Die psychisch vermittelte Kausalität im Zivilrecht. JuS 45(1):289–295

Medicus D (2007) Gesetzliche Schuldverhältnisse. Delikts- und Schadensrecht, Bereicherung, Geschäftsführung ohne Auftrag, 5th edn. Beck, Munich

Medicus D, Petersen J (2011) Bürgerliches Recht, 23rd edn. Vahlen, Munich

Meier-Hayoz A (1951) Der Richter als Gesetzgeber. Juris, Zürich

Meira Lourenço P (2006) A função punitiva da responsabilidade civil. Coimbra Editora, Coimbra

Mekki M (2008) La cohérence sociologique du droit de la responsabilité civile. In: Fabre-Magnan M, Ghestin J, Jourdain P, Labrusse-Riou C (eds), Borghetti J-S, Deshayes O, Pérès C (coord.) Liber amicorum: Études offertes à Geneviève Viney. LGDJ, Paris, pp. 739–762

Melo Freire P (1829) Institutionum Juris Criminalis Lusitani Liber Singularis, 2nd edn. Ex Typographia Academico-Regia, Coimbra. Available via Google books. https://books.google.de/books?id=EYRDAAAAcAAJ&printsec=frontcover&hl=pt-PT&source=gbs_ge_summary_r&cad=0#v=onepage&q&f=false. Accessed 31 Mar 2017

Melo Freire P (1853) Institutiones Iuris Civilis Lusitani, vol 1, 5th edn. J. A. Orcel, Coimbra. Available via Google books. https://books.google.com.br/books?id=MXcWAAAAYAAJ&printsec=frontcover&hl=pt-BR&source=gbs_ge_summary_r&cad=0#v=onepage&q&f=false. Accessed 31 Mar 2017

Menezes Cordeiro M (1984a). Da boa fé no Direito Civil, vol. 1. Coimbra: Almedina

Menezes Cordeiro MD (1984b). Da boa fé no Direito Civil, vol. 2. Coimbra: Almedina

Menezes Cordeiro A (1986) Direito das Obrigações, vol 1. AAFDL, Lisbon

Menezes Cordeiro A (1987) Teoria Geral do Direito Civil/Relatório. Separata da RFDUL. FDUL, Lisbon

Menezes Cordeiro A (1994) Direito das Obrigações, vol 2. AAFDL, Lisbon

Menezes Cordeiro A (1996a) A boa fé nos finais do século XX. ROA 56(1, December):887–912

Menezes Cordeiro AM (1996b) Da responsabilidade civil dos administradores das sociedades comerciais. Lex, Lisbon

Menezes Cordeiro A (1999) Tratado de Direito Civil Português, vol I-Parte Geral. Tomo I-Introdução. Doutrina geral. Negócio jurídico. Almedina, Coimbra

Menezes Cordeiro A (2002) Os direitos de personalidade na civilística portuguesa. In: Menezes Cordeiro A, Menezes Leitão L, da Costa Gomes M J (orgs.) Estudos em Homenagem ao Professor Doutor Inocêncio Galvão Telles, vol I-Direito Privado e vária. Almedina, Coimbra, pp. 21–45

Menezes Cordeiro A (2002–2003) Da reforma do Direito Civil Português. O Direito 134–135 (1):31–44

Menezes Cordeiro A (2004) Da modernização do Direito Civil, vol 1. Almedina, Coimbra

Menezes Cordeiro A (2009) Tratado de Direito Civil Português, vol II-Direito das Obrigações. Tomo 1-Introdução. Sistemas e Direito Europeu das Obrigações. Dogmática geral. Almedina, Coimbra

Menezes Cordeiro A (2010a) O sistema Lusófono de Direito. ROA 70(1, January–December):17–119

Menezes Cordeiro A (2010b) Tratado de Direito Civil Português, vol II-Direito das Obrigações. Tomo 3-Gestão de negócios, enriquecimento sem causa, responsabilidade civil. Almedina, Coimbra

Menezes Leitão A (2002) Os danos puramente económicos nos sistemas da Common Law-I. In: Moura Ramos RM, de Almeida CF, Marques dos Santos A, Pais de Vasconcelos P, de Lima Pinheiro L, de Brito MH, Moura Vicente D (orgs.) Estudos em homenagem à Professora Doutora Isabel de Magalhães Colaço, vol 2. Almedina, Coimbra, pp. 197–218

Menezes Leitão A (2005a) Os danos puramente económicos nos sistemas da Common Law-II (jurisprudência Norte-Americana). In: Miranda J (coord.) Estudos em homenagem ao Professor Joaquim Moreira da Silva Cunha. Coimbra Editora, Coimbra, pp. 19–38

Menezes Leitão LM (2005b) Direito das Obrigações, vol 1, 4th edn. Almedina, Coimbra

Menezes Leitão A (2009) Normas de protecção e danos puramente patrimoniais. Almedina, Coimbra

Menezes Leitão LM (2013) Direito das Obrigações, vol 1, 10th edn. Almedina, Coimbra

Mersinis TG (1999) The case for contractual solutions in the third party pure economic loss. Ant. N. Sakkoulas/Bruylant, Athens/Brussels

Mertens H-J (1978) Deliktsrecht und Sonderprivatrecht. AcP 178(2/3):227–262

Mertens H-J (1980) Verkehrspflichten und Deliktsrecht. Gedanken zu einer Dogmatik der Verkehrspflichtverletzung. VersRAI:397–408

Mertz J (1994) Der Schutz primärer Vermögensinteressen im niederländischen und im deutschen Haftungsrecht. Carl Heymanns, Cologne

Meyer O (2007) Principles of contract law und nationales Vertragsrecht. Nomos, Baden-Baden

Miller L (2011) The emergence of EU contract law: exploring Europeanisation. Oxford University Press, Oxford

Ministerio de Justicia (2009) Propuesta para la modernización del Derecho de obligaciones y contratos. Gobierno de España/Ministerio de Justicia, Madrid

Miranda J (2000) Manual de Direito Constitucional, vol 4, 3rd edn. Coimbra Editora, Coimbra
Miranda Barbosa AM (2006a) Liberdade vs. responsabilidade: a precaução como fundamento da imputação delitual? Almedina, Coimbra
Miranda Barbosa M (2006b) O papel da imputabilidade no quadro da responsabilidade delitual. Breve apontamento. BFD 82(1):485–534
Miranda Barbosa M (2015) Responsabilidade civil: um diálogo a propósito da ilicitude e da causalidade adequada entre o sistema Português e a tentativa de harmonização do direito delitual ao nível Europeu. TI 33(1):218–264
Möller R (2006) Das Präventionsprinzip des Schadensrechts. Duncker&Humblot, Berlin
Möschel W (1977) Der Schutzbereich des Eigentums nach § 823 I BGB. JuS 17(1, Januar):1–4
Möslein F (2008) Judikative Europäisierung - Der Beitrag der Gerichte zur Harmonisierung des Privat- und Wirtschaftsrechts. In: Liebscher M (ed) Harmonisierung des Wirtschaftsrechts in Deutschland, Österreich und Polen. Jahrbuch des Krakauer Forums der Rechtswissenschaften. Nomos, Baden-Baden, pp. 57–80
Moitinho de Almeida JC (n.d.) Seguro obrigatório automóvel: o Direito Português face à jurisprudência do Tribunal de Justiça das Comunidades Europeias. Accessible via STJ. http://www.stj.pt/ficheiros/estudos/moitinhoalmeida_seguroobrigatorio.pdf. Accessed 31 Mar 2017
Mommsen F (1855) Zur Lehre von dem Interesse. Schwetschke, Braunschweig
Monateri PG (1989) Cumulo di responsabilità contrattuale e extracontrattuale. Cedam, Padova
Montesquieu (1973) De l'esprit des lois, vol 1. Éditions Garnier Frères, Paris
Mota de Campos J, Mota de Campos JL (2010) Manual de Direito Europeu, 6th edn. Coimbra Editora (Wolters Kluwers), Coimbra
Mota Pinto CA (1966) A responsabilidade pré-negocial pela não conclusão dos contratos. BFD 14 (1):143–253
Mota Pinto CA (2005) Teoria Geral do Direito Civil. Coimbra Editora, Coimbra
Mota Pinto P (2008a) O Código Civil Português: "De uma possível tendência para o esvaziamento a uma também possível necessidade de reforma"? Algumas reflexões. In: Aa. Vv. Código Civil Português. Evolução e perspectivas actuais. Themis. Ed. especial. Almedina, Coimbra, pp. 25–46
Mota Pinto P (2008b) Interesse contratual negativo e interesse contratual positivo, vol 1. Coimbra Editora, Coimbra
Moura Ramos R (2002) Conclusões. In: Lopes Porto MC, Lacerda Machado D, Santos Justo A, Antunes Varela J, Hartkamp A, Spier J, von Bar C, Bussani M, Drobnig U, Oliveira G, Pamplona Corte-Real C, Ghestin J, McKendrick E (eds) Um código civil para a Europa. Coimbra Editora, Coimbra, pp. 307–317
Moura Ramos RM (2004) A reforma de 1977 e o Direito Internacional Privado da Família. In: Comemorações dos 35 anos do Código Civil e dos 25 anos da Reforma de 1977, vol I-Direito da Família e das Sucessões. Coimbra Editora, Coimbra, pp. 725–742
Moura Vicente D (2001) Da responsabilidade pré-contratual em Direito Internacional Privado. Almedina, Coimbra
Moura Vicente D (2008) Direito Comparado, vol I-Introdução e parte geral. Almedina, Coimbra
Müller P (2000) Punitive Damages und deutsches Schadensersatzrecht. De Gruyter, Berlin/New York
Müller J (2008) Der Allgemeine Teil im portugiesischen Zivilgesetzbuch. Entstehungsgeschichte und ausgewählte Einzelprobleme. Verlag dr. Kovač, Hamburg
Müller F, Christensen J (2007) Juristische Methodik, vol II–Europarecht, 2nd edn. Duncker & Humblot, Berlin
Münzberg W (1966) Verhalten und Erfolg als Grundlagen der Rechtswidrigkeit und Haftung. Klostermann, Frankfurt am Main
Mugdan B (1896) Motive zu dem Entwurfe eines Bürgerlichen Gesetzbuches für das Deutsche Reich, Recht der Schuldverhältnisse, vol 2. In: Mugdan B (coord., ed.) Die gesammten Materialien zum Bürgerlichen Gesetzbuch für das Deutsche Reich, vol 2. Guttentag, Berlin

Mugdan B (1899) Die gesammten Materialien zum Bürgerlichen Gesetzbuch für das Deutsche Reich, vol 2. R.V. Decker's Verlag, Berlin

Muñoz JI, Represas C, Suárez-Peñaranda JM, Rodríguez-Calvo MS, Vieira DN, Concheiro L (2000) La tercera persona en la ley española 30/95. Valoración médico-legal de los grandes inválidos. RDPC 9(10, November):99–105

Murillo ML (2001–2002) The evolution of codification in the Civil Law systems. Towards decodification and recodification. JTLP 11(1):163–182

Musielak H-J (1974) Haftung für Rat, Auskunft und Gutachten. De Gruyter, Berlin

Neuner J (1999) Der Schutz und die Haftung Dritter nach vertraglichen Grundsätzen. JZ 54 (1):126–136

Nogueira da Silva C (2007) Legal history. In: Ferreira de Almeida C, Cristas A, Piçarra N (eds) Portuguese law: an overview. Almedina, Coimbra, pp. 15–28

Nunes de Carvalho PP (1999) Omissão e dever de agir em Direito Civil. Almedina, Coimbra

Odersky W (1999) Harmonisierende Auslegung und europäische Rechtskultur. ZEup 2:1–4

Oliphant K (2011) Volume 4 (Book VI, Non-Contractual Liability Arising Out of Damage Caused to Another). Edinburgh Law Rev 16(1):309–311

Oliveira Ascensão J (2013) O Direito. Introdução e teoria geral, 13th edn. Almedina, Coimbra

Oliveira e Sá F (2007) Contrato e liquidação de dano de terceiro - Análise de uma hipótese. In: Morais Antunes AF, Taveira da Fonseca AM, Pestana de Vasconcelos MJ, Oliveira e Sá F (eds) Novas Tendências da Responsabilidade Civil. Almedina, Coimbra, pp. 207–251

Opoku K (1972) Delictual liability in German law. ICLQ 21(2):230–269

O'Sullivan G (1991) Negligence: is pure economic loss a lost cause? Recent changes in English law & their possible influence on Irish law. ISLR 1(1):109–125

Palmer VV, Bussani M (2007) Pure economic loss: the ways to recovery. In: Boele-Woelki K, van Erp S (eds) General reports of the XVIIth Congress of the International Academy of Comparative Law. Eleven International Publishing, Utrecht, pp. 189–273

Parisi F (2003) Liability for pure financial loss: revisiting the economic foundations of a legal doctrine. In: Bussani M, Palmer VV (eds) Pure economic loss in Europe. Cambridge University Press, Cambridge, pp. 75–93

Parisi F, Palmer VV, Bussani M (2006) The comparative law and economics of pure economic loss. IrLE 27(1):29–48

Pereira Coelho FM (1950) O nexo de causalidade na responsabilidade civil. Coimbra Editora, Coimbra

Pereira Coelho FM (1955) O problema da causa virtual na responsabilidade civil. Coimbra Editora, Coimbra

Pereira Coelho FM (1967) Obrigações: sumário das lições ao curso de 1966–1967. Photocopied, Coimbra

Pereira Coelho F, Oliveira G (2001) Curso de Direito da Família, vol I-Introdução. Direito Matrimonial, 2nd edn. Coimbra Editora, Coimbra

Pereira Neves V, Ferreira de Almeida C (2007) Portuguese legal system as civil law. In: Ferreira de Almeida C, Cristas A, Piçarra N (eds) Portuguese law - An overview. Almedina, Coimbra, pp. 29–33

Perry R (2004) Relational economic loss: an integrated economic justification for the exclusionary rule. Rut.LR 56(3):711–788

Pessoa Jorge F (1975–1976) Lições de Direito das Obrigações. Photocopied, Lisbon

Pessoa Jorge F (1995) Ensaio sobre os pressupostos da responsabilidade civil, repr 1968, 2nd edn. Almedina, Coimbra

Pestana de Vasconcelos MJ (2007) Algumas questões sobre a ressarcibilidade delitual de danos patrimoniais puros no ordenamento jurídico português. In: Morais Antunes AF, Fonseca AM, Vasconcelos MJ, Oliveira e Sá F (eds) Novas tendências da responsabilidade civil. Almedina, Coimbra, pp. 147–206

Picker E (1983) Positive Forderungsverletzung und culpa in contrahendo - Zur Problematik der Haftung "zwischen" Vertrag und Delikt. AcP 183:369–520

Picker E (1987) Vertragliche und deliktische Schadenshaftung. Überlegungen zu einer Neustrukturierung des Haftungssysteme. JZ 42(1):1041–1057

Pinkel T (2008) Das Buch VI des Entwurfs eines Gemeinsamen Referenzrahmens (DCFR): Nichtvertragliche Schuldverhälnisse aus Schädigung Dritter. Eine kritische Analyse des Modellgesetzes eines europäischen Deliktsrechts. ZERP-Diskussionspapier 6/2008. ZERP, Bremen

Pinto Monteiro A (1992) Sobre a reparação dos danos morais. RPDC 1(1):17–25

Pinto Monteiro A (1999) Cláusula penal e indemnização. Almedina, Coimbra

Pinto Monteiro A (2003) Cláusulas limitativas e de exclusão de responsabilidade civil. Almedina, Coimbra

Pinto Monteiro A (2006) A parte geral do Código, a Teoria Geral do Direito Civil e o Direito Privado Europeu. In: Faculdade de Direito da Universidade de Coimbra (ed) Comemorações dos 35 anos do Código Civil e dos 25 anos da Reforma de 1977, vol II-A Parte Geral do Código e a Teoria Geral do Direito Civil. Coimbra Editora, Coimbra, pp. 57–76

Pinto Oliveira NM (2002) Sobre o conceito de ilicitude do art. 483.° do Código Civil. In: Associação Jurídica de Braga/Escola de Direito da Universidade do Minho, Estudos em Homenagem a Francisco José Velozo. Universidade do Minho, Braga

Pinto Oliveira NM (2005) Direito das Obrigações, vol I-Conceito, estrutura e função das relações obrigacionais. Elementos das relações obrigacionais. Direitos de crédito e direitos reais. Almedina, Coimbra

Pinto Oliveira NM (2011) Princípios de Direito dos Contratos. Coimbra Editora, Coimbra

Pires da Rosa J (2008) Mudam-se os tempos, mudem-se as vontades! In: Aa. Vv. Código Civil Português. Evolução e perspectivas actuais. Themis. Ed. especial. Almedina, Coimbra, pp. 15–23

Pires de Lima FA, Antunes Varela JM (1987) Código Civil anotado, vol 1. Coimbra Editora, Coimbra

Pires de Lima FA, Antunes Varela JM (repr. 2010) Código Civil Anotado, vol IV. Coimbra Editora, Coimbra

Plötner M (2003) Die Rechtsfigur des Vertrags mit Schutzwirkung für Dritte und die sogenannte Expertenhaftung. Duncker & Humblot, Berlin

Poiares Maduro M (2006) A Constituição plural. Constitucionalismo e União Europeia. Principia, Cascais

Poiares Maduro M (2007) Interpreting European law: judicial adjudication in a context of constitutional pluralism. EJLS 1(2):1–21

Poiares Maduro M, Pereira Coutinho F (2007) EU law and Portuguese law. In: Ferreira de Almeida C, Cristas A, Piçarra N (eds) Portuguese law - An overview. Almedina, Coimbra, pp. 51–71

Posner R (2004) No thanks, we already have our own laws. Legal Affairs, July–August. Available via Legal Affairs. http://www.legalaffairs.org/issues/July-August-2004/feature_posner_julaug04.msp. Accessed 31 Mar 2017

Prata A (2007) Law of Torts. In: Ferreira de Almeida C, Cristas A, Piçarra N (eds) Portuguese law - An overview. Almedina, Coimbra, pp. 197–205

Prata A (2010) Dicionário jurídico, vol 1, 5th edn. Almedina, Coimbra

Rajski J (2006) On the need for a progressive harmonisation of private law in the European Union: the role of legal science and education. JI 11(1):20–24

Rajski J (2008) European initiatives and reform of civil law in Poland. JI 14(1):151–155

Ranchordás S (2014) Constitutional sunsets and experimental legislation: a comparative perspective. Edward Elgar, Cheltenham/Northampton

Rangel PC (2001) Repensar o poder judicial. Fundamentos e fragmentos. Publicações Universidade Católica, Porto

Ranieri F (1977) Le traduzioni e le annotazioni di opere giuridiche straniere nel sec. XIX come mezzo di penetrazione e di influenza delle dottrine. In: Paradisi B (ed) La formazione storica del diritto moderno in Europa, vol 3. Leo S. Olschki, Florence, pp. 1487–1504

Ranieri F (2003) Europäisches Obligationenrecht. Springer, Vienna

Rebmann K, Krüger W (2003) Münchener Kommentar zum Bürgerlichen Gesetzbuch, vol II-Schuldrecht Allgemeiner Teil, §§ 241-432, 4th edn. (cited here with the commentaries of W. Krüger). Beck, Munich

Rebmann K, Krüger W (2016) Münchener Kommentar zum Bürgerlichen Gesetzbuch, vol II-Schuldrecht Allgemeiner Teil, §§ 241–432, 7th edn. (cited here with the commentaries of S. Grundmann). Beck, Munich

Reinhardt R (1943) Beiträge zum Neubau des Schadensersatzrechts. AcP 148:147–187

Reinhard R (1961) Die subjektiven Rechte in § 823 Abs. 1 BGB. KF 1961 (Beiheft VersR). VVW, Karlsruhe, pp. 3–19

Reis Marques M (2006) Considerações sobre a vigência do Código Civil. In: Faculdade de Direito da Universidade de Coimbra (ed) Comemorações dos 35 anos do Código Civil e dos 25 anos da Reforma de 1977, vol II-A Parte Geral do Código e a Teoria Geral do Direito Civil. Coimbra Editora, Coimbra, pp. 89–102

Reis Marques M (2009) História do Direito Português Medieval e Moderno, repr 2002. Almedina, Coimbra

Remien O (2009) Der Gemeinsame Referenzrahmen im Unterricht-Szenarien, Fakten, Perspektiven. In: Schmidt-Kessel M (ed) Der Gemeinsame Referenzrahmen. Entstehung, Inhalte, Anwendung. Sellier, Munich, pp. 457–476

Ribeiro de Albuquerque JP (2011) "Critical legal studies": a indeterminação do direito e a função judicial. In: Manuel Hespanha A, Pizarro Beleza T (coords.) Teoria da Argumentação e Neoconstitucionalismo. Um conjunto de perspectivas. Almedina, Coimbra, pp. 215–237

Ribeiro de Faria JL (1990) Direito das Obrigações, vol 1. Almedina, Coimbra

Riesenhuber K (2009) Systembildung durch den CFR. Wirkungen auf die systematische Auslegung des Gemeinschaftsrechts. In: Schmidt-Kessel M (ed) Der Gemeinsame Referenzrahmen. Entstehung, Inhalte, Anwendung. Sellier, Munich, pp. 173–216

Rito S (1946) Elementos da responsabilidade civil delitual. Freitas Brito LDA, Lisbon

Roca Trías E, Fernández Gregoraci B (2009) The modern law of obligations in the Spanish High Court. ERCL 5(1):45–59

Rodotà S (1964) Il problema della responsabilità civile. Giuffrè, Milano

Rodrigues Basto JF (1988) Notas ao Código Civil, vol 2. Almedina, Lisbon

Röckrath L (2001) Die vertragliche Haftung für den Unterhaltsschaden Hinterbliebener. VersRAI 52(28):1197–1204

Rönnau T, Faust F, Fehling M (2004) Kausalität und objektive Zurechnung. JuS 44(1):113–118

Röthel A (2009) Integration durch eine unverbindliche lex academica: der Referenzrahmen als Modellgesetz? In: Schmidt-Kessel M (ed) Der Gemeinsame Referenzrahmen. Entstehung, Inhalte, Anwendung. Sellier, Munich, pp. 287–309

Rogers WVH, Bagińska E (eds) (2001) Damages for non-pecuniary loss in a comparative perspective, tort and insurance law, vol 2. Springer, Vienna/New York

Rogers WV, Spier J, Viney G (1996) Preliminary observations. In: Spier J, von Bar C (eds) The limits of liability: keeping the floodgates shut. Kluwer Law International, The Hague/London/ Boston, pp. 1–15

Romano Martinez P (2001) Cumprimento defeituoso em especial na compra e venda e na empreitada. Almedina, Coimbra

Rosas F (2001) O Salazarismo e o homem novo: ensaio sobre o Estado Novo e a questão do totalitarismo. AS 35(157):1031–1054

Rosenbaum I (2010) Hypothetische Kausalität und Schadensersatz. Verlag dr, Kovač, Hamburg

Rosengarten J (1996) Der Präventionsgedanke im deutschen Zivilrecht. NJW 30(1):1935–1938

Roussos K (1992) Schaden und Folgeschaden. Carl Heymanns, Cologne

Rudden B (1991–1992) Torticles. TulCivLaw Forum 6/7(105):105–129

Rübesamen R (2000) Das italienische Zivilgesetzbuch. Eine rechtsdogmatische und sozialhistorische Betrachtung. Lang, Frankfurt am Main

Rüthers B, Stasler A (2014) Allgemeiner Teil des BGB, 18th edn. Beck, Munich

Sá e Mello A (1989) Critérios de apreciação da culpa na responsabilidade civil (Breve anotação ao regime do Código). ROA 49(1, September):519–543
Sacco R (1960) L'ingiustizia del danno di cui all'art. 2043 cc. Foro pad. I:1420–1442
Sacco R (1984) Concorso delle azioni contrattuale ed extracontrattuale. In: Visintini G (coord.) Risarcimento del danno contrattuale ed extracontrattuale. Giuffrè, Milan, pp. 155–163
Sacco R (1991) Legal formants: a dynamic approach to comparative law (Installment I of II). AmJCL 39(1, Winter):1–34
Sacco R, Joussen J (2011) Einführung in die Rechtsvergleichung, 2nd repr. Nomos, Baden-Baden
Safjan M (2010) The universalisation of legal interpretation. In: Jemielniak J, Mikłaszewicz P (eds) Interpretation of law in the global world: from particularism to a universal approach. Springer, Berlin/Heidelberg, pp. 107–125
Samuel G (2001) Law of obligations & legal remedies. Cavendish Publishing Limited, London/ Sydney
Sandström M (1989) Der Herrschaft der Rechtswissenschaft. AB Nordiska Bokhandeln, Stockholm
Santos Júnior E (2003) Da responsabilidade civil de terceiro por lesão do direito de crédito. Almedina, Coimbra
Santos Justo A (2011) Direito Privado Romano II-Direito das Obrigações. Coimbra Editora, Coimbra
Santos Silva ML (2006) Cour de cassation, comm., pourvoi no. 02-19370 du 5 avril 2005 – Schadensersatzanspruch des einfachen Lizenznehmers für entgangenen Gewinn gegenüber einem nicht vertraglich verbundenen Konkurrenten-Portuguese case note. ERPL 14 (5/6):826–838
Santos Silva ML (2007) Anstiftung zur Verletzung von Vertragspflichten in Portugal. VersRAI:24–25
Santos Silva ML (2008) A ressarcibilidade dos danos económicos puros no âmbito do regime da responsabilidade civil extracontratual do Código Civil Português. RJVV 4(1):234–252
Santos Silva ML (2009) The compensation of pure economic loss in tort law in Portuguese legal scholarship. IJVO Jahresheft 16:52–62
Santos Silva ML (2010) O trust no Quadro Comum de Referência para o Direito Privado Europeu e as suas raízes históricas no Direito Romano. In: Aa. Vv. O sistema contratual Romano: de Roma ao Direito actual. Coimbra Editora, Coimbra, pp. 803–823
Schäfer H-B, Ott C (2005) Lehrbuch der ökonomischen Analyse des Zivilrechts. Springer, Berlin/ Heidelberg
Schildt B (1996) Der deliktische Schutz des Rechts am Gewerbebetrieb. WM:2261–2266
Schilling T (1994) Rang und Geltung von Normen in gestuften Rechtsordnungen. Berlin-Verl, Spitz, Berlin
Schilling T (1996) The authority of the Community legal order: an analysis of possible foundations. Harv.ILJ 37(2, Spring):389–390
Schlechtriem P (1972) Vertragsordnung und außervertragliche Haftung. Metzner, Frankfurt am Main
Schlechtriem P (1981) Vertragliche und außervertragliche Haftung. In: Bundesminister der Justiz, Gutachten und Vorschläge zur Überarbeitung des Schuldrechts, vol 2. Bundesanzeiger, Cologne, pp. 1591–1679
Schlechtriem P (1997) Schadensersatz und Schadensbegriff. ZEup 2:232–254
Schlechtriem P (1998) Civil liability for economic loss: Germany. Comparative law facing the twenty-first century. Unpublished manuscript
Schlechtriem P (2003) Schuldrecht Besonderer Teil, 6th edn. Mohr Siebeck, Tübingen
Schlesinger P (1960) L'ingiustizia del danno nell'illecito civile. JuS:336–347
Schlobach K (2004) Das Präventionsprinzip im Recht des Schadensersatzes. Nomos, Baden-Baden
Schmid CU (2002) Pattern of legislative and adjudicative integration of private law. Colum J Eur 8 (3):415–486

Schmid CU (2008) Judicial governance in the European Union: the ECJ as a constitutional and a private law court. In: Joerges C, Rödl F, Oddvar E (eds) Law, democracy and solidarity in a post-national Union. Routledge Cavendish, London, pp. 85–105

Schmid C (2010) Die Instrumentalisierung des Privatrechts durch die Europäische Union: Privatrecht und Privatrechtskonzeption in der Entwicklung der Europäischen Integrationsverfassung. Nomos, Baden-Baden

Schmid CU (2010) The "three lives" of European private law. In: Common Core Evaluating Group, Antoniolli L, Fiorentini F (eds) A factual assessment of the Draft Common Frame of Reference. Sellier, Munich, pp. 299–312

Schmid CU (2011) Legitimacy conditions for a European civil code. EUI Working Papers, European University Institute. Available via ResearchGate. https://www.researchgate.net/publication/5015180_Legitimacy_Conditions_for_a_European_Civil_Code. Accessed 31 Mar 2017

Schmidt K (1993) Integritätsschutz von Unternehmen nach § 823 BGB - Zum "Recht am eingerichteten und ausgeübten Gewerbebetrieb". JuS 33(1, December):985–992

Schmidt J (2015) The structure of the DCFR: borrowed from the German BGB or expression of a European common tradition? In: Afonso AI (ed) Um Direito Europeu das Obrigações? A influência do DCFR. Universidade Católica Editora, Porto, pp. 33–51

Schmidt R (2016) Bürgerliches Gesetzbuch: Allgemeiner Teil, 14th edn. Schmidt, Grasberg bei Bremen

Schmidt-Kessel M (2006) Reform des Schadensersatzrechts, vol I-Europäische Vorgaben und Vorbilder. Manz, Vienna

Schulte-Nölke H (2001) Schuldrechtsreform und Gemeinschaftsrecht. In: Schulze R, Schulte-Nölke H (eds) Die Schuldrechtsreform vor dem Hintergrund des Gemeinschaftsrechts. Mohr Siebeck, Tübingen

Schulte-Nölke H (2002) The new German law of obligations: an introduction. Available via the German Law Archive of the Oxford University Comparative Law Forum. http://www.iuscomp.org/gla/literature/schulte-noelke.htm. Accessed 31 Mar 2017

Schulte-Nölke H (2003) The Commission's Action Plan on European contract law and the research of the Acquis Group. ERA Forum 4(2, June):142–145

Schulte-Nölke H (2008) Die Acquis Principles (ACQP) und der Gemeinsame Referenzrahmen. In: Schulze R, von Bar C, Schulte-Nölke H (eds) Der akademische Entwurf für einen gemeinsamen Referenzrahmen. Mohr Siebeck, Tübingen, pp. 47–71

Schulte-Nölke H (2009a) Contract law or law of obligations? The Draft Common Frame of Reference (DCFR) as a multifunction tool. In: Schulze R (ed) Common Frame of Reference and existing EC contract law, 2nd rev. ed, Sellier, Munich, pp. 47–62

Schulte-Nölke H (2009b) Ziele und Arbeitswesen von Study Group und Acquis Group bei der Vorbereitung des DCFR. In: Schmidt-Kessel M (ed) Der Gemeinsame Referenzrahmen. Entstehung, Inhalte, Anwendung. Sellier, Munich, pp. 9–22

Schulte-Nölke H (2010a) Bausteine aus der Wissenschaft für die englische Vertragssprache. Der Gemeinsame Referenzrahmen als Toolbox für die Vertragsgestaltung. In: Schulte-Nölke H, Genzow F C, Grunewald B (eds) Zwischen Vertragsfreiheit und Verbraucherschutz. Festschrift für Friedrich Graf von Westphalen zum 70. Geburstag. Schmidt, Cologne, pp 609–620

Schulte-Nölke H (2010b) The European Law Institute. In: Cafaggi F, Francioni F, Micklitz H-W, Poiares Maduro M (orgs.) A European Law Institute? Towards innovation in European legal integration. RSCAS Policy Papers 2010/03. European University Institute, Robert Schuman Centre for Advanced Studies, Florence, pp. 55–62

Schulte-Nölke H (2011) "Restatements" in Europe and the US: some comparative lessons. In: Brownsword R, Micklitz H-W, Niglia L, Weatherill S (eds) Foundations of European private law. Hart, Oxford/Portland, pp. 11–30

Schulte-Nölke H, Schulze R (1999) Europäische Rechtsangleichung und nationale Privatrechte-Einführung. In: Schulte-Nölke H, Schulze R (eds) Europäische Rechtsangleichung und nationale Privatrechte. Nomos, Baden-Baden, pp. 11–20

Schulze R (1997) Vergleichende Gesetzesauslegung und Rechtsangleichung. ZfRV 38 (5):183–197
Schulze R (2011) Contours of European private law. In: Schulze R, Schulte-Nölke H (eds) European private law - Current status and perspectives. Sellier, Munich, pp. 3–26
Schulze R (2012) Non-contractual liability arising out of damage caused to another in the DCFR. In: Sagaert V, Storme M, Terryn E (eds) The Draft Common Frame of Reference: national and comparative perspectives. Intersentia, Cambridge/Antwerp/Portland, pp. 221–230
Schulze R, Schulte-Nölke H (eds) (2001) Die Schuldrechtsreform vor dem Hintergrund des Gemeinschaftsrecht. Mohr Siebeck, Tübingen
Schwab D, Löhnig M (2012) Einführung in das Zivilrecht, 19th edn. Müller, Verl.-Gruppe Hüthig, Jehle, Rehm, Heidelberg
Schwarz AB (1950) Das schweizerische Zivilgesetzbuch in der ausländischen Rechtsentwicklung. Schulthess, [n.p.]
Schweizer U (2005) Spieltheorie und Schuldrecht: der Ersatz reiner Vermögensschäden. Schöningh, Paderborn
Scognamiglio C (2000) Prospettive europee sulla responsabilità civile e disciplina del mercato. Europa e dir. priv. (2):333–356
Sefton-Green R (2009) The DCFR: a technical or a political toolbox? In: Somma A (ed) The politics of the DCFR. Kluwer Law International, Alphen aan den Rijn, pp. 39–50
Senden L (2004) Soft law in European Community law. Hart, Oxford
Senden L (2005) Soft law and its implications for institutional balance in the EC. UtrLR 1 (2):79–99
Senden L, Prechal S (2001) Differentiation in and through Community soft law. In: de Witte B, Hanf D, Vos E (orgs.) The many faces of differentiation in EU law. Intersentia, Oxford/New York, pp. 181–199
Silva Pereira T (2004) Proposta de reflexão sobre um código civil Europeu. ROA 64 (1, November):497–608
Sinde Monteiro JF (1983) Estudos sobre a responsabilidade civil. Almedina, Coimbra
Sinde Monteiro JF (1989) Responsabilidade por conselhos, recomendações ou informações. Almedina, Coimbra
Sinde Monteiro JF (1997) Manuel de Andrade und der Einfluß des deutschen Bürgerlichen Gesetzbuches auf das portugiesische Zivilgesetzbuch von 1966. In: Jayme E, Mansel H-P (orgs.) Auf dem Wege zu einem gemeineuropäischen Privatrecht. Nomos, Baden-Baden, pp. 29–49
Sinde Monteiro JF (2002) Manuel de Andrade, a "Europeização" do Direito Privado e o desafio de um código civil Europeu. Separata da obra Ciclo de Conferências em Homenagem Póstuma ao Prof. Doutor Manuel de Andrade. Almedina, Coimbra, pp. 43–53
Sinde Monteiro JF (2005) Rudimentos da responsabilidade civil. RFDUL 2:349–390
Sinde Monteiro JF (2007) Responsabilidade delitual. Da ilicitude. In Aa. Vv. Comemorações dos 35 anos do Código Civil e dos 25 anos da Reforma de 1977, vol III-Direito das Obrigações. Coimbra Editora, Coimbra, pp. 453–481
Sinde Monteiro JF, Veloso MM (2001) Portugal. In: Faure M, Koziol H (eds) Cases on medical malpractice in a comparative perspective. Springer, Vienna/New York, pp. 172–187
Sinde Monteiro JF, Moura Ramos R, Hörster HE (1993) Einführung in das portugiesische Deliktsrecht. In: von Bar C (ed) Deliktsrecht in Europa, Landesbericht Portugal. Carl Heymanns, Cologne/Berlin/Bonn/Munich
Smith A, Meek RL, Raphael DD, Stein PG (1978) Lectures on jurisprudence. Clarendon Press, Oxford
Snijderns H, Vogenauer S (2009) General introduction. In: Snijders H, Vogenauer S (eds) Content and meaning of national law in the context of transational law. Sellier, Munich, pp. V–VII
Somma A (2009) The politics of the DCFR. Kluwer Law International, Alphen aan den Rijn

Sousa Antunes H (2009) Nótula sobre as penas privadas na responsabilidade civil em Portugal. In: Leite de Campos D (ed) Estudos em homenagem ao Professor Doutor Manuel Henrique Mesquita-Studia Iuridica 95, vol 1. Coimbra Editora, Coimbra, pp. 133–145

Sousa Antunes H (2011) Da inclusão do lucro ilícito e de efeitos punitivos entre as consequências da responsabilidade civil extracontratual: a sua legitimação pelo dano. Coimbra Editora, Coimbra

Sousa Antunes H (2014) A alteração das circunstâncias no Direito Europeu dos Contratos. CDP 47 (July–September):3–21

Sousa Dinis JJ (2001) Dano corporal em acidentes de viação. Cálculo da indemnização em situações de morte, incapacidade total e incapacidade parcial; perspectivas futuras. CJ (ST) 9 (1):5–11

Sousa Dinis JJ (2009) Avaliação e reparação do dano patrimonial e não patrimonial (no domínio do Direito Civil). RPDC 18(19):51–68

Sousa Santos B (1987) Law: a map of misreading. Toward a postmodern conception of law. J.Law & Soc 4(3, Autumn):279–302

Sousa Santos B (dir.) (2005) Os actos e os tempos dos juízes: contributos para a construção de indicadores da distribuição processual nos juízos cíveis. Observatório Permanente da Justiça Portuguesa, Coimbra

Souza de Lobão M (1826) Tractado pratico das avaliações e dos damnos. Impressão Régia, Lisbon

Spier J (2000) Compensation for loss of spare time? In: Magnus U, Spier J (eds) European tort law. Liber Amicorum for Helmut Koziol. Lang, Frankfurt am Main/New York, pp. 299–305

Spier J (2005) The Principles of European Tort Law of the European Group on Tort Law. In: European Group on Tort Law (eds) Principles of European Tort Law: text and commentary. Springer, Vienna/New York

Spier J, Haazen O (1998) Preliminary observations. In: Spier J (ed) The limits of expanding liability. Eight fundamental cases in a comparative perspective. Kluwer Law International, The Hague/London/Boston, pp. 3–17

Spier J (ed) (1998) The limits of expanding liability. Eight fundamental cases in a comparative perspective. Kluwer Law International, The Hague/London/Boston

Spier J, von Bar C (eds) (1998) The limits of liability: keeping the floodgates shut. Kluwer Law International, The Hague/London/Boston

Stapleton J (2007) Extra-contractual recovery of pure economic loss in Europe. In: Bussani M (ed) European tort law: eastern and western perspectives, European Private Law 5. Stämpfli, Bern, pp. 225–247

Staudenmayer D (2005) Weitere Schritte im Europäischen Vertragsrecht. EuZW 4:103–106

von Staudinger J (Begr.) (2005) J. von Staudingers Kommentar zum BGB. Buch 2: Recht der Schuldverhältnisse, §§ 249–254, cited here with the commentaries by G. Schiemann. Sellier-de Gruyter, Berlin

Steiner GH (1983) Schadensverhütung als Alternative zum Schadensersatz. Carl Heymanns, Cologne/Berlin/Bonn/Munich

Stoll H (1970) Penal purposes in the law of tort. AJCL 18(1):3–21

Stoll H (1973) Begriff und Grenzen des Vermögensschadens. Müller, Karlsruhe

Stoll H (1984) Richterliche Fortbildung und gesetzliche Überarbeitung des Deliktsrechts. Müller, Heidelberg

Stoll H (1993) Haftungsfolgen im bürgerlichen Recht. Müller, Heidelberg

Stürner M (2010) Der Grundsatz der Verhältnismäßigkeit im Schuldvertragsrecht. Mohr Siebeck, Tübingen

Swann S (2003) Conceptual foundations of the law of delict as proposed by the Study Group on a European Civil Code. InDret 130:1–31

Tägert H (1938) Die Geltendmachung des Drittschadens. Boyens, Heide (Holstein)

Tamanaha BZ (2001) A general jurisprudence of law and society. Oxford University Press, Oxford

Tate CN, Vallinder T (eds) (1995) The global expansion of judicial power. New York University Press, New York/London

Teubner G (1997) "Global Bukowina": legal pluralism in the world society. In: Teubner G (ed) Global law without a state. Dartmouth, Aldershot, pp. 3–28
Teubner G (1998) Legal irritants: good faith in British law or how unifying law ends up in new divergences. MLR 61(1):11–32
Traugott R (1997) Das Verhältnis von Drittschadensliquidation und vertraglichem Drittschutz. Duncker & Humblot, Berlin
Trigo MG (2009) Responsabilidade civil delitual por facto de terceiro. Coimbra Editora, Coimbra
Trigo MG (2012) Adopção do conceito de "dano biológico" pelo Direito Português. In: Otero P, de Quadros F, Rebelo de Sousa M (coords.) Estudos de homenagem ao Professor Doutor Jorge Miranda, vol 6. Coimbra Editora, Coimbra, pp. 629–653
Trimarchi P (2007) Istituzioni di diritto privato, 17th edn. Giuffrè, Milan
Trstenjak V (2009) Der Gemeinsame Referenzrahmen und der Europäische Gerichtshof. In: Schmidt-Kessel M (ed) Der Gemeinsame Referenzrahmen. Entstehung, Inhalte, Anwendung. Sellier, Munich, pp. 235–253
Tunc A (1990) La responsabilité civile, 2nd edn. Economica, Paris
Tushnet M (2006) When is knowing less better than knowing more? Unpacking the controversy over Supreme Court reference to non-U.S. law. Minn.L.Rev. 90(1):1275–1302
Unberath H (2003) Transferred loss: claiming third party loss in contract law. Hart, Oxford
Valpuesta Gastaminza E (2011) Unificación del Derecho Patrimonial Europeo: Marco Común de Referencia y Derecho Español. Bosch, Barcelona
van Boom WH (2004) Pure economic loss: a comparative perspective. In: van Boom WH, Koziol H, Witting CA (eds) Bloch B (contrib.) Pure economic loss, tort and insurance law, vol 9. Springer, Vienna, pp. 1–40
van Boom WH, Koziol H, Witting CA (2004a) Outlook. In: van Boom WH, Koziol H, Witting CA (eds) Bloch B (contrib.) Pure economic loss, tort and insurance law, vol 9. Springer, Vienna, pp. 191–205
van Boom WH, Koziol H, Witting CA (eds) (2004b) Pure economic loss, tort and insurance law, vol 9. Springer, Vienna
van Dam C (2013) European tort law, 2nd edn. Oxford University Press, Oxford
van Gerven W (1994) Non-contractual liability of Member States, Community institutions and individuals for breaches of Community law with a view to a common law for Europe. MJ 1(1): 6–40
van Gerven W, Lever J, Larouche P (2000) Tort law. Hart, Oxford/Portland Oregon
Vaquer Aloy A, Bosch Capdevila E, Sánchez González MP (coords.) (2012) Derecho Europeo de los Contratos: Libros II y IV del Marco Común de Referencia. Atelier, Barcelona
Varela J (2011) A moderna integração das lacunas. O caso Português. In: Manuel Hespanha A, Pizarro Beleza T (coords.) Teoria da Argumentação e Neoconstitucionalismo, pp. 167–189. Almedina, Coimbra
Vaz Serra APS (1947) A revisão geral do Código Civil. BolMinJus 2(1):24–76
Vaz Serra APS (1955) Impossibilidade superveniente e cumprimento imperfeito imputáveis ao devedor. BolMinJus 47(1):5–152
Vaz Serra APS (1958a) Responsabilidade do devedor pelos factos dos auxiliares dos representantes ou dos substitutos. BolMinJus 72(1):259–305
Vaz Serra APS (1958b) Efeitos dos contratos (princípios gerais). BolMinJus 74(1):333–368
Vaz Serra APS (1959a) O dever de indemnizar e o interesse de terceiros. BolMinJus 86(1): 103–129
Vaz Serra APS (1959b) Fundamento da responsabilidade civil (em especial, responsabilidade por acidentes de viação terrestre e por intervenções lícitas). BolMinJus 90(1):5–322
Vaz Serra APS (1959c) Obrigação de indemnização (Colocação. Fontes. Conceito e espécies de dano. Nexo causal. Extensão do dever de indemnizar. Espécies de indemnização). Direito de abstenção e de remoção. BolMinJus 84(1):5–303
Vaz Serra APS (1959d) Reparação do dano não patrimonial. BolMinJus 83(1):69–111

Vaz Serra APS (1959e) Responsabilidade contratual e responsabilidade extracontratual. BolMinJus 85(1):115–342

Vaz Serra APS (1959f) Responsabilidade pelos danos causados por animais. BolMinJus 86(1): 21–99

Vaz Serra APS (1959g) Responsabilidade pelos danos causados por coisas ou actividades. BolMinJus 85(1):361–380

Vaz Serra APS (1959h) Responsabilidade de pessoas obrigadas à vigilância. BolMinJus 85 (1):381–444

Vaz Serra APS (1959i) Responsabilidade de terceiros no não cumprimento de obrigações. BolMinJus 85(1):345–360

Vaz Serra AP (1960a) Algumas questões em matéria de responsabilidade civil. BolMinJus 93(1): 5–79

Vaz Serra APS (1960b) Direito das Obrigações (com excepção dos contratos em especial): Anteprojecto. Separata do BolMinJus. Ministério da Justiça, Lisbon

Vaz Serra AP (1960c) Direito das Obrigações (Parte extensa) - Continuação. BolMinJus 100(1): 161–413

Vaz Serra A P (1960d) Requisitos da responsabilidade civil. BolMinJus 92(1):37–137

Vaz Serra AP (1962) Discurso proferido em Vila da Feira, na sessão comemorativa do centenário do nascimento de Guilherme Moreira, pelo Exmo. Senhor Doutor Adriano Paes da Silva Vaz Serra, em 1 de Dezembro de 1901. BolMinJus 112(1):19–29

Vaz Serra APS (1969) Anotação ao acórdão do Supremo Tribunal de Justiça de 11 de Fevereiro de 1969. RLJ 103(3406-3441):158–165

Vaz Serra A (1971) Anotação ao acórdão de 13 de Janeiro de 1970. RLJ 104(3442):12–16

Vaz Tomé MJ (1997) O direito à pensão de reforma enquanto bem comum do casal. Coimbra Editora, Coimbra

Vékás L (2008) Ist eine Konvergenz der nationalen Vertragsrechtssystem erkennbar? Betrachtungen aus der Perspektive der neuen Mitgliedstaaten Mittel- und Osteuropas. 4. Europäischer Juristentag. Manz, Vienna, pp. 67–83

Vendrell Cervantes C (2008) The application of the Principles of European Contract Law by Spanish courts. ZEuP 16:534–548

Viney G (2002) Un Code Civil pour l'Europe. Les perspectives dans le domaine de la responsabilité delictuelle. In: Lopes Porto MC (ed) Um código civil para a Europa. Coimbra Editora, Coimbra, pp. 211–225

Viney G, Ghestin J (1982) La responsabilité: conditions. In: Ghestin J (dir.) Traité de droit civil. Les obligations. LGDJ, Paris

Viney G, Jourdain P (2006) Traité de droit civil. Les conditions de la responsabilité, 3rd edn. LGDJ, Paris

Viney G, Markesinis B (1985) La réparation du dommage corporel. Essai de comparaison des droits anglais et français. Economica, Paris

Violante T (2011) A adjudicação constitucional e o Direito Comparado. In: Manuel Hespanha A, Pizarro Beleza T (coords.) Teoria da Argumentação e Neoconstitucionalismo. Almedina, Coimbra, pp. 337–359

Visintini G (1967) La responsabilité civile nella giurispudenza. Cedam, Padova

Vogenauer S (2001) Die Auslegung von Gesetzen in England und auf dem Kontinent: eine vergleichende Untersuchung der Rechtsprechung und ihrer historischen Grundlagen, vol 1. Mohr Siebeck, Tübingen

Vogenauer S (2009) Interpretation of the UNIDROIT Principles of International Commercial Contracts by national courts. In: Snijder H, Vogenauer S (eds) Content and meaning of national law in the context of transnational law. Sellier, Munich

Volens U (2010) Expert's liability to a third person at the point of intersection of the law of contract and the law of delict. JI 17(1):176–187

von Bar C (1980a) Unentgeltliche Investitionsempfehlungen im Wandel der Wirtschaftsverfassungen Deutschlands und Englands: ein Beitrag zur Ersatzfähigkeit reiner Vermögensschäden. RabelsZ 44(3):455–480

von Bar C (1980b) Verkehrspflichten: richterliche Gefahrsteuerungsgebote im deutschen Deliktsrecht. Carl Heymanns, Cologne/Berlin

von Bar C (1981) Deliktsrecht. In: Bundesminister der Justiz, Gutachten und Vorschläge zur Überarbeitung des Schuldrechts, vol 2. Bundesanzeiger, Cologne, pp. 1681–1778

von Bar C (1982) Vertragliche Schadensersatzpflichten ohne Vertrag? JuS 22(1):637–654

von Bar C (1983) Vorbeugender Rechtsschutz vor Verkehrspflichtverletzung. In: Hauß F, von Bieberstein WFM, Reichert-Facilides F (eds) 25 Jahre KF, Jubiläumsausgabe 1983. Beiträge zum Haftungs- und Versicherungsrecht. Verl. Versicherungswirtschaft, Karlsruhe, pp. 80–85

von Bar C (1986) Zur Bedeutung des beweglichen Systems für die Dogmatik der Verkehrspflichten. In: Bydlinski F, Krejci H, Schilcher B, Steininger V (eds) Das bewegliche System im geltenden und künftigen Recht. Springer, Vienna/New York, pp. 63–74

von Bar C (1988) Entwicklungen und Entwicklungstendenzen im Recht der Verkehrs(sicherungs) pflichten. JuS 28(1):169–174

von Bar C (1991) Die Überarbeitung des Schuldrechts am Beispiel der Überarbeitung des Deliktsrechts. In: Osnabrück-Emsland JG (ed) Dreher M, Benda E (authors) Vorträge zur Rechtsentwicklung der achtziger Jahre. Carl Heymanns, Cologne/Berlin/Bonn/Munich, pp. 211–223

von Bar C (1992a) Negligence, Eigentumsverletzung und reiner Vermögensschaden. Zu den Grenzen der Fahrlässigkeitshaftung für reine Vermögensschäden in der neueren Entwicklung des Common Law. RabelsZ 56(3):410–443

von Bar C (1992b) Neues Haftungsrecht durch Europäisches Gemeinschaftsrecht. Die Verschuldens- und die Gefährdungshaftung des deutschen Rechts und das haftungsrechtliche Richtlinienrecht der EG. In: Medicus D, Mertens H-J, Nörr K W, Zöllner W (eds) Festschrift für Hermann Lange zum 70. Geburtstag am 24. Januar 1992. W. Kohlhammer, Stuttgart/ Berlin/Cologne, pp. 373–395

von Bar C (1992c) Probleme der Haftpflicht für deliktiksrechtliche Eigentumsverletzung. Versicherungswirtschaft, Karlsruhe

von Bar C (1994a) Die Billigkeitshaftung in den kontinentalen Rechten der Europäischen Union. In: Hübner H, Helten E, Albrecht P (eds) Recht und Ökonomie der Versicherung. Festschrift für Egon Lorenz zum 60. Geburtstag. Versicherungswirtschaft, Karlsruhe, pp. 73–93

von Bar C (1994b) Liability for information and opinions causing pure economic loss to third parties: a comparison of English and German case law. In: Markesinis BS (ed) The gradual convergence. Foreign ideas, foreign influences, and English law on the eve of the 21st century. Clarendon Press, Oxford, pp. 98–127

von Bar C (1994c) Vereinheitlichung und Angleichung von Deliktsrecht in der Europäischen Union. ZfRV:221–232

von Bar C (ed) (1994d) Deliktsrecht in Europa: systematische Einführungen, Gesetztexte, Übersetzungen. Carl Heymanns, Cologne/Berlin/Bonn/Munich

von Bar C (1996a) A common European law of torts. Centro di Studi e Ricerche di Diritto Comparato e Straniero, Rome

von Bar C (1996b) Gemeineuropäisches Deliktsrecht, vol I-Kernbereiche des Deliktsrechts, seine Angleichung in Europa und seine Einbettung in die Gesamtrechtsordnung (English transl. Common European Law of Torts 1). Beck, Munich

von Bar C (1998a) The common European law of torts, vol I-The core areas of tort law, its approximation in Europe, and its accommodation in the legal system. Clarendon Press, Oxford

von Bar C (1998b) Germany. Antworten unter deutschem Recht. In: Spier J (ed) The limits of expanding liability. Eight fundamental cases in a comparative perspective, pp. 119–127. Kluwer Law International, The Hague/London/Boston

von Bar C (1998c) Verträge mit Schutzwirkung zugunsten Dritter, Drittschadensliquidation and extension of duty of care. In: Shiibashi T (ed) Toward comparative law in the 21st century. Chuo University Press, Tokyo, pp. 3–21

von Bar C (1998d) Vicarious liability. In: Hartkamp A (ed) Towards a European civil code. Kluwer Law International, The Hague/London/Boston, pp. 431–447

von Bar C (1999a) Außervertragliche Schuldverhältnisse, insbesondere Haftungsrecht. In: von Bar C, Barendrecht M, Basedow J, Drobnig U, van Gerven W, Hondius E, Kerameus K, Koussoulis S, Lando O, Loos M, Tilmann W (eds) (1999) Untersuchung der Privatrechtsordnungen der EU im Hinblick auf Diskriminierungen und die Schaffung eines europäisches Zivilgesetzbuches. Europäisches Parlament, Luxembourg. Available via the European Parliament website. http://www.europarl.europa.eu/RegData/etudes/etudes/join/1999/168511/IPOL-JURI_ET%281999%29168511_DE.pdf. Accessed 31 Mar 2017

von Bar C (1999b) Damage without loss. In: Swadling W, Jones G (eds) The search for principle. Essays in honour of Lord Goff of Chieveley. Oxford University Press, Oxford, pp. 23–43

von Bar C (1999c) Das deutsche Deliktsrecht in gemeineuropäischer Perspektive. Müller, Heidelberg

von Bar C (1999d) A European civil code, international agreements and European directives. In: von Bar C, Barendrecht M, Basedow J, Drobnig U, van Gerven W, Hondius E, Kerameus K, Koussoulis S, Lando O, Loos M, Tilmann W, in consultation with the Study Group on a European Civil Code (eds) The private law systems in the EU: discrimination on grounds of nationality and the need for a European Civil Code. European Parliament, Luxembourg, pp. 147–151

von Bar C (1999e) Gemeineuropäisches Deliktsrecht, vol II-Schaden und Schadenersatz, Haftung für und ohne eigenes Fehlverhalten, Kausalität und Verteidigungsgründe (English transl.: Common European Law of Torts 2). Beck, Munich

von Bar C (1999f) Non-contractual obligations, especially the law of tort. In: Offermann KH (ed) The private law systems in the EU. Discrimination on grounds of nationality and the need for a European Civil Code. European Parliament, Luxembourg, pp. 41–55

von Bar C (1999g) Schmerzensgeld in Europa. In: Ahrens H J, von Bar C, Fischer G, Spickhoff A, Taupitz J (eds) Festschrift für Erwin Deutsch: zum 70. Geburtstag. Carl Heymanns, Cologne/Berlin/Bonn/Munich, pp. 27–43

von Bar C (2000a) The common European law of torts, vol II-Damage and damages, liability for and without personal misconduct, causality, and defences. Oxford University Press, Oxford

von Bar C (2000b) Moderne Deliktsrechtspflege in den Zwängen einer wilhelminischen Kodifikation. In: Canaris CW, Heldrich A (eds) 50 Jahre Bundesgerichtshof. Beck, Munich

von Bar C (2000c) A new jus commune Europaeum and the importance of the common law. In: Markesinis BS (ed) The Clifford chance. Millennium lectures I: the coming together of the Common Law and the Civil Law. Hart Publishing, Oxford, pp. 67–78

von Bar C (2000d) Die Study Group on a European Civil Code. In: Gottwald P, Jayme E, Schwab D (eds) Festschrift für Dieter Henrich zum 70. Geburtstag 1. Dezember 2000. Gieseking, Bielefeld, pp. 1–11

von Bar C (2001a) Konturen des Deliktsrechtskonzeptes der Study Group on a European Civil Code. Ein Werkstattbericht. ZEuP (9):515–532

von Bar C (2001b) Le Groupe d'Études sur un Code Civil Européen. Rev.int.dr.comp. 53(1, January–March):127–139

von Bar C (2001c) Die Überwindung der Lehre von den Quasiverträgen in den Privatrechten der Europäischen Union. In: Hohloch G, Frank R, Schlechtriem P (eds) Festschrift für Hans Stoll zum 75. Geburtstag. Mohr Siebeck, Tübingen, pp. 93–112

von Bar C (2002a) Auf dem Wege zu Europäischen Grundregeln der außervertraglichen Schadenshaftung. In: Schlechtriem P (ed) Wandlungen des Schuldrechts, pp. 165–178. Nomos, Baden-Baden von Bar C (2002b) On drafting principles of tortious liability. In: Barrett G, Bernardeau L (eds) Towards a European civil code: reflections on the codification of civil law in Europe, pp. 67–74. ERA Forum, Trier

von Bar C (2002c) Paving the way forward with principles of European private law. In: Grundmann S, Stuyck J (eds) An academic green paper on European contract law, pp. 137–145. Kluwer Law International, The Hague

von Bar C (2002d) A plea for drafting principles of European private law. ERA Forum 3(2): 100–101

von Bar C (2002e) The Study Group on a European Civil Code. S.Iur 64 Colloquia 8: "Um Código Civil para a Europa". Coimbra Editora, Coimbra, pp. 65–78

von Bar C (2002f) Vom Europäischen Vertragsrecht zum Europäischen Vermögensrrecht. In: Schulte-Nölke H, Schulze R, in connection with Ludovic Bernardeau JPC (eds) Europäisches Vertragsrecht im Gemeinschaftsrecht. Bundesanzeiger, Cologne, pp. 263–269

von Bar C (2003a) The Common Frame of Reference and the works of the Study Group on a European Civil Code. ERA Forum 4(2):100–101

von Bar C (2003b) From principles to codification. Prospects for European private law. In: Alpa G, Danovi R (eds) Diritto contrattuale europeo e diritto dei consumatori. L'integrazione europea e il processo civile. Materiali del seminario del 12 luglio 2002, pp. 39–53. Giuffrè, Milan

von Bar C (2003c) Schadensersatzsrecht nach dem zweiten Schadensersatzänderungsgesetz. In: Lorenz E (org.) KF 2003: Das Zweite Gesetz zur Änderung schadensersatzrechtlicher Vorschriften. VVW, Karlsruhe, pp. 7–29, 65–67, 69–71, 97–99

von Bar C (2004a) Comparative law of obligations: methodology and epistemology. In: van Hoecke M (ed) Epistemology and methodology of comparative law. Hart, Oregon, pp. 123–135

von Bar C (2004b) Ein gemeinsamer Referenzrahmen für das marktrelevante Privatrecht in der Europäischen Union. In: Mansel H-P, Pfeiffer T, Kronke H, Kohler C, Hausmann R (eds) Festschrift für Erik Jayme, vol 2. Sellier, Munich, pp. 1217–1231

von Bar C (2005) Working together towards a common frame of reference. JI 10(1):17–26

von Bar C (2007) Coverage and structure of the academic Common Frame of Reference. ERCL 3(3):350–361

von Bar C (2008a) A common frame of reference for European private law - Academic efforts and political realities. EJCL 12(1):1–10

von Bar C (2008b) The launch of the Draft Common Frame of Reference. JI 14(1):4–9

von Bar C (2008c) Non-contractual liability arising out of damage caused to another under the DCFR. ERA Forum 9(1):33–38

von Bar C (2008d) Die Struktur des Draft Common Frame of Reference. In: Schulze R, von Bar C, Schulte-Nölke H (eds) Der akademische Entwurf für einen gemeinsamen Referenzrahmen. Mohr Siebeck, Tübingen, pp. 35–45

von Bar C (2009a) Das Europäische Projekt eines gemeinsamen Referenzrahmens. Ein "Werkzeugkasten" für das Europäische Privatrecht - oder doch mehr? TPR:185 0-1871

von Bar C (2009b) Die Funktionen des gemeinsamen Referenzrahmens aus der Sicht der Verfasser des wissenschaftlichen Entwurfs. In: Schmidt-Kessel M (ed) Der Gemeinsame Referenzrahmen. Entstehung, Inhalte, Anwendung. Sellier, Munich, pp. 23–33

von Bar C (ed) (2009c) Principles of European Law on Non-Contractual Liability Arising Out of Damage Caused to Another. PEL Liab. Dam. Sellier, Munich

von Bar C (2009d) Ein "Werkzeugkasten" für das europäische Privatrecht? In: von Bar C (ed) Recht und Wirtschaft. Carl Heymanns, Cologne, pp. 49–62

von Bar C (2010a) Außervertragliche Haftung für den Einem Anderen Zugefügten Schaden. Das Buch VI des Draft Common Frame of Reference. ERPL 18(2):205–225

von Bar C (2010b) Die Rolle der juristischen Zeitschriftenliteratur bei der Harmonisierung des Privatrechts in Europa. JI 17(1):4–10

von Bar C (2011a) Concorrência entre as ordens jurídicas e "Law made in Germany". BFD 87(1): 429–444 von Bar C (2011b) The notion of damage. In: Hartkamp AS, Hesselink MW, Hondius EH, Mak C, du Perron CE (eds) Towards a European civil code, 4th edn. Kluwer Law International, Alphen aan den Rijn, pp. 387–399

von Bar C (2011c) Preamble. In: Schulze R, Schulte-Nölke H (eds) European private law - Current status and perspectives. Sellier, Munich, pp. 265–267

von Bar C (2011d) Rechtsvergleichende Beobachtungen zum Ineinandergreifen von Vertrags- und Deliktsrecht in Europa. In: Schulze R (ed) Compensation of private losses. The evolution of torts in European business law. Sellier, Munich, pp. 201–212

von Bar C (2011e) Statements on perspectives for European private law: as much diversity as possible, as less uniformity as necessary? In: Schulze R, Schulte-Nölke H (eds) European private law. Sellier, Munich, pp. 265–267

von Bar C (2012a) The Draft Common Frame of Reference: scope and purpose. In: Sagaert V, Storme M, Terryn E (eds) The Draft Common Frame of Reference: national and comparative perspectives. Intersentia, Cambridge/Antwerp/Portland, pp. 3–6

von Bar C (2012b) Eine neue Vertragsrechtsordnung für Europa. In: von Bar C, Wudarski A (eds) Deutschland und Polen in der europäischen Rechtsgemeinschaft. Sellier, Munich, pp. 3–11

von Bar C (2013) The role of comparative law in the making of European Private Law. JI 20(1): 5–11

von Bar C (2014a) Privatrecht europäisch denken! JZ 69(1):473–479

von Bar C (2014b) Rechtsvergleichung ist nicht mehr genug! LR 3(1):3–9

von Bar C (2015) Gemeineuropäisches Sachenrecht, vol 1 – Grundlagen, Gegenstände, sachenrechtliches Rechtsschutzes, Arten und Erscheinungsformen Subjektivenrechte. Beck, Munich

von Bar C, Barendrecht M, Basedow J, Drobnig U, van Gerven W, Hondius E, Kerameus K, Koussoulis S, Lando O, Loos M, Tilmann W (eds) (1999) Untersuchung der Privatrechtordnungen der EU im Hinblick auf Diskriminierungen und die Schaffung eines Europäisches Zivilgesetzbuch. Europäisches Parlament, Luxembourg. Available via the European Parliament website http://www.europarl.europa.eu/RegData/etudes/etudes/join/1999/168511/IPOL-JURI_ET%281999%29168511_DE.pdf. Accessed 31 Mar 2017

von Bar C, Clive E (2009) Principles, definitions and model rules of European private law. Draft Common Frame of Reference - Full edition. Sellier, Munich

von Bar C, Clive E, Schulte-Nölke H (eds) (2009) Principles, definitions and model rules of European private law. Draft Common Frame of Reference - Outline Edition. Sellier, Munich

von Bar C, Clive E, Schulte-Nölke H, Beale H, Herre J, Huet J, Storme M, Swann S, Varul P, Veneziano A, Zoll F (eds) (2008) Principles, definitions and model rules of European private law: Draft Common Frame of Reference (Interim Outline Edition). Sellier, Munich

von Bar C, Drobnig U (2004) The interaction of contract law and tort and property law in Europe. Sellier, Munich

von Bar C, Lando O (eds) (2001) Communication on European Contract Law: Joint Response of the Commission on European Contract law and the Study Group on a European Civil Code. Available via SGECC. http://www.sgecc.uos.de/media/downloads/stellungnahme_kommission_5_final1.pdf. Accessed 31 Mar 2017

von Bar C, Lando O, Swann S (2002) Communication on European contract law: joint response of the Commission on European Contract Law and the Study Group on a European Civil Code. ERPL 10(2):183–248

von Bar C, Markesinis BS (1981) Richterliche Rechtspolitik im Haftungsrecht. Mohr Siebeck, Tübingen

von Bar C, Schulte-Nölke H (2005) Gemeinsamer Referenzrahmen für europäisches Schuld- und Sachenrecht. ZRP 38(5):165–168

von Caemmerer E (1960) Wandlungen des Deliktsrechts. In: von Caemmerer E, Friesenhahn E, Lange R (eds) Festschrift zum hundertjährigen Bestehen des Deutschen Juristentags, vol 2. Müller, Karlsruhe, pp. 49–136

von Caemmerer E (1965) Das Problem des Drittschadensersatzes. ZHR 127(1):241–279

von Caemmerer E (1968) Wandlungen des Deliktsrechts, vol 1. In: Leser HG (org.) Gesammelte Schriften, vol I-Rechtsvergleichung und Schuldrecht, Mohr Siebeck, Tübingen, pp. 452–553
von Caemmerer E (1970) Die Bedeutung des Schutzbereiches einer Rechtsnorm für die Geltendmachung von Schadensersatzansprüche aus Verkehrsunfällen. DAR:283–292
von Jhering R (1861) Culpa in contrahendo oder Schadensersatz bei nichtiger oder nicht zur Perfektion gelangten Verträgen in Jahrbücher für die Dogmatik des heutigen römischen und deutschen Privatrecht, vol 4. Gustav Fischer, Jena
von Jhering R (1867) Das Schuldmoment im römischen Privatrecht: eine Festschrift. E. Roth, Giessen. Available via Babel. http://babel.hathitrust.org/cgi/pt?id=mdp.35112104328911;view=1up;seq=1. Accessed 31 Mar 2017
von Kries J (1886) Prinzipien der Wahrscheinlichkeitsrechnung: eine logische Untersuchung. Mohr Siebeck, Freiburg
von Lillienskiold M (1975) Aktuelle Probleme des portugiesischen Delikts- und Schadensersatzrechts. Ing. H. O. Hövelborn, Bonn
von Savigny FK (1814) Vom Beruf unserer Zeit für Gesetzgebung und Rechtswissenschaft. Mohr und Zimmer, Heidelberg
von Savigny FC (1840) System des heutigen römischen Rechts, vol 1. Veit, Berlin
von Savigny FK (1951) Juristische Methodenlehre. Köhl, Stuttgart
Voss KU (1987) Fahrlässiges Delikt und reiner Vermögensschaden - Haftungsgrenzen in der deutschen, anglo-amerikanischen und niederländischen Praxis. Karl Ulrich Voss, Cologne
Wagner G (2006) Comparative tort law. In: Reimann M, Zimmermann R (eds) The Oxford handbook of comparative law. Oxford University Press, Oxford, pp. 1003–1041
Wagner G (2009) The law of torts in the DCFR. In: Wagner G (ed) The Common Frame of Reference: a view from law & economics. Sellier, Munich, pp. 225–272
Wallis D (2006) European contract law - The way forward. Political context, Parliament's pre-occupations and process. ERA Forum 7(1):8–11
Wallis D (2016) Concrete solutions for the EU facing challenges. Retrieved from http://www.europeanlawinstitute.eu/home/news-contd/article/concrete-solutions-for-the-eu-facing-challenges-opening-of-the-eli-annual-conference-and-general/?tx_ttnews%5BbackPid%5D=180991&cHash=9d73a6c21112f0f691f9188186e8b14a. Accessed 31 Mar 2017
Watson A (1974) Legal transplants: an approach to comparative law. Scottish Academic Press, Edinburgh
Watson A (1991) Roman law and comparative law. University of Georgia Press, Athens
Watson A (1996) Aspects of reception of law. AJCL 44(2):335–339
Watson A (2000) Legal transplants and European private law. EJCL 4(4):I–VIII
Weir T (1996) Pure economic loss in German law. In: Banakas EK (ed) Civil liability for pure economic loss. Kluwer Law International, London/The Hague/Boston, pp. 73–87
Weir T (1999) Book review of unification of tort law: wrongfulness. CLJ 58(3):643–645
Weitenberg M (2008) Terminology. In: Koziol H, Schulze R (eds) Tort law of the European Community. Springer, Vienna/New York, pp. 309–340
Weitnauer H (1969) Zur Lehre vom adäquaten Kausalzusammenhang - Versuch einer Ehrenrettung. In: Keller M (ed) Revolution der Technik: Evolutionen des Rechts. Festgabe zum 60. Geburtstag von Karl Oftinger. Schulthess, Zürich, pp. 321–346
Wendehorst C (2009) The CFR and the review of the acquis communautaire. In: Schmidt-Kessel M (ed) Der Gemeinsame Referenzrahmen. Entstehung, Inhalte, Anwendung. Sellier, Munich, pp. 323–364
Wengler W (1967) Der Entwurf für ein neues portugiesisches Zivilgesetzbuch. AcP 167:64–69
Wetterstein P (2001) Compensation for pure economic loss in Finnish tort law. ScanStudL 41(1): 565–580
Whittaker S (2006) Precedent in English law: a view from the citadel. ERPL 14(5/6):705–746
Widmer P (1999) Die Vereinheitlichung des europäischen Schadenersatzrechts aus der Sicht eines Kontinentaleuropäers. RHDI 52(1):87–102

Wiethölter R (1960) Der Rechtfertigungsgrund des verkehrsrichtigen Verhaltens. Eine Studie zum zivilrechtlichen Unrecht. Müller, Karlsruhe

Wilburg W (1941) Die Elemente des Schadensrechts. Elwert, Marburg

Wilburg W (1964) Zusammenspiel der Kräfte im Aufbau des Schuldrechts. AcP 163(4):346–379

Wilkinson AB, Forte AD (1985) Pure economic loss - A Scottish perspective. J.Rev 30(1):1–28

Windelen G (1996) Das Haftungsinteresse: Einfallstor für den Ersatz von Drittschäden? Pro Universitate, Sinzheim

Winfield PH, Jolowicz JA, Peel E, Goudkamp J (2014) Winfield & Jolowicz on tort, 19th edn. Sweet & Maxwell, London

Winiger B, Koziol H, Koch B A, Zimmermann R (eds) (2011) Digest of European tort law. Essential cases on damage, vol 2. De Gruyter, Berlin/Boston

Wissink M (2008) Overview. In: Koziol H, Schulze R (eds) Tort law of the European Community. Springer, Vienna/New York, pp. 341–363

Witting C (2004) Compensation for pure economic loss from a common lawyer's perspective. In: van Boom WH, Koziol H, Witting CA (eds) Bloch B (contrib.) Pure economic loss, tort and insurance law, vol 9. Springer, Vienna, pp. 102–140

Wolf E (1967) Das Recht am eingerichteten und ausgeübten Gewerbebetrieb. In: Esser J, Thieme H (eds) Festschrift für Fritz von Hippel. Mohr Siebeck, Tübingen, pp. 665–685

Würthwein S (2001) Schadensersatz für Verlust der Nutzungsmöglichkeit einer Sache oder für entgangene Gebrauchsvorteile? Mohr Siebeck, Tübingen

Wurmnest W (2003a) Common Core, Grundregeln, Kodifikationsentwürfe, Acquis-Grundsätze - Ansätze internationaler Wissenschaftlergruppen zur Privatvereinheitlichung in Europa. ZEuP 11(1):714–744

Wurmnest W (2003b) Grundzüge eines europäischen Haftungsrechts. Eine rechtsvergleichende Untersuchung des Gemeinschaftsrechts. Mohr Siebeck, Tübingen

Zemanek K (1998) Is the term "soft law" convenient? In: Hafner G, Loibl G, Rest A, Sucharipa-Behrmann L, Zemanek K (eds) Liber Amicorum Professor Seidl-Hohenveldern. Kluwer Law International, The Hague, pp. 843–862

Zenha Martins J (2011) Neoconstitucionalismo e interpretação conforme. In: Manuel Hespanha A, Pizarro Beleza T (coords.) Teoria da Argumentação e Neoconstitucionalismo, pp. 191–213. Almedina, Coimbra

Zeuner A (1964) Schadensbegriff und Ersatz von Vermögensschäden. AcP 163:380–400

Zimmermann R (2004) Principles of European Contract Law and Principles of European Tort Law: comparison and points of contact. In: Koziol H, Steininger B (eds) European tort law 2003. Springer, Vienna/New York, pp. 2–31

Zimmermann R (2008) European contract law: general report. In: European Jurists' Forum. 4. Europäischer Juristentag. Manz, Vienna, pp. 185–204

Zimmermann R (2012) Challenges for the European Law Institute. Edinburgh LRev 16(1):5–23

Zoll F (2009) The Draft Common Frame of Reference: an instrument of the autonomous qualification in the context of Rome I Regulation. In: Ferrari F, Leible S (eds) Rome I Regulation. Sellier, Munich, pp. 17–25

Zoll F (2011a) The influence of the chosen structure of the draft for the optional instrument on the functioning of the system remedies. In: Schulze R, Stuyck J (eds) Towards a European contract law. Sellier, Munich, pp. 151–160

Zoll F (2011b) A need for a new structure for European private law. In: Brownsword R, Micklitz H-W, Niglia L, Weatherill S (eds) The foundations of European private law. Hart, Oxford/Portland, pp. 555–562

Zweigert K (1949) Rechtsvergleichung als universale Interpretationsmethode. RabelsZ 15(1): 5–21

Zweigert K, Kötz H (1996) Einführung in die Rechtsvergleichung, 3rd edn. Mohr Siebeck, Tübingen

Zweigert K, Kötz H (1998) Introduction to comparative law, 3rd edn. Oxford University Press/Clarendon Press, Oxford/New York

Index

M. Santos Silva, *The Draft Common Frame of Reference as a "Toolbox" for Domestic Courts*, DOI 10.1007/978-3-319-52923-3

The manufacturer's authorised representative in the EU is Springer Nature Customer Service Centre GmbH, Europaplatz 3, 69115 Heidelberg, Germany. If you have any concerns regarding our products, please contact ProductSafety@springernature.com

Printed and bound by CPI Group (UK) Ltd, Croydon, CR0 4YY
30/09/2026
02225649-0018